Hornet's Nest

Hornet's Nest

The Experiences of One of the U.S. Navy's First Female Fighter Pilots

Missy Cummings

Writer's Showcase presented by *Writer's Digest*
San Jose New York Lincoln Shanghai

Hornet's Nest
The Experiences of One of the U.S. Navy's First Female Fighter Pilots

Published by Writer's Showcase presented by *Writer's Digest* an imprint of iUniverse.com, Inc.

For information address:
iUniverse.com, Inc.
620 North 48th Street
Suite 201
Lincoln, NE 68504-3467
www.iuniverse.com

ISBN: 0-595-00190-4

Printed in the United States of America

To all the square pegs
and bee girls who didn't fit the mold.

Suffer women once to arrive at equality with you, and they will from that moment on become your superiors.

—*Cato*

Contents

Preface

When I first approached various publishers and producers about publishing my story, the replies were almost identical across the board—it is a good story but can you change the ending so it is a happy one? This response was painful to me not because it was a rejection, but because the people reading it missed the point entirely. More than anyone, I wish my story had a happier ending, but if it did, then I wouldn't be writing about my struggles as one of the Navy's first female fighter pilots. In addition, life does not always follow a script in which the heroine faces adversity, suffers, overcomes all the odds, and lives happily ever after.

My story is real—almost brutally and painfully authentic. It is sometimes chair squirming and at times vulgar, but it is often exhilarating and also heartbreaking. I did not use fictitious or composite characters to provide a more exciting plot, promote a personal agenda, or to sell more copies of my book. All the characters in my story are real, and for the most part are people who still live and breath. Most of the names and callsigns have been changed to protect the characters' privacy, save for a few who have already established themselves as public figures and therefore do not need such protection. It is a genuine story and despite the intensity of my passions, I deliberately endeavored to maintain a detached and objective view into the more controversial events. The ending, while I wish it were more fairy-tale like, is not so much unhappy as it is unsettling. Thus is the reality of our existence.

Anytime a book is written about the military culture, it is full of acronyms and colloquial slang that is often confusing and distracting to the reader. In addition to defining certain phrases on their outset, I provided a glossary for quick reference in case the reader feels over-whelmed with the military jargon. I also included photos (courtesy of the U.S. Navy, Bruce Stevenson, and Jan Eric Krikke) of the various air-craft I flew to help illustrate the awesome flying machines that I so often reference.

I could not have either written my manuscript or survived the tumultuous period that led to this book without the support of my friends and family, especially my mother. They were the reason I was able to maintain some semblance of sanity throughout the trials and tribulations. There were a few people who were absolutely instrumen-tal in both providing support and the impetus to push forward with my book: my editor Carolyn Porter, Rear Admiral Paul Gillcrist, USN (Ret.) and Rosemarie Skaine, both established authors who were a great cheering section and inspiring mentors. David Day, a Psychology professor at Penn State, Bruce Fleming, an English professor at the Naval Academy, and Pete Crabbe, a screenwriter, were all essential in the shaping of my story and also my outlook towards writing in gen-eral. I also owe great thanks to my sponsor family, the Stevens, from Annapolis, Maryland who helped make all this possible.

Introduction

As I boxed my hand carved wooden airplane models of the A-4 and the F/A-18, vivid images and mesmerizing memories from my ten tumultuous years in the Navy raced across my weary and cynical mind. How young and naive I was when I took my very first plane ride to Annapolis, Maryland to attend the United States Naval Academy. How exhilarated and full of life I was when I graduated from that hallowed institution. The thrill and fear of my first solo flight during training only paled in comparison to the ecstasy and awe I felt after landing on a massive hunk of steel called an aircraft carrier for the first time— alone! I remembered how short-lived was my joy when just after I qualified and flew away, one of my friends died on that same carrier in one of the worst training accidents ever recorded. I recalled how I loved dropping bombs and dogfighting other aircraft. I laughed out loud when I thought of Tailhook and how much fun I had.

When I thought about my time in the present day Sodom and Gomorrah, the naval base at Subic Bay in the Philippines, it seemed like a dream or some bizarre time sequence out of a movie. Did I really live in a culture where women were ordered from a menu for only a few dollars? The young but weathered faces of the prostitutes who were really just children were emblazoned across my mind. The scantily clad girls hanging out of every doorway enticing sailors just off the ship, the sex games that were played at official Navy functions, the raw stench of sex that hung in the air, and the climactic volcano that ended it all, just like the biblical Sodom and Gomorrah—would these memories ever leave me?

Then I thought of Monterey, California and a peaceful calm fell over me. Just as the memories of the Philippines were ugly and appalling, the recollections of my time in one of the most beautiful spots on earth were nothing but of big band music and the sound of the ocean crashing on the beach just yards from my house. It was a brief respite, the calm prior to the storm—before I would make history as one of the first American female fighter pilots.

My memories of flying fighters were bittersweet and it still pained me to look up in the sky and see a military plane or watch the news about my comrades in action overseas. There was nothing more exhilarating than dropping a live bomb on a tank and scoring a direct hit, and I felt adrenalin coursing through my veins when I recalled maneuvering to gun a bad guy down out of the sky—but I would never be able to just enjoy the good memories about fighters. I would never forget the betrayal of the institution I dedicated my life to, and how close I came to losing that life. How did I ever make it through not only the blatant abuse and discrimination heaped on me by the Navy, but more importantly, four major medical operations in just two years? I was covered with frightening scars and forever cursed with an ambiguous and insidious disease.

The rush of memories and the emotional roller coaster that came with them left me feeling weak. Yes, my time in the Navy was certainly quite a wild ride and despite my anger with both the individuals responsible and the institution as a whole, I still felt loyal to the Navy. I spent my last two years in the Navy teaching, grooming, and motivating the Navy's future officers—hoping to instruct them how to avoid the pitfalls and mistakes I made in the past. For the first time in a very long time, I felt tears welling up. I never really wanted to leave the Navy; it had been my whole life. Born to an enlisted Navy man, I spent my entire childhood as a "military brat," moving every three years, and living the life of a nomad. I dreamed of deploying on aircraft carriers and making the Navy a 30-year career, just as my father did. However, my dreams were not to be, my career was over after only ten years, and it was time to leave. How did this happen?

I finished cleaning out my desk and said my good-byes to the other staff officers. The one staff member that meant the most to me was Gunnery Sergeant Sibley, a senior enlisted Marine and the NROTC drill instructor. Despite his lower rank, Gunny was the one person who possessed the power to truly motivate me and deeply inspire me. Gunny was an endless source of positive energy and the consummate picture of military discipline, and we worked closely together always trying to help the midshipmen achieve their full potential. He was one of the truly few "bullet worthy" individuals I ever met in the military. Bullet worthy means that because an individual is so exceptional and altruistic, I would gladly take a bullet to spare his life. I have only met a handful of these individuals in the military and unfortunately, very few were ever in any senior leadership positions.

Gunny once told me when he found out I was leaving, "LT Cummings, I think the Navy is losing one of the best officers I have ever met. You would have made a fine Marine, Ma'am." His opinion of me was perhaps one of the highest compliments I have ever received and it is not one that is given lightly. Despite my anger and disappointment with the Navy, I sometimes wished I could stay in the Navy for people just like Gunny.

Gunny wasn't the only one who didn't want me to leave the Navy. When several of my students found out I was leaving, they gave me little goodbye gifts and wrote me various thank you letters and cards. The letters were all poignant and heartfelt and every time I read one of them, I relived the pain and anguish over my departure from the Navy. In one of these letters, a very astute student recognized the value of discipline and my dedication to the midshipmen's education both as college students and future military officers. He said,

You were, and are, someone who cared about us genuinely. Even though you would be stern with us, and even send us to the Gunnery Sergeant, we knew that it was in our best interests…that you were teaching us for a reason. You have been a role model to all of us in understanding what it means to take care of your people and get involved with their lives…A thank you at this point would be trivial so I will say this: I will take everything I have learned from you and use it to improve the lives of my sailors and possibly midshipmen, as it has improved my life. And thank you anyway. Ralph Waldo Emerson said, among other things, to have changed the lives of young people for the better is to have succeeded. Congratulations. The Navy has lost a fine Lieutenant, I hope the world realizes what it has to gain. Fair winds and following seas.

My sorrow in leaving was almost unendurable. As I hastily gathered my personal belongings to leave as quickly as possible, I was stopped in the hallway by one of my freshman. He sheepishly handed me a letter and asked me to read it later. He told me he would miss me and wished me luck in the future. I shook his hand firmly, told him to keep working hard, and that I knew he would make an outstanding naval officer. As I made the long walk to my car, I read the letter.

Lt. Cummings,

There aren't many people that can change the world. There are even a fewer number that can change an individual. However, you rise as one of the few. I stepped through these doors of wisdom and challenge not too long ago, a boy. A boy with dreams and hopes. A boy without any proper direction in achieving those goals. You have taken me as far as you could and led me to the proper path where I myself can lead the way. I couldn't have done that without you. A forever-changed person, I see the world with calmer eyes. I see the goodness that individual wills possess. I have acquired a sense of confidence in my own abilities and you have guided me to find my own moral force to remain steadfast in my own convictions. By changing one person, indirectly [you] may have changed the world.

There aren't many people that can influence others. You did. By being open and caring while standing aside and giving the proper discipline at the proper time. You will forever be a United States naval officer, and you shall always remain a friend and guide. I stepped through these doors a boy, but I shall leave here a man. LT Cummings, best of luck in your new career, you will not be forgotten.

Despite the hardened shell that I nearly perfected over the years of strife, I was amazed that such simple letters could bring tears to my eyes. At that moment, I desperately wanted to somehow stop my departure from the Navy. All I ever wanted from the Navy was to know that I somehow made a difference. It was painfully ironic and bittersweet that I would not realize those goals until I actually left the Navy.

That evening I packed all my uniforms in a box that was unlikely ever to be opened again. As I carefully inserted my uniforms into protective coverings, I laughed at the irony and my almost childish inability to let go. It was as if I didn't really believe that my naval career was over. Why was I taking such great pains to preserve my Navy uniforms when in fact it was the Navy who betrayed me and was responsible for my departure?

As I methodically packed my black, white, and khaki uniforms, I could not help but reminisce about my more than ten years of commissioned service and the four that I spent at the Naval Academy. The torrential rush of memories came flooding back as I handled those same garments that I wore throughout my career and instead of fighting the onslaught of recollections, I let them engulf me. As I packed my dress white uniform, I vividly recalled the first time I ever wore it as a commissioned officer...

Chapter One

An Officer and A Gentleman

Sitting in my chair in my dress white uniform, I felt a surge of emotion come over me. It was May 25th, 1988 and I was about to graduate from the United States Naval Academy, the old school of old schools except for maybe West Point. It had been four long years and I was very ready to move on. I wouldn't say my college years were the best of my life, but they were critical in my transformation from a small town southern girl to a leader of men. I was thrilled with the prospects of a very exciting future, but a little sad that I was leaving behind some very close friends.

Our class of 1050 midshipmen sat in the middle of the stadium football field in our crisp dress white uniforms, eagerly anticipating the walk across the stage. I looked down my row of soon-to-be naval officers and winked to my roommate, Laura. She responded with a thumbs up and a tucking motion to keep her hair up inside her cover (the Navy word for hat). It was drizzling that gray day and many of the women in my class were concerned about the rain. All midshipmen, both male and female, must conform to certain hair regulations. While at the Academy, the women's hair was required to be above the collar, no buns or braids, and we were only allowed to use two barrettes. As soon as we graduated and became officers, we could have long hair if we pinned it above the collar.

In typical youthful rebelliousness, several of us decided not to cut our hair for the last few months before graduation and see how long we could grow our hair without getting in trouble. We each arranged our hair cleverly to appear to be within regulations. Many women used very small sponge rollers and slept in wet hair—the Shirley Temple approach. I kept a layer of hair in the back at the bottom of the collar. I then used a weaving technique with the two barrettes to keep the rest up.

This approach served me well at graduation because when it started raining, hair started falling. It was comical to watch several women's hair grow longer and longer as the graduation ceremonies progressed. The entire class and audience witnessed who won the contest, as one woman walked across the stage with her hair halfway down her back. Laura and I cheered for her and felt some sense of victory. After four years of living in an all male environment, we took our feminine victories wherever we could. My class was the ninth class to have women, so female midshipmen were still a relatively new concept at the Naval Academy.

So after what seemed like an eternity, the graduating class of 1988 held their diplomas in hand and stood at attention for the closing ceremonies. It is an impressive sight to see 1050 young men and women, a sea of white in their formal dress uniforms, standing at attention singing the Naval Academy Alma Mater. These young officers were the Navy's future, each sacrificing a great deal and dedicating their lives to the defense of our country. The closing tradition of the ceremony is to cheer those the departing class leaves behind. "Three cheers for those we leave behind us." Everyone removed their covers and lifted them to the sky after every cheer, "Hip Hip Hooray!" "Hip Hip Hooray!" "Hip Hip Hooray!" On the last cheer, 1050 hats went sailing in the air, as high as each person could throw.

The midshipmen hats are left behind for family and friends to pick up as souvenirs, a remembrance of a very special occasion. Many people sign their name in the hats, and some leave letters inside to whoever finds them. Laura and I put banana stickers in ours. Banana stickers were an inside joke at Annapolis. Supposedly, a Dole banana sticker meant a mid (shipman) had intimate knowledge of someone on the Academy premises. A Chiquita sticker was even more "prestigious"; it meant the mid had carnal knowledge of someone in Bancroft Hall, the huge complex of eight adjoining dormitory buildings that housed all midshipmen. In some form of bizarre harassment, women at the Naval Academy often woke to find their doors plastered with these stickers. Despite the message, Laura and I thought it a funny joke and wondered if the lucky recipients of our covers would even understand.

We parted ways that day, all excited about the future. Some of my peers would soon be Marines, some would drive ships, and some would become SEALs. I was off to learn to fly planes, something still new for women in the Navy. Women had only been flying in the Navy for little more than a decade and they made up less than 5% of all pilots. I knew that much like at the Naval Academy, a tough road was before me. But just as I persevered through four years at Annapolis, I would one day wear the Wings of Gold.

When I first considered a career in the Navy in high school, I did not know women could be pilots. I was raised in a very conservative family in traditional southern towns. I originally wanted to be a Navy intelligence officer, but found out at the Academy that I could actually fly high performance aircraft. From that day on, Navy Air was the only career I wanted. I dreamed of dropping bombs and dogfighting. I joined the Academy's aviation club and took extra aviation related classes to prepare myself for flight school. I shadowed the Academy officers who were pilots and hung on their every word.

Before reporting to Naval Air Station (NAS) Pensacola to begin flight training, I flew to New York City to take part in a weeklong celebration hosted by Glamour magazine. I was recently selected as one of Glamour's Top Ten College Women for 1988. It was quite an honor, and I was ecstatic beyond words. I was on top of the world as a recent graduate of the US Naval Academy, flight school bound, and somewhat of a celebrity. The week in New York was even more than I could possibly imagine.

When I arrived, I met the Glamour staff and the other winners. The other nine women were impressive but quite different from me. I spent four years at a military school repressing my feminism and building skills as a warrior. The other women were certainly more coiffured than I was, but not quite as assertive. I was disturbed by comments made by one of the women, a graduate of the University of Mississippi at Oxford. Her hair and makeup were always impeccable and her mannerisms were clearly those of a well-bred genteel southern belle. She said oh-so-matter-of-factly one day in her classic southern drawl, "Why, if ever one of us girls was caught leaving the sorority house without her hair and makeup perfectly done, she was surely in serious trouble."

I couldn't stifle my laugh and thought that our worlds were so vastly different. The irony was not lost on me that had I stayed in the South, I would be the same girl. At the Naval Academy, most women took pains not to wear noticeable makeup and played down the role of being a woman. I was shocked that in this day and age, women still thought like my southern friend. Make no mistake though, I did understand her. Originally from Memphis, Tennessee, I was quite southern by anyone's definition. In high school, I never left the house without applying an unbelievable amount of makeup (including the hideous blue eye shadow). I would spend an hour and a half every morning hot rolling my hair and I carried the biggest can of AquaNet™ hairspray that could fit in my purse. I understood my southern friend, but the military completely changed me and now makeup and excessive primping seemed almost ludicrous.

I met many incredible people that week in New York City—Gloria Steinem, Lisa Sliwa, a guardian angel, Helen Gurly Brown, editor of Cosmopolitan magazine, and a host of other successful New York women. At the week's end, I was exhausted yet charged. I spent the week rubbing elbows with some of the movers and shakers of New York's society, quite a new experience for a small town gal from Tennessee. I was very eager to report to flight school, take the proverbial bull by the horns, and start my flight training.

Just two weeks after reporting to flight school in Pensacola, I was flown back to New York City. Three of Glamour's top ten women were chosen to appear on NBC's Today Show, and I was one of them. My trip to New York was very quick; the Navy allowed me to miss only one day of training. The Today Show starts very early and before I knew it, I was on the set with Bryant Gumbel and Debra Norville. Though very nervous, I managed to stumble my way through the interview. In no time, I was on a plane headed back to flight school at NAS Pensacola. There was no time to wallow in any superficial glory because my aerodynamics final was in just two days.

The very first stage of flight training was called Aviation Indoctrination (AI). NAS Pensacola is nicknamed "the cradle of naval aviation" because all naval aviators must pass AI before they begin flight training. A five week program that introduced basic aerodynamics, propulsion and navigation, AI also provided numerous physical challenges. AI was a weeding out program, designed to attrite people who didn't eat, sleep, and breathe aviation. The physical program consisted of timed cross-country runs through sand, an extremely difficult obstacle course also through sand, and various water training devices. Most of my classmates were Academy graduates and still in excellent shape. August in Florida is the athletic equalizer though. No matter how physically fit we were, the heat, sand, and exercise humbled us all.

Because the Navy trains pilots who fly primarily over the water, all Navy pilots must be certified every four years in various water devices that to many, seem like torture. The Dilbert Dunker, made famous by the movie *Officer and a Gentleman,* is actually the simplest of the water training devices. Strapped into a mock cockpit with no canopy, the wide-eyed student is hoisted up a creaking rail twenty feet high and then dropped down a fairly steep incline. The steel cage plummets down the rail, hits the water, and then flips over. The pilot in training attempts to maintain a point of reference as the "aircraft" crashes, so he has his bearings and can calmly extricate himself. This just basically involves holding on to some structural object that is likely to remain intact, like the canopy rail. Once the aviator is underwater and all the motion has ceased, it's fairly easy to pull clear of the "wreckage." Very few people ever struggled with the Dilbert Dunker and for many, it was actually kind of fun!

After graduating from the Dilbert Dunker, the next water training device is the Helicopter Dunker. It is like going from kindergarten to college. The Helicopter Dunker is a big barrel with windows and a door cut out much like a real helicopter. All aviators must qualify in this, no matter what aircraft they fly since so much time is spent aboard helicopters flying over water. Strapped into one of ten seats, the barrel is dropped into the water from a height of about 10 feet. Once the barrel drops, it fills with water, but no one is allowed to move. Not one person can move until the barrel flips upside down, the motion stops, and five seconds have passed. That might not seem so bad, and actually at first it's not. The worst part is hitting the water and watching the water rise—unable to act and realizing what the victims of the Titanic might have been feeling. This ride is just the first; there are three more successively more difficult rides that must be passed.

On the first ride, everyone can go out the nearest exit, which is usually a window. Not everyone has his own window and some must share. On the second ride, everyone must go out the main doorway, in the center of the barrel. It may not sound too difficult, but when upside down, holding one's breath and waiting in line, seconds seem like an eternity. The first two rides leave everyone a little tired and with noses full of water. Then the real fun starts.

The last two rides are the same as the first two, only blindfolded simulating crashing at night in a helicopter. These blindfolded rides test the student's ability to use a reference point and stay calm as he exits. The last ride with everyone going out the same door blindfolded gets quite colorful. People claw over one another in desperation and undoubtedly someone is kicked in the face with a steel-toed boot on the departure. Divers are positioned in various places to rescue students in trouble, which happens quite frequently. Many people have to repeat certain rides until they pass which most eventually do. Some, however, never graduate past this point and are attrited from the program. A woman in my class started panicking during her first ride and the divers had to pull her out. She was hysterical and eventually she was taken to the medical clinic. We later found out that she almost drowned in a boating accident a few years prior. She was later medically disqualified for flying.

The dunking devices were just one aspect of the intense water survival training. Most of the students dreaded the water treading tests. Dressed in full flight gear that weighs almost forty pounds, each of us were required to tread water for five minutes and then drown proof for another five minutes. (Drown proofing is a face down relaxed float that uses the body's inflated lungs as the primary buoy.) One of the most difficult water tests was the mile long swim. While a mile might not seem like an arduous distance, we were required to swim the mile dressed in an oversized flight suit that acted as an anchor. The clincher was the distance must be covered in less than an hour, so fighting the clock and all the people in the pool made the mile swim extremely challenging.

For all the water exercises, the main lesson to learn is not the physical prowess needed to do these feats—no one can tread water for five minutes in full flight gear in arctic water or swim a mile with possible ejection injuries. The point is to learn to master fear of the water and that maintaining calm is paramount. Panic in a survival situation will almost always lead to death.

The end of the initial indoctrination training was marked by a three-day survival course in the woods of Eglin Air Force Base, forty miles from Pensacola. Our group of about sixty was dropped off at three different sites. Our mission was to survive on the land for the next three days. The survival course simulates ejecting or bailing out of a crippled aircraft in a remote area and staying alive until the rescue forces arrive. Air Force Captain Scott O' Grady's ejection, evasion, survival and rescue over Bosnia in 1995 was a textbook example of why this training is so important.

Survival instructors went with us to show us how to make traps, tents, fires and the general basics of survival. We were not allowed to bring any food with us, not even mints. Our task was to eat what we could forage or catch. The problem was that every week, a class of 60 hungry students came to the same spot for the same mission. There was not an animal around for miles and the area was stripped of all edible plant life.

The three days in the "wilderness" did expose me to the behavior of some people when they haven't eaten two meals in a row—probably the scariest part of the training. While we all pitched in to build campsites and find material, many complained incessantly about how hungry they were. They rambled on for hours about the first meal they would have when we returned to Pensacola. The descriptions were far more detailed than even a cookbook. I found this to be more torturous than helpful.

To combat the hunger, my group wove a fishing net using parachute lines. (We were allowed to have the materials we would have if we ejected from a plane.) We put the net into a little stream and after a few hours, caught eight minnows. They were smaller than goldfish but the men acted as though we landed eight of the biggest trout this side of the Mississippi. Like a pack of wolves, the guys fought over who would get the minnows, which were swallowed whole. I didn't even attempt to claim my share, which probably would have only been a mere fin. I was not starving and by sacrificing my share, I hoped to show the guys that I was a team player.

On the last day, the instructors brought strips of meat to the campsites to show us how to make beef jerky. We were each allotted two pieces, which for the most part, were gobbled up without hesitation. I actually became someone's hero when I offered up my second piece. I still was not dying of hunger like the guys. Years of not eating at the Naval Academy were effective survival training techniques.

Because of the fishbowl environment for women at Annapolis, most suffered from varying degrees of low self-esteem. Many women were extremely attractive and most were thin and in good shape, but the male mids still lumped us all in the "fat and ugly" category. The constant verbal abuse from our male peers was unrelenting. When we walked down the halls, many male midshipmen would often moo and oink at us. Because of the less than supportive environment, anorexia and bulimia were rampant at USNA and probably still is. In response to a particularly harsh verbal beating and the resultant low self-esteem, my roommate and I often just did not eat. Though I truly did not suffer from anorexia, I was accustomed to going days without food at the Naval Academy. Anorexia and bulimia at the Naval Academy were what we term in the Navy as "Standard Operating Procedures (SOP)," which are guidelines for normal operations.

Upon our return from the survival training, we headed to Quincy's, an all-you-can-eat joint and did some serious damage. After a few more academic classes, we graduated. The mental challenges of AI far outweighed the physical, and gender notwithstanding, if a student was not physically prepared and not mentally tough, he or she would not make it. Fortunately, I had no problems throughout AI. I was an excellent swimmer and my technical background and extra preparation from my days at the Naval Academy made the academics relatively easy. I graduated near the top of my class and was ready to put some of this training to the test in an aircraft.

AI was only an introduction into aviation and allowed the student naval aviator (SNA) to attain his swim and physiology qualifications before actually getting into a plane. After successful completion, the next step was primary flight training. All Navy student pilots spend their initial six months of training flying the T-34. Nicknamed the Mentor, the

T-34 is a single engine, two-seat, dual controlled aircraft. It is not much bigger than some Cessnas and Pipers flown in general aviation, but it is an excellent training aircraft. The T-34 is very forgiving; if the pilot makes a mistake, the consequences are not usually disastrous.

After the rigorous six months primary training syllabus in the T-34, all the students' grades were compared for selection to the next phase of training. This is a critical junction for all future pilots. This choice determines the "pipeline" or career track that will have a significant impact not only on a person's military career but potential civilian flying as well. Every student has three choices: jets, propeller driven aircraft (props), and helicopters. Jets were seen as fast, exciting, and glamorous. The prop community was seen as the best way to make extra money because of all the travel and excellent chance to transition to the commercial airlines. Unfortunately, the helicopter community didn't have any movies like *TOPGUN* to make it seem exciting so it was last on the totem pole of choices.

Typically jets were the most desired slots with props and helicopters usually the second and third choices respectively. Every student has input in the selection process and those students with the best grades usually received their first choice. For the most part, those students with the best grades chose jets, although some top students selected props or helos first. The needs of the Navy, however, far outweighed the students' preferences. If one week the Navy decided it needed a class full of helicopters, almost all students received helo orders. Despite this sometimes-random selection process, there is a perception in naval aviation that the jet pilots are the best of the best and the helo pilots are the worst pilots. It is a rivalry that can be felt at even the highest echelons of military politics in the Pentagon.

After the selection for jets, props, or helos, every student goes on to two more stages, intermediate and advanced, before graduating and becoming a designated naval aviator (DNA). This graduation is known as "getting your wings" and is the most defining event for a naval aviator. In a big ceremony, the soon to be DNA chooses a special person, usually a parent, spouse or fiancée, to pin on the coveted wings of gold. The recognized naval pilot then goes on to the fleet to perform missions.

The Navy has two locations for primary training. The first is located forty miles from Pensacola in a place called Whiting Field in Milton, Florida. The other location is NAS Corpus Christi, Texas. After graduation from AI in Pensacola, most students prefer to remain in the area. Pensacola is a party town with a year round spring break mentality. It is a dream come true for young, single people right out of college. This is especially true for Naval Academy graduates who are just released from their pseudo prison. Because of this ideal environment, most student pilots want to remain in the area and since 75% of all primary training is done at NAS Whiting, most are allowed to stay.

For several reasons, however, I wanted to go to Corpus Christi. Many of my friends who completed flight training told me that Corpus was the "gouge." (Gouge is Navy slang for good deal or good information.) They said the primary training squadrons in Whiting were impersonal factories and that the training in Corpus Christi was more laid back and individualized. The commute to work was a mere fifteen minutes for most in Corpus, as compared to the 45 minutes for the students in the Pensacola area. However, the biggest reason for my choice to relocate was to be near my dad. My father, who was also in the Navy, was stationed at NAS Corpus Christi. Unfortunately, my father and I were not on speaking terms.

My parents divorced in 1985, during my first year at the Naval Academy.My father was from a very rural and poor section of Arkansas. He did not finish high school, joined the Marines at seventeen (which was expected of his generation) and completed a four year tour. After his discharge, he went back home to Arkansas but work was scarce. In the early sixties, northwest Arkansas was still very much in a depression.

After struggling to find even a part time job, he decided that the military was a steady income source and not so bad after all.

He re-enlisted, this time in the Navy who was more than happy to have him. The Vietnam War was heating up, the draft was in full swing, and with his previous experience in the Marine Corps, the Navy thought my dad would make a fine electronics technician and aircrewman. As soon as he completed his initial training, he would be sent to Japan. His mission would be to fly cargo missions into Vietnam and deliver supplies to the forward-deployed troops. During my dad's training in Memphis, Tennessee, he made frequent road trips to outlying counties, and that's when he met my mom.

My mom was born and raised in Ripley, Tennessee, a small farming town two hours north of Memphis. Her father was Admiral Nimitz's meteorologist during World War II. After the war, he became the town's high school principal. My mother was an outstanding student and absolutely drop-dead gorgeous. She was a curvaceous blond with classic features—a Marilyn Monroe copy. Everyone in my father's family was tall and thin, but very gaunt through the face. As luck would have it, I inherited my mother's body and my father's face.

It was no wonder my dad was quite smitten with my mom. She was definitely what we term in naval aviation as a "trophy wife." My mom was equally intrigued with the stranger from out of town. To my mother, a small town girl, this worldly daredevil was all she ever dreamed of. Shortly after their introduction, they were married. My dad was a very junior enlisted man, an E-4 (on a scale from 1– 9). Just a month after the wedding, he received orders to NAS Atsugi, Japan, a naval airbase just outside Tokyo. Though my mother never ventured further away from home than Mississippi, she was now on her way to live in a foreign country.

My dad was shipped out early due to mission requirements. My mother made the trip a few months later, alone and pregnant. When she arrived, my dad took her to their first house, a two room shack with no running water, no indoor bathroom, no heat, and rice paper walls. Japan in 1966 was still very much in post World War II reconstruction. I can only imagine her despair. Here was the quintessential genteel southern belle in a world where indoor plumbing was rare and electricity the ultimate luxury. To make matters worse, she was forced to cope with her surreal surroundings alone a good deal of the time. My father was gone most of the time, flying in and out of a war zone. How stressful for my mother to know that her husband was in a war zone and there was always the chance he might never return.

Somehow they made it through those difficult years and eventually made it back to Memphis, Tennessee. We moved several times, as do most military families, but spent the majority of time in Memphis. As a child, the military was all I ever knew. My father ran our household like a little platoon. Sunday afternoon war movies were mandatory training periods for the entire family. My two brothers and I were expected to pay close attention because an oral quiz was given after the movie ended. Not only were we required to summarize the movie, we explained tactics, strategies and the historical implications. We watched all the classics, *Sands of Iwo Jima, Patton, Guns of Navarrone, Operation Petticoat*—the list is endless. I loved watching these movies and learned debate skills at an early age. The glory of fighting and defending the nation was emblazoned on my mind from the start and the most supreme sacrifice and honor was to die for one's country. I was a soldier from the time I was five.

My father was a very determined and headstrong man. Much to his chagrin, I turned out just like him. Ornery is the word my father used to describe me; he said I was more stubborn than a mule and I was too big for my britches. He was right but I learned from his mastery. My father made my brother and me brief him at the dinner table about current world events. Politics, religion, and money were mandatory topics. We were required to have an opinion and staunchly defend our positions. As each year passed, the discussions grew more heated and my debate skills sharpened, as did my tongue.

Always trying to best my father in our tête-à-têtes, I read voraciously. The one skill I struggled with then, and throughout my life was realizing when to retreat. It took me many years to learn that handing someone a humiliating defeat in battle would not necessarily win the war. Like many military men, my father was a very strict disciplinarian. If my brother and I were caught not showing the proper amount of respect or slacking off at our chores, punishment was severe.

The fate worse than death for me was not being allowed to talk on the phone. Phone restriction was not effective against my brother so when he really misbehaved, he was forced to get a crew cut. In the seventies, he felt this was cruel and unusual punishment. Report card day in my house was a day of terror. If I earned anything less than all A's, I was whipped and restricted for six weeks. I resented my parents' exacting demands and when I finally entered high school, I attempted to rebel and tried to enroll in the cosmetology school. That of course was not received well, and I ended up in the math and science trek. In retrospect, I am eternally grateful for their intervention—I never was handy with a pair of scissors.

In high school, my curfews were very strict, and I was not allowed to wear make-up until I was sixteen. Always the rebel, I could not wait to graduate from high school and move out of our house. Unfortunately, there was no money for college, so the onus was on me to earn a scholarship. I did very well in high school and in my junior year, my father suggested I look into the Air Force Academy. He thought the Air Force provided a better environment for women officers. In retrospect, I sometimes wish I heeded his advice.

I researched all the service academies, lured by the fact that they all advertised a "free" education. I narrowed my selection to the Naval and the Air Force Academies and received appointments to both, not an easy task. It was a tough decision but in spite of my rebelliousness, I still wanted to emulate my father. Hoping to win his admiration and respect, I chose the Navy because it felt like home to me. Since my father always worked around aircraft and ships, I knew that's where I wanted to be.

The last few months at home before I left for the Academy were not pleasant. Fighting between my parents escalated and they finally started discussing divorce. My older brother and I completely supported this decision. I left for Annapolis in July of 1984, and was glad to put my difficult home life behind me. After I left, a fierce custody battle ensued over my younger brother. I sided with my mother and my father, enraged with my decision, made it clear he wanted nothing more to do with me. My parents divorced a few months later; my mother retained custody of Matthew, and I did not speak to my father again until I saw him in Texas in September of 1988.

I reported onboard NAS Corpus Christi, fresh from AI graduation, still very much the brand new wide-eyed Ensign. I lived at the Bachelor's Officers Quarters (BOQ) where most officers stay for their first few weeks after reporting aboard a new station. I literally ran into my father at the front desk one day. He had no idea that I was coming and was genuinely glad to see me. He gave me his phone number and we met for dinner a few weeks later. We ended up spending a lot of time together and healed a broken relationship. I coaxed my older brother into a visit and they too mended their rift. We never really discussed my mother; there was still too much animosity on both sides to even broach the issue. In hindsight, I think that my choice of Corpus for my initial training was one of the smartest moves I ever made. My salvaged relationship with my father later became instrumental in the more difficult situations I faced during my naval career.

The transition from the structured Naval Academy life to living truly on my own was comical at best. At the Naval Academy, our laundry was done for us, our meals were always prepared for us, and almost every aspect of our lives was strictly regimented. In general, the Navy was our mother the entire four years at the Academy. When I moved to Corpus Christi, I found new and highly desired freedom in an off-base apartment! It seems laughable when I look back, but it was a great feeling to sign that first lease. I was free from both the watchful eyes of my parents and the Navy, and finally on my own. After a few cooking and laundry disasters like washing whites with a red shirt, I settled into my new life with an occasional call to Mom for emergency help.

I found a fantastic roommate, a girl who graduated a year ahead of me at the Naval Academy. Lisa was the best roommate; she was a bigger slob than I was and we got along famously. Lisa had finished primary and selected propellers, which allowed her to stay in Corpus Christi for the remainder of her training. Since she already completed the primary program, she was a steady source of "gouge." (In this sense, "gouge" meant she had all the old tests, knew what to study, and generally had a "clue.") One of the most important lessons of flight school is to learn both military lingo and aviation specific vocabulary.

For every new plane a pilot flies, the Navy first sends the aviator to "ground school."

This school is a series of classes that teach the particulars of an aircraft, the local flying area and the required procedures. In primary training, ground school is more comprehensive because it is initial training. A great deal of time is spent on meteorology as well as learning how to interpret the cockpit instruments that enable a pilot to fly in instrument conditions or "in the clouds." This classroom training takes about a month before any actual flying.

After a student passes numerous written tests, he is then allowed into the plane. This stage is called the familiarization (FAM) stage and is designed to do just that. During this phase, the student learns to start the plane, taxi, takeoff, fly to and from the working area, and last but not least, how to land. Because of the complexity, many students experience their first serious problems during the FAM stage. When a student has an unusual or unsafe problem, a "down" is issued. A "down" is a formal counseling sheet that documents the problem and allows the student extra training. While a down might not seem like a distressing occurrence, if a student gets too many, he will be dropped from the program. On average, every student receives one down in primary training. Two is not unheard of, but any more downs and the student is at risk for attrition.

The first few flights are probably pretty funny from the instructor's point of view. Flying and talking at the same time may sound easy, but for fledgling pilots, it can actually be the hardest technique to master. New students have a hard time talking on the radio and are always using the wrong callsign. The callsign, the plane's identification, is usually a set of numbers and letters that both the pilot and outside air controllers use. Each plane in every squadron has a similar callsign and students will often use the same callsign of another plane flying nearby. This juxtaposition leads to mass confusion and on some days can sound like a rendition of who's on first?

The funniest radio transmissions are those that are inadvertently broadcast to the world. On the throttle which is on the left side of the cockpit, there is a switch that lets the pilot transmit either to the outside controlling agency or to the other person in the cockpit. In a moment of frustration, it is quite easy to key the mike in the wrong direction. The funniest story all aviators tell regarding this mistake is about the landing pattern. A student completed a really "gooned" up approach to the field and said to the instructor, "Well, I guess I am really f—ked up sir." Unfortunately, he pressed the wrong button and transmitted that self-deprecating remark to the tower. Since it is against FAA rules to curse on the radio, the controller in the tower said, "Pilot who just cursed on the radio, identify yourself." After a long moment of silence, the instructor piped up and said, "He said he was f—ked up, not stupid!"

The most demanding aspect of familiarization training is learning to land. The landing pattern requires close attention to mandatory check-lists, looking out for other aircraft and the sometimes very vocal instructor in the back seat who is yelling at the student about nearly killing him. Usually four or more planes fly in the landing pattern at the same time with inexperienced pilots all at the controls. The highest potential for a mid-air collision exists in the landing pattern. It is very easy for a new student to become overwhelmed by the dynamic environment and drop something out of his scan. When overly taxed, the student pilot is highly likely to lose sight of other aircraft and not pay attention to his instruments, which can lead to a crash.

It is quite common to practice "touch and go's" at an outlying field and then return to the home field. "Touch and go's" are landings followed by an immediate take off for another loop around the landing pattern. After spending stressful twenty minutes in the landing pattern, the instructor often tells the student, "OK, take me home." This statement invariably brings a sigh of relief from the student because it means the flight is almost finished. It is this point in the flight that generates the second most told story in aviation.

As the student heads home, the instructor says, "Hey Joe, where are you from?" in the nicest, most polite manner. (Anytime the instructor strikes up casual conversation during a flight, the student gets a warm and fuzzy feeling that the flight is going well.) The student possibly replies, "Virginia sir!" The instructor then says, "Well, what do they raise in Virginia?" The student, thinking this was an odd question but programmed to respond, says, "Well sir, I think they raise cattle and maybe tobacco." Then the instructor yells out, "Well how about raising the f— king gear?" Invariably, students forget to raise the landing gear after the last touch and go, and can't figure why the plane just will not accelerate. Generally, that only happens once and the student never forgets the landing gear again.

Once the pilot has learned the fundamental skills of flying, the next phase of learning to fly is called basic instruments. In this stage, the student flies a simulator—a mock cockpit that moves a little in response to the student's inputs. It has no visual screen and is nothing like today's popular home computer flight simulators. It is designed to teach the student the skills necessary to fly in very disorienting weather conditions. The majority of time in basic instruments is spent turning, climbing, descending and performing other basic maneuvers. This intense instrument flying is intended to develop the pilot's scan (the rapid rate at which pilots disseminate cockpit instrument information). Though it sounds very elementary, it can be quite frustrating.

Once the fledgling pilot masters the basic instrument skills, he moves on to radio instruments. This phase teaches not only accurate interpretation of the instruments, but also the fundamentals of navigation, even in the most extreme conditions. The word "headwork" is introduced to the student pilot in this stage. Pilots live and die by checklists, but in instrument conditions, there is not a checklist to cover every situation. This phase is critical in developing headwork, the "thinking and flying at the same time" skills. This is also the phase where many students realize that the fast moving world of jets is maybe a little beyond their skills.

Since primary training is so overwhelming, every student is assigned an "on-wing" instructor. This instructor flies most of the initial FAM flights with the student to provide consistent instruction and mentoring. Often, the on-wing determines a student's eventual success in the program. There are three types of instructors; the laid back "Santa Claus," the middle of the road instructor, and the "screamer." Of course, we all hoped for Santas and dreaded the flights with the screamers. Some of the instructors possessed split personalities. They seemed like Santas on the ground but turned into monsters in the air. These closet screamers were the worst because a student never knew what to expect. The unfortunate students with screamers as their on-wings were always the ones sitting in the corner, looking shell-shocked.

My on-wing was a very laid back officer and truly loved instructing. He was older than the average instructor, and very comfortable letting the student screw up. I learned a lot from him and looked forward to our flights. In no time, I passed my first major checkride and was on my way to solo.

The stars and planets must be in almost perfect alignment for students to fly their first solo. The weather must be almost perfect, the student must have flown very recently, and no unusual conditions can exist that might possibly result in a lost sheep. Many students wait days and sometimes weeks to fly their first solo. I was very lucky; I flew my solo the very first time it was scheduled.

As I took off and headed out over the Gulf of Mexico, I was exhilarated. I was alone and flying an airplane with no one watching over my shoulder. It was actually very peaceful flying over the sparkling blue water dotted with boats making their way into the local ports. Sightseeing however was not my primary mission during my solo flight. The tradition for Navy student pilots on their very first solo is to take pictures of themselves in various attitudes. The quintessential picture is the upside-down, raised helmet visor, ear-to-ear grin shot that proves accomplishment of the first major step towards graduation.

After the first solo in a Navy plane, every proud student is rewarded with a tie cutting ceremony. Every two weeks or so, each student who soloed wears the most obnoxious tie he can find, and his on-wing cuts it in half. The cutting of the tie symbolizes the student's graduation to the ranks of solo pilots. After the tie cutting, every student then performs a little skit poking fun at his instructor, and generally a good time is had by all.

My tie cutting ceremony was my first glimpse into the darker side of naval aviation and how the guys really felt about women. Since not many women were in the program, I was the first woman to go through primary training in VT-27 since my roommate, which was six months prior. When I was called forward to have my tie cut, there was a lot of hissing and some outright booing in the audience. I didn't understand what was happening. I found out later the venomous reception was the typical reaction to women student pilots and was almost a tradition. I blew it off. My experiences at the Naval Academy served me well, so I really thought nothing more of it.

While I was there, the squadron's first female instructor arrived, LT Helen Coleman. There was much tittering upon her arrival because of the long-standing squadron tradition of "debriefing." During the tie-cutting ceremony, when an on-wing instructor's first student soloed, tradition mandated that the instructor stand up in front of the whole squadron and be "debriefed" (have his underwear cut off). This would be the real test of LT Coleman. If she went along, she was conditionally accepted. If she didn't, she would be ostracized the rest of her tour.

LT Coleman just came from the Philippines flying C-130's, large four engine cargo aircraft. The first detail I noticed about her was her flight suit. Baggy, one-piece overalls, flight suits were not made for women. A trip to the bathroom was a major expedition that required a woman to basically strip completely. While in the Philippines, LT Coleman altered her flight suits to incorporate a drop seat. Even though it was against the rules to modify flight gear, she was not reprimanded. LT Coleman was a very laid back and cool lady and the underwear ceremony did not faze her. She knew that going along with the squadron's games would gain her much more than bucking the system. In hindsight, this was an important lesson I should have paid closer attention to.

The day of her shorts cutting, the officers' club was packed to capacity to see the spectacle. The guys were keyed up to see what LT Coleman was going to do. When it came her turn, she strode to the front of the room, and about-faced. She dropped the drop seat on her flight suit to reveal a sexy pair of panties. The entire room roared with approval and her student grabbed the scissors, made two snips and pulled her panties away. Then the guys were treated to an additional thrill; earlier that day LT Coleman asked someone paint naval aviator wings across her butt. Mass chaos ensued and the camera flashes were blinding. The guys loved it. It was truly the event of the year and LT Coleman was accepted into the ranks. She was now known as a "team player."

This concept of "team player" would be repeated throughout my naval career. I respected LT Coleman immensely for her actions and admired her chutzpah. At the time, I was still very modest and don't think I could have acted so brazenly. I learned an important lesson that day about what it took to be one of the guys and be perceived as a "team player." Apparently to be a successful female naval aviator, the women must either act just like the guys, or sit and watch in silence.

My training finally came to a close. I did very well and was in the top of my class. I was overjoyed that I had the chance to fly jets, but was torn with my selection options. While jets seemed glamorous and exciting, helicopters and reconnaissance propeller planes provided the best career path for women. There was not a big selection of jets for women to fly and a very distinct glass ceiling was in place. Command of a squadron at sea was the precursor to long-term success in the Navy and it was completely closed to women jet pilots at the time. However, the helicopter and reconnaissance propeller planes women pilots had the opportunity to command a squadron. My failure to fully grasp the importance of this glass ceiling both personally and professionally at this critical juncture would be one of my greatest mistakes of my life.

To help me decide between the different platforms, I went to Kingsville, Texas to ride in the backseat of a TA-4J, the Navy's jet trainer. Only an hour away from Corpus, Kingsville really is in the middle of nowhere. I was ecstatic about my first ride in a Navy jet. When I arrived, I was even more thrilled to see another female student that was almost done with her training. Very few women were assigned jets so an opportunity to talk with another woman was rare. When we sat down to talk that day, I noticed how tired she seemed. Her face was drawn and she appeared very stressed. When I asked her how she liked it, her responses shocked me.

She had absolutely nothing positive to say about the squadron, the instructors, or her peers. She told me it was the worst decision she ever made, the guys, both instructors and students, obviously did not want her there. She enjoyed the flying aspect but could not stand the people she worked with and couldn't wait to leave. Finally she said she had no intention of staying in the Navy because of the way she was treated. She did eventually resign her commission.

I was shocked. Even with my less than positive experiences, I could not believe what I was hearing. After she left, I turned what she said over and over in my mind. It made no sense to me. Despite a few problems, I thought I was treated very fairly. I loved going in to work and thought my peers liked having me around. My class was very tight and I spent a lot of free time with the guys in my class. I finally came to the conclusion that this other female student was just something of a shrew and a bitter person. I categorized her as merely one of those people whose glass was always half empty. Surely she created her own hell. I promised myself I would never ever be like her. The sad reality is however, now I am that same woman, only exponentially more so.

After my flight in the sleek, responsive, almost mesmerizing A-4, I was able to put that talk with her even further out of my mind. I loved flying in the A-4, and was surprised how quickly I picked up on flying formation. As I flew the plane from the backseat that day, I fell in love and knew that flying jets was what I had to do. I loved the feel of the awesome power at my fingertips, the rush of speed, and the warrior spirit that emanated from the jet. After the flight, I drove home in a high, almost transcendental state. I knew that flying jets would be my future and that nothing could dissuade me.

Selection week came and everyone was on pins and needles. My choices on the official request form were: 1. Jets 2. Helos 3. Props. I had no real desire to fly propeller aircraft. I was attached to a P-3 squadron one summer as a midshipman and thought that the propeller submarine hunting community was very backstabbing and not really for me. The reconnaissance propeller planes also did not appeal to me. I wanted to operate with the fleet Navy, not just drill holes in the sky.

My wish was granted and not only was I going to fly jets, I was moving to Meridian, Mississippi, where another jet training base was located. Not many people really wanted to go Mississippi; the base was in the middle of a swamp. I was delighted because I would only be four hours from home in Tennessee and could visit my mom often. A friend of mine from the Naval Academy, Shannon Workman, was already stationed there and we would be roommates. It was rare for two women to go through training together, and I was grateful that we would have each other.

Though very excited with my new set of orders, I was saddened to leave Corpus Christi. I made a lot of good friends that I still keep in contact with today. My roommate Lisa was a source of strength and my Marine friends kept me laughing. I would miss the days a big group of us piled in a couple of cars and headed to Nuevo Laredo, Mexico for some shopping and Margaritas. One of the most rewarding aspects of my time in Texas was the renewal of my relationship with my father. He was to be transferred to NAS Memphis, and we would have more time to spend together.

When I left, I was the happiest person on the planet. All the pieces of my life were starting to come together and I felt grand. I saw my career really taking form and I envisioned a thirty-year commitment, just like my father. While I dated a little here and there, marriage was not on my list of priorities, and children were not even in the picture. My focus was on flying and my career, and that's exactly what I wanted. Life was perfect!

Chapter Two

The Turbo Guppy

The day I checked into my new squadron, VT-19, I learned the harsh realities of naval aviation. Earlier that day, two of the squadron's T-2's, the Navy's first jet trainer, crashed into each other in the training area. A student pilot and an instructor were in each. One plane was descending in the training area to go home, and the other was climbing into the area to take the departing aircraft's place. Not realizing the proximity of the entering aircraft, the bottom of the departing aircraft basically came down right on the other plane. The instructor and student pilots of the bottom plane were killed instantly. The other student and instructor safely ejected and suffered minimal injuries.

It was a rude awakening for all the young students. Up to that point, flying was fun and carefree; death was not something we considered. Naval aviation is an inherently dangerous business. Very complex aircraft operating in extremely hazardous environments (like an aircraft carrier) can spell disaster in just a moment's hesitation. We heard all the stories and watched the crash-and-burn films, but as is typical of youth, we never thought we could be victims.

The T-2 is a twin engine, jet powered aircraft that is lovingly nicknamed the "Turbo Guppy." Probably the ugliest aircraft in the Navy, it is nonetheless an excellent trainer and very forgiving. The T-2, plagued by extensive maintenance problems in the last ten years, will soon be completely phased out of the Navy's training program. As is true of most naval air mishaps, accidents are almost always related to pilot error; rarely are accidents due to faulty aircraft. The big difference between the T-2 and the T-34 (other than jet versus prop engines) is the addition of ejection seats and a tailhook. Equipped with very powerful rockets strapped underneath, ejection seats are designed to save the pilots in even the most extreme of circumstances.

VT-19 was a very somber squadron the day I checked in, but despite the tragedy that just occurred, it was still a busy squadron. A squadron, or any naval unit for that matter, cannot stop operating because of an accident, even when it involves death. Missions must be carried out, and time stops for no Naval Aviator. So, training continued. My class started our academic training; yet another "ground school," though this one focused on the new arena of jet aerodynamics. My class was even more focused than previous classes. Not only were we all highly motivated to fly jets, we now possessed first hand knowledge of the consequences of complacency in the air.

I took quickly to flying jets, and immediately found a new strength in the simulators. A product of the "Pacman" generation, I excelled in the simulators. Always the type of person who learned best from my own mistakes, some simulator flights were painful yet educational. I soon became the sim (ulator) building rat. If not flying or flight planning, I spent endless hours in the simulator building waiting for just a few spare minutes of trainer time. My dedication and tenacity paid off. I turned into a strong instrument and emergency procedures pilot, which helped me throughout my entire flying career.

The transition into the actual aircraft was not as smooth, unfortunately. Flying in the T-34 had been a breeze. I only put on a relatively light survival vest, donned a helmet, and jumped in the cockpit. Preparation for jets was not quite so easy. Getting ready for a flight in jet aircraft is an event in itself. We termed this preparation "walking."

When assigned a "training aid" (an aircraft), the students would then go to what is called the paraloft and start dressing at least forty-five minutes before the takeoff time.

In the paraloft, everyone's flight gear is hung on individual pegs. First a pilot zips on his "speed jeans," otherwise known as a "G-suit." Hooked to an air hose in the cockpit, these modern day cowboy chaps inflate to keep blood from pooling in the pilot's legs, which is a side effect from pulling against the force of gravity. The vice-like squeezing of the G-suit pushes the blood back to the heart and thus helps to prevent a black out.

After the G-suit, comes the torso harness. This is the most critical piece of gear since it attaches the pilot to both the ejection seat and the parachute. A complicated heap of webbing and straps, for the newest pilots it is the most difficult to negotiate. After much pushing and pulling in a dance that resembles an epileptic hula, the pilot is in the harness. If strapped in correctly, a pilot cannot stand erect and has to walk around in a pseudo hunchback of Notre Dame manner.

Next comes the survival vest. It contains everything needed in an ejection and possibly hostile environment including signal flares, shark repellent, Chiclets and even condoms. Supposedly these prophylactics are included as a water receptacle! The crucial part of this vest is the self-inflating life preserver. When immersed in water, the vest will automatically inflate, saving the unconscious pilot's life.

One drawback to all this extra equipment is that it weighs between 35–40 pounds and is quite uncomfortable. Donning the helmet is the piece de resistance. In the little propeller driven T-34, the pilot wears a helmet with a little microphone in front of his lips. In jets, the pilot graduates to the oxygen mask. Because jet aircraft can fly to much higher altitudes than props and the cockpits are not pressurized like commercial airliners, pure positive flow oxygen must be used. While the oxygen is nice and cool, the mask is bulky and uncomfortable. The microphone is in the mask, so a pilot has to keep it on most of the time to talk. A jet pilot sounds and looks remarkably like Darth Vader when flying.

This process of simply walking is very time consuming at first. The older instructor pilots jumped into their gear in five minutes, so it must have been painful watching students fumble around like a bunch of circus clowns. Learning to move around in the intimidating survival gear and actually fly the aircraft is the biggest challenge of the first few flights. After much wailing and gnashing of teeth and a few scares for my instructors, I finally got the hang of flying in the less-than-glamorous getup and talking on the radio.

Life in VT-19 was a dream. The instructors were even more laid back that the ones in Texas, and the atmosphere was very positive and supportive of the students. I learned an enormous amount of information in those six months. I really loved going to work and the instructors took a lot of time to show us the ropes. I felt totally accepted by both the instructors and the students, and never once felt as if my sex was ever an issue.

We were a very tight group of students. Since there was really nothing to do in Meridian, we hung out at one another's houses watching the Twin Peaks TV series or we headed down to Pensacola where all the real action was. It was on these trips that I was introduced to a seedier side of naval aviation, which were bar games. The object of the guys' favorite bar game was to pick up a girl and score a quickie that night. This was generally not a very tough challenge because Pensacola is known far and wide for its young, dashing aviators and the women who flock to the bars to meet them. Pensacola is what aviators like to call a "target rich environment," which means the ladies are plentiful and very willing.

To make the game a little more interesting, the pilot-to-be could not tell the girl what he really did for a living. Each guy contributed ten bucks to the kitty. The one to walk away with the cash (usually somewhere around $150) would be the guy who used the lowliest of positions to sleep with a girl. On the fringes of this game, knowing full well what the unsuspecting girl did not, I found the whole game sad but pretty funny. Aviators are a very gregarious, charming group who are also very entertaining. The winner of more than one of these little games was a very irresistible Romeo, Rick, who always told a girl what she wanted to hear. Rick's "winning" occupation that worked on several women? A garbage man.

Several weeks later, back in Mississippi, Rick continued the fulfillment of his life's motto, "Quantity not quality." A hero among the guys in my class, we tagged along with Rick just to see what new tricks he pulled. After one particularly successful evening at the local comedy club, Rick decided to take his antics to a new level. He persuaded one of the local civilian women to accompany him to the flight line in the middle of the might where all the T-2's were lined up for the next day's launch. His mission? To have sex in the cockpit of the T-2.

The star-crossed lovers sneaked out to one of the planes. Rick opened the cockpit and in they climbed. The event must have been awkward in the ejection seat, with long metallic safety pins installed to keep it from firing on the ground, not to mention the control stick—somehow they managed. In the middle of the act however, a night security guard happened by and caught the two. Clearly understanding youth, he told Rick to just zip up and get out and he would forget it. Rick, not a candidate for diplomacy in the State Department, told him to "F—k off" until he finished. Rick did finish but quickly found himself hauled into jail.

We found out later that this was not Rick's first offense and as a result, the Navy kicked him out. In Meridian, Mississippi, the Navy could ill afford any more bad press. Just recently one girl who was a victim in one of these little sex trysts attempted suicide due largely in part to the brusque and callous treatment she received once she was passed around. The image of naval aviators as dashing gentlemen was quickly wearing thin on the local population.

The squadron was shocked at Rick's punishment. Many applauded Rick, including the instructors. These types of wild antics were not unusual, they were encouraged. We didn't necessarily disagree with the Navy's punishment, but it was viewed as extreme and a "raw deal" for Rick. The other training squadrons in Texas heard of Rick's act of bravado and made a T-shirt to commemorate the event, which portrayed a naked girl hanging out of the cockpit of the T-2 with the phrase, "The seat's not safe until the pin is in."

Not all naval aviator bar games are crude and demeaning, some have happy endings. One night, this same group of student pilots gathered in a Pensacola bar and decided to play the dog tag game. To play, the very daring and masochistic pilot swallowed his dog tag chain and coughed one end up through his nose. Then the showman pulled one end through his mouth and the other through his nose in a seesaw-like maneuver. While seemingly very gross, we were all mesmerized by those individuals with such command over their gastrointestinal systems.

As we were standing around, applauding Vic, the king of the dog tag game, a civilian girl approached the group. She started giving us and especially Vic a hard time for acting so childish and gross in a public setting. With the chain still running through his nose and mouth, he looked at her sideways, and said, "Oh yeah? Well, I bet you can't do it."

Not to be outdone by the handsome aviator, she said, "OK, give it to me!!!!" He pulled out the chain through his nose. She took it from him and without cleaning it or even wiping it off, she swallowed the chain. After a lot of coughing and gagging, to everyone's amazement, she produced one end out her nose. Thunderous applause greeted her victory, and Vic was extremely impressed. Six months later, they were married. That's true love, aviator style.

My introduction into this enlightening locker room side of men was in a squadron room called the "Ready Room." Originally the room on carriers where pilots briefed en masse for upcoming missions, the tradition of meeting in the Ready Room continued at all land based squadrons. The Ready Room is the heartbeat of the squadron and the focal point of all squadron social interactions. Not only are briefings conducted in these rooms, but all officer meetings and training sessions are also held here. The Squadron Duty Officer (SDO) mans his post in this room, monitoring all in and outgoing aircraft, and is the first person notified in the event of an emergency.

When no group activity is scheduled in the room, it becomes the "water cooler." Men like to tease women about gossiping, but they are just as guilty, if not worse. Everything is discussed in the Ready Room and no subject is taboo. Much professional learning occurs in the Ready Room, but far more important are the social interactions and the war stories shared between pilots.

It is also in the Ready Room that callsigns are usually assigned. No self-respecting pilot ever assigns himself his own callsign. Occasionally, a new guy would try to do just that and announce his callsign as, "Killer", "Ace", "Iceman," or some other manly-man name. In a pseudo knighting ceremony, someone else would typically assign a callsign and the more a pilot hated his callsign, the more it stuck. Most callsigns are a play on the pilot's last name. Brown might yield "Charlie" as a callsign, Rink was dubbed "Roller," and Bright became "Notso."

Sometimes a pilot's actions earned him a callsign. A lost pilot was labeled "Magellan"; the big, slightly overweight easygoing guy with a mustache became "Bear." Any one who threw up on a flight was immediately christened "Chunks." Some names begged for X-rated but hilarious callsigns. Cuny became "Lingus", Bates was known as "Master", and Bush was called "Jeeter" (Ju eat her?) I never knew a woman pilot that was offended by these; we thought they were hysterical as well.

I did not have a callsign for the longest time. I just used my first name, Missy, because it is really a nickname for Mary Louise. I knew that sooner or later I would be given one that probably wouldn't be pretty. Such is life in naval aviation. That day came when I was late for a brief. My alarm didn't go off and I dressed in the car while racing to work. The day before, I went to the beauty parlor for a permanent. Picture if you will, a person running into the Ready Room with a new perm that hadn't been brushed after a night of sleeping on it. The Ready Room was packed to capacity and when I walked in, one of the guys said, "What up with that Medusa hairdo?" The guys fell out of their chairs laughing and "Medusa" stuck. I actually thought it was a great callsign. I love mythology and sometimes secretly wished I could turn guys into stone!

In training squadrons, there are two Ready Rooms, the instructor and the student ready rooms. This separation is necessary because it allows the instructors to complain about the students and compare notes in an uninhibited environment. The students also welcome the separation because the students likewise compare notes, discussing the personal idiosyncrasies of specific instructors and the pitfalls of trickier flights. Just as in the instructor Ready Room, the student Ready Room was filled with all sorts of manly-man "social" behaviors, meant not only to show off but entertain as well. Probably the most lewd and crude bunch of people, naval aviators are also some of the funniest.

It was here in the Ready Room that I learned the importance of burping and farting between male buddies. Two bodily functions almost never discussed in groups of women, they are at the forefront of all Ready Room discussions. Contests were routinely held; who could let out the longest burp, who could say the alphabet while burping, who delivered the smelliest fart. The best was who could clear the Ready Room with particularly malodorous gas. Exposed to this behavior earlier through my brothers, it was still amazing to me that men in their forties still loved the camaraderie of bodily functions.

This room of profound professional and social learning was also the place I first learned about Ball Walking. Made famous in the Tailhook scandal, Ball Walking was not an everyday occurrence but it happened fairly frequently. Ball Walking was somewhat of a rite of passage and gained the daring student entrance into the Boys Club. To Ball Walk, the brave soul wore no underwear underneath his flight suit, took only his testicles out, and positioned both flight suit zippers in such a way that only the testicles were exposed. The guy then walked around the squadron and chatted with everyone as if nothing were amiss. The guys, both students and instructors, roared with laughter and approval whenever anyone accomplished this feat. The guys never Ball Walked to solely embarrass the women (there were only three of us)—they did it just to impress one another.

At the time, I was young, gullible and very naive on many levels. Embarrassed by the bawdy jokes and fraternity like pranks, I still was very much in the trenches, soaking everything up like a sponge. I learned quickly that to survive in this environment, a woman must just go along with everything and never make a fuss. This acceptance made her a "team player." I remembered LT Coleman and tried to follow her example. I also liked a lot of the jokes and stories and I loved being included in the group activities. During one phase of training, we each stood up and told a dirty joke. They were typically gross and vulgar, and when my turn came, I said, "What's the different between like and love?" No one answered, and I then said, "Spit or swallow!" The guys howled with approval and I got a standing ovation. If I had to do it again, I would do the exact same thing.

Despite my clever joke, I was still as green as they come, and I bought into everything the guys said, hook, line and sinker. Because we missed out on the very important socialization years of college, most of the Naval Academy graduates were behind our peers from civilian schools. For the guys, this often translated into severe alcohol abuse. For me, I always seemed to embarrass myself in the silliest of ways. A perfect example was the coffee machine incident.

One day I was the assistant duty officer, a job that required me to assist the primary duty officer in the instructor Ready Room. Part of my duty was to make coffee in an industrial sized coffee machine. I had not made coffee in a machine before since my parents always drank instant coffee and I was not a coffee drinker. I went to the machine and figured out where the grounds went and how much water I needed. My first pot was a success and the instructors told me it was tasty. Feeling pretty good about myself, I quickly ran to make the second pot. While my coffee experience was severely lacking, I did have a lot of tea training. Using the deductive skills of a math major, I decided that since tea bags could be reused, coffee grounds must be recyclable as well. The result was disastrous. The coffee looked like weak tea and I was the laughingstock of the Ready Room. Though embarrassing, there was a silver lining; I was fired from ever making coffee again.

My class finally finished ground training and graduated to the flying stages when tragedy in the air struck again. Another Naval Academy graduate in my class and my neighbor, Lucky, was on his fourth flight when he and the instructor found themselves in what aviators call an "unusual attitude." It is not extraordinary for an aviator to become disoriented in clouds or after hard maneuvering. To combat any cockpit confusion, pilots often practice recovering from this disorientation. During Lucky's flight, his instructor told him close his eyes while the instructor flew the plane to a nose-high, slow, inverted position. He then instructed Lucky open his eyes and attempt to recover, which he did.

What neither expected was that when Lucky pushed the stick forward, he accidentally ran the trim to a full nose-down position. When he tried to roll upright and bring the wings level, the plane did not respond. The instructor then took control of the aircraft and also tried to pull the plane out of the dive. Unable to control the spiraling plane, the instructor followed the established procedures and ejected them both from the plummeting, spiraling aircraft.

The ejection seats and parachutes worked as advertised and in no time both pilots were hanging in their parachutes, headed for the ground. The instructor made a textbook landing and after getting out of his harness, he started to look for his student. Lucky lost consciousness during his ejection, which is fairly common, but most pilots eventually regain consciousness before they hit they ground. Unfortunately, Lucky did not. Generally it is not critical for a pilot to be conscious when they hit the ground. If ejection occurs over water, the life preserver will automatically inflate when immersed in water.

Lucky was not so fortunate to land in water, or on open land for that matter. He came down in the middle of a grove of trees, still unconscious. Because Lucky's legs were limp and spread apart, when he descended into the trees, he was gored in his groin. The instructor saw this happen and immediately radioed for help. As quickly as possible, Lucky was taken to the local hospital. Word of the accident spread like wildfire and my class of seven gathered at the hospital. Lucky was in very serious condition. When he was gored, he severed a major artery and was in danger of bleeding to death. He suffered additional serious ligament and muscle damage, and was in the ICU for several days. Always quick with a joke and a smile, he put on a happy face and acted as if this would hardly slow him at all. We nervously stood around, not knowing what to say or do; mostly thankful it hadn't been us.

Now a class of six, we progressed through all the instrument and familiarization stages. The intermediate syllabus is designed to teach the basics of flying jet aircraft and introduces just the beginning of tactical flying. The final two stages are the gun flights and carrier qualifications. The gun portion of the syllabus is the first introduction to dynamic flying and is probably much more scary for the instructors than for the students. The object of these gun flights is to set up a simulated gun shot on a banner towed behind another T-2. Four planes fly a figure eight pattern that moves with the towplane and the aircraft come very close to one another. These gun flights are the first real test of a pilot's ability to fly in a demanding, fast moving environment. After eight harried gun flights, students then proceed to the most demanding of all training evolutions, landing on the aircraft carrier.

A floating city that carries not only 5000 people, but also enough firepower to decimate a small country, the aircraft carrier is the primary weapon for current naval policy. Aircraft carriers provide the United States with the ability to insert air power into any area without the need

for landing strips on foreign soil. Each of the twelve carriers can carry
as many as eighty fighter, attack, and support aircraft and launches
these planes around the clock in even the worst weather.

Landing aboard an aircraft carrier is what sets Navy pilots apart
and above all other military pilots. Landing an aircraft on a runway
only 900 feet long that pitches, heaves, and rolls both day and night is
an act of intense precision, flying ability, and courage. It is the one
area of training that causes most student pilots to attrite and is the
most difficult of all training phases. Up to this point, my grades were
excellent and I was a well above average student. Named Student of
the Month during September of 1989, I possessed the best academic
and flying grades of all the students that month in VT-19. Although I
was doing well, I occasionally flew an ugly flight and never felt that I
had the program wired. My confidence up to this point was a little
shaky and I could not yet see myself as a real naval aviator.

There is significant preparation before a solo student is sent to the carrier. It seems almost insane that the Navy sends young students to the carrier their very first time, alone. However, no instructor is stupid enough
to ride along for what is destined to be a very scary flight. Despite the fear
and anxieties of the fledgling carrier aviators, their intense training takes
over and usually leads to varying degrees of success.

The training starts with a series of lectures about the techniques of flying the "ball." The ball is actually a lighting system that tells the pilot
whether he is high or low on the landing glide path. In addition to the
light aid, there is another system of checks and balances called the LSO,
the Landing Signals Officer. The LSO is a highly trained professional in
the art of carrier landings and can tell just by looking at the attitude (nose
position) and height of the aircraft if the landing will be successful.

The deck of the carrier is basically divided into two sections—the
takeoff and the landing. The takeoff section is where the steam driven
catapults (called cats) shoot the departing aircraft off, accelerating
them from zero to 150 knots (170 mph) in just two seconds. The

landing section is an angled portion, ten degrees from the centerline, which catches incoming aircraft. Stationed along this landing section are four high-tension wires, spaced about twenty-four feet apart, numbered one through four. An arriving aircraft catches one of these wires with a tailhook that hangs down from the back of the plane. The wire that provides the best margin for safety is the three-wire. While catching any of the wires will work, everyone aims for the three-wire. The most dangerous of the four wires is the one-wire. Catching the one-wire means the pilot just barely cleared the end of the ship and is highly discouraged.

To train student aviators to hit the three-wire, the squadron holds FCLPs, or Field Carrier Landing Practices. The students will fly the landing pattern at a remote land runway over and over again, intensely focusing on landing techniques and landing in the same spot. After two weeks of this intense landing practice, the students go to the real carrier—alone, never before having seen the back of the boat.

My class was combined with two other classes, so there were about twenty students qualifying. After completing our FCLPs, we flew from Mississippi to Pensacola where we waited our turn at the carrier. The ship was the USS Lexington, the only remaining carrier from W.W.II. The Lady Lex held the distinction of having the smallest landing area of any of the carriers, so our task would be that much more difficult. High on nervous energy, none of us slept very well, and we anxiously waited.

Finally, the call came in. Since I was at the beginning of the alphabet, I was in the first wave of three. We jumped in our jets and headed out to the Gulf of Mexico. My group headed out in a four plane formation. An instructor was in the first aircraft, leading his three chicks to "mother," the callsign of the carrier. Very nervous students, who at times seemed to be hanging on for dear life, flew the other three planes.

As we circled overhead the carrier waiting our turn, I dared a peek outside the cockpit. The sight shocked me. We were holding at 8000 feet overhead and when I saw the carrier for the first time, it looked tiny. I said to myself, "There's no way, I will end up flying right over it." It was inconceivable to me that I would take my aircraft and land it on that hunk of steel. When we got the signal to "Charlie," which means it is time to land, my stomach jumped into my throat and my heart was pounding.

We flew over the carrier and separated the flight into the four individual planes. I was number three. The instructor in the first plane flew out of the pattern to wait for us overhead. We were on our own. Dash two, the second plane, made his approach and was waved off. His initial approach was out of the set limits, very common for the first time around, and he was told to go around and try it again.

I was next. This was it and I was on my own. As I was nervously making my turn to final, I heard all the radio chatter about my friend who was just yelled at for screwing up his approach. Now the pressure was on. As advertised though, my superb training took over and I was on autopilot. I made my approach, which was far from perfect, but well within limits. I saw the ball and I saw the back of the ship—but I never saw anything else because I was so intensely focused. In less than fifteen seconds from the time I made my turn, I flew over the back end of the ship. No one was more surprised than I was when I hit the deck and went from 130 mph to zero in an instant. I was scared, unsure of where I was, and froze. I kept the power at full throttle, which is the correct procedure in case I missed and needed to go around again. However, I didn't miss and I needed to clear the landing area but I was still in shock that I was actually there! The Air Boss, a senior aviator who watches all the operations on the deck from the tower, said, "OK 734, we've got you, you can come back on the power."

It took me several seconds to realize he was talking to me but when I did, I immediately brought the power back to idle. The Boss said in a very stern voice, "734, look to your right." I did, and all I saw was the centerline of the landing area. Then he said, "Look to your left." I did, and all I could see was shimmering blue water. Since the landing area is ten degrees off the forward movement of the ship, it is easy to drift left if a pilot doesn't pay attention. I drifted left and was a little too close to the edge for comfort. The Boss then yelled, "Don't be there again!!!" I managed to muster a weak "Yes Sir" and taxied out of the landing area, tail tucked between my legs with my heart still beating a million times per minute. I never did land that far left again.

I then taxied over to the catapult, still dazed and amazed that I was actually there. The flight deck seemed very surreal—a maze of planes and people with steam flowing around both man and machine. A little overwhelmed, I followed the directions of the very brave enlisted handlers who understand they are taxiing inexperienced and apprehensive students. In what seemed only a split second, I was hooked up to the catapult, ready to be shot off the front of the carrier for the first time. In reality, about five minutes passed but I felt as if time were on fast forward. It was all I could do to get over the shock at having successfully landed, follow the taxi directions, and then prepare for the cat shot.

My first cat shot took me by complete surprise. Because the USS Lexington has the smallest deck, the catapult shots must be very powerful to ensure the aircraft has enough flying speed at the end of the stroke. The T-2 accelerated from 0 to 170 mph in about two seconds. I was holding on for dear life, and I couldn't breathe. The force of launching was so powerful that I was literally pinned in the seat and the air was forced out of my lungs, like an anvil just hit me square in the chest. Just when I thought I was going to die, the plane was released from the cat and I was off flying, almost floating in a dream-like sequence. In actuality, the student isn't really flying and probably isn't really thinking that first time either. The plane is able to complete the takeoff sequence without the pilot's intervention, a fortunate technological advance because most of us were brain dead on our first launch anyway.

After I reasoned I wasn't going to die and was safely flying, I was ecstatic. It was the same feeling most people have after a really fantastic roller coaster ride—"I WANT TO DO THIS AGAIN!" To me, cat shots are much more fun than the traps. There is relatively no work involved and it is pure elation going down the track. I have always thought the only way to make it better was to eat a piece of Godiva chocolate at that same instant.

I completed the next three traps and shots without incident. I was not the best 'hooker' out there, but I was very consistent and very stable. In what seemed like no time at all, I was commanded to RTB, Return To Base. I wanted to stay and do more, but I knew I did well enough to qualify and I passed the biggest hurdle of my jet training. I returned to Pensacola as a single plane, nearly out of my skin with excitement. As I was flying away from the carrier, I heard the next group of student pilots from my class check in for their turn. When I landed, some of the guys met me at my plane and we jumped up and down, hugging each other in pure joy. It was an unforgettable moment. In just those few hours, my self-confidence skyrocketed and for the first time, I really believed I was a naval aviator.

The next few hours held the most violent swings of emotions I have ever endured in such a short period. After the initial excitement wore off, I called my mom to tell her but she wasn't in. I left her a message saying I was a Qual, and it had been absolutely fantastic. It turned out to be the most important message I would ever leave her.

A couple of hours after I landed, the squadron received a transmission which no one was prepared for. There was a crash at the carrier, not just in the general vicinity, but actually on the deck of the carrier and five people were dead. We all looked at one another, immediately realizing that the flight of students who passed us on the way out were all people from our squadron. One, if not more of the deaths would be someone we knew.

We quickly found out the details. The flight of four made it to the carrier, and the instructor dropped off his three chicks for their shot at landing on the boat. The first pass for the lead student in the group went OK and then the second pilot, Steve, made his approach. Every approach to the carrier is filmed, and we were able to watch the actual events just days later. Steve's approach initially seemed normal and well within parameters. At only a quarter of a mile away from the ship, Steve started to go low. Going low is a mistake that can be corrected and still safely land, but if not corrected immediately, the consequences can be deadly. Steve didn't respond like the LSO's wanted, so they told him to wave off and go around.

Waving off means that the pilot goes to full power and aborts the landing attempt. The accident investigation was never able to determine what exactly happened, but Steve started his wave off late. The nose of the T-2 came up—Steve was trying to fly away from the carrier. He heard the frantic screams on the radio and tried to put distance between himself and both the steel deck of the carrier and the water. He knew that hitting either would be deadly. Trying to gain altitude, Steve drifted to the right and flew dangerously close towards the control tower. The LSO's, fearing a collision, warned him to turn away. No doubt in a panic, he pulled the nose of the plane up even more and desperately tried to bank sharply to the left.

Steve was in a very precarious position with no experience in this slow flight arena. When he pulled up and left, he was at a very slow speed. The plane stalled and experienced an "adverse yaw departure." When the T-2 stalls in an angle of bank, it flips over in the opposite direction and loses all lift. This is exactly what happened to Steve. He flipped and the plane fell upside down, almost one hundred feet and crashed on the carrier, killing Steve and four maintenance personnel who were underneath.

The fire crews responded in amazing lightening speed, but no one under the wreckage could be saved. Two students in planes on the deck refueling were struck by falling debris, but they managed to eject their canopies and emergency egress away from the flames. Because of the quick response of the fire teams and other flight deck personnel, many lives were saved and a more catastrophic disaster was averted.

Almost immediately CNN broadcasted the news of the accident, and repeated it every thirty minutes. The Navy's worst training carrier accident and the five deaths were headline news for days. My mother was besieged with phone calls from around the country and overseas. Fortunately, she received my earlier message so she knew I was OK, otherwise the time delay would have been unendurable.

When the other pilots in Steve's formation returned to Pensacola, it was a somber reception. No one really knew what to say. Just that morning Steve's fiancée brought us all orange juice and cookies as a good luck send off. Steve was a class favorite. He was a strong student, with above average grades. We were also concerned about another classmate who didn't return and was last seen near the fireball of the accident. We later found out he was okay, but it was torture waiting for the news. The entire group met that night at a beach bar, but the mood was hardly one of celebration. Only three of us qualified, and we didn't feel much like reveling in our accomplishments. We all drank way too much that night and mostly just stared at one another in disbelief that one of our classmates was dead.

There was little time for grieving. Just two days later, I checked into a new squadron, VT-7, and started ground school for the last stage in training, Advanced Strike in the TA-4J. I grew up a little that day when I realized that my entire training in the T-2 was marked by death. The day I checked in, two pilots died, and my last day was marked with the worst training carrier accident in modern naval aviation history. My class of seven had not fared well through the past six months. One student pilot was dead, one was seriously maimed, and another was attrited. In the end, only three of us would get our wings.

Chapter Three

Wings of Gold

Just three days after the accident on the carrier, I was back in the classroom, going through the final stage of training. The last stage of training in the jet pipeline is called Advanced Strike. At this point, the student has learned all the basics of flying jet aircraft, including carrier operations. The last hurdle before the winging, Advanced Strike introduces tactical flying. The student learns basic bombing techniques, air-to-air fundamentals, low-level flying, and must have one more successful repeat performance at the carrier.

The plane flown in Advanced Strike is the TA-4J, a two-seat training version of the A-4. The A-4 is one of the most versatile planes ever flown in the military. First designed in the 1950's, the plane is still flying all over the world today. The A-4's days of glory were in Vietnam when it was the cornerstone of the Navy's light attack inventory. The A-4 is a single engine, highly maneuverable delta wing jet used in the 1980's both by the Blue Angels and the top notch adversary pilots of TOPGUN. Moving from the T-2 to the TA-4J was like moving from a tricycle to a Harley-Davidson. The TA-4J was unstable, fast, and unforgiving compared to the slow but stable T-2.

The new squadron of planes and instructors was called VT-7, housed in the same building as VT-19, just down the hall. Even though only a hallway separated the two squadrons, the difference was like night and day. The atmosphere in VT-7 was antagonistic when compared with VT-19, and the instructors were not the laid back teachers of the T-2's. There was no joking around in VT-7, no horseplay and certainly no ball walking. The students did not speak unless spoken to, and when talking to each other, it was in the hushed tones of a library or church.

There were two primary reasons for the difference in squadron atmospheres. First, the instructors of VT-19 had different backgrounds than those in VT-7. The T-2 instructors generally came from the support communities of tankers and patrol craft. In some cases, outstanding propeller pilots were allowed to transition to jets as instructors. These communities are, for the most part, more relaxed than the fighter and bomber (attack) squadrons. Fighter and attack communities fall into a different category and are considered "tactical" aircraft, otherwise known as TACAIR.

At the time, these aircraft were the F-14 Tomcat, the F/A-18 Hornet, the A-6 Intruder, the EA-6B Prowler, and the A-7 Corsair. (The A-6 and A-7 are no longer active aircraft and the F-14 has only a few years left.) The pilots of carrier-based tactical aircraft are a breed apart from all other pilots. Known widely for their arrogance, loud mouths, and cavalier attitudes, these men flew fast, unforgiving aircraft in very dangerous environments with millions of dollars worth of missiles and bombs attached to their planes. Confidence is the most basic requirement of this job; dropping bombs and then landing on a pitching, heaving carrier deck in total darkness is not for the indecisive and faint-hearted.

These fighter and attack pilots were the instructors in VT-7. They took their job very seriously and subscribed fully to the notion of survival of the fittest. Unfortunately, in a training environment, this egotism and bravado would sometimes become warped and misdirected. If an overzealous instructor perceived a student, male or female, as weak, that student stood a slim chance of graduating. The advanced stage was much more evaluation than instruction, and those that did the best were the fastest learners.

The second reason for the antagonistic and unfriendly student environment was a surplus of students. During that time I was in training, the Navy just had too many students in the jet pipeline. When a glut occurs, the instructors are ordered to weed out those students who are average to below average. During my time in VT-7, the attrition was 30%, an unbelievably high percentage. A normal loss rate from Advanced Strike was closer to 8–10%. Because of the surplus, one in every three students in the pipeline would not make it.

This incredibly high attrition rate led to fear and dread among the students. We started calling NAS Meridian, NAS Attridian. There was only a single Ready Room in VT-7, and only the instructors were allowed to sit on the couches. The students could only sit in the straight-backed chairs lining the walls. Cowering in the background, the students tried not to be noticed. "Downs," the paperwork that documented unsatisfactory performance and led to a student's attrition, were commonplace. The "down" was actually a pink sheet of paper and when the instructors slipped into their Darwin mood, the students told each other, "Stay away because pink is flying!"

Not all instructors were so threatening, but it only took a handful to create such a fear-inspiring environment. Graduating and earning the coveted Wings of Gold during that time was a big deal. Because of the us-versus-them environment, the students hung together even tighter, making sure the gouge network was solidly in place. I could not have made it through this stage without the guys in my class.

Ground school went well for me, as did my simulator training. Always a strong instrument pilot, I passed my very important instrument checkride and was on my way to the tactical stages. The very first tactical stage is called TACFORM, or tactical formation. This stage teaches the student pilot to maneuver in close proximity to one or more aircraft while maintaining certain strategic positions for defensive or offensive situations. It is the first dynamic stage in Advanced Strike and is the building block for all other tactical evolutions.

The first flight in this stage is absolutely critical. The stage only consisted of two flights before the checkride, so every minute and maneuver counted. The instructor who was assigned to a student's first TACFORM flight was crucial and played a key role in the student's understanding and progress.

I was sitting nervously in the straight-backed chair against the wall waiting for my instructor before this important first tactical flight. I never flew with this instructor before and knew nothing about his techniques or preferences. He came barreling in the Ready Room and said, "CUMMINGS, WHO THE HELL IS CUMMINGS?" I knew right then I was in trouble. I meekly said, "Here, Sir." He turned and gave me a look to kill. It was obvious to everyone in the room that he did not like me from the very beginning. He walked up to me and yelled, even though I was sitting right in front of him, "CUMMINGS, WHAT THE F—K IS YOUR CALLSIGN?" I flinched, but not because he cursed. F—k is a word that is a noun, verb, adjective and adverb in naval aviation. I balked because I never encountered an instructor so openly hostile. For the first time in my flying career, I was really scared of my instructor. I managed to squeak out a reply, "Medusa, Sir."

He sneered at me and screamed, "MEDUSA, WHAT THE F—K KIND OF CALL SIGN IS MEDUSA? CALLSIGNS CAN ONLY HAVE ONE OR TWO SYLLABLES, NOT THREE LIKE THAT F—KING CALLSIGN OF MEDUSA!"

I was speechless. I had never been told of the callsign syllable requirement, but even more important at the time, I knew I was going to have to fly with this screamer. I wasn't the only one without anything to say. The entire room was deathly quiet. Even in VT-7, this outbreak was unprecedented.

Finally another instructor broke the silence. An instructor who flew with me often and did not buy into the student harassment package said ever so matter-of-factly, "That's right MON–TAN–A, you tell her!" The instructors howled with delight over this faux pas on Montana's part. Clearly not a rocket scientist, Montana was now madder than ever. He embarrassed himself in front of not only the instructors, but the students as well. He blamed me, and the next three hours were some of the worst in my life. He yelled at me through the entire brief and he screamed at me during the whole flight. I did not hold up well under his assault.

Not surprisingly, I flew the worst flight of my life, and it was the first time I felt like crying since I was a little girl. I was angry with him and angry with myself for letting him affect me. Up to that point, I thought I was impenetrable. Clearly, this was not so. I did not receive a "down" that day, but I did miss out on some very important learning. Two days and two flights later, I did receive my first down on my TACFORM checkride. The instructor told me, "You didn't do anything unsafe, but the overall flight was not pretty, and I think you just need to see this again."

He was absolutely correct, and while I did not want a down on my record, I knew I had not yet bounced back from the beating I received two days prior. During the two years and three stages of training, most students did not make it without one or two downs, so I wasn't too alarmed. However, I was ashamed. Always the perfectionist, I hate sloppy performance. I knew I was not ready for the next, even more demanding stage of air-to-air combat.

I flew two practices that went very well, and I felt ready for my next checkride. I flew again with a new instructor, and unbeknownst to me, he was a good friend of Montana's. My second check ride was a repeat of the flight with Montana. The instructor, "Hacker," yelled and cursed at me through the entire flight. Just as we were about to land for the final time, he took the controls from me and finished the landing. Though the flight was not my best, it was much better than the last checkride. When we climbed out of the plane, Hacker said, "If it's the last thing I do, I am going to see to it that you are kicked out of this program. As long as I am around, you are not going to get your wings." I was totally flabbergasted. Other than Montana, no one had been so vicious with me, but now Hacker spelled out just exactly what he had in mind.

He failed me on my checkride and a few instructors privately discussed my situation; the next day, I would be given a "special" checkride. Very nervous and not knowing what to expect, I went on this special checkride with an instructor who was infamous for giving downs. On this flight, I was instructed to perform many maneuvers that I had never before performed. With less than 200 flying hours, I wasn't experienced enough to shoot from the hip. I was very much still a student and a parrot. I needed to see something first before I could do it. It seemed that Hacker's promise was coming true; I was given another down for this special checkride. Despite my position in the top of my class and my exemplary performance throughout the entire training program, it looked as if I was the next to be attrited.

I was in a state of total confusion. Three downs in six days were totally unheard of. I knew I made mistakes, but I didn't know enough at the time to reason through the entire situation. I started to believe I was the worst pilot in the world and wondered how I made it as far as I did. I knew Hacker and Montana hated me, and I also knew that once a few instructors had it in for a student, he was a goner. I could not believe that after such stellar performance up to this point in flight school, I was about to be another statistic.

The training office reviewed my case and because I received so many downs so close together, a special progress board was convened. Three senior instructors reviewed the flights, spoke with the instructors involved, and then met with me. They forwarded their recommendation up to the Commodore, a Captain who was in charge of the entire airwing. Captain Beatty called me into his office to give me the final decision. I stood at attention while he read his verdict.

All three of the instructors and Captain Beatty agreed that I should be returned to flying, and that the senior pilot in VT-7 would give me my next checkride. The senior pilot possessed the most experience and was highly respected in the airwing. I was relieved and knew absolutely that I was given the fairest deal possible.

After he told me of his decision, he asked me to sit for a more informal discussion. He apologized for Montana's behavior on my first TACFORM flight. It turns out that Montana was not supposed to fly with women. The year prior, the same circumstance occurred with another woman and the other instructors turned Montana in for his abuses. Montana did not like women and did not think they should be flying. Captain Beatty then told me that he was very upset with the highly questionable events that transpired over the other two flights and that he personally was going to put a stop to it. His last words to me were, "Ensign Cummings, I want you to go back down there and show them you are not going to take any of their Sierra!" (Sierra is the Navy's word for S—t.)

I went into Captain Beatty's office expecting the worst. I did not tell anyone what Hacker said to me, but obviously he said it to others. I learned a great deal that day about leadership and the wisdom of senior leaders. Captain Beatty inspired and motivated me that morning. After I left his office, I was impressed that he saw the situation for what it really was, and then built me up after I was so decimated by Montana and friends.

My next check ride with the senior pilot was eye watering. Because I flew so many extra practice flights and the trial by fire, I was totally locked on. The senior pilot said my tactical formation flying was the best he'd ever seen in a student. Every since then, TACFORM has been one of my strongest skills. Montana, Hacker and the gang were told to back off and were not allowed to fly with me again. I then graduated to the most exacting stage, Air Combat Maneuvering.

When I started the Air Combat stage, I was a little intimidated. This was an extremely demanding stage. Two and three aircraft hurling themselves at one another in a small piece of sky is thrilling but dangerous. The pilots cannot lose concentration for even a second or risk certain death. After my first two flights where I flew the moves correctly but cautiously, one of the F-14 pilots pulled me aside. LT Cherry, callsign Buster, was very concerned about my overall understanding of air-to-air combat. In truth, I did not have the big picture and was just flying to please the instructor.

Buster sat me down and talked to me like no other instructor. He took some models and started moving them through the air, giving me all types of hypothetical situations. Buster talked me through an actual real world engagement, explaining the how's and why's. In the two hours we spent just discussing the whole concept of fighter combat, I learned more than in all the academics. He wasn't the only pilot who mentored me. Maybe out of pity over the Montana incident, two Marine Captains took extra time in the briefs and debriefs to make sure I understood completely where I made mistakes. Because of all the coaching and one-on-one attention, I ended up one of the best dogfighters in my class.

These skills also helped me in other stages. I was an outstanding bomber and received a special award for precision bombing. I also did very well in the very demanding low-level flights, able to fly low and fast without getting lost. In the most demanding of all stages, the carrier, I again did very well and was above the class average. This was no small feat because landing the A-4 on the carrier was much more difficult than the T-2 and required much greater skill.

When I landed on my last flight, I felt a huge weight lifted from my shoulders. I did it; I earned my wings after two long years. I despise the phrases, "It was a character building experience" and "What doesn't kill you only makes you stronger," but they were absolutely true in this case. If I hadn't experienced all the nastiness, I don't think I would have finished so strongly. Not only did I finish strong, but also my best performances were in the tactical portions of the flying, and I finished in the top of the class.

As I climbed out of my plane on that last flight, I saw them waiting for me. When a student finishes his last flight, all the other students come out and hose the new naval aviator down with fire hoses. I was pleasantly surprised with the turnout. I knew that my peers were rooting for me throughout all the problems, and there they were, celebrating my victory with me. Soaking wet, I shook everyone's hands. We were beyond the hugging stage of the T-2 celebration; we were real pilots now. The last person to shake my hand and slap me on the back was my good friend, callsign Stiffy. Another Naval Academy graduate and quite a man with the ladies, he was my best friend through training. Stiffy also just finished, and was on his way to Tomcats.

When pilots finish their training, they put in their dream sheet. This is a list of preferences for new aircraft. Everyone wanted the fighters, F/A-18s and F-14s. In 1990, selection was quite competitive. Those with the best grades got what they wanted. Even though I finished second in my winging class of eighteen, I could not have premium orders like Stiffy's. I was a woman, and women were not allowed to fly aircraft that possibly ventured into combat.

At that time, women were allowed to only fly a handful of support jet aircraft and the selection was extremely limited. My choices were further limited due to the fact that many of the squadrons open to women were shutting down due to the post-cold war military drawdown. I asked to fly single seat A-4's in either Hawaii or the Philippines. These squadrons were adversary squadrons that simulated enemy operations. The adversary squadrons were the closest parallel to tactical flying for women. I found out a few days later that I was headed to the Philippines. It was not my first choice; I wanted to live in Hawaii. However, professionally, it was the better choice. The squadron in the Philippines traveled often, and many more qualifications were available. I was excited and ready to leave the country. The farther away from Hacker and Montana, the better.

After the last student pilot finishes his final flight and is hosed down, the next ritual is the Winging ceremony. This is a formal ceremony held in the base chapel. My "Winging" ceremony was held on a picture perfect Mississippi summer day. All eighteen wingees and their families packed the church to capacity. In front of God, country, and family, a specially chosen person pins on the new naval aviator's wings. Usually this person is a mother, father, wife, or fiancée. My mother pinned on my wings, and it was a very proud moment for my family and friends who came from Tennessee on my behalf. After the ceremony, in the middle of all the hugs and well wishes, Hacker approached me. (I already pointed him out to my mother and I was shocked that he reached out to shake my hand.) As he shook my hand, he said, "Good Job Medusa, I always knew you could do it." I was stunned and speechless. I never have been able to figure out if he told me he wanted me kicked out to motivate me, or if he really meant it and just felt guilty after I performed in such a stellar fashion.

My orders to the Philippines would not take effect until the new fiscal year, in October. In the interim, I needed to find a job somewhere in the area. Most wingees just hang around the squadron helping with menial tasks like administering urinalyses. I went home to Memphis, Tennessee to work in the same command as my father, the Naval Air Technical Training Center (NATTC). This is the advanced school for all aviation enlisted personnel. NATTC is where the Navy trains their people to fix aircraft, repair electronics, install components, and work with ordinance. It is a massive organization and I worked directly as the Commanding Officer's assistant.

I enjoyed the two months I worked at NATTC. The Marines kept a reserve A-4 squadron there that was very similar to the one I was going to in the Philippines. I hung around with them, listening to their sea stories and flying the simulator to keep my skills honed. I carpooled with my Dad every day, and he showed me the ropes. One of my best girlfriends from the Naval Academy also worked in NATTC and it was fun working with a peer and a good friend.

One of my principal projects at NATTC was to administer a command wide survey on Sexual Harassment and Fraternization. I knew nothing about the Navy's policies and procedures for this type of project, and not only was I supposed to conduct the survey, I was to investigate any discrepancies. In a command of over 3000 people, my work was cut out for me. It took me about a month to complete the project. The Commanding Officer, Captain Tom Finta, was so pleased with my work, that he awarded me a Navy Achievement Medal (NAM). This is a very important personal award that signifies its wearer as a hard charging, dedicated sailor or officer. I was elated because I was a very junior officer, and this was my first real job outside of flying.

During this waiting period to go to the Philippines, I decided to go to my first Tailhook Convention. It was September 1990, one year before the Tailhook Convention that shook the Navy to its core. This convention is legendary among naval aviators. Now that I was winged, "real" aviator, I decided to see what all the hubbub was about. My roommate from flight school, who also finished that summer, was going, as well as some other girlfriends from the Naval Academy. It would be a big WUBA convention in addition to the Tailhook convention.

WUBA is a Naval Academy acronym that stands for Working Uniform Blue Alpha. Because there were apparently not enough derogatory names to call us, the men changed WUBA to mean Women Used By All and taunted us with this nickname. To show them we didn't care, we adopted the name and changed it to mean, Women Underestimated By Assholes.

From all over the country, carrier pilots piled into the Navy's C-9 transport planes, bound for Las Vegas. The convention was held annually in Las Vegas, and every year it was hosted by the Hilton. Despite the losses the Hilton knew it would incur, the money and notoriety that came with the Tailhook Convention were worth the damages. The Tailhook Association, the professional society of carrier pilots, fronted money every year to cover the expected losses and imminent destruction of hotel property. In the land of risk taking, this was a sure thing for the Hilton.

While Tailhook was a convention open to all naval aviators, its primary focus was carrier aviation. Those pilots who proved their mettle by landing on a carrier were "Hookers," and Tailhook was the opportunity for the Hookers to let it all hang out—literally and figuratively. I heard all the wild stories about Tailhook; now, I wanted to see it for myself.

The Tailhook Convention was ostensibly advertised as a "professional" convention, paid for with taxpayer dollars. To a large extent, it really was. One lecture hall was packed to full capacity with representatives from both the Navy and the corporate world. McDonnell Douglas, Grumman, and Northrop were just a few of the defense contractors that set up booths advertising their affiliations with the Navy.

We loved these booths because they gave out cool accouterments like pictures, T-shirts, hats, beer holders, and the rest of the typical conference propaganda. The Navy also occupied a few representative booths that were useful. Personnel from Washington were there to advise aviators on their careers and possible job openings. My personal favorite naval exhibit was the Safety Center booth. They set up a large screen TV showing all the famous crash and burn clips. I sat in front of this TV for hours, mesmerized not only with the aspect of death, but also with sometime survival in horrific situations.

Two of the films I saw always stuck out in my mind. The first was a C-2 launched from the deck of a carrier. A C-2 is a propeller-driven cargo plane that can carry up to 40 people. The film showed the C-2 taxiing to the Cat. The weather was bad; the visibility was low, and the waves were causing the deck to pitch and heave. Captured on film, the C-2 was launched off the carrier at exactly the wrong time and flew directly into a gigantic wave. The plane disappeared completely and then…miraculously, it emerged from the other side and kept flying. I can only imagine the thoughts that coursed through the minds of the pilots and did the passengers ever realize how close they came to death? Had that been a jet, it would have crashed, and it was incredulous that the C-2 remained airborne.

The second accident is my all time favorite because it demonstrates the funny side of technology. A guy was landing his F/A-18, which is equipped with a camera that films what the pilot sees in his windscreen. During the rollout on the runway, the pilot mistakenly thought something went wrong and the aircraft was about to flip. He pulled the ejection handle and went shooting up 200 feet in the air. The pilot's parachute deployed and he plunged back to earth, slow enough to live but fast enough for the fall to be painful. Proving that it needs no pilot, the faultless plane rolled to a stop, just in time to film the embarrassed pilot hitting the ground right in front of the aircraft. The pilot was a little bruised and shaken up but OK. It's not every day your plane gets the best of you and then films your screw-up for all to see.

After a group of us finished watching these rubbernecking films, there were various symposiums we could attend. The most popular was the question and answer session held by the Navy's senior leadership. The open forum allowed the lowliest of officers to ask admirals any question without fear of reprisal. The questions usually focused on deployment schedules and lack of money for training. Occasionally, a woman asked when more planes and jobs would be opened to the female tailhookers. The unsuspecting female pilot would be loudly booed down. The message was loud and clear—women aviators were clearly second-class citizens who were not considered "real" aviators by either our peers or the Navy's leadership.

The majority of every pilot's time during Tailhook was spent socializing and drinking. Tailhook was not known primarily for the professional opportunities; Tailhook was known as the party of all parties, and that was the chief focus. When we arrived and checked in, the first place we went was the infamous third floor of the Hilton. Held on the same floor every year, squadrons throughout the Navy and Marine Corps reserved rooms on this floor, and these rooms were the heartbeat of the party. Called "Admins," the beds were cleared out to make room for the kegs, bars, and any other special paraphernalia. Half of the rooms on the third floor hallway opened onto the pool. Booze, pools and aviators are a deadly mix. I am surprised no one has ever died at these conventions.

Each squadron paid for the liquor available in each room, so there was no shortage of alcohol. In the true spirit of aviator competitiveness, each squadron tried to outdo the other in outrageous acts. Strippers were routine and actually somewhat blasé in the "Admins." Really now, anyone can come up with a stripper, how unoriginal! Strippers were part of the regular Friday night routine at any US Navy Officer's Club at bases. Tailhook demanded new and unusual forms of entertainment, and aviators are clever enough to meet that challenge.

My squadron's room was best known for the Margarita machine that ran 24 hours. Liquor was free flowing and highly encouraged at all hours of the day. Another room offered the infamous rhino penis that served up beer. It was not uncommon to see furniture launched out of windows. In the evening, the pool turned into an X-rated chicken fight contest. The guys put the willing women on their shoulders, and in no time, the women's tops were gone. (The women voluntarily removed their own tops.) Quintessential Mardi Gras lovers, aviators' chants were heard all over the hotel, "Show us your tits!!!"

One of the more popular rooms was the leg shaving room. The squadron that ran this room was an S-3 squadron. (S-3's are anti-sub-marine and tanker (fuel) aircraft.) In the food chain on the carrier, they are the amoebas, the stepchildren in the jet community. A lack of respect for the S-3 community does exist in the Navy, so no doubt the S-3 aviators wanted to prove they could party as hard, if not harder than the fighter guys.

The S-3 aviators invited any and all women into the room and offered them anything they wanted to drink. Those that accepted the free leg shavings sat in a chair in the middle of the room. The lucky guy then lathered the girl's legs up and started shaving. The other guys stood around, transfixed on the task in a voyeuristic stare. The aviators that did the shaving were very adept. I never saw them nick one girl. The women ranged from giggly to orgasmic. I was not around for the more graphic episodes, but I understand much more was shaved than just legs.

Women were not the only recipients of the shaving cream and razor. While I was watching the leg shavings from the hallway, an unfortunate aviator made the mistake of passing out right in front of the door to the leg shaving room. The rest of us were all so wasted that we just looked on, laughing. No one checked to make sure he was still breathing. Lucky for him it was only a mild loss of consciousness due to alcohol. While the rest of the aviators took no notice of him, a few brave women in the leg-shaving room did. When they saw him fall and determined that he was not going to be getting up anytime soon, they sprang into action.

In the middle of the hallway, with hundreds of people milling about, they stripped him buck-naked from the waist down. The poor guy was laying face up, exposed to the world, with no fighting chance. The imaginative and industrious duo whipped out two razors and a can of shaving cream and proceeded to shave him clean; they were not shaving his legs. He lay there for hours, oblivious to what transpired. The passersby made all kinds of clever comments, "That's going to itch when the hair grows back in!" and "That looks like a penis, only smaller!" For all the accusations of assault and lewd behavior after the Tailhook '91 scandal, I wondered why this guy didn't come forward and let everyone know the shavings were equal opportunity.

When most people recall stories of the infamous Tailhook, they think of the Gauntlet and the women who were assaulted and raped as they were forced down it in 1991. Everyone I spoke to who went to both Tailhook conventions in 1990 and 1991 said the 1990 Tailhook was by far more out of control than the one that caught the attention of the press. The Gauntlet in 1990, in place every night by 11 PM, was the hallway of the third floor lined with drunk, depraved, and defiant aviators, just waiting for girls to venture down. Any woman who dared run the Gauntlet would not make it to the end with all her clothes, that much was clear to me.

As barbaric as it sounds, many women voluntarily went down this chute, egging the guys on for more and willingly took off their own clothes. Tailhook was known across the country as a place to meet dashing, handsome, and fearless naval aviators, glorified in the still very popular movie, *TOPGUN*. Women with groupie mentalities, from all walks of life flocked to the convention. Because so many commercial pilots are former naval aviators, both the commercial pilots and hoards of flight attendants also attended. The aviators knew this, and it was sport to "bag a stew" (sleep with a stewardess). Not all women who attended were willing to do anything to catch a pilot, but many were and made their intentions quite clear.

I was not there the entire time to see all the shenanigans, but I was in that hallway every night and knew what was happening. I personally did not object to the game; I never saw anyone go down the Gauntlet that objected either. When the elevator doors slid open, no girl was immediately forced to go down the Gauntlet. Everyone left the elevator area, and walked around a wall to the entrance of the hallway. One of two choices was made at the hallway's entrance. I could take my chances down the Gauntlet, or I could skirt out a glass door that led to the outdoor pool area. I always chose the patio route.

Even in my most drunken state—which was more time than I care to remember—I never dreamed of going down this hallway. Those women who elected to go down that hallway were poor choosers. No doubt alcohol clouded many women's judgments, and I am not attempting to downplay their suffering, but they were clearly not paying attention to their surroundings. I am not defending what the perpetrators did. Raping and assaulting women is morally uncon-scionable, illegal, and many women were assaulted. However, the men in the Gauntlet were drunk and getting mixed signals. With many girls welcoming the groping of the Gauntlet and voluntarily stripping, it is easy to see how the situation quickly spun out of con-trol. The crimes of Gauntlet were not as cut and dried as reported, and while a few individuals were guilty, the real blame should fall squarely on the shoulders of the Navy's leadership.

The Gauntlet was a tradition planned and executed in full view of senior officers, with many actively condoning it. I witnessed a plethora of commanders and above watching from the sidelines, getting a good laugh, and egging on their young protégés. Not one of these naval offi-cers who understood the importance of strong leadership, command presence and moral courage ever elected to do the right thing and stop the madness. Even though twenty years had passed since My Lai, it is amazing that seemingly law abiding, model citizens can turn so quickly to their animal instincts.

I was no angel during the convention and alcohol dominated my time at Tailhook just as it did for most of the men. I loved getting into the thick of the partying, and while not involved in any of the sex games, I was doing tequila shots in the middle of a group, trying to fit in and just be one of the guys. This desire to be accepted and liked by my peers would dominate my social interactions for some time to come. Just like the guys, I drank like a fish the entire four days. I stayed out until five in the morning, slept for a few hours, got up and imme-diately started drinking, just like my male counterparts. Tailhook was a colossal party, and I was not going to miss a minute. Furthermore, I was going to prove to the men that I was a team player.

Gambling was a new concept to me, and I was the person that Las Vegas loves, just off the farm, ignorant and drunk. Fortunately, losing 20 or 30 dollars seemed like a huge loss to me so I did not find myself in any financial predicaments. I knew I reached bottom at the convention though one night at the Blackjack table. Actually it was morning, about 4 AM and a group of us were going strong, totally wasted. I was sitting on a stool, actually ahead for the first time, with my legs tucked up against the bottom of the Blackjack table.

I was wearing black fishnet pantyhose and a mini skirt, dressed to let the guys know that I was a "player." Unfortunately, I was a very drunk player. I was so drunk in fact that I fell off the stool. That is not an unusual occurrence in and of itself really. However, one leg of my fishnet hose caught on a staple underneath the table. As I fell, the right leg of my hose ripped off. Everyone turned to watch what I would do. I was now standing with only half a pair of fishnet hose. I grabbed the intact leg, ripped it off, threw it at a group of guys to resounding applause, climbed back on my barstool and said, "Hit me!"

When Tailhook was over, not a sound was heard on the flight home. We all experienced severe hangovers, and it was a miracle that none of us died from alcohol poisoning. I was actually physically ill for several days after. Despite my attempts to fit in, I was not a drinker, and my body was not prepared to handle that level of abuse. Notwithstanding how sick I felt, I still had a marvelous time. Except for the few confrontations like the question and answer session, I loved hanging around with all the aviators. They were very raw, but they were hilarious.

When the Tailhook Convention was exposed in the press a year later, I was actually sad. I wasn't ready for the party to be over, and I was very sorry that it ended in such a negative fashion. I never thought anything of the lewd charades and wild antics; as far as I knew, this was all normal behavior, part of the Navy's SOP (Standard Operating Procedures). A few weeks later, I was headed overseas where the antics of Tailhook would severely pale in comparison to daily military life in the Philippines.

Before I reported to my first fleet squadron, I was required to go through the Navy's SERE school—Survival, Evasion, Resistance and Escape. Located in Maine, this is one of the Navy's Prisoner of War schools where each aviator is forced to take a long hard look at his intestinal fortitude. It was one of the best Navy schools I ever attended, and I learned a lot about myself. Despite thinking I was savvy, I learned I was still very naive, trusting and downright gullible. Unfortunately, I cannot go into detail about this school because it would compromise the training, but after some mild torture and abuse, I emerged even stronger and smarter than before.

After SERE school, I headed for California. Before I flew to the Philippines, I was required to attend Spin School at NAS Miramar. Spin School lasts only one day and involves a single flight. The flight is performed in a T-2 because of the stability and survivability of the aircraft. During the flight, a very experienced instructor takes the student up and places the plane in a series of spins and out-of-control flight. The student then must recognize certain spin modes and demonstrate proper recovery procedures. It is a very violent flight, but the lessons learned are essential.

When I arrived for Spin School, the squadron was abuzz with cameras and civilian people frantically scurrying about. Brad Johnson, the star of the soon-to-be-released movie, Flight of the Intruder, was in the middle of a photo shoot in the cockpit of an A-6. Preoccupied with my upcoming flight, I did not pay much attention to the ruckus. The flight went well, but upon my return, I felt sick to my stomach as I was climbing out of the cockpit. Feeling sick after an out-of-control flight is very typical, especially after not flying in a few months. I ran into the paraloft, just in time to throw up in a big garbage can. I did not see Brad Johnson standing just a few feet away. There I was, heaving my guts up in front of a bona-fide movie star. So much for rubbing elbows with the rich and famous.

The next day I flew to LA where I picked up the cattle car to the Philippines. Cattle car is Navy slang for commercial personnel transport aircraft. I was turbo-charged for the future. I was a Naval Academy graduate, and earned my Naval Aviator wings with blood, sweat, and tears. I acquired my first Navy Achievement Medal for superior performance, and I made it through SERE school. Despite my less than glamorous brush with Hollywood, I felt good about myself and was ready to take on the world.

Chapter Four

Mabuhay

When I stepped out of the plane into the Philippines, the first word I read was "Mabuhay" on signs all around the terminal. I found out later that this was the Philippine word for "welcome." The heat and intense sunlight took me by complete surprise. It was December, and while I knew the Philippines was a tropical climate, I did not know what to expect. It was my birthday, Sunday, December 2, 1990, and I was twenty-four years old.

I deplaned and went through customs, dazed and exhausted. The trip is well over twenty-four hours, and the time difference is +13 hours (EST). After clearing customs and finding my bags, I stepped outside the terminal without a clue as to where I would go. Fortunately, one of the helicopter pilots in the squadron, Dave, who was also a Naval Academy graduate, took pity on me and met me as I came out of the terminal. Dave drove me to the Bachelor Officers' Quarters (BOQ), which would be my home for the next 19 months. I shadowed him very closely over the next two months because I was so lost, and he was the one person to initially show me any kindness.

The Philippines was a very strategic naval location, and one of our greatest prizes of the Spanish American War. The name of the naval base was Subic Bay. Sixty-five miles northwest of Manila, Subic Bay was within a day's flight from both China and Japan. What made Subic Bay even more desirable was its protected, deep-water port surrounded by 300 degrees of mountains. Even in the worst typhoon, ships at anchor were not in desperate peril. Entire battlegroups could pull into port with plenty of room to spare.

There were two sides of Subic Bay Naval Base—the piers and the airfield. The airfield was completely separate from the ship side and even boasted its own name, Cubi Point Naval Air Station. The runway was built on a landfill after W.W.II. The runway and airfield facilities were at sea level, but all the housing and dining facilities were located on the 600 foot mountain chain that was the original coastline. There was always an intense rivalry between the aviators of Cubi Point and the surface officers of Subic Bay. This rivalry is as old as naval aviation. Like all traditions, while it may seem silly, it sure was fun to uphold.

While separated by only two miles, going from one side to the other was portrayed as an arduous task. Each side provided separate dining, medical, recreation and lodging facilities, and while everyone was allowed to use both, no self-respecting aviator would find himself in the "shoe" Officers' Club. (The word "shoe" is derived from the difference in color of shoes.) In the Navy's working khaki uniform, all naval officers wore black shoes. Only aviators were authorized to wear brown shoes, which of course were more stylish and looked better. When aviators referred to surface officers, they used the word "blackshoe." Because aviators love one-syllable words, the reference was eventually shortened to "shoe".

The battle over uniforms was not limited to footwear. Flight suits and the extremely cool leather flight jackets were always (and still are) at the center of controversy both in stateside stations and overseas. Only aviators are allowed to wear flight jackets, which perpetuates the rivalry. Since it was hotter than Hades in the Philippines, the jackets were not much of an issue, but flight suits were. The Commanding Officer of

Subic, a Captain, promulgated (a very Navy word) that no aviator or crewman was allowed in any facility wearing a flight suit.

This created a stir because many of the aviators lived on the Subic side and "commuted" to Cubi Point. Also, the only commissary (food store like a Giant or Safeway) was on the Subic side, so if a pilot needed to go shopping, he was required to change. While this seems petty, it was a thorn that only widened the gap between communities. The pilots in my squadron often rebelled and wore their flight suits at the commissary, and then all hell would break loose! When stationed overseas in an isolated, remote environment, it is amazing what people will do for entertainment.

The focal point of all real social activity for officers in Subic Bay and Cubi Point was the Cubi Point Officers' Club (O Club). The Cubi Point O Club was THE place to be when any carrier pulled into port. The shoe Navy had their own officer's Club in Subic, but its atmosphere was more of a genteel Southern country club compared to the "anything goes" attitude of the Cubi Point O Club. The difference in clubs was another perfect illustration of the difference in community attitudes. In the Cubi Point O Club, aviators earned their reputations as fast living, skirt chasing, and hard drinking killers. I always wondered if pilots were born hell-raisers or did they act that way because they thought it was expected of them? Despite the public's perception, compared to everyday life in the Philippines, Tailhook. '91 was a church picnic. Even well after Tailhook '91 caught the attention of the American public, the Navy was still supporting prostitution on the base. Admirals and senior officers of all ranks attended these parties and were frequent guests of honor.

The Cubi Point O club sat on the top of the 600 foot mountain that paralleled the runway. The club was eye level with aircraft coming in for final landings. In the Navy, aircraft don't just do a nice, easy gradual descent to a landing. They fly at 800 ft above the ground until at the airfield, and then execute a break maneuver that consists of a 180-degree sharp turn, designed to bleed off airspeed before the turn to final. This break maneuver is primarily designed for carrier operations, but because it is fun and a display of showmanship and piloting prowess, all fixed wing pilots like to do them at home fields. This was especially true at Cubi Point because the O Club had a large patio that overlooked the airfield. Anyone flying in at 5 PM on a Friday afternoon knew everyone at the club was looking. The aircraft with afterburner capability would come into the break, very, very close to the club, and light the afterburners just as they started their turn to slow down. Lighting afterburners is contrary to attempting to slow down but the light display and the deafening noise was always applauded. Those pilots who executed these "s—t hot" breaks were at the club within a half-hour to cheers and drinks.

Because helicopters do not have the same need to slow down before landing, this break maneuver is pointless. The most memorable approach to the field and the club was performed not by Navy or Marine Corps helicopters, but by Army Blackhawk helicopters. One Friday afternoon, as the usual large crowd of aviators from all over the world gathered for the evening ritual of drinking and debauchery, two Army Blackhawk helos approached the field. To everyone's amazement, they did not fly to any of the helo pads. Instead, they flew straight to the outside patio of the club. When a helicopter hovers low to the ground, the noise is deafening and the vortex of wind and disrupted air sends everything within a hundred yards flying. The Army helos flew straight to the patio and hovered like birds over the crowd. Everyone was holding on, mostly to their drinks, and the helos dipped their noses in a bow, then flew away. All the umbrellas flew away, windows were shattered, and the place looked like a war zone, but the crowd loved it and howled for more.

The Army pilots drank for free that night, with no hint of being in trouble despite all the damage. This was the type of flying expected and encouraged in the Philippines. The FAA does not regulate the airspace there, and the Philippine air controllers ignored the airspace within

American control. Flying in the Philippines was often compared to the wild, wild west. There were few rules, and the ones that existed were routinely broken with no fear of reprisal. Almost completely lawless, it was by far the most fun I ever had flying. Coming from flight school and the US airspace system where flying is incredibly structured, I was given a taste of flying freedom in the Philippines. All the pilots loved it. Aircrews from other countries and the incoming carrier air groups all anxiously waited for their time in the PI. The flying was not just a lot of hot-dogging and showing off (which is termed as "flathatting" in the Navy). The lack of formal structure gave the Navy the opportunity to provide very realistic training scenarios. Not having to restrict airspace, modify strike plans, and limit the number of aircraft in a particular area, carrier airwings could train and practice real scenarios that would be used in conflicts like Desert Storm.

Besides the strategic location of the O Club overlooking the runway, it was a unique building both inside and out. The top floor of the club contained the main dining room and the Plaque Bar that led to the out-side patio. The Plaque Bar was and still is world famous. For as many years as the bar has been in existence, squadrons and support units that passed through Cubi Point left wooden plaques to mark their presence. Every inch of wall and ceiling space was covered with plaques from years past, listing the names of all the individuals in each unit. When the walls filled to capacity, squadrons became very inventive. The bar itself became a plaque, the tables were plaques, and wooden statues adorned the bar. My personal favorites were the plaque toilet seats in the ladies' room, courtesy of a Marine Corps squadron. They always did know how to treat a lady!

The Plaque Bar was the ultimate aviator shrine. Many famous naval officers passed through those doors and left a small remembrance of their junior years. When the treaty with Philippines was not renewed in 1992, the Naval Aviation Museum based in Pensacola, Florida, packed up the entire bar and moved it to the new wing of the museum. It looks almost exactly as it did in the Philippines, so much so that when I walked into the museum years later, I got goose bumps down my arms. The same cappuccino machine that never worked was there, as well as the shuffleboard game, and all the plaques. The only piece missing was the old jukebox that always skipped and played the same music since the early 80's! This is not a paid advertisement, but if anyone really wants to see a genuine piece of aviation history, go to Pensacola Naval Aviation Museum!

The bottom floor of the club was the nightclub section, complete with a cockpit of a C-2 jutting out one side of the bar. It was in this section that the Tailhook machine, (made famous in Stephen Coonts' book *Flight of the Intruder*) existed in the late 1970's and early 1980's. Essentially it was a chair, hanging from a rope. When it was released, the chair slid down a wire into a pool of water. The pilot in the chair could stop himself by dropping a "tailhook" just in time, snagging a wire that stopped the chair just shy of the pool. Usually the pilots daring enough to tempt fate drank quite a bit before they strapped in, and more aviators ended up in the pool than snagged the wire. In the mid 1980's, the contraption was removed and the pool was filled with cement to prevent injuries. But, in typical aviator fashion, other games replaced the missing tailhook chair. Carrier landings across tables were the natural replacement, as were a myriad of drinking games.

The first month I was there was very exciting. Desert Shield had just been declared, and the Navy was in the process of mobilizing its forces. Subic Bay and Cubi Point had not seen such a volume of traffic since the Vietnam War. Subic Bay was not just a mere gas station for ships and planes. It was also a major artery in the Navy's supply system for parts, weapons, people, and most importantly, ship repair facilities. If a ship experienced any structural, engine, or support systems problems anywhere in the Western Pacific (otherwise known as WESTPAC), it could come to Subic for repairs. The Subic Bay workforce were highly skilled, but very cheap, Filipino men. They were paid very well, far above what the average Filipino made, but much less than Americans.

Desert Shield had been in effect for four months, but it was clear to me that something much bigger was on the horizon. Ship after ship pulled in, taking on trucks, tanks, troops, and every weapon imaginable. Another strategic aspect of Subic Bay was the impressive weapons compound. Ships and aircraft did not have to ferry dangerous weapons over seven thousand miles; they could one stop shop in the Philippines for whatever was needed.

New Year's Eve, 1990, marked the most ships in the port of Subic Bay since the Vietnam War. Thirty-three ships were in port, all headed to the Gulf and surrounding areas. While not official, everyone there knew that war was going to be declared any day, and that this Philippine port call would probably be the last one for some time. Tension was in the air, and the time was right for some serious partying.

When no ships were in port, Americans numbered only a few thousand. One aircraft carrier employs 5,000 people, so when thirty-three ships pulled in, the entire base was bursting at the seams. The New Year's Eve Party was the mother of all parties. I had only been "in country" for four weeks and was still clueless about my surroundings, both professionally and socially. I attended the previous Tailhook convention just four months prior, but it could not hold a candle to the events of that New Year's evening. I ran in to people that night that I had not seen since my days at the Naval Academy. It was a fantastic party, full of life and wild antics.

An entire squadron of S-3 pilots and flight officers stripped from the waist down, put their shorts on their head, and ran amok through the crowd. The streaker wannabe's eventually scaled a gazebo and displayed all to the world below. Having very limited knowledge of the male anatomy, I learned a lot that night. I had not yet really ventured into town and only heard stories of what went on, but the quest for sex was definitely in the air. As a "round-eye" (a Caucasian woman), I quickly found out that I was a much sought after commodity. The only white women on the base were wives, Department of Defense teachers, Navy nurses, and a handful of other active duty military women. At the time, the three women in my squadron were the only female pilots stationed there.

I received enough proposals that night to last a lifetime. The stream of would-be suitors was flattering but while fairly naive in the realm of sex, I was not stupid enough to fall victim to their wiles. Some of the men were very creative in their lines of reasoning. My personal favorite was, "Please make love to me tonight. I am getting ready to go to war, and you'll be the last woman I'll ever sleep with. Don't you want to be the last woman I ever think of?" Generally that speech, made by more than one beau to many other women, occurred after consuming large amounts of alcohol.

Months later, when the ships pulled into port on their way from the Gulf back to the States, the nurses and I were able to reunite with these depraved veterans. We reminded them they were very much still alive. In true aviator style, they brushed aside our scolding and told us that we should sleep with them because they were now war heroes. Their favorite chant was "We are liberators of Kuwait and saviors of Bangladesh, Kiss me!" On the ships' way back from the Gulf, Bangladesh suffered horrific typhoons, and the Navy provided some humanitarian support. While we did admire them for their unequaled bravery and amazing courage, we still didn't sleep with them, :(

During the week long New Year's party, it was easy for me to ignore the pursuits of others. A sometime boyfriend, Carl, from Tailhook '90 pulled into port on the carrier, USS Ranger. I decided to prove to the guys in the squadron that I was a "player" and be just as wild in the sex arena. My tawdry and less than discreet affair with Carl was a huge mistake. The sad part was I did not really like him, and I was basically prostituting myself for an image. To make matters worse, another pseudo boyfriend, Ted, showed up that week as well. I was caught red-handed playing the field.

The worst part about my dating two guys at the same time was the fact that they were in the same airwing. Unbeknownst to me, they knew each other well. Unlike Carl, I really liked and admired Ted. We knew each other at the Naval Academy, and I considered Ted a soulmate. He knew me better than any person I ever met and probably ever will. When he found out about Carl, Ted graciously departed stage left with an "I am really disappointed in you" speech. Ted was on his way to war and he wasn't about to ruin his friendship with Carl. They were both aviators and would fly into battle together.

I felt absolutely sick over not just the loss of a really remarkable guy, but also the loss of the respect Ted once held for me. I ended the relationship with Carl and turned over a new leaf. From that point on, I never played the field and never ever jumped into a relationship to prove something to my peers. God has a funny way of punishing us for our sins though, because two years later I found myself not only in graduate school with Carl, but also in the same department. I was tortured daily with the reminder of one of my greatest follies.

This prostitution of one's morals, principles, and values to "fit in" is one of the most disturbing trends I have seen in female naval aviators. This behavior was the norm and was expected in my squadron. When I arrived, I did not know the other two women were in a myriad of relationships with guys in the squadron. While I certainly was no angel, I drew the line at sleeping with the guys in my squadron. I knew enough about myself to know I could never sleep with someone, break up, and then see him day after day. That policy was hard because I initially had a crush on Dave, the helo pilot who met me when I first arrived. I quickly got over the crush a few weeks later when. In a show of bravado, he humiliated me in the Ready Room for an inconsequential paperwork mistake.

The wild parties finally came to an end, and it was time for all the ships to go to war. After the squadrons and battle groups headed for the Gulf, life in the PI quieted down on the base. I then decided to see what the town of Olongapo was all about. When I walked outside the gates of the base into Olongapo, the stench of raw sewage hit me hard enough to make me gag. A river, known as "S—t River," separated the town and the base, which was used by the town of Olongapo as a dump for raw sewage. The water was absolutely disgusting and no doubt carried enough diseases to wipe out an entire country. As late as the mid 1980's, military personnel crossing the bridge threw coins into the river and watched as young children dove into this same sewage to find the coins. It was merely sport to the soldiers and sailors, and the children lined the banks at the chance to earn some money. Finally, the practice was forbidden and high walls were erected on the bridge to prevent any more temptation.

Once I crossed the bridge and moved away from the stench, the next assault on the senses was the food vendors lining the streets. One of the most popular stands was the meat on a stick stand. One of the guys in the squadron said the meat was monkey meat or dog meat, whatever was handy for a kill that day, even roadkill. I was never that hungry so I always passed on the mystery meat.

One of the most popular Philippine delicacies is balut. It is a chicken egg with a partially formed embryo that was soaked in a vinegar solution. The smell is enough to make a person sick if not already after walking over S—t River. Again, not much for tasting such exotic culinary delights, I did not partake of the balut. It was a rite of passage for the guys in the squadron, and those that passed the test said the balut tasted better than it looked or smelled.

Not all Filipino food is so revolting. I loved going out in town and tasting the local fare. Because we lived on the water, the seafood was excellent. I still enjoy many Philippine dishes today—pancit, lumpia and adobo. I was a finicky eater as a child, but I surprisingly started eating sushi in the PI. That was probably not the smartest of decisions because refrigeration in town was a crapshoot, and restaurant hygiene was not regulated by any organization.

I discovered during my time overseas that some of the most interesting restrooms are in Asia. The standard eastern toilet for women is either a hole or a trench that a woman squats over to do her business. Western sitting toilets were still somewhat of a new concept in parts of the Philippines. On the base in almost every female toilet, a sign was posted that said, "Huwag kang tumayo sa upoan nang kubeta!" Translation: Don't stand on the toilet seat. The Philippine girls who had never seen a Western toilet squatted on the seat lid and tried to pee into the toilet. Because the angle wasn't quite right, it made a huge mess. It was in the Philippines that I completely mastered the hover technique.

Transportation in town was a sight to behold. There were primarily two ways to travel around, the suntok, and the jeepney. The suntoks, also known as trikes, were small motorcycles with sidecars attached. For a few pennies, anyone could hire a trike driver to go anywhere in town. The trike drivers were absolutely insane drivers. There were no rules of the road in Olongapo, and the Philippine trike drivers should have been pilots, embodying the "speed is life" principle. They had no regard for personal safety, and it was common for the trike drivers and their passengers to end up in the hospital. It became so dangerous that eventually the Navy prohibited its personnel from riding in them.

The other safer and equally cheap mode of transportation was the Jeepney. From the front, the Jeepney looks very much like an American Jeep that has been stretched into a long bed truck. Each Jeepney sat about twelve people, but then an additional ten could cram in the bed. Hanging from the outside was also not discouraged. The Jeepneys ran certain routes just like buses and were color-coded. An expression of personal wealth, each driver owned his own Jeepney. They were flamboyantly decorated with fringe hanging from all sides. The color schemes alone rivaled the tie-dye artists of the 60's. On the hood of each Jeepney stood one or more horse statues. Much like the Jaguar of the American culture, these horses represented wealth and status. More than one horse symbolized great wealth. A display of multiple horses was quite a statement for a business that generated a fare of one peso per person, or about three cents.

Shopping in the PI was amazing and I loved having all my clothes made. The one true talent of the Philippine people is to copy anything and everything. I took a Victoria's Secret catalog to my seamstresses and showed them a picture of what I wanted. The next day, I had a completely new outfit. Their ability to replicate was not just limited to sewing. Furniture, shoes, almost anything that could be described was made. At night, anyone walking down the street heard music spilling out from all the local dives that sounded like the real artist. Despite the fact that few Philippine bands spoke much English, they could mimic almost any band from Simon and Garfunkel to Metallica.

Because there are no copyright laws in the Philippines, the bars and restaurants had very familiar sounding names. The Hard Rock Cafe Olongapo was nothing like in the US and not part of the chain. Some of the more popular clubs were Michael Jordan's, California Jam, and the Rock Lobster. My personal favorite hangout was Rolling Stones because they played alternative and progressive music. It was in this bar that I learned the very valuable lesson of not doing anything worth regretting if a camera is around.

Dave, the helo pilot, also liked to hang out in Rolling Stones and felt very comfortable there—too comfortable, in fact. One night after imbibing large amounts of alcohol, he decided to jump on a speaker and show us what he was made of, literally. Dave stripped, bare ass naked, and danced on top of the speaker. Another pilot in my squadron was clever enough to snap a shot for posterity. Always the practical jokers, the picture fell into the wrong hands, was blown up and then posted in the Ready Room for all to see. Yes, we all knew Dave far better than he probably would have liked.

Days in Olongapo were fairly tame; this is when most of the vendors did the majority of business. When night fell, the music started pumping; the women started gyrating in the doorways, and hello wild, wild west! Bar brawls were routine, and if we wanted to see any real intense fights break out, we headed over to the bar where the Navy SEALs made their home. Trained assassins, these guys were actually very low key when it came to picking fights. However, there was always some very drunk Marine who was eager to prove to his buddies that SEALs were all pretty boys and tried to pick a fight. Move over Mike Tyson and Evander Hollyfield! These fights were far more exciting, and a lot more blood was shed.

I befriended several native Filipinos, which gave me additional insight into their culture. My maid Remy was a lovely young woman in her thirties who managed to avoid the life of prostitution by working as a maid in the officers' quarters. She was married with children, and invited me to dinner in her apartment in town. I loved going out in town with a native because I was able to experience far more than the disgusting barbaric debauchery of Olongapo, rivaled only by Sodom and Gomorrah. Her family, like most other Asian families, was very tight-knit. They, like the rest of us who did not partake of the forbidden fruit, ignored what they saw happening in the streets and just tried to live a normal life.

Another of my favorite Filipinos was Rico, a ski boat driver. The day I arrived in the Philippines, Chris took me to the beach where all the single people hung out and water-skied. I only skied a handful of times in my entire life and always on two skis. The atmosphere of a group of pilots skiing is just as competitive as flying, so skiing on two skis was just not allowed. When it was my turn, I was handed one ski with the statement, "Nobody here skis on two, in fact we don't even have a combination set." Trial by fire has always been one of my strongest suits, and after being dragged a hundred or so yards, I finally got up and was elated. It was the beginning of my favorite pastime and became one of my strongest sports.

Rico was the driver of boat 18. It was the most powerful ski boat, and he knew exactly how to pull a skier. This was no easy feat because we came in all sorts of shapes and sizes, but Rico always remembered specific idiosyncrasies about each person. We always tipped him well and brought food for him and his family. When we all left, we took up a collection of several hundred dollars and baskets of food for him. In return, he made all the skiers little wooden personalized water skis that were Christmas ornaments. Our informal ski club was known as the Gucci Ski Team because of our colorful and varied ski collection. For the Plaque Bar, Rico made a plaque of a ski with not only our names but his as well, and it is now hanging in the bar today in the Pensacola naval aviation Museum.

The Filipina I spent more time with that any other and someone whom I still keep in contact with is Norma. She was a masseuse who worked in the officers' quarters. There were basically two types of massages in the Philippines; real therapeutic massages and "special" massages. Norma was a genuine masseuse who trained in Manila. She was older, in her early forties, with a grip that could bring even a large man to tears. Norma was not a Filipina that would ever engage in any type of prostitution, and therefore was known across the base for her professionalism. I never experienced a massage prior to Norma's and was a little suspect at first. After the first massage, I became an avid fan.

Norma's massages were ten dollars an hour (compare to fifty or more in the US). She also did manicures, pedicures and facials, which were divine. Because she was so good at what she did, she became a very wealthy woman by Philippine standards. She actually saved enough money to buy a house with concrete walls and wooden roof. In the Philippines, houses are not bought on credit so all money must be paid up front. Norma was very successful; she saved enough money to have a well installed on her property as well as an indoor toilet. She lived in a small community and was the richest woman in the neighborhood as well as a community leader. She shared everything with her neighbors, letting anyone who asked have water.

Norma had a son who was eighteen years old. His father was an American sailor who befriended Norma during his tour in the PI. She became pregnant, and unlike most of his peers, he supported his son until his transfer back to the States. When he left however, the father did not take this new family with him. This abandonment was not uncommon, and when strolling down the streets of Olongapo, I noticed the beautiful Amerasian children hanging on their mothers or playing in the filthy, stench filled streets.

Norma often invited me to her house for dinner, and once I took her flying in a rented Cessna, a small four-seater, single engine plane. She had never flown before, and I took her to see the local volcano, the mountainous countryside, and the Mount Rushmore of the PI, a mountainside carving of Ferdinand Marcos' head. Even though he was a corrupt leader and helped keep the country entrenched in its third world status, the people still loved him and his wife, Imelda. (I saw the 3,000 pairs of shoes and actually, I was not too shocked. Imelda kept every pair of shoes she ever owned. I will probably have owned close to 3,000 pairs when I die!)

Norma and I enjoyed a wonderful afternoon, although she was a little airsick. I was completely charmed by watching her face as we flew over her homeland of forty years. She was amazed and awestruck with the very skill of flying that I took for granted. Few flying experiences are that rewarding.

Not only did I enjoy meeting the locals and experiencing their way of life, I also very much enjoyed the amazing history lessons that the Philippines provided without all the tourist busses and souvenir stands so well known elsewhere. The region that surrounded Subic Bay and Manila, just 60 miles away, was overflowing with historical treasures from World War II that remain essentially untouched and unspoiled, as if the War had just ended a few years before.

With permission from the U.S. government, diving trips were organized in Subic Bay that allowed those lucky participants to dive the shipwrecks that resulted from the intense fighting during the Japanese invasion in the early part of the war. I can not adequately express in words the feelings of awe and trepidation I felt as I swam down the diving line through the murky, almost incandescent green water to find myself staring down the huge guns of a battleship resting on the sea floor. It was an experience that every American should share in to appreciate the freedoms that we have today.

One of my favorite destinations was Corregidor, a tiny crescent shaped island that marks the entry to Manila Bay, which had been a military stronghold since the Spanish conquests. During W.W. II, Corregidor was converted into an American military post during the W. W. II and housed thousands of American troops as well as munitions and other war fighting equipment. It was eventually lost in a fierce struggle in 1942 when the Japanese invaded and was regained in yet another bloody battle when MacArthur returned in 1945.

Since the island was not easily accessible and protected by the Philippine government, Corregidor was in almost pristine condition and was a dream for any W.W. II buff. The beaches were littered with armament and tanks, abandoned in one of the last desperate battles to keep the Japanese at bay. The tunnels that housed the headquarters and communications center still contained all the original furniture and equipment, and the monstrous defensive guns were still in place, with nearby bomb craters that signaled a fierce struggle. My squadron's helicopters would often fly to the island and I was moved every time I saw the rows of barracks that still exhibited blast marks and collapsed walls as if the battle had just taken place. Occasionally we would transport veterans of the Corregidor battle back to their haunts and the stories they told were chilling and riveting.

Across the Bay from Corregidor lay the Bataan Peninsula. The peninsula was the site of one the most horrific and inhumane events of W.W. II—the Bataan Death March. When the Japanese successfully gained control of the Manila Bay area in 1942, they took prisoner over 60,000 Philippine and about 12,000 American soldiers.[1] The Japanese forced the POWs to march sixty five miles across the Bataan Peninsula in intense sun and scorching heat without food or water. Over 5000 Americans and 3000 others died on the march

To honor those brave men, both American and Filipino, who suffered and died in the Bataan Death March, a 311 foot cement and steel cross was erected on the top of Mount Samat, which is the mountain that marks the Bataan Peninsula. The cross is referred to as the "Shrine of Valor."[2] The pilots in my squadron flew by this cross almost every day as it was on our path for reentry into the airfield landing strip at Cubi Point. I never failed to remind myself of the bravery of those men and of the atrocious acts of cruelty they endured every time I flew by the cross. Fifty years after the war and the horrifying loss of life, the Bataan peninsula was a site of honor and reflection. It was one of my favorite places in the Philippines.

After witnessing firsthand those sites that marked some of the most famous and critical battles of World War II, I had a newfound and significantly deeper respect for those veterans of the War. Prior to my tour in the Philippines, the war in the Pacific was some abstract, unrealistic concept from the history books and movies. As I dove on the wrecks, walked through battle fields strewn with shrapnel, and flew by the cross of Bataan almost every day, I was constantly reminded of the great human sacrifice of our veterans and felt extremely privileged to be a part of such a tremendous and honorable organization.

Chapter Five

Me Love You Long Time

Sex was THE hobby for Americans in the Philippines. It was highly advertised, plentiful, and dirt-cheap. The town outside the gates of Subic Bay, Olongapo, was an adult Disneyland, surpassed only by Thailand. Any sexual fantasy could be satisfied for around ten dollars. The prostitutes in the Philippines who provided these services were for the most part, young girls. The girls ranged anywhere in age from eleven to early thirties. By the time these women reached their middle thirties, they had numerous children and had battled most known sexually transmitted diseases. By their middle thirties, they just couldn't keep up with the competition from the highly desired young girls.

When a sailor walked by a bar, several scantily clad "hostesses" surrounded the doorway, calling and teasing these potential customers. Their most famous phrases were, "Me love you long time" and "I love you no s—t!" Inside most bars, the girls were positioned on the bar top, tabletops, speakers, or wherever any conspicuous display room was available. They all wore numbers so any interested party could order them much like ordering a beer. In fact, the prostitutes were often ordered along with a beer. When looking at a menu in a booklet or up on the wall, it read, "San Miguel 10p, Margarita 30p, Bar Fine 100p."

"Bar Fine" was another phrase for hooker. The bar fine was the cornerstone of Olongapo's economy. At the time, about 30 pesos equaled one dollar, so the bar fines were not very expensive. The Bar Fine charge was usually for only an hour, but the patron could haggle with the mama-san if he wanted more time with his girl. Guys in my squadron would routinely "bar fine" a girl for weeks at a time. Maybe it made them feel as if they were making some kind of commitment.

The name of the prostitution game in the Philippines was "quantity, not quality." (This motto was one of the favorites boasted by men all over WESTPAC.) Since the sex was so cheap, the volume was increased to turn a profit. These earnings were split between the bar owners, the mammalian, and last and certainly least, the girl. On weekend nights when battlegroups pulled into port, these women slept with ten to twenty men in one night, depending on their skill level. Rooms were located on the premises for convenient and quick rendezvous.

One of the most colorful and popular phrases the men used to refer to the bar fines was LBFM's (little brown f—king machines). These girls were experts in their field. Since the primary object of the girl was to rotate through partners as quickly as possible, they learned to bring the lucky sailor to orgasm in seconds. Masters of pelvic control, these women knew how to achieve results—fast. However, they were not sluts without any morals or upbringing. Most of these women were devout Catholics that attended church every Sunday. They did not view their jobs as shocking or immoral; they viewed their lives and profession in terms of survival.

The Philippines, especially in that area, is a third world country whose population lives by sweating, scavenging, and slaving. Many of these girls were sent to Olongapo by their parents and families to earn a living. The prostitutes did not pocket their money to buy new clothes or in hopes of finding their way to a better life. They sent a large portion of their wages home to support their often large families in other provinces.

These women were considered property by both their owners and the sailors who "bar fined" them. They were often treated like ignorant mutes, better to be seen and not heard. However, they were far smarter that anyone suspected. These women, who slept with hundreds of men, remembered names and details of individual customers from years back. It was fairly routine for a sailor to deploy through the Philippines at one, two, and even ten-year intervals. No matter how long a customer was absent, his girl always remembered him and was waiting to make up for lost time.

I generally only ventured into town with either my nurse girlfriends or the ski team. White women were a premium and many entrepreneurial enlisted round-eye women made a pretty penny turning tricks. I was quite naive when I arrived in the PI. I was overwhelmed by it all. My blond hair was perceived as good luck in the PI, so the bargirls would often sneak up behind me and stroke my hair. I let them because it obviously meant a lot to them. I was amazed at their superstitions and felt sorry for them. I remember fixating on their pantyhose. The dancers wore very skimpy thong outfits with pantyhose. Not only was it around 100 degrees all the time, but their pantyhose had built-in briefs and the lines just looked horrible. That was how hardened I was becoming. Children were parading in front of me on a bar, prostituting themselves for pennies, and in some strange denial, all I concentrated on were their fashion mistakes.

I tried not to pass judgment on those who "bar fined" the girls. If I distanced myself from everyone who paid for sex, there wouldn't really be anyone to talk to except other women. I saw friend after friend fall to the easy temptations. After I living in the PI for a month, a friend of mine from flight school was ordered to my squadron. When everyone found out he was coming, the betting started. For new guys, the bet was how many hours passed before the guy was with a hooker. Since he was a friend of mine and I thought I knew him well, I staunchly defended him. I actually made the statement that never in a million years would my friend from flight school take part in such debauchery.

I was only partially right. He was in country less than twelve hours before he succumbed to Olongapo's offerings. His first night, he didn't actually have sex with the girl. (He waited to do that the next night.) Instead, he let a girl give him a hand job that later led to his callsign, "Handy." He eventually turned into the biggest whoremonger (a term the round-eyes gave to the guys who liked the prostitutes) and always found on the prowl out in town.

The guys in the squadron liked to play all kinds of sex games. The on going game in the squadron was the alphabet game. Because the jet pilots in our squadron traveled so much to so many different countries, there was a lot of opportunity to mingle with many exotic women. The object of the game was to sleep with a different girl in every country, which gave the pilot the letter "qual" (ification), for that country. There was no restriction against paying for sex so it was fairly easy for the guys to get the J(apan) and K(orea) quals. The leader of the pack, of course, had the most letters in the alphabet. He swore he earned over half the letters, but he was always struggling with the Q, Y, and Z letters. He hoped to travel to Africa to win some of those quals as well.

At the time, I thought all these antics were very funny. Frankly I was just glad to be included in any of the "reindeer games." I was never allowed to play, because they said, "women can get laid anytime they want." I didn't mind, I was happy enough observing on the fringes. However, after the incident with Ted, I was very unhappy with my behavior and I drew the line after Bar Golf.

Bar Golf was a game all the officers would play. Modeled after regular golf, eighteen bars in town were mapped out. (There were literally hundreds, so this was never a problem.) Each bar had a Par, which meant a player must drink a certain amount of drinks in a certain amount of time. If he went over the time limit, he was penalized strokes. The winner had the lowest number of strokes. In reality, few guys made it to the end without passing out or throwing up. What made the game interesting were the ways in which a player could score an Eagle or a hole-in-one. For a one under par, a guy received a blowjob in the bar. For a hole-in-one, he would "do a hook" on the premises. At least one other guy, if not all, had to witness the act.

These Bar Golf outings were a regular part of squadron life and my first CO was an avid supporter of the game. After I saw just some of what went on, I absolutely refused to take part. I was a big drinker in the PI but not only could I not handle 18 bars of drinking, the sex side of it thoroughly disgusted me. The majority of guys only took part in the drinking, but they certainly cheered on the others who were more daring.

Another popular game for men in town was the game of "smiles." A group of guys went to a bar and asked for an equal number of girls. The guys sat around a circular table and the girls climbed underneath and started giving the guys blowjobs simultaneously. The first guy to smile lost and paid for the round of women.

This culture of sex and drinking permeated every aspect of life in the PI, especially in my squadron. Most of the guys in the ready room talked about nothing else. They loved comparing stories and discussing their conquests. Of the five department heads in our squadron that were the most senior personnel next to the CO and XO, three were heavily involved in the bar fine culture.

My boss was one of the men who at forty would bar fine the youngest girls for weeks on end. When he tired of one, he traded her in like a used car. Another department head, fifty years of age, flaunted his twelve-year-old girlfriend with much fanfare. She spoke little English and he loved to bring her to official squadron functions. She would occasionally throw a temper tantrum, but what twelve-year-old doesn't? When she did this, the LCDR loved to say to everyone, "When she hits thirteen, I'm getting rid of her for an eleven year old."

The last department head not only enjoyed the pleasures at hand; it was his business as well. One of the most senior officers in the squadron, he owned and operated a brothel in town. Our squadron routinely held official and unofficial functions at his bar and he saved the best and newest girls for his squadron buddies. He was married to a Filipina, which was how he was allowed to own property in the PI. He intended to stay in Olongapo once he retired. He was not my boss, so fortunately he never wrote any of my evaluations. He bitterly divorced a "round-eye" a few years prior and reminded the squadron repeatedly that "round-eyes" were just a bunch of gold diggers.

I had been in the squadron for a few months when my first evaluation was due. The Commanding Officer told me that I was doing very well as a pilot and in my ground job, but he didn't think I hung out enough with the guys in the squadron. I told him that Bar Golf and outings to the department head's brothel were not really activities that I cared to participate in. He told me then that I was not a "team player" and I needed to rethink my priorities. I did rethink my priorities and out of spite, I went to even fewer squadron functions. In the end, it was not the best way to handle the situation. My father always said I would cut off my nose to spite my face and he's a very wise man.

While the sex games during my flight training seemed relatively harmless, the Sodom and Gomorrah environment of the Philippines overwhelmed me. I tried my best not to let the revolting actions of my peers affect me, but it became hard for me to separate my feelings for them personally and professionally. Because I refused to take part in the debauchery, the guys in the squadron thought I was "holier than thou" and they started attaching the word "feminist" to me. While I believe in equal treatment, I have never been a card carrying "feminist", just an independent thinker. Unfortunately, many women in the military are unfairly branded as feminists merely for just joining! This label as a feminist was one more problem that would come back to haunt me later in my career.

Leadership in my squadron was anything but consistent. My first Commanding Officer was the consummate "team player." His executive officer that eventually became the CO was a family man who truly loved his wife and kids. He never played out in town and wanted no part of the sordid adventures. His replacement, "Dice", liked to define himself as a party animal and loved to tell stories. He loved to espouse the famous Navy saying, "What goes on detachment stays on detachment." I was never sure whether Dice's disgusting sex stories were true, or if they were just an attempt to bond with the other male pilots. Formerly an F/A-18 pilot, he loved to tell stories about flying from city to city just to "bust the cherry" of a new girl. I found Dice to be particularly revolting because he was married. His wife was an extremely nice woman, another officer, and a new mother. While she was at home nursing their little girl, he was playing the Alphabet game.

In truth, Bar Golf, Smiles, and the Alphabet Game were actually quite tame compared to other activities available to the more perverse. Potential customers, both men and women, could bar fine any age and any sex in any quantity they desired. The homosexuals of the PI were called "Beni boys." In a section of dilapidated concrete block buildings, the young boys hung in the doorways, just like on the main strip. Some dressed in drag, but all were very young and very willing to please. This district also happened to be located near a large number of beauty parlors where many of the Beni Boys made their living cutting hair. In some of the bars, if a hook approached a guy and he turned her away, she either asked him if he preferred a boy or sent one of the young boys over to him.

Perhaps the most famous sex parlor in the Olongapo area was Marilyn's, which was right next door to Blow Heaven. The business cards for Marilyn's read, "Home of the #1 cocksuckers—with some new cocksuckers just out of boot camp." It was in this fine establishment that customers, both male and female, watched the legendary ping pong ball shows. The women who worked at Marilyn's completely mastered control of their pelvic muscles. They inserted Ping-Pong balls into their vaginas and shot them across the bar, with amazing precision and accuracy. Ping-Pong balls were only a warm-up, though. They also smoked cigarettes and opened beer bottles. One of the most requested tricks was for a woman to squat over a beer bottle with a quarter on the top. She picked the quarter up and gave the lucky recipient change, two dimes and a nickel.

I have always been amazed at these feats and I can only imagine the training program. While these acts seem lewd and lascivious, they pale in comparison to the red light districts of Bangkok and Pattaya Beach, Thailand. Pattaya Beach continues to be one of the Navy's most popular ports of call. Some of the guys in my squadron tired of the amateurish pornography, prostitution, and child molestation of the Philippines, and headed to Thailand for the professional version. Ping Pong Ball shows were just the tip of the iceberg. The streets in the red light districts are littered with live sex shows featuring both humans and animals.

One of the favorite rites of passage for aviators in Thailand is the "Foamy Bath." When a guy goes to the Foamy Bathhouse, he starts in the selection room. There he has his pick of scores of women, all wearing numbers. Buying more than one is highly recommended and not very expensive. Once he chooses his girl(s), he then enters a tiled shower room and gets in a rubber boat in the middle. His hostess then comes in, buck naked, sprinkles soap flakes all over, starts the water, then proceeds to scrub him all over with her body—all parts of her body. They are very thorough in their bathing and all customers leave very satisfied.

One of my ex-boyfriends showed up in the PI one weekend after his battlegroup left Pattaya Beach, Thailand. He came knocking on my door, hoping to rekindle our flame for just a couple days. I knew he just came from Thailand because his battlegroup made such a ruckus while they were there, they were restricted to the base in the PI as punishment. When he approached me with THAT look in his eye, I said, "Can you look me in the eye and tell me you did not have a Foamy Bath in Thailand?" His mood visibly changed and he stammered a bit before blurting out, "OK, I did have a Foamy Bath, all the guys did, but

I didn't have the special!" All Foamy Baths are specials, so unfortunately for him, there was no round-eye love that weekend.

The Philippine women who took part in all these activities didn't disgust me. I felt sorry for them and in some ways, I admired them. The Philippines is a very matriarchal society. The women in Philippine families bear the brunt of not only raising the children, but also supporting the entire family including grandparents, great grandparents, siblings, cousins, and often the illegitimate offspring of their young daughters. The women of Olongapo worked hard, sometimes for an entire community. The women who worked the clubs both on and off base had American names that they used instead of their real names. Often the boys and young men who tended to lawns and washed cars also had American names. However, they weren't normal names, they were names like Baby, Girl, Boy, Precious, Princess, Milady and Bong. These names seemed like an attempt on the part of the Americans to dehumanize the Filipinos, making their actions seem almost excusable.

Not all women who worked in the clubs and facilities on base were prostitutes. Many were wives of sailors they married while stationed in Subic Bay. These quickie marriages were common in the PI. The Philippine women were not stupid. They knew that if they married an American, they could not only go back to the US with their husband, they could also take several members of their families. A visit to any naval installation in southern California is testimony that this practice was rampant. From the men's perspective, Philippine women were a dream come true. Small, thin, sexually knowledgeable, these women were very hard working and willing to do almost anything their husbands requested. The men in my squadron bragged that they never listened to nagging, or really any conversation in general because many of the girls could not speak or understand English. Despite their lacking communications skills, they tried very hard to please their men.

One afternoon, one of the jet pilots, LT "Bug" Roach brought his "hook" into the Ready Room. It was a slow day in the squadron, so most of us were just hanging around, shooting the breeze. The conversation turned to parasites in the food and how to avoid them. We were comparing gross stories when Bug pointed to his girlfriend and said, "She has some kind of worm right now!" We all recoiled a little bit and turned to her. Someone asked, "Why don't you go to the doctor and get some medicine to kill it?" She replied, "I don't want to kill it because it helps me eat." I didn't understand at first, but Bug explained that she meant having a worm in her stomach kept her thin. I was thoroughly disgusted at both her indifference and his approval of her self-destructive behavior.

As willing as the Philippine women were to please their men, most American men did not find out about their one disagreeable trait until after the wedding: Philippine women have terrible tempers and are like caged tigers when they are upset. It was not uncommon to see a fair number of dishes and glasses hurled at an unsuspecting American husband. The Filipinas were not afraid to hit their men. One of my favorite memories of the female Philippine temper was directed towards my Chief, who assisted me in running the administrative division. His wife was a Filipino and she discovered that while she was out of the country, he enjoyed a little fling in her absence. She decided to confront him at the squadron. In the middle of the office, his wife whipped out a butcher knife and started chasing him around the office. I was sitting at my desk in my office when I saw him run by. She then flew by in hot pursuit with a giant knife, not too far behind. It took one of the helicopter aircrewman to restrain and calm her down. It seems funny that in a culture of rampant prostitution that the women were so unforgiving. Actually maybe it's just poetic justice.

The women I felt the most sorry for were the American wives both in the PI and back in the States. They had no idea what they were up against. While not official statistics, I would wager that 80% of the married men partook in the town activities to some extent. Some men actually rationalize that getting a blowjob does not violate any marriage vows. The wives of the pilots in my squadron were very tight and very supportive of one another. I loved hanging around with the wives. They were not intimidated by the presence of women in their husband's work place; they had much bigger problems to worry about.

One of the wives was rushed to the hospital during my time there with a fever of 104 degrees. She was very sick and was hospitalized for some time. She was later diagnosed with gonorrhea. I did not know until this occurred that women can contract gonorrhea internally and never know it. Left untreated, gonorrhea is a fatal disease. Her husband contracted the STD in town, and men know almost immediately if they have it. He went to see the squadron flight surgeon, who treated him with antibiotics. Even in the PI, doctors are legally and morally bound to ensure that all partners of a person with a STD are treated, much like in the US. Unfortunately, this flight surgeon felt no obligation because the pilot in question knew that if his wife found out about his extra-curricular activities, there would be hell to pay. So instead of facing his punishment, the pilot almost killed his wife. When I asked her why she stayed, she told me with three kids and no work experience, she had nowhere to go. It was heartbreaking watching her sob at her kitchen table. I only became more resolute not to participate in any more of the "reindeer games."

Not surprisingly, Sexually Transmitted Diseases (STD) in the Philippines were a big problem. Attempting to combat the potential epidemic of diseases, prostitutes who worked in bars were required to carry health cards. These cards were issued by Navy sponsored (translation, taxpayer supported) clinics who mandated that any professional hooker must come in every two weeks for a complete checkup. If a girl was discovered to have AIDS, she was sent back to her province immediately. After that, I don't know what became of them. Military men who contracted HIV were eventually processed out of the Navy. The Cubi Point STD clinic was always packed. When any of my sailors didn't show up for morning muster, they were most likely in the STD clinic. Often, when other women or I were in the medical building, we would swing through the clinic. If we recognized any officers, we added them to the "stay away from" list.

It was very difficult for the "round-eyes" in the Philippines to date. Absolutely none of us wanted anything to do with any whoremongers so we created a pretty tight network. Privacy meant nothing in the PI. If a guy was diagnosed with a STD, the word spread like fire through the round-eyes. If a guy was seen out in town with a LBFM, that piece of information was dispersed quickly so he would not ever be able to date a round-eye. The ethical violations were debatable. Should a patient have complete confidentiality or should women be warned that a guy is a walking STD? One pilot bragged that during his six months in the PI, he slept with over 200 women, both Asian and American. He also single-handedly spread chlamydia to an alarming number of women.

The Navy knew exactly what was going on both in town and on the base. In addition to heavily subsidizing the sex clinics in town, the senior leadership also turned a blind eye to active duty personnel running houses of ill repute. When large battlegroups pulled into port, the Morale, Recreation, and Welfare department hired extra "hostesses," otherwise known as "hostitutes," to help with the special events. In every officer barracks, a massage parlor was available. The massages were legitimate for the most part, but "specials" were always within reach. Tailhook '91 was nothing compared to the average PI Friday night party at the Officer's Club. I even knew of an officer who was the local pimp for the officer barracks. Once contacted, this officer would have a girl at another officer's door in twenty minutes.

A very senior officer on Subic Bay loved his massages and made no attempt to hide it. He was a Captain who was always setting absurd flight suit policies, so all the pilots from the Cubi side hated him. It became almost a past time to hate this Captain and finally the SEALs drove us to action. The Navy stationed a platoon of SEALs in Subic Bay and since our squadron always flew them on missions, we became good friends. The SEALs hated this Captain as much as we did, and planned the ultimate revenge.

The Captain was religious about his massages, which were administered just a stone's throw from his office. He left his office promptly and walked to the massage parlor. He stripped in the dressing room and then entered the massage room in nothing but a towel. After an hour he emerged, no doubt refreshed, and headed back to work. I can't say for sure he was getting a special, but that was the rumor we liked best.

One day, some of the SEALs and guys from my squadron lay in wait in nearby bushes. When the Captain went into the massage room, the guys went into the dressing room and stole all his clothes. After his massage was finished, the Captain, in a panic, strategically arranged two towels around him and awkwardly made a dash for his office. The towels the Navy used were small, and not big enough to cover everything.

The SEALs and the guys from my squadron actually erected a viewing area for the mad dash. As the Captain bolted out of the massage parlor, the cameras captured the event for posterity. Everyone was long gone by the time he emerged from his office, fully dressed. The Captain was so mad that he threw us all out of the Subic Club, not that we ever went there anyway. These zany antics were what I loved most about the PI.

In this land of cheap booze and even cheaper women, it was difficult for us round-eyes to have even a somewhat meaningful relationship. We were all extremely distrustful of the American men but as women so often do, we ignored glaring character flaws of our chosen beaus. What should have been a single woman's paradise was really more of a hell. Even if the men we chose to date did not partake of Olongapo's offerings, they more often wanted only sex.

I, like many other round-eyes, fell victim to the sex plagued environment. Within just a few weeks of my arrival, I fell in lust with a Marine navigator, John. He was stationed in Japan but because both of our squadrons traveled so much, we saw each other frequently. While I wasn't in love with John, I idolized him, his career, and his whole out-look on life. He was a very laid back guy and was the first boyfriend I truly wanted to emulate. John despised the entire prostitution culture, and after extensively checking his background, I decided he was a worthwhile risk.

After dating for three months, he received his orders to go home. Upon his return, John planned to leave the Marine Corps and go to graduate school. John made it clear to me I was nowhere in his future plans. I was crushed. I didn't expect to marry him, but I was shocked and devastated that he dismissed me without any remorse. John headed home without so much as a "let's keep in touch."

A couple of weeks later I flew to Okinawa for an exercise. While I was there, I went to the Marine Officer's Club one night with a big group for the typical Friday night blowout. That memorable night, I ran into a group of DOD (Department of Defense) teachers. These teachers are hired by the to teach the children of American service personnel sta-tioned overseas. They were all in their middle twenties and generally a very fun group.

I was talking with a group of the teachers when one of them men-tioned that she had been seeing a Marine navigator who recently left for the states. I almost threw up. I turned to her and asked her if her boyfriend's name was John, and yes, they were one and the same. We talked and drank for a long time that night. It was a very painful but enlightening evening. Since John was stationed in Japan, whenever he flew to the PI, he stopped in Okinawa first for fuel. So he would spend one night with her when he made the transit to the PI, and then spend the next night with me.

The worst part about finding out he cheated on me was realizing what a fool I was. Everyone else knew. Had I looked a little harder, I would have recognized the truth as well. In discussing my unfortunate choice of boyfriends with a male friend of mine, he pointed out that no actual promise of monogamy occurred between us. Since we were neither married nor engaged, he said, then no cheating took place. It was an insight into the male thought process that I quickly dismissed, but probably should have listened to more closely. John probably did justify his actions this way, so we clearly came from two different moral backgrounds. I slept with very few men prior to John and was still very naive about such matters. I thought that once a man slept with a girl, it didn't mean marriage, but it did mean monogamy. Sex definitely meant the two were a couple. Even in such a hard core pornographic society as the PI, I managed to hold on to my southern upbringing and never really got over these innocent romantic expectations.

I was still in a state of shock over this relationship when I met the man who tremendously impacted my personal life. Freshly wounded, I decided to go on a ski trip arranged by my nurse and doctor friends. Stress from both my hostile work environment and my dismal personal failures were reaching a pinnacle. I was glad to go to the northernmost island of Japan, Hokkaido, and learn to snow ski. On the trip, one of the doctors, Bill, started to shower me with interest, compliments, and attention. I was thoroughly infatuated. Even though I had known him for some time, I never really considered dating outside the aviation community. I was even more flattered that a surgeon was so interested in someone as "common" as I was. I held doctors up on pedestals and believed they held the noblest of all professions. We had a fabulous time and when I flew back to the PI, I was extremely happy.

We dated for the next eight months, and I knew Bill was the man I wanted to marry. I shadowed him much like a fawn does its mother and hung on his every word. Prior to meeting Bill, I never really wanted children. Now that our relationship was growing (or so I thought) every day, I started to reconsider. We discussed our future together and he made it very clear that he wanted me in it. We traveled quite a bit; me flying us all over the Philippine islands in a little plane I rented. It was a wonderful time in my life and I was never happier. Life even improved in the squadron. I was moving quickly through the ranks and was finally recognized for my dedication and efforts.

What is amazing to me is how quickly women can forget the lessons they learn in previous disastrous relationships. I jumped into the relationship with Bill with no life preserver and no reflection on what just happened to me. Big red flags stared me in the face from our very first weekend together, but I chose to ignore them. He was very self-centered and only thought how a given situation affected him. Bill often disregarded the established curfew when we were in town. In Olongapo, all US service personnel were required to be on base by 1 am due to suspected terrorist activity. Because he was a doctor, Bill routinely ignored the regulation, knowing he would never be punished. I however, could have been court martialed for this offense but he didn't care. If he wasn't ready to go home, Bill wouldn't leave, and often I returned home alone.

These minor infractions bothered me, but I excused them away. I was very infatuated with Bill who so effortlessly said all the right words to make me think our future held much promise. When we fought, I always gave in and was willing to do whatever he wanted to make sure everything ran smoothly. In hindsight, I find it interesting how much I mirrored my mother. Only a few months later, the most significant relationship of my life ended disastrously. A mutual friend of ours decided to clear her conscience. She told me that Bill was having an affair with another friend of hers, and had been the entire time we were dating.

After my relationship with John, I should have been prepared for this type of news. I wasn't. I cried a river of tears that eventually ended in numbness that lasted for years. When I confronted him, Bill denied it at first and then eventually admitted his guilt. He then told me, "It wasn't like I did anything wrong. We weren't married so how could I be cheating on you?" The betrayal and sense of failure were almost more than I could bear. This infidelity coupled with what I witnessed in the Philippines impacted me enormously. Besides occasional brief relationships, I never really dated anyone seriously again.

Chapter Six

Land of the Misfit Toys

Not only do pilots have callsigns, but all squadrons have particular callsigns or nicknames as well. Fighter and attack squadron callsigns are usually very macho names like the Gunslingers, the Dragonslayers, and the Black Knights. Some are very clever like the Grim Reapers and the famous Marine squadron, the Black Sheep. My favorite callsigns are the funny and apropos, for instance, the VF-143 Pukin' Dogs. In the same vein, I always loved the callsigns of fighter squadrons that seemed completely out of place, like the Chippy Ho's. Obviously, these guys have a sensitive side after all.

Once over a target area I heard, "Gladiators approaching the target." "Roger that, the Sidewinders are on station, keep a look out for the Bulls." All voices were deep, full of testosterone and the warrior spirit. Then came a voice out of nowhere, "Dolphins checking in!" No matter how manly the pilot said that, he would not be taken seriously. Ah the frustration of a fighter pilot with the callsign of Dolphin!

The squadron callsign for VC-5 was the Checkertails. There is absolutely no hidden or clever meaning to this callsign; the tails of our aircraft were painted in a yellow and red checkered pattern. It was a bit of a letdown after flying with the VT-7 Screaming Eagles, but at least we didn't have a callsign like Dolphin.

VC stands for a fixed-wing composite squadron. The squadron was composed of about 14 A-4E's and 5 SH-3's. A-4E's are single seat, light attack bomber planes introduced in Vietnam, but they are incredibly versatile aircraft. They make excellent fighter aircraft because they are highly maneuverable, and are also used to train student pilots. The TA-4J was the two-seat trainer version that I flew in flight school. While the US is now phasing out all versions of the A-4, many countries like Singapore and New Zealand still use them for combat aircraft.

The SH-3's were passenger transport, and search and rescue helicopters. They were primarily used in the Philippines for VIP transport, but were often involved in humanitarian and rescue missions. The Navy is also in the process of phasing the SH-3 out of service. Still, it is a very safe and dependable helicopter, and a workhorse in the Philippines.

VC-5 and the A-4 flew many missions. We primarily provided adversary support. This meant we pretended to be the bad guy. Air-to-air combat was a very small part of our mission and for safety reasons, was phased out in 1991. We also towed a myriad of targets for other planes and ships to shoot. Sometimes we used our planes to act as missiles to give other planes and ships practice in tracking high-speed targets. We shot a few missiles and dropped a lot of practice bombs. The missions the pilots loved the most were the air-to-air engagements.

I had only been in the squadron just a few weeks when I went on my first real mission as an adversary pilot. I was ecstatic when I found out I would be dash 4 (the last plane) in a four plane low level that would be going against some Air Force fighters. We were supposed to ingress into "enemy" territory, very low through a very narrow valley, simulate dropping bombs, and then try to egress without the Air Force planes finding us. It was a very exciting mission because we would be flying as fast as possible, as low as possible, through mountainous terrain and as if that weren't difficult enough, we would have to maintain a formation designed to protect one another called the "battle box."

The battle box formation requires four planes to take up the imaginary corners of a box, typically about one mile from each other at each point although the distances can vary depending on the scenario. Dash four is a difficult position to fly because it is not easy to maintain sight of everyone and stay in this mutually supportive formation. While everyone in the box is responsible for looking out for the enemy, it is up to dash four to make sure no other aircraft attack from behind. What made our particular mission even more demanding and dangerous was that we were flying the battle box at speeds greater than 500 mph in and out of mountains, only 500 feet above the ground. I was now a single seat pilot and there would be no instructor in the back to bail me out. I would solely determine my success or failure on this flight. For this flight, my pucker factor would be high.

Pucker factor is a classic aviator phrase that represents how tight a person holds his buns together because a flight regime is so scary or dangerous. Most pilots have a high pucker factor around the boat at night and all pilots would have a pucker factor of 100% if a missile targeted them. While the other seasoned pilots in my squadron may have had only a mild pucker factor for our low level flight, mine was high. This was my first real mission—myself and three other planes were going to be screaming across a jungle floor, with an unknown number of bad guys trying to bag us, while also trying to negotiate mountains that routinely claimed the lives of many of my peers.

We took off, slowly circled overhead our ingress point like vultures over a rotting carcass and then at the appointed time, sharply split into our box formation, put the throttles at maximum, and started our push to the target area. My heart was thumping out of my chest. I had flown fast and low before, but I was not experienced at flying through mountains while trying to watch three other aircraft. Every time unavoidable smaller mountains split the formation, my heart skipped a beat while I momentarily lost sight. Inevitably though, I regained sight and maneuvered back into position, feeling relieved only to find myself confronting another killer mountain in my path.

While we were flying at the speed of heat, weaving our way through the narrow valleys and imposing mountains in almost a choreographed ballet, enemy planes were descending on us like flies on honey. I was so focused and scared, that I never saw another plane while our flight leader took evasive maneuvers with the formation. All I knew was that we were yanking and baking all over the place and it was all I could do to keep from hitting the ground. We finally successfully egressed and returned to base less than an hour after we took off. I was still out of breath when we landed but electrified beyond words. I was no Chuck Yeager on the flight but I hadn't fallen out of the formation, which was common for new pilots. I proved I was no wuss and the flight leader seemed genuinely pleased with my performance, especially for someone so new.

I loved flying these exciting missions but I soon learned that in naval aviation, my squadron was at the bottom of the totem pole. While the phrase "adversary squadron" sounds impressive, the Navy's VC squadrons were for the most part dumping grounds for the Navy's marginal jet pilots. The Navy did have a few adversary squadrons affiliated with TOP-GUN, but these were VFC squadrons and were for the elite pilots. Most of the jet pilots assigned to the VC squadrons had major flight-related shortcomings. Most VC-5 pilots either did very poorly in initial carrier qualifications, or in later requalifications. A few were just overall marginal performers out of flight school. The bottom line was that if a male jet pilot was assigned to a VC squadron, he screwed up somewhere.

This, however, was not true for female pilots. Women trained to fly combat aircraft, but the irony was that women were not allowed to fly in combat. When I was assigned to VC-5 in 1990, VC squadrons were the most tactical squadrons in which a woman could fly. Consequently, VC orders were the best orders a woman could hope to obtain. Of all the VC squadrons, VC-5 in the Philippines offered the most tactical missions and a variety of qualifications. Women pilots could not achieve these qualifications anywhere else in the Navy. Consequently, the Navy's worst male jet pilots were sent to the same squadron where the best women pilots were also ordered.

This "land of the misfit toys" (as the A-4 pilots liked to refer to themselves) was not true of the helicopter pilots. They ended up in the squadron generally not because of performance problems, but because of luck of the draw (otherwise known as "Needs of the Navy.") When these helicopter pilots received their wings, if the Navy needed to fill a vacancy, they were on the next cattle car out of LA bound for the Philippines.

The jet side of the squadron traveled frequently, providing adversary services to Naval, Marine, and Air Force units all over WESTPAC. These deployments generally included Japan, Korea, Okinawa, Thailand, Singapore, and Brunei with an occasional diversion to Australia. The helicopter pilots resented the jet pilots on many levels. The jet pilots flew a more glamorous mission and got to fly all over the world. Also, the helo pilots were left to pick up the slack when the jet pilots went on these international deployments. Most of the time, however, we all got along. However, when our evaluations were due, there was always a lot of tension in the squadron. The number one or two ranking was very important for promotion and almost always both spots went to jet guys. This infuriated the helicopter pilots, especially when the number one and two slots were given to jet guys with applications into the airlines. These jet pilots made it clear they were getting out of the Navy. I was not privy to all the deciding factors, but it seemed the helicopter pilots made some valid points.

The squadron encompassed about 40 officers and 220 enlisted personnel, which made it a medium-sized squadron. All of the officers comprised the "wardroom." This is a traditional nautical term that formerly describes the place where all the officers gather at sea. In a squadron, it merely means the group of officers.

The man in charge of both the wardroom and all the enlisted personnel was the Commanding Officer (CO) who held the rank of Commander (O-5). He was the person ultimately held responsible for everything. In a perfect world, the CO is supposed to concentrate primarily with operational concerns. The second in command, the Executive Officer (XO) who is also an 0-5, is in charge of the administrative aspects of the squadron, basically looking after the nuts and bolts of daily operation. Reporting to the XO are the department heads, usually Lieutenant Commanders (O-4).

The departments of VC-5 were divided into operations (OPS), administrative (ADMIN), safety, training, and the largest of any naval organization, maintenance. Each department was segmented into divisions and headed by the junior officers. Mostly the senior enlisted personnel managed the maintenance department, where the majority of the enlisted personnel work. Only a handful of officers worked as division officers in maintenance for overall supervision. Unlike the Air Force where pilots do nothing but fly, Naval aviators have "ground jobs" in addition to their flying duties. Division officers, department heads, and even the XO and CO are expected to maintain a myriad of flying qualifications in addition to their very demanding ground responsibilities. These dual hats leave little time for family, which is also the reason most aviators leave the Navy.

When I first checked into the squadron in December of 1990, I was amazed to find my picture posted all over the squadron. The picture was from the US Naval Academy yearbook from my junior year. I was on the Judo team at the Academy and actually won a medal at the Eastern Collegiate tournament that qualified me for Nationals. The caption on the reproduced picture was something along the lines of "You're next!" It was funny and I laughed it off. It turned out that Dave, the same guy who picked me up my first day, made the poster and put it up. That's how he knew what I looked like.

I immediately took to the helo guys. They were laid back and seemed to have a collectively good sense of humor. The jet half of the squadron was a little different. We were all single seat pilots, an aggregate type A group who were competitive by nature. There was always a lot of one-upsmanship between the jet pilots, but no more than in any other jet community. Of the eighteen or so jet pilots, three were women. The guys in the squadron had a slew of pet names for us; squatters, split-tails, and my personal favorite, booze hags.

The other two women had been "in country" over a year and were much more familiar with the surroundings. They both shunned me on arrival, which actually took me by surprise. I never really had the opportunity to work with any other women and looked forward to it. They made it clear that they did not like me and so did not include me in their outings. In retrospect, I don't think they were territorial as much as they were solo operators. We all went through flight school alone, so female bonding was not important or even possible. All three of us were survivors in a very anti-woman world and excelled by whatever means necessary. I did not see it that way then however, and I looked at them as traitors and downright mean-spirited.

Because of the lack of genuine friendship in a very competitive environment, I ended up hanging around with my suite mate from the BOQ, Elaine, who was a Navy nurse. A natural nurturer, Elaine introduced me to her circle of nurse and doctor friends. They took me in like a lost pup and truly made my life not only bearable but great fun. I enjoyed an almost normal life in the PI. The people I worked with were my peers, but at the end of the workday, I met with a different set of friends. What I didn't know then is these friendships further alienated the pilots at work. Although they did not want me in their club, they nevertheless expected me to hang around them. This was yet another illustration of the dichotomy of a woman in a man's world.

When new pilots report in, they are usually not assigned a very demanding ground job until they have their initial qualifications. They are also given time to acclimate to both their living and working environments. When I arrived in 1990, I was assigned the Command Managed Equal Opportunity (CMEO) position. Initially, I was relieved. While I was assigned to NATTC in Memphis just a few months earlier, I acted as the CMEO. Because of my big project there, I was very familiar with all the instructions and duties. It was not a very demanding job. All it really required was making sure sexual harassment posters were made public, annual training was held, and a yearly command climate survey was conducted. If any sexual harassment complaints were made, the CMEO investigated the claim and referred the findings to the Commanding Officer. I never personally witnessed any complaints and thought that my job as the VC-5 CMEO would be a cakewalk. Little did I know then that my insignificant position as CMEO in VC-5 would eventually affect my entire naval career.

I was only on board for three weeks when the Legal Officer came to me with not one but two complaints. Two of the enlisted women came forward accusing their department head, LCDR Baker, of locking them up on separate occasions in the squadron communications office and assaulting them. The communications office was essentially a safe the size of a room and a person must possess a combination to gain entrance. I was flabbergasted. I thought that the days of being chased around a desk by the boss were long gone. I was wrong. When LCDR Baker was confronted with the charges, he admitted his wrongdoing, excusing his behavior by stating, "I only did it because my wife is pregnant and I didn't want to go out in town." His wife was a lovely person, thin and beautiful who already had two children. His town comment clearly referred to the rampant prostitution outside the gates of the naval base.

Because LCDR Baker was senior to these women, he was initially removed from his department head position and later from the squadron entirely. He was sent to work at the airfield operations center during the investigation. This is a typical and entirely appropriate response to such serious charges. The Uniform Code of Military Justice (UCMJ), the laws that govern all military personnel, clearly states that this type of sexual harassment is unlawful and can be punished by dismissal.

As the CMEO, I worked with the squadron Legal Officer on the pending case. A squadron legal officer is not a lawyer, but usually a pilot with four weeks of legal training. Legal Officers are only supposed to assist the naval lawyers on pending cases, not decide their outcome. LCDR Baker's case should have been referred to the base lawyers for handling, but the CO insisted that it be handled at the squadron level. The squadron legal officer drew up three charges of sexual harassment and one charge of fraternization against LCDR Baker. When the legal officer showed me the charges, I was dumbfounded. How could LCDR Baker be charged with fraternization?

The Navy defines fraternization as "personal relationships between officer and enlisted members which are unduly familiar and do not respect differences in rank and grade." These two young women, nineteen years old and both black were very upset over the entire affair. It was clear that they did not want the attention of a forty-ish married white man who was their boss! By even listing a charge of fraternization, the accusation was on the table that these women asked for his unwanted advances! I found out later in my career that this was a typical method for handling these types of situations. Fraternization was seen as a much lesser crime than sexual harassment, and was often the charge pressed in these situations.

This turned out to be true when the CO dismissed all three sexual harassment charges. Despite LCDR Baker's confession, he was charged with fraternization. I was furious! The message that the CO sent the women and the squadron was that this type of behavior was tolerated and swept under the rug. LCDR Baker was brought back into the squadron and was again the department head of one of the enlisted women. He received no punishment except for a non-punitive letter of reprimand. (A non-punitive letter is merely a letter from the CO to the accused expressing dismay at the conduct of the accused.) A slap on the wrist, it carries absolutely no penalty.

As the CMEO, it was my job to advise the CO throughout all these proceedings. I told him that legally he could not uphold the fraternization charge, especially when neither of the enlisted women was charged. I told him that if any organization from outside the command were to investigate the allegations and results, he would be in trouble. The CO told me that it was his call to make (which it was) and the way he saw it, no harassment took place, only fraternization. The CO then went on to tell me that Baker did not deserve any further punishment. Anything more punitive, he said, would ruin his career. He actually pulled out a calculator and tallied up the potential loss of wages and said Baker did not deserve to lose these as well as the retirement benefits that accompanied promotions. The CO obviously did not care about the careers of the two enlisted women involved. The women subsequently resigned from the Navy after Baker was brought back into the squadron.

I found out later that before I arrived, bets were made in the squadron about whom I would sleep with first. When it never materialized, I was termed a "cold bitch" and referred to as "not a team player." I only became more resolute in my non-participation after witnessing a particularly disgusting exchange between two of the guys who slept with one of the women in the squadron. I was the duty officer, which required me to be in the Ready Room all day. It was routine for pilots to hang around in the Ready Room while waiting for planes to be readied or conduct general squadron business.

This particular day the conversation turned to sex, which it often did. The two guys starting discussing their respective relationships with this woman and then the discussion turned in a very graphic direction. They actually started comparing notes, discussing their favorite positions, how flexible she was and how good her blowjobs were. The conversation was both nauseating and degrading. I don't doubt they embellished for my sake and it achieved the desired effect.

Beyond the revulsion for the language, I saw something new. Previously I didn't care for this woman because of her brusque treatment of me, but after that day my attitude changed. I realized that both her flings and her treatment of me were attempts to fit in with the guys in the squadron.

I also realized that no matter what a female pilot did, she would never be in the "club." This particular woman was a gifted pilot, what we term in the Navy as a "great stick." She was thoroughly professional to fly with and I really looked up to her abilities as a pilot. She was head and shoulders above the guys in skill, but they shunned her. She stooped to their level and as a reward for her "team player" conduct, she was completely debased and degraded behind her back. I will never forget that day because I realized that this was a no-win situation. I would never break into the club, no matter what.

In our squadron, there were two rituals that made a pilot a "real man" and gained him entrance into the "club." The first was flying so low across the ground or water that rooster tails were produced. Rooster tails are the deflection of the exhaust of an aircraft off the ground or water that produced a horizontal spiraling vortex of air and water or dust. It is very cool to see but it requires the pilot to be as low as approximately twenty feet. For a helicopter going less than 100 knots (114 mph), it is exciting but not fantastically so. Our pilots sometimes raced down a ravine at the required 20 feet, at speeds of greater than 400 knots (455 mph). This of course required a very steady hand and a very big set of balls. I rode with one of our senior pilots when he did this, and while incredibly nerve wracking, it was intensely electrifying.

The second rite of passage was taking the A-4 supersonic. The A-4 is a fantastic plane with more roles than originally designed. However, going faster than Mach 1 was not one of them. The planes we flew were very old. Some flew in Vietnam and had bullet holes patched with strips of metal. Our A-4's with no external tanks and full internal fuel weighed around 20,000 lbs. The engines were only rated at about 9,000 lbs. of thrust. Mach

1 was impossible at sea level and at any other altitude, flying straight and level. Despite the lack of thrust and design for these speeds, it was possible for a pilot take the light A-4 to almost 40,000 ft and push it over in a 45-degree dive at full power. Mach 1 could then be achieved with a pullout that kept the pilot from planting it in the ground. The pilots who dared to attempt this feat returned and told everyone in the wardroom, thereby gaining entrance into the boys' club. Occasionally, pilots returned with mangled wings or missing components from solo flights. No questions were asked and the damage was chalked up as inevitable for old aircraft. We never did have any fatal accidents, so we were very lucky. The planes very easily could have catastrophically failed in flight.

I never did have the gonads required to do these feats. I have always been a more conservative pilot who firmly believes better safe than sorry. Maybe if I had flown more hours in the Navy, I would have felt more comfortable. After just six months in the squadron, I only had around 400 hours of flight time, which is not much, so I didn't feel the need to press my luck. Because I just came from a very regimented environment in flight school, it was hard for me to break the rigid habits. I also carried Murphy's Law around like a black cloud. On occasion I would "come into the break smoking" (faster than 450 knots, 511 mph). Sometimes the breaks were very impressive, but if it was a Friday night at 1700, it was certain that I would goon it up and look ridiculous.

The jet guys were not the only pilots in the squadron who flew by the seat of their pants. Occasionally, the helo pilots would have an impressive story as well. In fact, the only real kill in the squadron came from a helicopter. The helo was flying in the local area when the pilots decided to fly into a gorge. They flew down into and across the gash in the earth. They decided to leave the gorge by ascending straight up. As the helicopter rose from the pit below, it spooked a cow who was tethered to a tree just above. The terrified cow bolted towards the cliff. Unfortunately, the owner of the cow didn't measure the rope, which turned out to be longer than the distance to the cliff. The crazed cow hung itself, right in front of the mortified helicopter crew. After paying the Philippine farmer for his cow, the maintenance guys painted a little cow below a window of the helo, just like a kill from W.W.II. For once the helo guys showed up the jet pilots.

Despite the differences in flying jobs, both the helo and jet pilots all worked ground jobs. In 1991, just a few months into my tour, the previous ADMIN division officer, another Lieutenant and a jet pilot, was fired for general incompetence and gross negligence. The squadron failed its administrative inspection, one of the major inspections for a squadron. Failing it sends waves throughout the entire Navy. Personnel were consistently late or just flat out absent, embarrassing correspondence was sent out, and there was a general lack of accountability on everyone's part. Both the department head and division officers were fired, and I was assigned my first division.

My job as the administrative division officer was definitely one of the biggest leadership challenges I have ever faced. About 25 enlisted personnel worked for me, ranging in age from eighteen to mid-forties. The administrative department is primarily responsible for personnel issues; all incoming and outgoing correspondence; and the massive amounts of paperwork that the Navy loves to generate. It is not a glamorous job, but it is essential. The enlisted personnel who are assigned to ADMIN departments are generally called yeoman. Their computer and writing skills are above average, and while not the cream of the enlisted crop, certainly a more educated bunch. In normal squadrons, the yeomen were usually well behaved kids that rarely got into trouble. I was not so lucky when I was appointed as the ADMIN division officer.

At first, I was a little intimidated and at a loss where to even start. One of the best petty officers in the division loved to bring in pictures of him and his "bar fine" engaging in "golden showers." He was eventually officially punished for bringing this same girl into the classified safe room and having sex with her on classified documents. Half of the rest of the division was on restriction, and a few were headed to the brig (jail).

These yeomen were the same yeomen that would be no problem in any other command. What was different now was the fact that the squadron was in the Philippines. The temptations were too great for young kids from small towns with money burning holes in their pockets. For around ten dollars, these kids could have any of their sexual fantasies fulfilled, night after night. Most of the men in my division were frequent visitors of the STD clinic and some married the Philippine girls who showed them a whole new world. One of my sailors actually tried to "defect" to the Philippines. He claimed the squadron was treating him inhumanely. I am not sure if he ever really understood the concept that a person couldn't defect to a democratic allied country, but we flew him out on the next cattle car to the US anyway.

Despite the seemingly overwhelming task, I learned a very important lesson about the menial and unpleasant jobs that no one wants: You cannot fail, you can only improve. After a lot of hard work and enforcing military discipline, I was able to turn the division around. A year later during the next inspection, the department was graded outstanding in EVERY category, which numbered around fifty. I was very happy, as was my Commanding Officer, since it made him look good. The inspection team, from the headquarters in Japan, was so impressed with the turn-around, that they recommended me for a Navy Commendation Medal. This is a very prestigious medal, usually reserved for senior lieutenants and LCDRs. I was still a Lieutenant junior grade (0-2) and was delighted that someone outside my command recognized my performance.

When I received the award, I was shocked to find out it was downgraded to a Navy Achievement Medal, which is significantly less meaningful. I found out later (because I was the ADMIN officer) that my own Commanding Officer downgraded the award, which is unheard of. Usually an officer's own command really goes to bat for him, and some staff person in an unknown office downgrades the award, not his own skipper. This was the first indication that I was to be punished for my lack of participation in the squadron's extracurricular activities.

I was definitely not in the "in-group" in the squadron. Because I chose not to participate in the lewd drinking games in town, and I would not sleep with any of the guys, despite several unsuccessful attempts, I was relegated to the fringes. That suited me just fine. Because of the Sodom and Gomorrah environment many of the male pilots loved to be in, I certainly didn't want to socialize with them after hours. I was not alone in my exile; some of the guys chose to be on the fringe as well. They were typically the newly married guys who also preferred not to take part in the town activities. The married guys and I got along famously and often dined at each other's houses. However, because of our "uncoolness," we were always given the worst flights. We called ourselves the blue-collar pilots of the squadron and wore patches that said "Skeet for the Fleet." Those of us not privileged to be part of the "club" pulled all the targets for other planes and ships to shoot at. It was a thankless task, droning in circles, sometimes very close to the water with people we never met, firing live ordinance at us.

I was pulling a banner for some F-14's once who consistently disregarded all the flight rules. When planes fire at a banner towed behind another aircraft, the name of the game is to always approach the banner from a perpendicular angle. This allows the bullets to pass well clear of the towing aircraft which is only a very short 2000 feet away. The F-14s I pulled for that day were struggling with correct positioning. Instead of flying at a perpendicular angle, they would fall behind, and then fire from behind the banner with the two fuselages of the planes aligned, in what we term as a "sucked" position. If a pilot's aim was off, which it often was, the bullets would go flying over our cockpits. After a half an hour of some really scary runs, I ended the exercise early because the F-14 pilots would not quit firing from the sucked position. After that, I was coined the biggest bitch in WESTPAC because I terminated training early. The other male pilots would have taken the same action and often did, but I heard about that incident for weeks.

I was an above average pilot in the squadron, but that wasn't saying a lot. Because the Navy's bottom of the barrel male pilots were sent to VC-5, the number of "incidents" was higher than the Navy average. When our pilots went to the tanker which is another larger plane that is the big gas station in the sky, they were usually unqualified and downright scary. The tanker pilots always cringed when they heard our squadron check in. We were famous for taking home "party hats" from the tanker. A Party Hat is the basket that is originally attached to the tanker that engages the fuel probe. Some of the pilots in the squadron unintentionally rammed the basket, ripped it off, and sent fuel spraying everywhere. The lucky pilot then got to take the basket home, still attached to the fuel probe.

I was far from perfect and had my share of learning experiences. Fortunately nothing major occurred. My worst mistake was caused by my over cautious approach to flying. I aborted a takeoff at a fairly high speed, 110 knots (125 mph). I mistakenly thought the horizontal stabilator (which is what makes a plane go up and down), was not working properly and decided to abort the takeoff rather than having to eject later in the flight.

This dilemma of a high-speed abort is one that every pilot quarterbacks. If not done exactly right, the pilot risked running off the runway and flipping the aircraft. Even though I executed it flawlessly, in retrospect, I probably wouldn't do it again. At the time I had less than 500 flying hours, which is considered very inexperienced. (This is called a typical "nugget" mistake.) A "nugget" is a new pilot with little experience, a term appropriate for me and most of the other pilots.

One of the other nugget pilots, "Fergie" Ferguson, made a major mistake that almost cost him his life. On a clear day after a successful mission, Fergie landed with his landing gear up. This is perhaps the most senseless mistake a pilot can make, and many safeguards are installed in the plane to remind the pilot. Despite all the bells and whistles, Fergie landed with his gear up anyway and was very lucky to escape with his life. He was a nice guy on the ground and knew he made a mistake that would probably cost him his wings. Because Fergie was such a popular guy in the squadron, the Commanding Officer allowed him to continue flying, which is generally unheard of for this type of accident. Fergie, a very intelligent and introspective person, turned in his wings anyway, stating he knew he shouldn't fly anymore. It was one of the bravest acts I have ever witnessed in the Navy. I doubt any of the other pilots in the squadron would have been able to come to the same conclusion.

Another one of the squadron's shining star pilots was the senior pilot, LT Mike "Razor" Sharp. Not only was he responsible for safety in the squadron, but he also administered all the check rides to the other pilots, called a NATOPS checker. (Naval Aviation Training & Operating Procedures Standardization) This is the most respected of all piloting positions in any squadron and carries with it an abundance of responsibility.

My first clue that Razor was probably a little overwhelmed was when he ran off a runway in Japan. He blamed it on the aircraft, stating that one of the control surfaces caused him to inadvertently run off the side of the runway. Other pilots were landing at the same time and knew this was not true. When the plane was tested for this problem, the supposed cause was never found. It is a big deal when a plane runs off the side of the runway. The landing gear are not made for four-wheeling, and the A-4 is especially susceptible to flipping on unprepared surfaces. Because he was the senior pilot, no investigation was held and Razor was allowed to continue flying without recourse.

A few weeks later, Razor flew into another airport in Japan and landed in a closed section of the runway. This was very serious because the runway was closed due to construction. When Razor touched down, he landed in construction material and put a 2X4 through the wing. No one is quite sure why he did this; all pilots were briefed before takeoff not to land in that particular section of the runway. If Razor had been in the United States and did this, his wings would have been pulled. Because Razor was the "senior pilot" and "one of the boys," he was again allowed to continue flying. Clearly safety was not a priority in the squadron. We were extremely lucky no one was killed.

Chapter Seven

The End of Sodom and Gomorrah

I progressed quickly through the squadron's training programs and flew in several major exercises. The jets in the squadron were constantly on the go, but I loved living out of a suitcase and flying from country to country. Because there are so many US air bases in Japan and Korea, the majority of our exercises took us away from the PI. After participating in several of these exercises in just a few months, we came home to the Philippines to regroup during the summer. The Gulf War was over and the Navy was concentrating on bringing unnecessary troops home, so there wasn't much demand for my squadron's services.

We worked with a few ships enroute to the US via the PI, but there wasn't much business. After dragging a few targets for live-fire practice, we sometimes finished our missions early with spare gas. In May of 1991, the number one place to go if fuel supplied allowed was the volcano, Mount Pinatubo. Dormant for 500 years, its recent activity caught the attention of seismologists and volcanologists all over the world. They flocked to the PI to observe the volcano, so our helicopters were employed full time taking the scientists to strategic locations.

There are basically two types of volcanoes, lava and ash. Mount St. Helens in Washington was an ash volcano, and the volcanoes in Hawaii are lava. While hot, molten lava seems more threatening, actually ash volcanoes do the most damage because their explosions are much more devastating. Mt. Pinatubo was only about 25 miles northwest of Subic Bay. It wasn't considered a big threat to Subic Bay because of the prevailing winds and the topography. The prediction was that any explosion would send ash and lahar north, away from Subic. (Lahar is the mixture of ash and water and is much like cement.)

The big concern for the US government was Clark Air Force Base (AFB). Only 10 miles from the volcano, it was in the direct path of any potential ash fallout. By the beginning of June there was grave concern by the scientists and volcanologists that the volcano could catastrophically erupt. In response, all personnel from Clark AFB were evacuated to Subic Bay. The volcano started spewing small amounts of ash into the air, forming little mushroom clouds. It was very surreal but breathtaking.

Families in Subic opened their doors to the families from Clark, and all singles were double and triple bunked in both the enlisted and officer's barracks. The mood was one of disbelief and skepticism. No one really expected anything too terrible to happen. Everyone hung around the bar; drinking, laughing and basically thinking the evacuation was yet another knee jerk reaction to a little earthquake and some ash. We couldn't have been more wrong.

One day I came back from a flight and my CO grabbed several pilots, including me. The volcano was going to massively erupt any second and we were given twenty minutes to pack an overnight bag and fly to Okinawa. All the jets were to be evacuated in the event of an eruption. Because of our departure, all the helicopters would then fit into the hangar. We grabbed a change of clothes, toiletries, and a gas card and took off. We still didn't think the situation was too serious and that we would be back in a day or two. As all the jets were reaching altitude, the volcano erupted in what we thought was "the big one." The brilliant blue sky turned gray. The ash cloud expanded and rose to more than 30,000 ft—very impressive and awe inspiring. We knew then that we would be gone for more than just a few days.

When we landed in Okinawa, we called home immediately. The damage was not too severe, and the evacuated Clark AFB sustained the brunt of the fallout. Everything at Subic was just fine. In fact, there was a big volcano party at the club where Jimmy Buffet's volcano song was played over and over. The mood was akin to that of the Titanic on its sinking—the band still played as the world around it was collapsing.

Three days later, all hell broke loose. The huge eruption on the day we left was just a burp compared to what was in store for the area. On 15 June, 1991, the top third of the volcano literally blew off, sending 18 million tons of ash into the air. Mt. Pinatubo sent a cloud of ash that peaked at over eleven miles into the atmosphere[3], well into the stratosphere. Commercial airliners as far as the Chinese mainland lost engines due to the ingestion of the ash. In a one in six million chance, right at the same time the volcano erupted, typhoon Yunya struck the Subic Bay area. Not just a problem because when the ash mixed with water, it fell like cement blocks, but the typhoon also caused the winds to shift 180 degrees. In full accordance with Murphy's Law, Subic Bay, not Clark AFB, was now in the direct path of the falling cement bricks.

The earthquakes that accompanied the explosion were 5.6 on the Richter scale, not the most powerful but they continued for days. The explosion occurred in the morning, but in mere minutes, day was turned to night. In darkness as black as a night with no moon, the water-soaked ash pummeled the earth already heaving and groaning from volcano ejecting tons and tons of ash. The eruption of Mt. Pinatubo was ten times more explosive than Mt. St. Helens. While I was not there, my friends who were say the entire experience was terrifying.

On the base, there were surprisingly few deaths. Only two dependents were killed when the ceiling of the high school gym fell in. Roof cave-ins were the big fear for everyone. In large amounts, dry ash alone is enough to cause a weak roof to fall in, but with the wet ash falling, the danger was increased exponentially. Commercial airliners and large military cargo planes left in the open ended up scattered around the airport like toys, comically all popping wheelies. The ash was so heavy, when it fell on the rear tail horizontal surface; it caused the plane's nose to come up.

While the loss of life on the base was minimal, it was more devastating in the outlying areas. Many of the aboriginal Filipinos, called Aetas, refused to leave the mountain slopes during the evacuation. Deeply superstitious people, they believed no harm would come to them. The death count totaled 737; only half of these were due to the eruption, the rest died of disease in evacuation centers.[4] Despite the poverty of the region and lack of shelters for the Filipinos, the loss of human life was relatively light.

The lahar flowed from the northern edge of what remained from the volcano. A river of oozing gray mud, it quickly overwhelmed any structure, animal, or person in its path. The saddest pictures I saw were those of fleeing Filipinos on foot or on mule. The imprint of a prone person's body under the ash could be made out and sometimes the bodies just lay on top of the mud, moving with it, eventually discarded much like pieces of driftwood.

The property damage was measureless. Clark AFB was abandoned completely and it was decided that the lease, under renegotiations, would not be renewed. Subic Bay was different. Far more strategic than Clark, the US government determined that Subic Bay could be salvaged, at the cost of hundreds of million dollars. The clean up effort began, but it was slow work moving thousands of tons of ash.

Because significant amounts of ash might cause an engine to seize, the single engine A-4's were not allowed to return for several weeks. When we finally were allowed to return, I was amazed. It looked like I landed on the moon. Everything was gray and a strong musty smell permeated the air. Everything we touched was gritty. Ash is really very fine sand and ended up in everything we ate and drank. Water was at a premium and strict conservation measures were in effect.

The dependents evacuated to the United States remained there because of the lack of support facilities. The only people left were the active duty military personnel and the Filipinos. Many of the men took advantage of their wives' absence. They fired their wives' matronly older maids and hired new, young ones from town. Despite the devastation, drinking and carousing were at an all time high, as was the number of patients in the STD clinic. These new live-in "maids" as they were referred to, presented an ugly problem when the wives came back. When the husbands found out their wives were returning, they kicked out their newly acquired "maids" with minimal compensation and rehired the old ones. Scores of these spurned young Filipinas were furious, and after the wives returned, many found the scorned young "maid" on their doorstep, telling all. The counseling center was overwhelmed with domestic disputes, as were the base chaplains.

When I first looked at the volcano damage, I thought it would take years before the place would even somewhat resemble the old Subic Bay. Prior to the eruption, the base was gorgeous, containing hundreds of square miles of tropical jungle with colorful birds and monkeys galore. After the eruption, environmentalists speculated it would take more than ten years to restore the original splendor of the jungle and surrounding bays. Nature has a funny way of compensating, though. Just two long months after the volcano erupted, the mother of all monsoon seasons began. Almost as if Mother Nature knew the area needed to be cleaned, the monsoon season that year was particularly fierce. It rained for twenty or more days at stretch without stopping. When it finally did stop after about four months, the results were amazing. A few remnants of ash remained on distant mountaintops, but for the most part, the landscape was thoroughly scoured. The jungle looked even better than before because ash is also very rich soil. The sunsets were tremendous due to the residual ash in the air, and the wildlife both in the jungle and in the bays completely rebounded. Even the scientists were awed at the renewal.

The area close to the volcano still resembled a moonscape with lahar continuing to tumble out of the center. Earthquakes were still so routine that people didn't even acknowledge their occurrence in casual conversations. At the club when earthquakes hit, people simply picked up their drinks. (Spilling alcohol was considered alcohol abuse.) If an unlucky soul was caught abusing alcohol, it meant a round for everyone in the bar. In a very surreal way, life quickly returned to normal. The town of Olongapo rebounded even quicker than the base and was back in full swing within just a few short weeks of the eruption.

The A-4's were finally allowed to return six weeks after the eruption just in time for the beginning of monsoon season. When a monsoon hits, it rains and rains and rains and rains, and just when it stops, it rains some more. When the rain is severe and thunderstorms hit, flying the A-4 is dangerous and what we call "varsity" flying. "Varsity" means even the best, most experienced pilots struggle with the conditions. If the rain were particularly fierce, we wouldn't fly. Because of the lack of flying during the monsoon season, I took the opportunity to attend the TOPGUN Training Officers' Ground School in Miramar, California.

Not everyone in my squadron was allowed to attend the TOPGUN training. The Commanding Officer thought any candidates must be above average pilots. Upon his return, the pilot then moved into the more tactical phases of flying and began air combat training. The TOPGUN training was a prerequisite for the tactical training, and reserved for those pilots who demonstrated the most potential.

Made famous in the movie *TOPGUN*, the real name of the school is the Navy Fighter Weapons School. It was instituted after the poor showing of naval aviation in Vietnam in the air-to-air arena. TOPGUN is the Mecca for all fighter pilots and produces the finest fighter pilots in the world. The pilots who attend this school are supposed to return to their units and share their new knowledge with the rest of the squadron.

Most of the pilots who attend TOPGUN go for the academic and flying portion of the syllabus, as depicted in the movie. Unfortunately, not all pilots who attend are allowed to participate in the flying portion of the syllabus. Like everything in the Navy and in life, it all comes down to money. Each pilot's respective squadron pays for the pilot to attend, and if the money isn't available, there is no flying.

That is in fact what happened to my entire TOPGUN class. It was the end of the fiscal year and there was no money for anyone. I wasn't disappointed because my squadron NEVER had money and only one individual from the squadron actually graduated from the flying part of the syllabus. I knew before going that I would only attend the six weeks academic training, but I was thrilled to do just that. Only a handful of women had previously attended TOPGUN, and none were allowed to execute the flying portion. I felt lucky and privileged to be there. I was a sponge, soaking in every bit and morsel of information.

I learned more that six weeks about tactics and strategy than I ever even suspected existed. Primarily, I learned what a rag tag outfit VC-5 really was. Compared to TOPGUN, my squadron was an embarrassment and its training program was laughable. During the TOPGUN Training Officers' Ground School (TOGS), I learned professional briefing techniques, the nuts and bolts of defensive maneuvers, and a slew of information that falls under the classification, "if I told you, I'd have to kill you" (a famous *TOPGUN* movie quote). I learned that I really didn't know anything about fighter tactics, both the enemies and ours. I left knowing I needed to study quite a bit. I was embarrassed with how ill prepared I was, but when I left, I felt I at least knew where to start. I finally had a clue. I still wasn't the best pilot in WESTPAC, but when I heard the discussions of F-14 and F/A-18 pilots, I could at least understand them and appreciate the points they were making.

My experience at TOPGUN's TOGS was overwhelmingly positive. For the most part, all the instructors and other pilots treated me with respect and were more than willing to explain concepts I did not understand. I loved it and really looked up to the other pilots. I was the only VC pilot there. Everyone else was a "real" pilot who flew F-14s and F/A-18s. I respected them immensely and saw them as role models. I think their treatment of me was sincere. As a VC pilot, I was no threat to them. I think most of them looked at me like a kind of kid sister. This would all change when women were allowed into combat aircraft.

One evening, the school sponsored a lecture by a former naval aviator who actually fought in Vietnam, Willie Driscoll. A radar operator in an F-4 Phantom, Willie and the pilot, Randy Cunningham, are true aces—a rare commodity in today's military. His speech was riveting, and he also played a tape of actual radio transmissions of a dogfight over Vietnam. The lesson of his lecture was the "team" concept and why a maverick would not cut it in aviation. On the tape, we heard the transmissions of a pilot who broke off from his division to chase a North Vietnamese plane. He was so engrossed with the potential kill, he didn't notice he flew into a trap. I will never forget hearing the giddy delight of the pilot who thinks he is going to be a hero, and the screams of his division leader trying to make him to break off the attack. In the end, the cowboy was shot down and killed, an effective illustration of what can happen when unit integrity is violated.

Another memorable incident of my time at TOPGUN was a conversation I had with the Commanding Officer. During the reception that followed the lecture on unit integrity, we were all standing around, discussing the lecture. The TOPGUN CO came up to me and asked me how I thought the training was going so far. I gushed about how much I loved it and how much I was learning. He then asked me, "Do you really have what it takes to kill a man?" Unfortunately, I have always had the propensity to be a smart-ass and I replied, "Do you have a gun?" We were all drinking and everyone standing around—including the skipper—thought that comment was uproariously funny. We both just left it alone and moved on to another topic. Little did I know that this comment would come back to haunt me six years later.

Prior to my leaving for TOPGUN, the entire wardroom of VC-5 in the PI went to lunch together—a fairly rare occurrence. The topic of conversation was the upcoming Change of Command. These ceremonies are very traditional in the Navy, symbolizing the passing of leadership from the old CO to the new CO. Usually concurrently held with the Change of Command ceremony is another tradition called the "Hail and Farewell." This is an informal party that recognizes both the officers that are leaving the command and those that are arriving. Since the average tour in the PI was two years, Hail and Farewell's were frequent.

The discussion at lunch that day revolved around the entertainment portion of the Hail and Farewell. One of the officers suggested that the squadron hold a drawing, with a hooker from the bar owned by the department head as the winning prize. The kicker was that the girl would be paid for using the money that all officers were forced to donate as dues. It must have seemed like a grand idea at the time, because most of the guys at the table applauded the suggestion. I looked on in amazement. Finally, one of the guys asked me what my problem was. I told everyone that not only was it in extremely poor taste to use a bar-fine as a door prize at an official function, but it was definitely illegal to use the officer's recreation fund to pay for it. My statement was met with a lot of nay saying and I reiterated my position once more stating, "If you do this, you are setting yourself up for big problems."

A few days later I was on the next plane bound for California so I was not at the Hail and Farewell. Because all the wives and dependents were still in an evacuation status, they were not around to object and the drawing was held. I don't know who the lucky winner was, but I heard a stupendous time was had by all. I returned from TOPGUN, knowing nothing of what transpired. A few weeks later, I received a phone call from headquarters in Japan. Someone called the Navy's Sexual Harassment Hotline and reported not only the hooker incident, but also the fact that an officer in the squadron was sleeping with an enlisted woman. Since I was the Equal Opportunity officer, I was in

charge of the subsequent investigation. In addition, my equal opportunity program was to be inspected since it seemed the squadron was having a lot of difficulty with sexual harassment issues. After I hung up, I
had a headache for the next four months.

During this time period, annual training on the prevention of sexual
harassment and fraternization was held throughout the entire Navy. As
the Equal Opportunity officer, it was my job to arrange a meeting hall
for the entire squadron, show them the videotape prepared by the Navy's
EO office in Washington DC, and field any subsequent questions.
Because all squadrons work in shifts, I scheduled two different training
sessions. It was customary for all the officers to attend one session
together. The only officer who did not show up was LCDR Baker, the
same officer who recently was found guilty of fraternization.

The Commanding Officer later told him he must attend the second showing, which he did. When LCDR Baker arrived in a flight
suit, he took a seat in the first row. The rest of the audience was
enlisted personnel, so it was quite obvious who he was. When I
started the videotape, LCDR Baker made a big production out of
finding ear plugs, sticking them in his ears, and reading a newspaper.
I was standing in the back of the lecture hall and clearly saw the spectacle below. There was much grumbling from the enlisted ranks.
LCDR Baker's reputation was well known and the enlisted personnel
did not like him. Now, instead of showing professional courtesy and
at least acting like he was paying attention, he flaunted his position
in front of his subordinates. He sent the clear message that he
thought he did not need the mandatory training, and would blatantly
ignore all training on sexual harassment and fraternization.

I could not believe my eyes. I have seen a lot of officers mentally blow
off this training and just vacantly stare straight ahead. In fact, I have
done this in similar training sessions. What really angered me was his
clear breaking of both rules and professional conduct in front of the
enlisted personnel as well as the very same women he abused. Later that

day, I told the CO what happened. Both the CO and XO told me that LCDR Baker was just very busy and obviously had a lot on his mind. I reiterated my position that an officer who was recently found guilty of fraternization should at least act as if he was paying attention, if for no other reason than to set the example for the enlisted personnel. They agreed and told me to give LCDR Baker the videotape so he could watch it on his own time.

When the inspectors from headquarters in Japan arrived, they initially were investigating the charges that the squadron used a hooker as a door prize. It was an open and shut case and the Commanding Officer who recently departed was held responsible. I heard later that he was asked to retire, which he did.

The inspectors also began investigating my Equal Opportunity programs and the command climate. In doing so, they heard all the "Baker" stories. They reviewed the charges and legal proceedings against LCDR Baker and found that the entire affair was grossly mishandled. He was ordered immediately to leave the squadron and go back to the United States. Quickly moving an officer was a form of punishment, one that the Navy uses often to diffuse potentially embarrassing situations. While I thought the right action finally was taken, I found out later that he was ordered to a training command as an instructor. I thought this was a very poor decision. LCDR Baker was a below average and dangerous pilot in the squadron and clearly did not exemplify the characteristics the Navy is trying to teach its young officers. Now he would be responsible for teaching both young men and women how to fly. The irony was never lost on me.

After the inspectors settled the Baker situation, they came back to me with the charges that one of the pilots, "Pops", was sleeping with an enlisted woman in the squadron. At the time, Pops was married, but it was a very rocky marriage. She left him several times while living in the PI, and when the volcano blew, she left, never to return. Pops was one of the squadron's best pilots and he got along with everyone. He was very funny and I enjoyed both flying and working with him.

In our squadron, it was commonplace for pilots to sleep with the enlisted women. It never became a problem in the workplace, and while I didn't agree with the practice, I never said anything. Again I was desperately trying to fit in with the other pilots and I did not want to create any more enemies. The CO and XO did not seem to care, abiding by the infamous, "Don't ask, Don't tell" policy now used for homosexuals. I never dreamed of pursuing any legal proceedings as the Equal Opportunity officer. It was clear that I would not be supported by the command.

In truth, Pops had been sleeping with an enlisted woman, Kathleen, for some time. It was common knowledge in the command. While I never witnessed the actual act, Pops lived down the hall from me, so I often saw her coming in and out of his room. It was openly discussed in the wardroom, and I am sure many enlisted personnel also knew.

The inspectors led me to believe that an enlisted woman reported this fact to the Navy's Hotline for sexual harassment in conjunction with the phone call about the hooker door prize scenario. The rumor in the squadron was that Pops' wife actually made the call. I was brought into a room and asked point blank if I knew he was involved in an affair with an enlisted woman.

I felt like I was suddenly in the worst Scruples™ game of my life. I absolutely possessed first hand knowledge of their relationship. However, I knew what would happen if I turned Pops in. I would become completely ostracized by the command and the other pilots would absolutely hate me. Pops was a hero in the command and anyone who turned him in would not be tolerated. In addition, his career would be destroyed.

I lied and told the investigators that I had seen nothing and heard nothing to implicate him or any of the other guys. I felt cornered in an impossible situation. I am not proud of what I did, but at the time I felt there was no other choice. It was an ethically wrong decision, so I won't try to qualify it. It was the decision I made. After the inspectors left, satisfied that there was no fraternization, Pops came to me. He thanked me and told me that he knew I was the one that saved him from any legal or administrative proceedings. We shook hands and never spoke of it again.

Overall, the inspection went as well as could be expected. In my opinion, the only true offender was Baker, and he was gone. No one else got in trouble and the inspectors were satisfied that I was doing my job. What I didn't foresee then was that when Baker was abruptly removed, the rest of the male pilots would hold me responsible. I never considered the possibility that I would be the person they thought called the hotline, but that's exactly what happened. All my fears of ostracism and isolation from turning Pops in came true anyway. Now I was the ultra-feminist bitch who turned in Baker and was responsible for his removal.

The next few months were very difficult in the squadron. Many of the jet guys did not speak to me, but I didn't really care. These were the guys who were the biggest whoremongers and never did their ground jobs anyway. The helo guys hated Baker and were glad to see him go, so they didn't seem to care who turned him in. The real problems started in the flight schedule. I was scheduled for the absolute bare minimum for flights and when I did fly, it was only with the two other women in the squadron. After a week of this treatment, I tried to individually approach some of the guys and make them see that I had nothing to do with Baker's departure. The perception was that since I spent so much time with the inspectors, I was the one that "ratted him out." They never stopped to think that my competence was actually called into question over the entire affair, and that I had only done my job as the Equal Opportunity officer.

The harassment did not let up and actually got worse. I was having no luck with individuals so I decided to talk to the CO about it. I showed him a month of flight schedules where I was only scheduled with the other women. He agreed that there seemed to be a problem. The XO was in the room, but he did not think there was a problem. In exasperation I said, "I am being abused because they think I made a hotline call. These flight schedules undeniably prove harassment that could make a real hotline call." The CO then told me he was very happy with my performance, both in the cockpit and in my ground job, and he thought I was one of his best officers. He admitted that the guys might be displacing their anger onto me, and said he would stop it. That's exactly what he did. The CO called all the jet guys together who were responsible for scheduling and told them to cut it out. They did. In addition, since I recently returned from TOPGUN, I was allowed to begin the squadron's in-house fighter training program. Life dramatically improved from that point, and my career seemed to be back on track.

Just a few weeks later, our squadron was involved in a massive air exercise that included an entire air wing from Japan. I was very excited about the exercise since my Commanding Officer told me I was now a section leader because this is the first major milestone in a pilot's career. For single-seat squadrons, it meant leading two planes, both aircraft and people. I flew in several missions, both as a wingman and as a section leader and when the final exercise was scheduled, I was pumped and ready to go.

The airwing was split in half, the good guys (blue air) and the bad guys (orange air). The scenario was a simulated air strike on Cubi Point. The bad guys developed a strike plan to completely bombard the base and all ships in port with simulated bombs. Accompanying the bomber aircraft would be the sweepers, the planes responsible for air-to-air defense. The good guys were the home field players. When the strike was initiated, the good guys would launch in defense and try to shoot down both the bombers and the sweepers. The goal of the defense was to let no bombers through, and sustain no damage to the base.

I was very motivated when I was assigned to not only the good guys, but also to a three-plane division. The other two planes were F/A-18's. I was in awe of the F/A-18 and the pilots. I thought they hung the moon. I flew some missions with this particular squadron before and believed I held the respect of their pilots.

We briefed the mission together, discussing the game plan. Since the A-4 has only one radio and no radar, frequencies were important. A more modern jet, the F/A-18 has two radios. Our plan was to takeoff and hold over a strategic point that would allow us to intercept any stray interlopers. Once the F/A-18's picked the incoming targets up on their radars, they would give me a heads up and we would then attack. This exercise was the graduation of a three week long training evolution, and there were going to be at least forty airplanes in the same piece of sky. This can very dangerous, but with proper briefing and professionalism, these exercises are the most educational and stimulating.

The F/A-18s and I took off in a three-plane formation, flew to our pre-briefed point and held. I followed the communications plan as briefed, but when we got to the designated frequency for the exercise area, I heard nothing. Having flown in few of these "gorilla" exercises, I was a little concerned. However, I also knew that radio silence and communication discipline were also very important. We held at our point as briefed, but I still heard no communications. What I expected to hear was a call from one of the F/A-18s giving me a heading and distance to the incoming strike package and sweepers. The two F/A-18s started a lazy turn to the west and I knew something was up, but because we were still relatively slow (300 knots, 341 mph). I didn't think we were very close to the action. When aircraft fight other aircraft, they like to be as fast as possible. This is where the aviator motto, "Speed is life" comes from.

Just a few seconds later, the F/A-18s went into afterburner. Not only is that easy to see because of the bright light behind the plane, but since an A-4 has no afterburner, they went flying by me. I knew then that I was in over my head because the F/A-18s were taking off and I had no clue how many planes were in front of me. I should have called them on the radio and asked them for help, but in classic aviator style, I didn't want to sound or look stupid.

Just as I saw the F/A-18s pulling away from me, I was frantically looking around the sky, trying to see what they were after. The next thing I knew two enemy F-14s were right in front of me, flying within a half mile of each other at the same altitude. I split the section (meaning I flew right between them and came very close to hitting one of them). I was furious. It is possible that the F-14s may have seen me, either visually or on radar, but an A-4 is almost impossible to see head-on. The F-14 radar is not as refined as the F/A-18's, so my guess is the F-14 guys had no idea I was there. I don't know any pilot who intentionally tries to have a mid-air collision.

What was clear is the F/A-18 guys knew exactly what was going on and had no reservations about putting both the F-14s and me in danger. I pitched out of the fight because not only was I shaken up from the unexpected near collision, I had no SA. (SA is the aviator term for situational awareness). Most pilots who crash into other aircraft or mountains are faulted for not having enough SA. As a conservative pilot, I extracted myself from the fight and held overhead, watching the ensuing melee, trying to figure out who was who. Eventually the engagement was over and I returned home by myself, furious at what just took place.

In the debrief that followed, my first words to the F/A-18 pilots were, "What happened to our briefed frequency and the supposed radar calls?" The executive officer of the squadron was one of the pilots. He turned to me, shrugged his shoulders, and said, "Well, we switched off that freq. Sorry." That made me even madder. Not only did we not even come close to the briefed flight, but he also thought it was no big deal that he put me and the four aircrew of the F-14s in real danger. After the debrief, I went to my Commanding Officer to express my outrage at what just happened and how unsafe it was. He turned to me and said, "Missy, Boys will be boys."

I was no longer upset; I was stunned beyond belief. I had always been taught that in aviation, safety was paramount and it could not be compromised. Obviously this was a naïve misconception on my part. The whole incident was emblazoned in my mind. It left a bitter taste in my mouth not only for the F/A-18 community, but also for naval aviation in general.

During this time period, negotiations between the US and the Philippines to renew the treaty for Subic Bay fell apart. The Philippine government asked for an astronomical amount of money for treaty renewal, despite severe property damage in the wake of Mount Pinatubo. The US military was in a state of drawdown after the Gulf War, and despite all the strategic aspects of Subic Bay and Cubi Point, the treaty was not renewed and the base was slated for closure. What started 91 years ago finally came to an end. Subic Bay was the genesis of many Navy traditions and sea stories, and it was a sad day when the last ship pulled out. Despite the difficulties I encountered there, which I considered inconsequential and part of life, I really enjoyed my time there. I flew all over the Western Pacific, flew with all the aircraft in the Navy's inventory, did a little hot-dogging, and was allowed to go to TOPGUN. I traveled extensively, learned to water and snow ski, biked across southern China and shopped like a madman in Korea and Hong Kong. I lived through a volcano, drank way too much, and most importantly, made lifelong friends. I wasn't ready to go, but I was glad that I at least was a part of history.

When the word came down that the base would be closed, most of us just looked at each other in amazement. We never thought it would happen and were caught off guard regarding our future. Flying billets in a downsizing Navy become a very hot commodity. Since the selection for jet women was very small to begin with, my choices were quite limited. I was offered various training command billets, meaning I would become a flight instructor. One of these training squadrons was the same squadron that LCDR Baker was in and the same squadron that many of the other whoremongers were headed to. I wisely decided this was not the place I wanted to be. I asked to go to a different training squadron in another state, but because of the military drawdown and the unexpected closure of Subic Bay, I would have to wait several months before I could start flying again. In addition, I would probably be working with some of the same people.

A friend suggested that I look into the Navy's graduate school, cleverly named the Naval Postgraduate School in Monterey, California. I always dreamed of the astronaut program and I knew that at a minimum, a Master's degree in a technical field was required. I thought long and hard about this option. I did very well academically at the Naval Academy, and my undergraduate degree in Mathematics allowed me entry into several engineering programs, specifically Space Systems Engineering. This was the choice degree for all hopeful naval astronauts. I was intimidated at first. I originally started as an Electrical Engineer at USNA and eventually dropped out so my GPA would remain high. Because of this setback in college, I was afraid that I might not cut it in the engineering world. It was also a little early in my career to leave flying and attend graduate school. I was now just a frocked Lieutenant, which meant I wore the rank of LT but was still paid as a LTJG. Professionally, I wasn't ready to stop flying. I just started flying as a section lead, and was really gaining experience. What clinched my decision was the continual asinine behavior of some of the guys in the squadron.

I walked into the ready room one Saturday morning to take care of some squadron business. One of the jet pilots was sitting at the table making copies of the tape that held some fantastic flying footage. Over the years, many of the pilots accumulated very motivating but very illegal film images of various stunts and dangerous maneuvers. Since the squadron was to be decommissioned, everyone decided to pool their film clips. The result was an impressive video album of our flying experiences in the Western Pacific set to music.

Next to one of the blossoming Francis Ford Coppola's was his hook, a girl who spoke no English and just sat there like a good dog. She was one of his more permanent hooks, meaning she was his steady bar fine until he tired of her. Another one of the senior pilots came in and they started discussing the dilemma of what to do about their various hooks once they left the Philippines. They decided that they owed these women nothing and planned to leave without as much as a good-bye. They callously laughed and I felt like throwing up. The conversation wasn't anything new or worse than usual, the difference was this poor girl was sitting right there, oblivious to the degrading and demeaning statements about her.

The next Monday I told my Commanding Officer I wanted to go to graduate school. I felt that I needed to better myself and I absolutely wanted to get away from these people and the whole Sexual Disneyland atmosphere. He looked at me and said, "Well, you always did seem smarter than the rest, and more of an intellect." I suppose I was looked at as an intellect not because I walked around espousing Shakespeare or Einstein's theories, but because I took pride in all my work and didn't participate in dehumanizing behavior.

Despite all the problems with the guys and not really being a part of the in-group, I did very well professionally in the squadron. I acquired all the flying qualifications available to first tour pilots. I earned a personal medal, and was very proud of my division. My Commanding Officer routinely rewarded me with exceptional evaluations. When I left, I was the number one ranked, frocked Lieutenant, a highly coveted position. I felt I earned it, but I wasn't really a phenomenal officer. I was merely an officer that cared about my troops and did all my jobs to the best of my ability. It wasn't hard to shine in such a dark, perverse world.

So I left the Philippines, both sorry and glad. I would miss all my friends, the flying, and all the fun activities. In the end though, I thought it was better for both the Navy and the Philippines that this Sodom and Gomorrah would finally come to an end. I boarded the same cattle car I flew in on, no longer the gullible, naive small town southern girl. I was a lot smarter about all aspects of life, but unfortunately quite cynical for one so young. No woman at that stage in her life could have walked away any different. I made a lot of mistakes, demeaned myself in various ways to fit in, and I wasn't exactly happy with the person I had become. On that 24-hour plane ride back to the states, I made a promise to God and myself that my life would be different now. I would do everything in my power to become the model naval officer that I always aspired to be.

Chapter Eight

The Taming of the Shrew

The Naval Postgraduate School (NPS) is the Navy's premier school for graduate level education. Not only do Navy officers make up the student body, but also officers from the Marines, Air Force, and Army, as well as many civilians. NPS offers both Master's and Doctoral degrees ranging from National Security Affairs to numerous engineering disciplines. NPS is predominantly known for its meteorology and oceanography research and degree programs, but the engineering disciplines are highly respected as well. While sponsored by the Navy, the faculty is composed of civilian professors from all over the country. They must "publish or perish" and fight for research grants just like professors at any other institution.

The Naval Postgraduate School was established in 1909, originally located in conjunction with the Naval Academy in Annapolis, MD. In 1951, the Navy moved the school to Monterey, California, after landing one of the best real estate deals of the century. Monterey is now one of the most expensive places to live in the country and the school is located on pristine land in the middle of town bordering the water-front. Originally a lavish resort built in the 1880's, the school includes the Hotel Del Monte, beautifully manicured gardens, and a Greek revival swimming complex. Some of the original buildings of the resort remain standing today including the old hotel, which contains the student center and administrative offices. The campus of NPS is gorgeous and because of its prime location, many students walked to school every day.

When I first arrived in Monterey in a twin-engine puddle jumper, I knew right away that I was unprepared. For the past two years, I lived in a tropical climate and thought any temperature below 90 degrees was chilly. The air temperature in Monterey rarely reaches the seventies during the summer months, and because of its location on a bay surrounded by mountains, Monterey is cold and foggy most of the summer. Having not researched my new duty station enough, I brought only shorts, tank tops, and sandals. I envisioned Monterey as the stereotypical "sunny" California. I could not have been more wrong. I was immediately reminded of Mark Twain's debated quote, "The coldest winter I ever spent was a summer in San Francisco." Monterey is only eighty miles south of San Francisco and the climate is very similar. The first purchases I made in the United States were sweaters, pants, and turtlenecks.

Despite the fact that I was now back in "civilization," I was in for yet another culture shock. When I left the Philippines, I was a fast-living, hard-drinking, obnoxious pilot—just like the guys. My language was abhorrent; I used the word "f—k" in almost every sentence. Another girlfriend of mine also came from the Philippines at almost the same time, and a conversation between the two of us was usually much less than proper. When mothers picked up their children and dragged them away from us, I knew it was time for a change.

My lifestyle completely changed as well. My mother spent my first summer with me, setting up house. My personal belongings were stored the entire time I was overseas, so it was Christmas when I received my shipment. I would not characterize myself as the Martha Stewart type, but it was nice having a place for my belongings and choosing the decor. In the Philippines, not only did I live out of a suitcase, I also never cooked or did laundry. In Monterey, I was surprised at how much I enjoyed cooking for myself again. I grew up in a very southern family and I was expected to cook by the time I was nine. Much to everyone's surprise, I turned into an excellent cook, not a chef or culinary expert, just a good home-cooking kind of gal. I like to cook meals for a crowd, and it was in Monterey that I started throwing dinner parties.

My social life in Monterey was very different from that in the Philippines. Gone were the days of hanging out in the trashiest bar around, drinking, and playing silly games. The biggest changes were in the people I associated with. Up to this point in my naval career, I worked only with aviators. At NPS, I attended classes with surface, submarine, Marine, Army and foreign officers. It was an eye-opener for me to realize not everyone in the Navy operated on the crude level that I experienced in the PI. While different from what I was accustomed to, it was a welcome change.

Another dramatic difference was the actual landscape. Monterey Bay is perhaps one of the most striking features of the West Coast. It is known throughout the world as a prime diving spot and a haven for oceanographers and marine biologists. The Bay itself is a mystery for scientists. The undersea Monterey Canyon is just off the coast, and reaches depths of up to 11,000 feet—quite remarkable, especially so close to the shore. The nearby Monterey Bay Aquarium is one of the best in the world, not just for tourists, but also for research.

The vast resources of the bay provided numerous activities. I often went kayaking with my friends to watch the seals and the sea lions. If the waves were particularly treacherous, we instead sat on the beach and watched the whales move through the kelp beds. On sunny days, I rented a plane with some friends and went whale watching from the air. It was awe-inspiring watching the mammoth creatures swim in schools of dozens. While I missed the fast, dynamic flying of the A-4, buzzing along in a Cessna while watching whales was almost as satisfying. I did not recognize then that I was starting to change.

The Monterey Peninsula is a haven for artists of all types. During my time there, I was able to recapture my love of the theater. An

Anglophile, I absolutely love any and all Shakespeare productions. I discovered that the University of California in Santa Cruz is world renowned for its Shakespeare productions. The reputation is well deserved and I spent my summers making the 40-minute trip to see many impressive performances. San Francisco was only two hours away and I made several trips to see productions like *Phantom of the Opera*. In the Monterey area, I was a patron of several local theaters that never sat more than 30. After starved of such cultural experiences in the Philippines, I more than made up for lost time.

On the other side of the mountains that bordered Monterey, Carmel-By-The-Sea is nestled in the most picturesque setting imaginable. Made famous by the actor-turned-politician, Clint Eastwood, Carmel contains more artists and restaurants in one square mile than in all of some southern states. Carmel maintains it storybook charm through very strict zoning laws. It's against the law to walk along a sidewalk and eat an ice cream cone at the same time! Just as I was wide-eyed in the Philippines, I was equally overwhelmed by the beauty and culture of Carmel and Monterey. Because of the ugliness and depravity of the Philippines, I truly appreciated the aesthetics of the Monterey Peninsula.

Always a fan of outdoors sports, I rollerbladed and biked along some of the most scenic spots in this country. In the spring, a sea of pink, purple, and white wildflowers surrounds the bike paths along the bay's edge. The beach is rocky, and the waves crash against the shore, sending spray high into the air. As I made my way down the paths, I heard the familiar clanking of the sailboats' masts and the loud barking of the sea lions. If we felt particularly energetic, my friends and I biked the famous and breathtaking Seventeen-Mile Drive.

Seventeen-Mile Drive is a road that begins in Monterey and winds its way along the coast, ending at Pebble Beach Resort. A Mecca for golfers, Pebble Beach has the distinction of one of the most difficult and beautiful golf courses in the world. Every year, the PGA's AT&T National Pro-Am golf tournament is held in Pebble Beach. Pebble Beach and

Seventeen-Mile Drive are very exclusive and boast some of the most spectacular houses on the West Coast. I loved biking along this road, awed by the beauty and power of nature. My biking group would often take a break and eat lunch at the resort, watching the golfers who pay over $200 for just one round of golf.

Despite the majestic beauty of the Monterey Peninsula, the friends I made are what I remember and miss the most. A group of about ten, we were very much a family. We were, for the most part, all students in the Space Systems Department. There were more men than women and most of us were aviators, both pilots and Naval Flight Officers (NFO's, navigators and radar operators). We all loved the outdoors, and we met through snow skiing trips sponsored by the NPS recreation department. However, our most common denominator was not our hobbies, but our failed relationships. All of us were on the rebound in some fashion. Half of the group was going through painful divorces and the other half just ended serious long-term relationships. We were no doubt drawn to one another because of our similar situations and needed a support group.

My roommate, Diane, was a member of the "recently divorced" club. Both an NFO and a test pilot, she married an F-14 pilot early in her naval career. Diane was on the fast track for success, and was destined for prominent leadership positions in the Navy. Her husband, however, was not as successful. He was an average pilot with an average record. After his initial commitment, he left the Navy with plans of hiring on with the commercial airlines. Frank was a typical F-14 pilot: obnoxious, arrogant, and self-centered. His transition into the civilian world was not smooth and no airline would hire him. Instead of turning a critical eye inward, he turned it to Diane instead, making her life a living hell. Frank was extremely jealous of her success and her accomplishments. She eventually left after years of mental abuse.

The most disturbing part of their relationship is what happened after Diane filed for divorce. Frank took Diane to the cleaners. I heard bizarre

tales of men suing their wives for alimony and such, but I never
dreamed a former fighter pilot would stoop that low. He did and it was
shameful. Frank was completely capable of working but took half of
everything she owned and she paid him alimony. He also tried to take
half of her retirement pay after only five years of marriage. Diane struggled financially for some time, but eventually landed on her feet. She
even managed to put her negative feelings aside and two years later
married a "bullet worthy" friend of mine. I was amazed not only with
Frank's pathetic and greedy manipulations, but also with Diane's ability to persevere and triumph. Watching her suffer through a nasty
divorce, coupled with what I witnessed in the Philippines made me very
distrustful of men.

Through my friendships with my men friends, I realized an entirely
different side of the other sex. Coming from the Philippines, I stereo-
typed men in the "they all just want one thing" category. I didn't believe
that men really held any true feelings for women and commitment was
a word that meant nothing to them. My male friends showed me that I
was very wrong, especially Todd and Greg.

After ten years of marriage, Todd's wife left him after he received
orders to Monterey. She didn't really explain; she just said she could not
be the wife of a Marine officer anymore. Todd, a Marine's Marine, could
not comprehend why she left him and did everything he could to persuade her to return. She spurned him and broke his heart. He tried to
be the stoic Marine, but I saw the pain in his face. I just recently found
out about Bill's infidelities, so I was equally suffering. Todd and I took
long walks on the beach, held hands, and cried on each other's shoulder. I was deeply moved by his anguish over the loss of his wife and his
sense of commitment. Until I met Todd, I didn't think it was possible
for a man to love a woman so completely.

Through the divorce of another friend, Greg, I realized that men
were not the only ones who cheated on their spouses. When Greg left
the country on various deployments, his wife cheated on him with not

one, but two other men. Just like Todd, Greg was incredibly devoted to his wife and went to great lengths to salvage his marriage. His wife unfortunately did not feel the same sense of commitment and they eventually divorced. The split was very hard on Greg. Both Todd and Greg were like loyal dogs who kept coming back after even the most flagrant abuse. I was again amazed at the depth of Greg's emotion and devotion. I didn't think it was possible. Todd and Greg were my two best friends in Monterey. I hated to see them suffer but in the end, their pain gave me hope that I might find a husband with such noble qualities.

I did not date for a year and a half after the Bill episode. When I eventually did go out again, I dated a very nice guy, a helicopter pilot. Scott was in the Aeronautical Engineering Department that shared the same office as the Space Engineers. We had a lot in common; mostly we loved to spend time outside. We both flew small planes, in fact, Scott owned his own Cessna 172. We dated for six months and had a fabulous time flying all over California. During the summer of 1994, we spent a week flying from California to Ohio. It was an easy relationship with few complications and a lot of pure fun.

Scott lived in the elite Pebble Beach area. He rented a small guesthouse from a very well off older couple. One afternoon, the owners invited us in to show us around their palace. The tour ended with their piece de resistance; a curio cabinet of lighted shelves displaying treasures they accumulated in their travels around the world. They pointed out their most prized possession—a Chinese miniature terra-cotta soldier about a foot high. I recognized it immediately; I owned one just like it. Scott looked at me in alarm when he saw the soldier. Our eyes met with the same thought, "The Missy Cummings greatest haggling story of all time."

When I traveled through China with three of my doctor friends, we stopped in Xian, the gateway to the Silk Road. One of the most remarkable archaeological finds of this century, the tombs of the terra-cotta soldiers, is located in Xian. China's first emperor (circa 220 BC),

Emperor Qin Shi Huandgdi knew that he was dying. It was the custom for a dead emperor to be buried with his entire palace staff and army (complete with chariots and horses) for protection in the afterlife. Not wanting to die a horrible death, Emperor Qin's advisors were very clever. They convinced the Emperor that he could appease the gods if he was buried with lifelike terra-cotta replicas of every man and animal. In 1974, a farmer digging a well discovered this amazingly intact burial ground. The burial ground has yielded over 8000 terra-cotta soldiers, horses, and chariots, and only half of it has been excavated. Amazingly, the archaeologists discovered that every terra-cotta soldier is different in size, dress and facial expressions.

No strangers to capitalistic ideas, the marketplace of Xian is overflowing with soldier replicas of all sizes. As the four of us made our way through the crowded marketplace, we were inundated with these clay soldiers. My boyfriend Bill was the first to fall victim of the persuasive Chinese salesmen. The original asking price was $25, and Bill haggled him down to $10. Because Bill bragged so much that he was the best haggler of the group, Steve decided to show him up. At the next stand, Steve managed to buy his for five dollars—what a coup! At the next stand, Steve taunted Amy and told her that no woman could outdo his shopping prowess. She stepped up to the challenge and completely shamed him; she bought the exact same soldier for one dollar. It was the deal of the century, and she squelched the over-inflated male egos.

I watched all these deals with disdain. I told them these soldiers would never make it back in one piece and this one-upsmanship was ridiculous. Steve replied, "You're just saying that because you know you can't get a better deal than Amy." It would be farcical for me to deny my competitive spirit, and on the triple dog dare, I started haggling. Since I spent so much time in Korea, I perfected the art of haggling and knew just when to walk away. In the greatest shopping moment of my life, I bought the same terra-cotta soldier (that cost Bill 10 dollars) for a

QUARTER plus a cloth bag thrown in for free! Only women can truly understand the joy of an unbelievable shopping purchase.

After my flashback to this scene, I found myself standing in front of this curio cabinet looking at the identical soldier. Scott and I were thinking of this same story, which I just told him only days before. The wealthy woman said in a very proud tone, "And this is our terra-cotta soldier from Xian, China. They are quite valuable you know. We managed to haggle a very low price for this one. We only paid $250.00 for it, and we have the papers to prove its authenticity."

Scott looked at me pleadingly, desperate for me not to tell the story. After choking back laughter, I just nodded my head and complimented her on her haggling skills. She beamed with pleasure and we left shortly after. Scott thanked me profusely in the car for not telling her. I told him I would never have told her; every woman needs to think she got the ultimate deal.

Scott treated me very well and was the man my father wanted me to marry. Unfortunately, despite our good times, Scott and I knew very early on in the relationship that we were not soulmates. Scott and I did not communicate on the same level and often fought over the stupidest events. We knew that our relationship would reach its finite limit when I graduated. Though we broke up, Scott and I remain friends. The classic bridge burner, I have never been particularly adept at ending my love affairs. Scott was different. I truly care for him and think he is a wonderful person, just not the person I want to marry. Scott has the distinction of being the only ex-boyfriend I still speak to.

So I spent the first year of my time in Monterey putting together the pieces of my life's puzzle. Socially, I reached an all-time high. I attended plays and musical events almost every weekend. When not attending a cultural event, my group headed to the local dance hall on a Saturday night to go ballroom dancing. We initially took lessons at the local community college and got the bug. With more men in our group than women, we never lacked for dance partners. When my group went to the local dance hall, we were the only ones younger than 60. We didn't mind because the older dancers enthusiastically welcomed us, encouraged us, and taught us new steps. Often the older women cut in, stole our young studs and refused to give them back. After an evening of dancing to big band music of the 1940's, we went for ice cream. It was hard to believe we were all in our late 20's and early 30's. It was almost as if we were living in another time. My life of drinking and carousing in the Philippines now seemed like a distant bad dream.

Academically, I was doing very well. My undergraduate degree in mathematics served me well. Because I was pursuing a master's degree in astronautical engineering, I first needed to have another undergraduate degree in aeronautical engineering. This required me to take extra classes to catch up with my peers. My first year was difficult, but when I finally moved into my space classes, life improved dramatically. I felt for the first time in my academic career that I actually understood most of the material and theory.

I enjoyed not only my classes, but also my peers. The Space and Aero students all shared the same lounge area. Because most of us were aviators, the atmosphere in the lounge was much like that of a squadron Ready Room. We studied in the lounge, shared the "gouge," and reminisced about "the fleet." Just like in a Ready Room, people gave each other a hard time about various aspects of graduate school life, but that's where the similarities ended when compared to the Philippines.

Unlike the PI, everyone at Postgraduate School was very interested in their professional careers. Only the cream of the academic crop was allowed to attend NPS, so the average IQ was about 30 points higher than in the VC-5 Ready Room. I never heard any vulgar stories in the NPS Aero lounge and if anyone accidentally cursed, he apologized. It was a complete turnabout from my professional life in the PI, and a very welcome change. Conversation in the lounge centered not on hookers or Bar Golf. Instead, we talked politics, engineering dilemmas, and new technology. By no means was this a nerdy or geeky crowd. Jokes and double entendres flew around at lightening speed, and a listener had to be very clever to understand. Often a group of us ventured to the outdoor cappuccino bar to continue our lively debates so other departments could join us.

It was during one of these debates that I earned my last callsign in the Navy. A group of us were discussing our research projects and the problems associated with graduate level work. I was on my soapbox, ranting about the lack of computer facilities and other such inane points. My good friend Eric, always quick with funny jabs, said to me, loudly so everyone heard, "Missy, listening to you, I would think I am watching the play, Taming of the Shrew!" The group exploded with laughter and a new callsign was born, "Shrew." Eric was right, and I didn't try to fight it. I thought his parallel to Shakespeare's Kate was accurate and actually a compliment. I actually liked "Shrew" much more than Medusa. I now had the highly coveted one syllable callsign and wore it like a badge of honor.

I soaked up this environment like a sponge. I loved learning, I loved flying, and I loved bantering and clever humor. I was in my element in Postgraduate School. I think of my time in Monterey as the "Missy Cummings Renaissance" years. During my two years there, I lost the hard edge I gained in the Philippines, and I learned that flying in the Navy was not the meaning of life. Because Monterey matured me both socially and professionally, I quickly made up for my lost years in the Philippines. I volunteered to lead the school's remedial physical training program, tutored on the weekends for disadvantaged students, and organized a software donation program for local area high schools. I was the ugly duckling that finally turned into a swan.

In April of 1993, almost a year into my master's degree, a momentous event occurred that changed my life forever. The Combat Exclusion Law was repealed in a hallmark decision; women were now allowed in all branches of the military with few exceptions. I believe the repeal was a direct result of the Tailhook '91 debacle and the election of President Clinton. If both of those events had not happened, I do not think the law would have been repealed. Typical of naval officers, I usually vote Republican, and it is ironic that the Democrats enhanced my career.

The repeal rocked all the services that were unprepared for such a sweeping change. Prior to the repeal, the Presidential Commission on the Assignment of Women in the Armed Forces was appointed to study all sides of the women in combat issues. The Navy's aviation branch fought viciously against the repeal to block women's entry into the combat aviator ranks. Both senior and junior officers across the Navy vehemently vocalized their anger and opposition against women combat pilots. In fact, all the TOPGUN instructor pilots signed a petition unconditionally against women in combat aircraft and gave it to the commission. Signing petitions in an official capacity is against military regulations, but because the TOPGUN pilots were so respected, the petition was allowed to stand. One instructor made the statement to the commission, "We don't believe that you can act as a unit unless you keep it the way it is, where it's the bonding—it's that intangible, the bonding, that makes a squadron good, better, and we don't believe you can have that go on if we have females in aviation." Perceived violations of this nebulous and mystical "bonding" by the presence of women would eventually be the toughest obstacle for fledgling women fighter pilots.[5]

Unaware of the raging controversy in the dreamy fairyland of Monterey, I was ecstatic that my dreams of flying a fighter were now a reality. For me, the repeal meant that I could transition to a "real" aircraft and actually go to sea on a carrier. I was shocked when the actual decision was handed down. I never thought I would see women in combat aircraft during my lifetime. Despite my surprise, I was elated and was one of the first women to put in a request to fly fighters. I loved going to the carrier, and I very much wanted to actually be a real Navy pilot. As an Academy graduate, it was drilled into my head the need to have sea time to make Admiral. I put my dreams of the space program on the back burner so I could concentrate on becoming a carrier pilot.

Just a few short months later, the Navy convened a board to decide who would transition to the fighters and bombers. I specifically requested the F/A-18 Hornet. It was the newest of the Navy's fighters and was capable of performing more missions than any other naval combat aircraft. My fitness reports were all outstanding and since I placed in the top of my flight school class, I knew that my chances were high for selection. I thought my luck was really changing when I got the news. Not only was I going to be one of the Navy's first women fighter pilots but I would also fly the F/A-18, one of the world's premier fighters. I was out of my skin with excitement.

I was so excited and motivated to start flying that I tried to leave NPS right away. I was only half way through with my degree, but I wanted to fly more than go to school. The Navy vetoed my idea of postponing completion of my degree, stating that the F/A-18 community needed pilots with advanced degrees. I was required to finish my degree before I could leave. I understood my marching orders clearly, but not easily dissuaded, I decided to double up on some of my course work so I could finish early. Through many long hours and full course loads, I was awarded my Master's degree in Astronautical Engineering six months early.

The days following my selection into the F/A-18 community were heady. I worked hard trying to finish early, always dreaming of the reward at the end. I was on cloud nine. My social life was hectic as well, but despite running around like a chicken with my head cut off, I was incredibly happy. When I look back on my two years in Monterey, I have almost nothing but fond memories. Unfortunately though, the few bad memories I do have all resulted ironically from the event that made me so happy: chosen as one of the first female combat pilots in the history of the United States.

While I was thrilled beyond words, not all of my male peers were delighted with the repeal. The issue of women in combat was debated hotly in our department, but the arguments were polite and quite intelligent. It did not bother me that some of the men did not support women in combat. I completely understood and respected both sides of the issue. I just hoped that military men who disagreed with women in combat could put aside their prejudices and work together towards a common mission. It generally wasn't an issue at graduate school, but for my friend Rob, women flying fighters was a big problem.

Rob and I started graduate school together. He just returned from the Gulf War and was a bona fide hero. A quiet, reserved man, he was also a Naval Academy graduate. I really looked up to Rob. I thought he was a model officer and knew he was an excellent pilot. When Rob spoke, I listened and he was someone I wanted to emulate. Few men have that effect on me. When he found out I was going to fly F/A-18's, he didn't speak to me for days. Rob was an A-6 bomber pilot, and also asked to transition to F/A-18's but he was not selected. Instead, he was going to sea in a non-flying billet. I knew Rob was angry because he thought he deserved the spot I received, and was also vehemently opposed to women in combat.

At first, I didn't resent his reaction. As a war hero, I thought Rob deserved whatever he wanted. I figured he would be angry for a few days and then realize I personally didn't set the policy. When his "forgiveness" did not surface after a few weeks, I was dismayed. One day when a group of us were standing around in the lounge, I tried to pay him a compliment. I wanted to bury the hatchet and resume life as normal. We were in uniform and a star fell off one of my ribbons. To the group I said, "Well maybe I can just borrow one from Rob. He has so many, he probably wouldn't even notice one missing." I gave Rob a genuine smile. He coldly turned to me and said, "Not a chance. I actually earned all my medals, not like SOME people."

I was absolutely crushed. I considered Rob my mentor, big brother, and friend. His insult hurt me deeply, so I walked away, afraid I might cry. I didn't mind the slings and arrows of idle banter, but Rob really meant what he said and I knew our friendship was over. A few more days passed and I made it clear I was still upset with him. He stopped me one afternoon and curtly apologized. Although I was surprised, I think he knew he went too far. But the damage was already done, and I felt betrayed by someone I trusted. Our friendship was only superficial from that point.

Men were not the only people outraged that women were going into combat. One Sunday morning as I was leaving the school chapel, a woman whom I had never met approached me. Without so much as an introduction, she said, "How could you possibly do this to your family?" I didn't know her and had no idea what she was talking about. I said, "Excuse me?" and she replied, "Flying F/A-18's in combat is a man's job. How does your family feel about your leaving them?" I was still confused and answered, "Well, my parents are divorced and I haven't lived at home since high school. I am sure they'll miss me but they are actually happy for me."

My accuser then appeared equally perplexed and said, "What about your husband and children?" A friend of mine was standing nearby and he started laughing. I looked at her hard and said, "I'm not married and have no kids, so if you don't mind, my friends are waiting." I found out later she was the wife of another officer and a member of CWA, Concerned Women for America. (CWA is a conservative right wing political group that opposes women in combat.) I was shocked that this woman accosted me outside my own church. I realized then that my path as one of the first was going to be more difficult than I originally suspected.

My most memorable confrontation after my F/A-18 selection took place in the NPS library. One evening as I was entering the library to tutor a high school student, a man whom I vaguely recognized physically stopped me by grabbing my arm. I was very taken aback. He angrily said, "Are you that girl who was in the newspaper?" He was referring to an edition of the Monterey newspaper that was about a week old. My two roommates and I were asked to speak to a class of kindergartners about flying. A local reporter covered the event and put an article and picture of us in the Metro section. The article contained many misquotes and mistakes. Most notably, the writer wrongly referred to me as a TOPGUN. I was unhappy with that title because I really wasn't a TOPGUN, despite the fact that I attended TOPGUN ground school. However, the overall message was positive with a "Navy supports community" twist. The three of us thought it was silly but fun, and were thanked by the school for our efforts.

I slowly replied, "Yesssss," wondering where this conversation was headed. He then harshly stated, "I am the senior strike fighter representative here at the Naval Postgraduate School. The article proves what a disgrace to the light attack community you are and we don't want your kind flying with us." I was completely floored. I never heard of any "senior strike fighter representative" and had no clue who this challenger was. I tried to tell him the article wasn't accurate but he cut me off, "I made sure everyone in the community knows about this little incident, now everyone knows who you are."

I was still confused but I understood that threat. I asked him if he faxed the newspaper article to the F/A-18 training squadrons and he just slyly smiled at me. He then said, "I have friends in Lemoore." There are only two Navy F/A-18 training squadrons; one in Lemoore, California and the other is in Jacksonville, Florida. I reached my limit of this abusive exchange and told him, "Save your breath, I am going to Jacksonville." I then turned on my heel and entered the library. My student was waiting for me and I was trying to maintain a professional level of composure. Inside, I was seething. I did not know this person who was clearly trying to make trouble for me and I didn't understand his hostility over a silly speech to five-year-olds. I later told my roommates about it and they told me to laugh it off. The guy was obviously some loose cannon with no life, they said, and no real threat. None of us could conceive of the devastation he would cause later in the future.

Despite these seemingly insignificant negative incidents, my peers were overwhelmingly supportive of my new transition. Life was so fabulous that I quickly forgot these seemingly insignificant events. I put my nose to the grindstone so I could graduate as quickly as possible. Earning my master's degree in Astronautical Engineering was a gigantic boost for my self-esteem. No one could look at me anymore and say, "She's no rocket scientist!" I conquered my fear of engineering and was ready to meet new challenges.

When I briefed my last design project and thesis, I packed my dog into my car and started the long drive across the country to Florida. I was on top of the world. I put the negative experiences of the Philippines behind me, and shed the rough and tough image. I was finally a real person, confident and secure about my future and myself. A friend of mine who was already an F/A-18 pilot sent me several manuals of emergency procedures that must be memorized. I spent the six days of driving memorizing and rehearsing my emergency procedures. I was glad to be out of the nebulous world of academia and concentrating on flying again. I was ready to strap on a jet and find out what real flying was all about.

Chapter Nine

The Gladiators

After a long drive across the country, I reached my destination—Jacksonville, Florida. After two years of the damp, windy weather of Monterey, I was now back in tropical weather. Jacksonville is still incredibly hot and humid in September. I dug out all my Philippine clothes again, and wore shorts and tank tops almost year-round. I was pumped when I checked into my new squadron, VFA-106. VFA means Navy fixed wing (V), Fighter (F), Attack (A). Another name for VFA is "Strike Fighter" which is indicative of the F/A-18 Hornet's dual mission. The F/A-18 can drop bombs (strike) while nearly simultaneously battling other aircraft (fighter).

The F/A-18 is a landmark aircraft because of the duality of its design. Prior to the Hornet, planes were designed with a single mission in mind. Because the strike mission cannot occur without fighter support, a large number of aircraft were required to safely execute a strike plan. The carriers are severely restricted in the aircraft they can carry due to the limited deck space. When the F/A-18 was introduced, it allowed the Navy to meet two missions with one aircraft. This combination was also essential for a post Cold War shrinking military and saved billions of dollars. Once the F/A-18 proved that it really could perform both missions, all the older fighters in both the Navy and Air

Force were eventually reconfigured to do the same. None however, could surpass the F/A-18 that was an aircraft far ahead of its time.

The F/A-18 is an aircraft for the computer generation. Not only is the cockpit completely digital, but the plane's flight controls are computer driven. In fact, the pilot of an F/A-18 does not actually fly the aircraft. As far as the computers are concerned, the pilot is only a voting member and doesn't even wield the deciding vote. The plane will only allow the pilot to do what he wants when the computers have approved his vote. Known as "fly by wire," this computer command of the aircraft's control surfaces allows planes to fly more efficiently and out maneuver conventional aircraft. Engineers are still learning the complex nuances of such an advanced system, but the results thus far have been astounding. Once in a mid-air collision, an F/A-18 lost its entire tail control surface. Normally this would cause an aircraft to spin out of control and crash. In the F/A-18, the computers figured out that they didn't really need the tail surface to fly, and quickly corrected all the other surfaces to maintain balanced flight. The pilot never even knew the tail fell off and flew home unscathed. The F/A-18 is truly a remarkable aircraft.

VFA-106 is one of two Navy F/A-18 Fleet Replacement Squadrons (FRS). The FRS is designed to train already winged pilots to fly the F/A-18. The training or "transition" is usually accomplished in six months. After completion, the pilot is then assigned to a "fleet" squadron and deploys on carriers throughout the world. The callsign of VFA-106 is the very macho "Gladiators," and its most prized possession is a gladiator helmet worn by Charlton Heston in the movie, Ben Hur. It is placed in a glass case that sits in the middle of the Ready Room.

When I checked in, I was glad to find out three women just completed the program and were going to make the next cruise to the Mediterranean. When I introduced myself to them, I was only slightly surprised by their reception. All three made it clear that they did not want to socialize with each other, so I was on my own. I recognized right away what was happening. I remembered this phenomenon from the

Philippines; the women wanted to be perceived as "team players," so hanging out with the other women was taboo. I was somewhat disappointed but I didn't really give it a further thought. It was clear to me this behavior of female jet pilots ignoring one another was "Standard Operating Procedure."

I was assigned to class 2–95 that would begin training in November. I had two months to find a place to live, unpack my belongings, and find my way around Jacksonville. I was very concerned that my two years out of the cockpit made my flying skills rusty so I quickly found the simulator. I used my two months of dead time to practice and study. From my experiences in flight school, I knew I could never get too much simulator time. Just like in flight school, I lived in the simulator building, waiting for even fifteen minutes of spare time. I spent most of my initial time just learning my way around the cockpit.

Moving from the A-4 to the F/A-18 was like moving from a Model-T to a Ferrari. The cockpit of the A-4 was antiquated, as were all the avionics. With only one radio and no radar, there wasn't much else to do but fly. The exact opposite is true of the F/A-18. The F/A-18 has one of the most advanced radars of modern technology. What makes the F/A-18 so exceptional is the radar's ability to track in the air-to-air mode as well as the air-to-ground mode. The F/A-18's ability to drop bombs and shoot down incoming aircraft is what makes it one of the United States' most versatile aircraft. Because of its dual role, there is twice as much information for the pilot to learn.

I felt overwhelmed at first. I had never flown an aircraft with a HUD, a heads-up-display. The HUD projects in the aircraft windscreen all the information a pilot needs to constantly keep track of; airspeed, altitude, heading, horizon, and other targeting information. When I first started flying the simulator, I turned the HUD off, because it was too distracting. Eventually though, I succumbed to technology and became a "HUD cripple." Every F/A-18 pilot at some point in his career begins to rely on the HUD for this critical data. If something goes wrong with the

HUD projection system, the plane operates just the same, only the pilot is not quite as steady.

In no time I got up to speed. I learned my way around the cockpit and all the many functions of the three computer screens. The F/A-18 has what is termed a "glass cockpit." Older aircraft displayed all-important information with dials and gauges; the F/A-18 displayed all this same information on three computer screens. Much like navigating through Microsoft Windows, the pilot can fall into many glitches and traps if not careful. A major part of the battle in learning to fly the F/A-18 is learning to be an effective systems operator. After two months of practice, I was still no expert but I felt I'd mastered some basics.

I met the rest of class 2–95 on our official starting date. With ten people in the class, we were a diverse group. The senior member of the class, Lizard, was a commander (O-5) who was transitioning from A-6's. Because the Navy was getting rid of all its old attack planes, there were several older pilots that needed to be reassigned to new aircraft. Because of this downsizing, my class had two other attack transition pilots in it. Two other transition pilots made up Class 2–95, an S-3 pilot and myself. The remaining five members were brand new pilots who recently finished flight school. Three were Marines and the other two were Navy pilots.

One of the Marines, a black man had the callsign "Road." (Black pilots in the Navy are rare commodities and black female pilots are essentially non-existent.) Road earned his callsign in flight school when he was lost on a solo flight and followed a well-known road home. Road and I immediately became fast friends. He was an easy-going guy and because the two of us were in such a clear minority, we stuck together.

I was not really close to anyone else in my class. Most of the guys were married, with multiple children. I was five years older than the newly winged group who were mostly single. Unfortunately, they were still very much in the fraternity frame of mind, so I didn't really socialize with these guys outside work. It was no slight to them; I had my fill of wild parties and after graduate school, drinking until I puked was not fun anymore. The Jacksonville area boasts four major naval bases and because I had been in the Navy for ten years, several of my good friends lived nearby. I spent the vast majority of my personal time going to the surprisingly fantastic cultural attractions of Jacksonville with old friends.

My reception in the squadron was somewhat standoffish at first, but nothing I perceived as hostile or abnormal. The fighter community was not ready for women when they finally arrived and I am sure many instructors did not like having women forced on them. I tried to lay low. I worked hard in the simulators and my peers seemed open to my numerous questions and pleas for help. The instructors greeted me in the hallway and the senior leadership seemed positive about having women. When I was asked to participate in the upcoming Strike Fighter Golf Tournament, I jumped at the chance. I thought it would be the perfect opportunity to meet the community. My Executive Officer (XO) then made it clear that I would not be playing. I would instead drive the beer cart. I did not even bat an eye. I am a terrible golfer and thought this would be an even better chance to show everyone what a "team player" I was.

When I showed up to the golf shack, I was in for a big surprise. One of the instructors attempted to persuade both me and another female ensign to change into Hooter's outfits. Known worldwide for their well-endowed waitresses in very tight, skimpy outfits, Hooter's is very big in the naval aviation community. I was shocked that he would even ask. I was a senior lieutenant here to fly fighter aircraft, not thrust my breasts into the faces of my peers. I flat out refused and told the other girl she would not participate either.

The instructor was obviously miffed with us, but when I explained the gravity of asking his fellow female officers to dress in such a degrading manner, he acquiesced. Eventually, one of the male junior officers was made to wear the Hooter's outfit. I thought that compromise was funny and appropriate, but many of the players complained. They were used to women baring all serving them beer on the golf course. In fact, when I approached a foursome, I was often ordered to "bring me a beer," and treated like somebody's beer wench. I was shocked at how poorly my peers treated me, even knowing I was a pilot just like them. It was a humiliating and degrading experience but I learned to really appreciate waitresses after that debacle. Probably the most disturbing lesson of that fateful afternoon, I was reminded of just what second class status women held in these men's eyes. It was very clear to me that day that my time in VFA-106 and the fighter community as a whole would be a trial.

I was only in the squadron for a month when an event occurred that changed the environment of acceptance and camaraderie for women tactical pilots all across the United States. On October 25, 1994, during a sunny brilliantly blue day over the Pacific Ocean, Lieutenant Kara Hultgren crashed her F-14 while attempting to land on the carrier, USS Abraham Lincoln. She was the first female naval combat pilot to die and immediately became the lightening rod for both sides of the "women in combat" issue.

The Navy's F-14 Tomcat, made famous in the movie *TOPGUN*, is the Navy's oldest fighter and will be taken out of service by the year 2005. Despite the glamour of Hollywood's depiction, the F-14's have suffered serious engine and avionics problems. The capabilities of the F/A-18 and other more modern USAF aircraft completely eclipse the F-14. Well known for its unsafe track record, many of my friends who were F-14 aviators called it the "Flying Coffin." The Tomcat's engines were underpowered for the airframe, and while not a problem in most flying regimes, the lack of power could become lethal when flying around the aircraft carrier. As a result, almost one-quarter of the Navy's F-14's have crashed.

The Navy knew about the F-14's lack of thrust, and also an equally dangerous and unpredictable flight control system. The F-14 is also a "fly by wire" plane but the technology is older and not as reliable and redundant as the F/A-18. Instead of fixing the F-14's costly problems, senior Navy officials consciously chose instead to spend valuable tax-payer dollars on the newer F/A-18 Hornet.[6] Just like the Ford Pinto scandal of the 1970's, the Navy's "corporate" brass decided that they could put a price on life. The F-14's safety record is the worst of all modern day naval aircraft and many men have died operating the problem-ridden aircraft. One of these 'flying coffins' claimed the life of yet another of my peers from flight school in a mysterious disappearance over the ocean. The wreckage and the body were never found. F-14 pilots were obviously not as indispensable as portrayed by both the movie *TOPGUN* and the Navy.

The day Kara attempted to land on the carrier, this problematic engine was a factor. When Kara made her turn to the carrier's final approach course, she experienced what carrier aviators call a "mildly overshooting approach." Kara failed to make a tight enough turn and overshot the centerline of the carrier. She recognized this mistake and responded in a very typical manner by making a harder left turn. Her approach was far from perfect, but well within limits and her responses were completely appropriate. Unfortunately almost simultaneously, Kara's F-14 experienced a "bleed air failure" of her left engine.

Bleed air is designed to augment thrust and support various external systems. Not a serious enough problem to cause a catastrophic engine failure or complete loss of thrust, bleed air failures can lead to more grave difficulties. Depending on the circumstances, the consequences could result in engine failure in slow flight regions like landing. There is no way of knowing absolutely whether or not she recognized her left engine was experiencing this failure, but certainly her attention was on landing. In those last few critical seconds before landing on a carrier, a pilot's attention is completely focused on the back of the carrier. Kara no doubt failed to recognize her left engine was in trouble.

What is known without a doubt is that as Kara "wrapped up the turn," her left engine lost airflow and stalled. The bleed air failure played a role, but that alone would not cause the engine to stall. Kara did not recognize the stall in time to respond. The backseat radar officer, LT Matt Klemish, reacted late and realized they were not going to make it. He pulled the ejection handle and expelled them both from the plane. The back seat is shot out of the plane first, and then .4 seconds later, the pilot is ejected. Matt made it, Kara did not. Typical of most naval aviation mishaps, less than a second does mean the difference between life and death.

The initial reaction to Kara's death was shock and disbelief across the country for both military and civilian people. Kara and I were not best friends but our paths often crossed. Women jet pilots are a very small group so most know one another. Kara was full of life and exemplified carpe diem. When it came to verve, I pale in comparison to Kara. She was very quick-witted and always ready with clever comebacks. When she first reported to the F-14 training squadron, Kara's commanding officer pulled her into his office for a "counseling session." Without directly confronting the issue, the CO wanted to ensure that Kara understood the rules concerning fraternization. With the influx of women into the Navy's traditional jobs, there was much concern that the females would resort to their womanly wiles to get ahead. After much hemming and hawing from the CO, Kara seized the reins and asked, "So what you're saying Sir, is don't f—k the help?" The CO turned beet red and thanked her for her clarity. Kara was a straight shooter and a hard charger. She was as close to being one of the guys as any woman pilot could ever be. Unfortunately, even Kara could not break the mystical "bond" of male naval aviators.

Almost immediately after Kara's crash, an intense controversy erupted again over the "women combat pilot" issue. Conservative groups held Kara's crash up as evidence that women were not capable of flying fighter aircraft. The Center for Military Readiness, a one-woman "think-tank" headed by Elaine Donnelly, spearheaded the attack. She claimed that Kara was unqualified and was allowed to fly the F-14 solely based on the fact that she was a woman[7]. Since there was such an outcry both for and against Kara, the wreckage of the plane was salvaged from the ocean, an unprecedented move. When aircraft are lost at sea in deep water, the plane and the pilot are usually left in their watery grave—the ultimate burial at sea. In an attempt to appease both sides of the debate, the Navy salvaged the plane at great expense and then investigated the wreckage.

Whenever a plane crashes, the Navy begins a Mishap Investigation Board which consists of several aviators and a flight surgeon. This group attempts to reconstruct the accident, find the cause, and assign blame to someone or something. The official report of the board is called a Mishap Investigation Report (MIR). Only personnel with a need to know have access to this very sensitive, protected document. This level of confidentiality is required to insulate the investigators and Navy from legal reprisal. Aviation is an inherently risky business, with new and cutting edge technology. The Navy absolutely must be allowed to determine the cause of crashes without concern for lawsuits. It's critical that the Navy and the civilian defense contractors who design these aircraft find out exactly what went wrong. If family members and the general population were allowed access to these documents, the Navy and the aerospace industry could find themselves besieged with lawsuits and unable to find the cause of crashes.

In most crashes however, mechanical or technical difficulties are NOT the cause. 89% of naval crashes are due to human error.[8] The pilot makes a mistake that eventually causes the loss of the aircraft and/or crew. Just as in Kara's case, some mechanical or computer problem exacerbates the problem, but in the end, the pilot makes the wrong choices. Kara failed to recognize her bleed air malfunction. Because of her overshooting start, she aggressively maneuvered the jet, which stalled the engine. Kara failed to recognize the stall, and finally, she failed to recognize an unsalvageable situation and eject. The MIR spelled out these findings in clear black and white, ultimately laying the blame on Kara. The board was not unfair in its assessment. Kara's MIR read no differently than any other MIR of any male pilot in the past. The difference was how the MIR was handled.

After the MIR was completed, the Navy prepared an official statement for the press. The higher-ups in the Navy decided to soften the impact of the MIR in an attempt to quell the anti-female pilot sentiment that was picking up speed. The Navy, still reeling from the fallout from Tailhook, mistakenly decided to tell the press the accident was due mostly to mechanical malfunction with only a small part due to pilot error. When the pro-Kara statement was made public, the aviation community was in an uproar. The aviators all knew that most plane crashes were due to pilot error. The rosy picture painted in the papers was ridiculous to naval aviators, no matter which side of the fence they were on. Everyone knew the Navy's official statement that the crash was due primarily to engine failure was incorrect and that the Navy was afraid of political fallout. Without realizing the consequences of their actions, by glossing over Kara's role in her crash, the Navy made life miserable for those female aviators still left to face the angry masses. One F-14 aviator was so outraged at the public misrepresentation that he decided to take matters into his own hands.

An aviator somehow connected to the investigation obtained a copy of the MIR and anonymously disseminated it across the Internet. This rash and criminal act reverberated through the entire Navy and public arena and only intensified an already contentious situation. Now everyone knew the Navy covered up the cause of the accident, which only fueled the anti-female pilot sentiment further. Elaine Donnelly and others of the same opinion used this fact to support their belief that the Navy was allowing unqualified women to fly.[9] In its attempts to sail in calm waters, the Navy created two immense problems. Senior officers were forced to respond to allegations that a cover up occurred, but even more troubling was the breach of security. A naval officer seriously violated the Navy's aircraft safety system and compromised the entire investigation process.

In response to the charges that Kara was unqualified, her mother released her training records that showed she did well in training, finishing third out of seven. Kara experienced a few difficulties and took two tries to carrier qualify. She was not the only one because almost half of all F-14 pilots fail their first attempt at the carrier. Kara possessed 2000 flight hours prior to transitioning to the F-14, so she was an experienced pilot. Because she was not allowed to fly on the carrier prior to 1993, she was not an experienced carrier pilot but Kara was very qualified to fly fighters. However, the Navy's knee-jerk reaction to potential unfavorable press caused an even greater problem. The Navy was no doubt fearful of more backlash and did not want another black eye after the Tailhook '91 scandal. Unfortunately, by not publicly stating that Kara's accident was primarily due to pilot error, the Navy's own pilots became very distrustful and wary of the system. Despite Kara's more than qualified status, the Navy's attempt to prevent dissension both inside and outside aviation only made life worse for the rest of the Navy's women combat pilots.

On the East Coast, Kara's crash definitely impacted the lives of the women pilots aboard the USS Eisenhower (nicknamed the Dyke for the women on board). During the winter of 1994, the Ike made history by deploying with women of all ranks aboard. Initially the cruise went very well, with few problems. After Kara's crash though, intense scrutiny was focused on the next potential Kara, Shannon Workman. Shannon and I had been friends since the Academy and lived together through most of flight school. When the combat exclusion law was repealed, Shannon was then selected as the Navy's first woman combat pilot.

Due more to timing and location than any other factor, Shannon was selected to fly the EA-6B Prowler. She just happened to be the next woman available for orders when the combat exclusion law was repealed. The Prowler is the Navy's electronic jamming platform, and while not a fighter or a bomber, it is capable of carrying radar homing missiles. While not as glamorous as the fighters, the EA-6B is known as a "high value unit." Fighters exist to protect these types of aircraft because they are absolutely critical for any attack mission. Not only is each aircraft worth 60 million dollars, but they are also one of the most difficult planes to land aboard the carrier.

Landing on the carrier was not Shannon's strong suit. She was a top-notch pilot, but she, like many other Prowler pilots, struggled when landing the 55,000-pound aircraft aboard the carrier. Her training was not made any easier by the Navy's insistence that she be the poster child for women in combat aviation. As she progressed through her training syllabus, she was besieged with press and photo requests. One day she came home from work to find ABC's TV magazine Behind Closed Doors news crew on her doorstep. Shannon was overwhelmed with both the relentless press and the pressures of learning to fly a complex aircraft. At the same time, her marriage was falling apart and she was struggling to hold her personal life together.

Her initial carrier qualifications were not eye watering, but with some solid practice, she qualified. Despite all the hardships, she persevered and was assigned to the first squadron that deployed women aboard the Ike. She was not the best pilot landing aboard the carrier, but she held her own. The senior pilots are always concerned when a pilot is struggling, but their attention became sharply focused on Shannon after Kara's crash. With all the rumors sweeping the Navy about the cover up and whether or not Kara was really qualified, Shannon became the target for the "I told you so's."

Within just weeks of Kara's crash, Shannon was removed from flight status for inconsistent trends when landing on the carrier. After all the intense scrutiny and pressure—both personally and professionally—she was then fired and sent home. Another male EA-6B pilot, also earmarked as a potential problem, was also not allowed to fly. The male pilot however, received extra training, with a guaranteed return to carrier aviation. Shannon was never allowed to fly carrier aircraft again.

In deliberations to remove a pilot from flight status, usually all aspects of a pilot's life are examined. If some medical or personal problem was adding undue stress to the pilot, he was usually allowed to return in a probationary status. This is why the male pilot was allowed to return. However, no consideration was given to Shannon's stressful life. While going through a bitter divorce, she was forced into the public's eye by the Navy. From early in her training, the Navy identified her as their first female combat pilot and allowed film crews to film her constantly. Every time she took off or landed, she was filmed and the Navy frequently asked her to do interviews. After all the extreme pressures put on her by the Navy, she was hung out to dry in the end. If Kara had not crashed, I am sure Shannon's career would have been much different.

Because of Kara's crash and the subsequent furor over the release of the MIR, all women combat pilots were under intense scrutiny. At the time, there were less than fifteen of us and we all felt the hatred and condescension of our peers. In VFA-106, Kara's crash marked a definite change in the squadron's atmosphere towards women. Immediately after the accident, the walls of the Ready Room were plastered with anti-women newspaper and magazine articles. When the illegal MIR was released, it was copied and passed around like candy. As the details of the Navy's mishandling of the press became known, it was all anyone in the squadron talked about. The discussions were very pointedly, "I told you so." Since I was the only woman in the squadron, I ran for cover. It seemed as if the conversations became more opposed to women in combat when I entered a room. I don't doubt the male pilots were trying to see what I would say or do, but I knew I was in a lose-lose situation. Instead of dealing with the hostility that confronted me at every turn, I ran away. I spent my days studying in vacated classrooms or in the simulators. If I was in the Ready Room when these conversations started, I simply left.

Not only did I feel like the next witch in line to be burned, but Kara was also someone I knew and respected. She made a mistake that cost her life and no one else's. I felt she paid her dues for pilot error. What really disgusted me was not how the guys felt about the Navy's ill-advised public statements; I agreed with them on that issue. I was sickened by how they talked about Kara after she was dead. I had been in the Navy a long time and seen many pilots die. Not once, no matter how badly the guy screwed up, did I witness such a complete assassination of another pilot's character. In naval aviation, it is an unwritten rule that aside from the MIR, no one speaks ill of a fallen comrade. Following Kara's death, it was fashionable to denigrate her both personally and professionally. After Kara's crash, I knew it was a completely different ball game and I was ill prepared.

The double standard for women pilots was only highlighted one year later when naval aviation experienced one of the worst mishaps in its eighty-five year history. On January 29, 1996, LCDR Stacy Bates and his backseater took off in their F-14 Tomcat from Nashville's commercial airport. He flew into Nashville for the weekend to visit his parents, which was common for cross-country training missions. In what would be his last show of bravado, LCDR Bates requested a "high performance takeoff," which is an almost straight up vertical climb. It is a legal maneuver, but the Navy has issued strict guidelines on how and when these maneuvers can be performed. The weather was bad in Nashville, but the air traffic controllers approved his request. When LCDR Bates took off, he executed the high performance takeoff very aggressively and almost immediately was vertical. Seconds later he became very disoriented, lost control of the Tomcat, and crashed into a Nashville neighborhood. Both he and his backseater were killed, along with three civilians who were in the house the plane hit. Five people were dead because one pilot wanted to look cool.

The crash eventually gained notoriety in the press not only because of the senseless loss of life, but also because of the parallel between Kara Hultgren and LCDR Bates. He was also in the same squadron as Kara, the VF-213 Fighting Blacklions. In the fighter community, word of this crash spread quietly in the typically reverent tones in remembrance of a fallen comrade. The contrast between Stacy Bates and Kara was like night and day. I never heard an ill word spoken about LCDR Bates and there was no discussion in the ranks about his qualifications or lack thereof.

It turned out that a year prior, LCDR Bates crashed an F-14 due to negligent, flagrant pilot error. With a long flying record of near mishaps, several backseaters refused to fly with him. Surprisingly, he was not grounded for his loss of a $25 million dollar aircraft. Instead, he was slapped on the wrist and was back flying within a few days. LCDR Bates was clearly a member of the "boys' club," which protected him from discipline that another, less popular aviator might receive. I find it ironic that Kara was posthumously crucified for her mistakes, while LCDR Bates was allowed to keep flying after negligently destroying one aircraft. Unlike Stacy Bates, Kara was not hot-dogging. This clear double standard in the fighter community cost four innocent people their lives.

After Kara's crash, the Commander in our group, Lizard made sure everyone knew that he didn't support women in combat. He had a field day with Kara's crash. As our class leader and an O-5, he was in a position to influence us in both thought and deed. I tried not to let his opinions affect me, but because he was the class leader, it was difficult. One afternoon my class was sitting in a classroom, waiting for our instructor when the conversation turned to women on ships. Another Lieutenant and I were discussing berthing problems on the ships. He said that women received preferential berthing and it wasn't fair. He was basically saying women were very disruptive and didn't belong on ships because of the accommodation problems. Eventually I told him that everyone on the ships was going to have to grow up and deal with it since women were here to stay.

Lizard, who was listening the whole time, interrupted me and announced, "LT Cummings, this is the end of this conversation." I was stunned. I didn't really know what his problem was since I wasn't even talking to him. I turned to him and said, "Lizard, this is just a conversation between two Lieutenants." He said, almost yelling, "I order you to shut up!" The room was deathly quiet and all eyes were on me. In my entire naval career, I have never been specifically "ordered" to do anything, especially to end a private conversation. I looked at him with steely eyes, understanding the line in the sand was drawn. I responded, "Aye Aye Sir" which is the robot response of new recruits in boot camp. The instructor entered the room soon after.

I was furious. How dare he ORDER me to end a conversation with someone else! A couple of my classmates later expressed dismay with the Commander's behavior. I classify that type of leadership as Captain Queeg leadership (from *Mutiny on the Bounty*). It is the perfect example of how not to lead. Many months later, Lizard again attempted this type of bizarre authority and he eventually became the laughingstock of the carrier. It was clear to me then that he did not like women, and he was willing to go to extraordinary lengths to prove it. His later attempts to discredit both me and my reputation would become central in the fight for my career.

After Kara's crash and my class leader's display of his scorn of me, I buried myself in work. I knew there was nothing a solitary woman could do to affect a change in a sea of machismo except to lay low. I worked diligently throughout ground school and was very excited to finally fly the real plane. I practiced the start up procedures so much in the simulator that my first flight went smoothly. When I taxied onto the runway, my heart was furiously beating. Never having before flown an afterburner aircraft, I didn't know what to expect. When I was cleared for takeoff, I jammed the throttles full forward, in breathless anticipation. I was not disappointed. The afterburners kicked in and the plane jumped forward, racing down the runway. I know the instructor hated hearing my giggle of delight as we roared down the runway, but I couldn't help it. It was a fabulous experience and one of sheer, unadulterated joy.

When we returned, I was tired but exhilarated. The flight went well and the instructor seemed pleased with my progress. After our debrief, I headed to the Officer's Club for the weekly night of drinking and carousing. I knew the guys didn't want me around, but I always showed up for at least a few minutes to prove to them I very much wanted to be a part of the team. I was excited and when I walked into the club, the first person I saw was one of my friend's ex-boyfriends, Luke. Besides our mutual friend, Pam, we had a lot in common since Luke also previously flew the A-4.

Luke asked me how everything was going and I gushed about the flight. He was genuinely happy for me and was very supportive. He then asked me how Pam was doing and I was immediately reminded of an earlier conversation. Pam told me she recently spoke to Luke and he told her that he thought all women F/A-18 pilots (myself included) were dogs. When Luke asked me about Pam, all I thought of was the dog comment. Not one to let an opportunity slide by, I replied, "ARF ARF." Luke blushed, an unusual occurrence for a fighter pilot, but then he slapped me on the back and said, "You're a good sport Shrew." We both laughed at ourselves and started talking shop.

I left the club that night on cloud nine. I knew that performance in the squadron was what counted and so far, I was on the right track. Despite the animosity in the squadron, I was able to approach a few pilots so I felt I was making some progress. Driving home that night after flying one of the world's greatest fighters, I knew that I finally found my calling.

Chapter Ten

Trouble in the Hornet's Hive

My first indication that all was not well was my first major checkride in the simulator. A pilot's annual checkride to ensure he has thorough knowledge of normal and emergency procedures is called a NATOPS check. In the old days, the checkride was flown in the plane, but now NATOPS checks are flown in very realistic simulators. I studied very hard for my first checkride, wanting to show everyone how serious I took my flying. The NATOPS checkride brief is an oral examination to make sure the pilot knows every minute engine and flight control parameter. The flight is then conducted in the simulator to determine if a pilot can actually handle emergencies. The event is concluded with a debrief in which the student learns if he passed or failed.

My instructor, Comet, and I already knew each other because we flew together in Meridian, MS. However, Comet made sure I knew I wouldn't get any breaks because of our prior acquaintance and grilled me in the brief for an unusually long time. However, always the first student with my hand up, I enjoyed showing him I could recite cold every parameter and procedure. My oral quiz took so long that we were late getting in the simulator.

The actually simulator portion of the checkride was an eye-opener. The checkride was supposed to be a review of everything learned up to that point. Comet spent an inordinate amount of time showing me very unusual and unrealistic scenarios instead of actually testing me. I did not mind because I was always eager to learn the nuances of the complex F/A-18. In the middle of the flight, the HUD (heads up display) quit working, which was not part of the intended checkride. The simulator technicians were called in the middle of my flight so there was a lot of confusion about which emergencies were real, and which were the fault of the simulator.

Eventually it was all sorted out and I flew the rest of the checkride with no HUD and a quirky simulator. Just like all high tech simulator games and computers with problems, the simulator needed to be rebooted but we wanted to finish the checkride first. We finally completed the "hop,"—another name for flight. It was not the smoothest checkride. The problems with the simulator combined with the verbal miscommunications between everyone made it more like a sitcom than a checkride. In our debrief, Comet told me I did well despite all the problems and I passed my checkride. I now had the requisite green light for my solo flight.

A pilot's first solo flight in the F/A-18 is a little anti-climatic. The wonder of flying alone has long passed since the days of first soloing in the little T-34C. The F/A-18 solo flight is designed to allow the nugget (new) pilot a chance to explore the plane's capabilities. The F/A-18 was designed to fight combat missions in groups, so going out alone is just not as much fun as going out with another F/A-18. On my solo, I spent most of my time playing with the radar. Never having flown with radar, I found it fascinating and quite helpful. I practiced locking up aircraft flying nearby and taking simulated missile shots. Modern day radar is so advanced that planes can fire missiles at targets from distances greater than forty miles.

After playing with the radar, I headed back home to practice some landings. Landing the F/A-18 is relatively easy. Unlike the F-14, the F/A-18 has plenty of power and flies exceptionally well in slow flight regimes like landing. The true challenge of carrier aviation is precision landing. Navy pilots always like to pick on Air Force pilots, saying, "Any pilot can land on a three mile long Air Force runway. Only carrier pilots can land on a floating postage stamp."

Carrier pilots only have a landing margin of plus or minus 40 feet so it is important to practice. So that's what I did for the remainder of my solo—practice landings. A smooth aircraft to fly and land, the F/A-18's number one problem is gas. Always critically low on fuel, F/A-18 flights last barely an hour with any heavy maneuvering. Because of this limitation, I was only able to squeeze in three or four landings before I ran out of gas and was forced to land. I was very motivated after my solo and looking forward to the next stage of flying in the F/A-18.

A few days after my solo, the Training Officer approached me. The Training Officer was a Marine and made it clear he didn't think women should be flying. He loved sitting in the Ready Room spewing forth his theories on Kara's crash and her perceived lack of qualifications. He told me that he heard I failed my NATOPS checkride and that I would be required to refly it. I was completely stunned. I was told that I passed and had flown several times since then, including my solo. When I questioned him further about my checkride, he wouldn't elaborate, only saying that Comet told him so.

I tracked Comet down in the Ready Room and asked if we could chat in private. Because we had known each other for so long, I felt I could talk candidly with him. When I asked him what was going on, Comet told me that the Training Officer approached him and asked him if I experienced any trouble on my checkride. When Comet told him about the flight, the Training Officer decided it was unsatisfactory and that I would have to repeat it. I pointedly asked Comet if he thought my checkride was unsatisfactory. Comet, clearly uncomfortable with the unfolding of events, squirmed and said, "Noooooo, but because the simulator broke, you probable should refly it. Just look at it like a practice." I accepted his response, knowing that something was wrong but powerless to do anything about it.

In naval aviation, if a pilot is told he successfully completed a flight or checkride, it is unheard of for an instructor to change his mind several days later. Instructors are taught that if a flight is questionable, they are not to pass the student. I discussed my predicament with another senior pilot in the squadron who agreed the events sounded suspect but told me just to refly the checkride to remove any doubt. I thought his advice was very wise. I was very aware of the post-Kara crash fallout and knew the instructors were watching me very closely to make sure I wasn't the next Kara Hultgren.

I was nervous for the refly of my checkride. The pressure was on and only I could make the situation right. My instructor for my refly was a LCDR, which made him one of the senior pilots. He was highly respected in the squadron and what he said was gospel. He was the pilot who gave the instructors their checkrides—he was the man. Our brief went well, and I was able to parrot all the parameters again flawlessly. We flew the flight with no interruptions and it went very smoothly. After the flight was over, the LCDR and I sat down for the debrief. He looked at me and asked me how I thought I did. I was still a little nervous and said, "OK I guess." He smiled at me and said, "It went much better than OK. I don't know what the problem was with your first one, but that was one of the best checkrides I have ever seen."

I felt great after this positive reinforcement. I started to doubt myself after finding out I would have to refly the checkride. Now the senior pilot who administered instructor checkrides told me my second checkride was outstanding. It was a good feeling and my self-confidence was restored. I was glad to know not everyone thought of me as the next Kara Hultgren.

My elation with my checkride and the improvement in my confidence did not last long. On my next flight in the aircraft, I received my first SOD. A SOD is a signal of difficulty, and is much like the "down"

of the training command. It is an event that stops the student in training for reflection on why the student didn't perform up to standards.
More than two SOD's during the course of training is cause for alarm.

The flight was my sixth flight in the plane and was designed to practice
carrier landings at the field. Because of an unprecedented wind shift, the
runways were changed. Pilots like to land with a headwind to shorten both
the takeoff and the landing rolls. The new landing runway was rarely used
and I had not seen this particular one before. When I made my first
approach to the field, I was confused. With parallel runways and a taxiway
that looks like a third runway, I wasn't sure which runway to line up
behind. I picked the wrong one and was immediately corrected by the LSO
(Landing Signals Officer) who was watching from the ground. It was a
"bonehead" mistake, but typical for students who had never flown at a
particular airfield before.

I felt terrible about this mistake because if other aircraft were
landing simultaneously, the situation could have been dangerous. In
the debrief, the LSO, "Bull" Durham told me he understood my confusion with runways but he thought overall my landings were not as
precise as he liked to see. Bull knew I had not flown in two and a half
years, and thought I needed more landing practice. I hated receiving
a SOD, it was embarrassing and painful, but I also knew he was right.
I hadn't seen the back of the carrier in four years and did need extra
practice. Bull flew in my backseat during my extra practice flight so
he could see for himself what I was doing. He showed me where I was
going wrong and my landings improved dramatically. They were so
much better that I required no more extra flights and I was able to
keep pace with my class.

The next major hurdle for class 2–95 was learning to bomb. Once
we all learned the basics about flying the F/A-18, we graduated to
learning the strike half of the F/A-18's Strike Fighter mission.
Learning to drop weapons is a complicated process that takes numerous flights to accomplish. The student first starts out "circling the

wagons." These flights consist of four aircraft flying in a circular pattern, taking turns at dropping bombs on a designated target. Once the student demonstrates proficiency in basic bombing, he then graduates to more complicated bombing missions. These include bombing with a wingman, night bombing, and bombing from the radar display. When practicing bombing, pilots almost always carry practice bombs, small 25-pound hunks of steel that carry a smoke charge for spotting. Only when a student has proved his proficiency at dropping practice bombs, is he then allowed to carry any live bombs.

Because teaching pilots to bomb for the first time in an F/A-18 is an inherently risky process, all Navy pilots head to the desert for practice. The Navy has two primary bombing complexes: one in El Centro, California and the other in Fallon, Nevada. Students and instructors do occasionally make mistakes and bomb the wrong target, so practicing in the vacated desert is the best idea. When a group of pilots head to Fallon or El Centro to practice, the whole relocation is called a detachment or "det." My class went on our bombing det to Fallon, Nevada for two weeks. We were looking forward to it because Fallon was our first opportunity to fly the plane like it was meant to fly.

In sharp contrast to the flat, sparse Florida landscape, the mountains and cool clear air of Nevada were a welcome change. No wives or significant others accompanied anyone. Dets are serious training evolutions and no one wants to be bothered with outside problems. My focus was completely on learning to bomb and I was glad to leave the rest of my life behind in Florida. We lived in meager quarters and ate our food in the local chow hall. The students didn't care about the lack of amenities. All we did was sleep, study, fly and eat. There wasn't much time for anything else.

Learning to bomb in the F/A-18 is not an easy task. The flights begin with weaponeering. This means figuring out the loading of weapons on the aircraft and the specific drop parameters that vary with each weapon and each mission. Then the pilot must successfully find the target. As simple as it sounds, target recognition is one of the biggest problems in strike aviation today, as evidenced by the inadvertent bombing of the Chinese embassy in Yugoslavia in 1999. Finding and recognizing a specific target from either a verbal description or even a picture from 16,000 feet in the air is hard on a clear day. Throw in marginal weather conditions and potential threats, and finding the target becomes a difficult challenge.

Once the pilot finds the target, he must then actually release the bomb. Because the F/A-18 is such a complex computer-driven machine, it is easy for a pilot to miss one step in a checklist and not drop the bomb. The flight is far from over after the bombs are off. Assuming the correct target was selected and the bombs worked as advertised, the pilot still has to make it back to the carrier. The departing aircraft must find each other and join back up before heading for home. In a real life scenario, the enemy is likely still trying to kill the bomber so egress can be pretty hairy.

The planning for these flights was long and intensive. The briefs were long because the instructors wanted to make sure we understood all the nuances of the complicated missions. The flights, in comparison, were relatively short—sometimes not even an hour long. Speed is life and when learning to bomb, the plane's engines run almost at maximum the entire flight. The pilot routinely pulls 5 to 6 G's throughout the flight, so even though bombing flights are short, they are exhausting. I came back from these fights drenched in sweat even though the outside air temperature was below 30 degrees.

My "circle the wagons" bombing wasn't shabby but it wasn't outstanding either. I was an average nugget bomber, some days I was right on and some days I would have only been a decent nuclear bomber. One of my strong skills that emerged in Fallon was "strafing." The F/A-18 is equipped with a Gatling machine gun that can fire up to 6000 rounds per minute. Missions concentrating on learning to fire this gun were called strafing missions. Our strafing target was a large banner-like target that was stretched across a small hill. We flew low and fast to find the target. Once the target was sighted, the pilot had maybe three seconds to acquire an accurate firing solution.

I loved the strafing missions. I was reminded of all the World War II movies I watched as a child. In my head, I envisioned myself rolling in on the target, hearing all the sound effects of those W.W.II movies. I loved the sounds of the machine gun rat-a-tat-tat and the whine of the engines. I was in for a big surprise in the actual plane. From the cockpit, the pilot can't hear the roar of an engine down low. Even worse, when the gun fires, it doesn't sound cool and lethal at all, it really just sounds like a kiddy pop gun. Despite my disappointment with my expected sound effects, I still did very well. For whatever reason, I strafed better than anyone in the class, even besting the older guys.

So I was great at some aspects and just OK with others. Always the perfectionist, I wanted to do better but I was already putting out maximum effort. Though the flying was exhilarating, I was physically exhausted at the end of each day. I just chalked up the fatigue as my body's reaction to the new stresses. After the day's flights were over, most of the instructors and students gathered at the Officer's Club to unwind at the bar. Because I was so tired and needed to study, I rarely attended these group sessions. When I did go, I had maybe one drink and a few laughs, and then headed back to my room.

Once when a group of us were discussing the next day's events, betting came up. In a typical group of four pilots that bombed together, many different bets were made: whose bomb would be the closest, who would have the best overall score, etc. One of the students in my class, Seal, had over 1000 hours in the F/A-18 so he was a sure winner against all the nuggets. Seal had been out of the cockpit a couple of years so all his training was just a refresher. When discussing the bets, I winked at Seal in a flirting manner and said, "I don't know if I want to bet with Seal in the flight, bombing with him is like playing pool with Minnesota Fats."

Seal, still single (for a reason) at 30 years old, didn't recognize the praise and started calling me a whiner. He didn't just call me a whiner; he said it in a singsong taunting manner as if we were kindergartners on a playground. Sick of the immaturity, I turned to Seal and announced in front of the group, "Seal, you need to dial 1-800-compliment and learn how to take one." The instructors thought that was funny but unfortunately, while Seal could dish it out, he couldn't take it. He never really spoke to me again.

Seal was not my only enemy. My class leader Lizard was still making sure everyone knew he didn't like me. One day as I was studying in one of the empty rooms, Lizard came in and said he wanted to speak with me. He told me there was a problem with my hair. My hands immediately flew to my bun. Always extremely conscious of my appearance, I thought maybe my bun was unraveling. Navy regulations state that in uniform, women's hair will be either no longer than the collar, or in a bun. Since my hair was two inches longer than my collar, I wore it up. He then said, "No it's fine now but it's completely unsat(isfactory) when you fly." I looked at him quizzically, what did he mean?

He quoted the Navy's hair regulations and told me my hair must be in a bun when I fly. He saw me climb out of a jet and a two-inch pigtail of hair was sticking out the back of my helmet. I worked hard to stifle a laugh. Helmets are individually fitted to each person's head and there is absolutely no room for a bun. Most women who wear these helmets have hair in buns and must let their hair down to strap on the helmet. They then take the remaining hair and tuck it up inside the helmet.

My hair was not long by any stretch of the imagination and I wondered where this criticism was coming from. I explained to him that women could not wear buns inside a helmet and if my hair came out of the helmet, it was an accident. He then again "ordered" me to keep my hair properly restrained and left. I was again amazed at his lack of leadership ability despite his seniority in rank. I just shook my head as he left and took greater pains to make sure all my hair was tucked up in my helmet.

Several days later, Lizard got the opportunity he was waiting for—a chance to ridicule me in public. It was "live day," the day all the pilots got to drop real 500 pound bombs on real targets—tanks. Everyone was very excited. We went through our grueling preparation procedure and jumped in our jets. I was number four in the four plane flight so was the last to roll down the runway. As I took off and put the landing gear up, I saw a light in the gear handle. The gear safely came up and nothing else was wrong, just the light in the handle.

I saw this a long time ago in A-4's. Sometimes when the pilot threw the handle up, it did not go up all the way. In that case, the light came on and the pilot had to cycle the handle to reset the light. In a split second, I cycled the handle without thinking. The light still didn't go out so I circled the field while radioing the duty officer for help. The problem was not an emergency, but I needed to clear it up before I could drop my live bombs.

The duty officer was an instructor with years of experience. He told me to take the same action I first tried, which was cycling the handle. While I was circling the field, we were not able to make the problem go away. I would not be able to complete my mission. In the meantime, a real emergency occurred. A freak weather storm was inbound and suddenly the winds blew in with almost hurricane force. While I was circling overhead all the other airborne planes landed, so I was the only one left. All airplanes have wind limits they can land in, and high crosswinds have flipped countless F/A-18's. Now I was in trouble. The winds were greater than seventy-five knots in a 15-degree crosswind. Those are very dangerous conditions, not to mention the fact that I still had two 500 pound LIVE bombs attached to my plane.

All Navy airfields have wires at the end of each runway for just such emergencies. The wires work just like those on an aircraft carrier. The incoming plane snags the wire with its tailhook, significantly reducing the rollout distance. The concern was that if I did not catch the wire immediately, the seventy-five knot wind could flip a wing. If the plane flipped, the two 500 pounders could explode in a deadly fireball.

Everyone was on edge as I made my final approach. I was a nugget pilot with less than 35 F/A-18 flying hours and I was going to take an arrested landing. The crash crews were stationed and all eyes were on me. While my approach was not eye watering, it was on target. All the extra landing practice paid off and I snagged the wire and quickly came to a grinding stop. Everyone breathed a deep sigh of relief, especially me. The weapons crew quickly "dearmed" me and I taxied back to the hangar.

When I walked back into the squadron spaces, many of the instructors congratulated me on a job well done. It was a "varsity day" out there, they said, and I hung in there. When I checked in with the squadron duty officer (SDO), he also was complimentary of my approach but wanted to discuss the light in the handle problem. During the event, the SDO researched the problem in the manuals and found we both made a mistake. Sometimes the light in the handle can be indicative of a more serious problem, one where a pilot should not cycle the handle. I listened closely. The SDO also had not grasped the danger of cycling the handle at the time, so it was a big learning point for both of us. I personally felt very bad that I made the mistake. I consider myself a very safe pilot and hate it when I do something without understanding the full consequences.

After our discussion, I went into the planning room to do some research for the next day's flight. After studying for a half-hour, Road, my other minority student friend sat down next to me. We were the only people in the room but he said in low tones, "Missy, I just want to tell you Lizard is not your friend. He really hates you and is doing everything he can to make you look bad." My stomach was in an immediate knot and I asked him to elaborate. Road then went on to tell me he was in the Ready Room during and after my gear incident. He heard Lizard tell all the instructors what a dirt bag I was and how I did not belong in a cockpit, etc. Road told me Lizard's comments were pretty hateful and

I needed to watch my back around him. As he left, Road said one more time, "Missy, just remember, LIZARD IS NOT YOUR FRIEND!"

After Road left, I felt very ill. I knew Lizard didn't like me but I didn't think he would stoop to such levels because of personal differences. Though Lizard was himself a student, he was a Commander and soon to be the Commanding Officer of an F/A-18 squadron. The really alarming part of the whole sordid affair was the possibility existed that Lizard would be my CO. Just a couple of weeks prior, I discussed my future with my detailer. (In the Navy, detailers are the people that assign an officer from job to job.) They control the destiny of officers and because of their power, they are often feared. My detailer told me there was a strong possibility my next squadron would be commanded by Lizard. Now I knew Lizard would stop at nothing to besmirch me and my flying reputation. I was very concerned.

Shortly after my disturbing conversation with Road, Comet, the NATOPS checkride instructor, pulled me aside. He also wanted to discuss the gear incident with me to ensure I understood the landing gear system of the F/A-18. Despite the checkride incident, I still considered Comet a confidante and someone who was looking after my best interests. Comet was going through a very nasty divorce and we often commiserated together about the lack of quality mates. Our relationship was completely above board, but I felt we were not just instructor and student; I also looked to him as a mentor. When Comet spoke, I listened.

After discussing the gear incident, he turned to me and said, "Missy, you don't seem yourself. Is there something else bothering you?" Generally I am not an emotional person, but after stewing over Lizard's comments, I felt a little teary. I told Comet about the conversation with Road and he seemed sympathetic. I ended the conversation with the statement, "What am I going to do? Lizard is in the Ready Room verbally assaulting me and he might be my CO?" Comet told me to just shake it off, because it wasn't certain I was going to Lizard's squadron. I felt better after talking to Comet and went back to studying. Not an hour later, I was told to stand tall in front of Lizard. Comet told Lizard what I said and Lizard was furious with me. He accused me of trying to ruin his career and claim sexual harassment. I didn't know what to think at first. I still don't know what he hoped to achieve with his ranting, so I just stood and took it. When given an opportunity to speak, I said, "I am not sure what was said. I wasn't here. I do know something must have been said, or else why would Road have told me what he did? It doesn't really matter though Lizard, you don't like me and you're a commander so what can I say about anything?" Lizard became more enraged with this statement and the situation was never really resolved. I left the Ready Room understanding that Lizard could talk ill of me all he wanted, but I obviously could not counter.

Even more than the continuing Lizard-Missy battle, I was upset that Comet told Lizard everything I said. I trusted Comet and thought he was someone I could confide in. I clearly misjudged him and wondered at my own stupidity. One of my biggest character flaws is shooting off my mouth without accurately measuring up my audience. I did it again and this time pissed off a lot of powerful people in the process. I spent the rest of the det laying low and licking my wounds.

Class 2–95 wasn't the only group of pilots in Fallon. Squadron detachments from all over the fleet were also there to practice their bombing. I ran into a lot of old friends while in Fallon. On the evening of the gear incident, one of these friends came calling. It was about 8:30 PM and I was already in bed. It was a long day and I was still shell-shocked from the day's events. I was just about to drift off to sleep when I heard a very discreet knock on the door. I was surprised to find my old friend Kevin at the door, sporting a sheepish grin. Another F/A-18 pilot, he asked to come in and I reluctantly accepted. I was still on East Coast time and very tired. I wasn't sure what Kevin wanted and I was a little leery of that familiar little soft knock which says, "I want to see you but I don't want any of the other guys to know I am here."

Kevin and I had been friends a very long time. We hung out together at the Naval Academy and were in flight school at the same time. He was already married, divorced, and recently remarried. I loved Kevin on many levels but we never dated. Our timing was always off. When one of us was available, the other had a partner. We sometimes chatted about a potential relationship, but timing and distance made it impossible. We both cared more for our careers than our personal lives and it was a choice we both were well aware of making. Kevin is someone I considered as a soulmate. We always knew exactly what the other was thinking and we connected on a deeper level that is indescribable. Despite the fact we would never really be a couple, I still loved him because when I looked at him, I was looking in a mirror.

We chatted about life in general, catching up on old times, and then of course we started talking about flying. I told him about the events of the day. Kevin knew I felt sick over my mistakes, both personally and professionally, and tried to console me. He told me stories of other F/A-18 pilots who made the same mistakes so I felt a little better. I then asked about his day of flying and as he talked, he was virtually transformed.

Kevin told me that he flew to a special range reserved for the smart bomb training. The F/A-18 is capable of carrying a myriad of bombs ranging from gravity (dumb) bombs to laser, self-guiding (smart) bombs. As he described the flight, it was obvious he relished in the telling. I was fascinated with the mechanics of the story at first. I would soon be flying these same flights so of course I wanted the "gouge." But as Kevin continued with his story, I noticed a not-so-subtle change come over him. His words started to run together, clearly his mind was racing along and his mouth couldn't keep up. His expressions were very animated and his face became steely and hard.

Kevin told me about his earlier live Walleye mission. A Walleye is a TV-guided bomb that the pilot watches from the cockpit. His chosen target was an abandoned semi-tractor trailer. He dropped the Walleye and the bomb guided right to his chosen targeting point, the semi cab.

I will never forget his statement, "And then as I watched the bomb hit, I knew that if a person had been in the truck, there would be nothing left but hair, teeth, and eyeballs!!" He followed this bizarre statement with a maniacal laugh and I was deeply disturbed with Kevin's transformation. Prior to flying F/A-18's, Kevin was a life-loving guy who I always respected for his ability to keep life in perspective. Now my Rock of Gibraltar was a Dr. Jekyll/Mr. Hyde who relished in the thought of mass destruction.

Kevin then continued to verbally hemorrhage about numerous other flying events. The theme was clearly how much he loved to destroy military hardware, buildings, and people. He looked at me with glazed eyes and told me of his recent trip to Europe. He said, "I went to Paris and all I could see around me were targets. I saw beautiful bridges and buildings that were there for centuries, and all I could see were targets. I just kept thinking to myself what kind of bomb would be best for that target and how I could destroy it. Missy, you know what I am?"

At this point, I was completely speechless. I just shook my head no and Kevin continued, "Missy, I am f—king lethal. I am truly a warrior, a god of death from the sky. I am f—king lethal." Kevin was in a pseudo-mantra like state, stating over and over again about how "f—king lethal" he was. He left my room shortly thereafter, which brought me a sigh of relief.

Kevin's visit was not consoling after all. Instead, it was very disturbing. What happened to the man I knew and loved? Kevin was not my soulmate. He was now a brainwashed, but legal killer. I have no problems using the F/A-18 for its mission, but I am not the type of person who ever relished the certain death that accompanies dropping bombs. Kevin's clear and unmistakable change deeply troubled me and I started to suspect that I would never fit in with "f—king lethal" warriors of the F/A-18.

The detachment soon came to an end. My last flight in Fallon was a make-up live weapons day. Since I never did drop the 500 pounders, my make-up day was the last day of the det. This time I took off and headed to the target area with no problems. The plane flew significantly different with the two massive bombs hanging on the wings and I was in for a big surprise when I dropped the first one. On my first drop, the plane surged and snapped rolled to the opposite side, catapulting me out of my seat, only to be restrained by the ejection seat harness. It was a little wake up call for me that this was no longer pretend practice bombing and this was what bombing was all about.

After the initial shock of the first drop wore off, I got my score. My target was a tank, and my first hit fell 75 feet short. I was a little frustrated, again just an average hit. The next time around I completely focused on my targeting and flew a perfect pattern. As I pulled off the target, fighting the more than 5 G's that was pulling my mask, helmet, and head into my lap, I heard the call, "Direct hit, you smoked the tank." I was ecstatic. I did it, and a direct hit on a tank is no easy task. There is no better feeling in the world when a pilot finds out he has scored a direct hit. I felt good because I finally felt like a real bomber pilot with the ability to do my mission. I smiled in my mask all the way home.

The joy of my direct hit didn't last long. I was on the ground less than an hour when the call came in. Another Marine F/A-18 pilot just flew into the side of a mountain. Most of the deaths in the F/A-18 community are due to CFIT—controlled flight into terrain. These deaths are always particularly sad because they are so preventable. The pilot usually loses his reference to the ground and doesn't realize where he is until it is too late. Nugget pilots are not the only victims. Just a few weeks later the Navy lost an admiral and the Commanding Officer of an F/A-18 squadron. The CO took the admiral out for a show-and-tell flight to demonstrate just what the F/A-18 could do. With more than 4000 hours of flying time, the CO flew them both into a mountain.

I left Fallon a much wiser pilot. I made my share of mistakes but I learned a great deal, both personally and professionally. I was still highly motivated and despite all the troubles, I felt I was making significant progress. Now the focus of my class was on learning the fighter aspect of the F/A-18's Strike Fighter mission. We had just a month to prepare for our next upcoming detachment, Key West. Just as Fallon allowed us to practice our bombing mission, Key West, Florida would allow us to concentrate on the more difficult and intangible air-to-air aspects of the F/A-18.

During our month long preparation, I flew numerous preparatory flights and studied quite a bit. Success in the air-to-air arena requires a lot of studying and memorization. When a pilot expects to fight another aircraft, he must completely understand both his and the enemy's radar and missile capabilities. It is one thing to sit on the ground and be able to instantly recall a parameter but it is completely different when bearing down on the bad guy with over 1000 knots of closure.

I was an average student on my simulators and flights but I was still very tired. In the past, I could fly twice a day and still go for a run. Now just flying once a day was almost all I could handle, and to make matters worse, I thought my hair was falling out. I began to notice clumps of hair coming out in my brush while in Fallon. Not wanting to believe anything was wrong with me, I thought I was just imagining my hair loss. If anything, I thought my exhaustion and possible hair loss were due to the stress of even more dynamic flying and squadron life. Fallon in particular had been very stressful for me, especially due to the Lizard incident. When I returned to Florida, I hoped to put all the ugliness behind me, but the Commanding Officer, Captain Moffit had other, more Machiavellian plans for me.

Three weeks after my return from Fallon, Captain Moffit issued me my second SOD (Signal of Difficulty). He told me he reviewed the events of the flight and thought I deserved a SOD. At no time in the history of the squadron had a SOD been issued a month after the fact. The fact that I received my second SOD was upsetting, but it was not the worst of the news. In a conniving and cunning manner, Comet told Captain Moffit about the confrontation between Lizard and me upon our return from Fallon. Comet, quite the busybody, also told Captain

Moffit that I accused Lizard of verbal assault. Captain Moffit decided he would hold an investigation to look into my "charges" despite the fact I had not charged anyone with anything.

I was horrified when he told me of the pending investigation. I knew instantly that if a CAPT Moffit initiated a public investigation, all the instructors would look at me as some kind of militant and radical feminist only trying to ruin the career of a commander. If Captain Moffit went through with the investigation, he would in effect destroy my reputation and career. The squadron was so rife with hatred for women pilots, that if the instructors perceived me as a troublemaker, I would never survive.

I begged and pleaded with Captain Moffit not to hold the investigation. I explained to him just what would happen. I told him I was not upset with the events in Fallon. I repeated over and over that I never made any charge of "verbal assault." I told him Comet and I just had a private conversation and I never meant for it to leave the room. Now I really was close to tears. I knew all too well what the ramifications would be in the wake of an investigation. Captain Moffit just looked down at me with a condescending, knowing look and said, "I am holding this investigation regardless. I need to protect my command."

After I was dismissed, I ran from his office, looking for Lizard. I eventually found him in the club. He already knew about the investigation and was not happy. I told Lizard that I had nothing to do with the investigation and in the course of any interviews, I would minimize our friction. I told him I absolutely did not want this to affect his career and I never dreamed such an innocuous comment would lead to such disaster. I poured my heart out and apologized profusely. Lizard seemed to accept my apology and it appeared that we had a truce.

The investigation was performed by one of Captain Moffit's lackeys, his administrative officer. There was no real attempt to find the real facts. The investigation was purely directed at what a poor officer I was for making such charges and completely cleared Lizard of all wrongdoing.

The actual report was absurd and completely unprofessional. Here are some of the more enlightening excerpts from this report:

"[Lizard's] remarks, as innocent as they may have been, were misconstrued into a lot more second hand in LT Cummings' estimation."

"It was very unprofessional for LT Cummings to use the 'verbal assault' accusation."

"[Comet] handled the situation very well."

Despite some glaring inaccuracies and outright lies in the report, I didn't fight it. I promised Lizard I wouldn't make any waves and I kept my promise. I just wanted the whole incident to go away so I could concentrate on flying and salvage my reputation.

My greatest fears were realized almost immediately after the investigation was concluded. Almost all of the instructors and most of the students started giving me the silent treatment. No one would shoot the breeze with me any more and some of the instructors seemed to enjoy staring me down. I was under immense stress now. I knew the instructors hated me and the Commanding Officer was doing everything he could to make my life miserable. It was very lonely and I acutely felt the ostracism. By the time class 2–95 left for Key West, I really felt ill. Always the armchair therapist, I chalked up my fatigue and general ill feelings towards the recent turn of events. I knew I was the only fish in the bowl, and was even madder at myself for letting it show so clearly.

My grandfather during W.W. II.

U.S. Marine Corps Photo

My father as a young Marine.

My mother in a beauty contest

Christmas in Japan.

My first year at the Naval Academy.

The judo throw that won me third place in the Eastern Collegiate Championships in 1987.

A school magazine interview with the three big men on campus: the Brigade Commander, Napoleon McCallum, & David Robinson.

Two T-34's flying in formation. The T-34 is the Navy's first trainer.

My first solo in the T-34

U.S. Navy Photo

My initial jet class.

Photo courtesy of Jan Eric Krikke, Aviaworld

The Navy's intermediate jet trainer in 1989—the T-2C.

Photo courtesy of Bruce Stevenson

The Navy's advanced jet trainer,
the TA-4J on the catapult of the USS Lexington.

Photo courtesy of US Navy

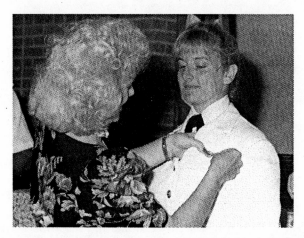

My mom pinning on my wings during flight school graduation.

U.S. Navy Photo

My Winging Class, July of 1990

My dad and I just before my move to the Philippines.

At an airshow in Atsugi, Japan in 1991 in front of the A-4E I flew.

Photo courtesy of Jeff Goerges

Learning to water-ski.

Learning to fly one of my squadron's helicopters.

U.S. Navy Photo

Mt. Pinatubo erupting as one of the squadron's planes hastily heads to Japan.

Flying over the volcanic crater of Mt. Pinatubo after the eruption.

Shaking the hand of a Terra-Cotta soldier in Xian, China.

U.S. Navy Photo

A U.S. Navy F/A-18 Hornet dropping a bomb

Showing the F/A-18 on one of my cross-country trips

U.S. Navy Photo

My last tour in the Navy as an assistant professor at Penn State.

Chapter Eleven

Gunned by A Girl

The Key West detachment is a two week exercise designed to concentrate on the air-to-air mission of the F/A-18. Shooting down other aircraft may seem simple on a home computer but in reality, it is one of the most complex evolutions of flying. Orchestrating multiple aircraft in a small piece of airspace is much like a well-rehearsed ballet. Even a split second mistake can result in disaster. Unlike bombing a stationary target, enemy aircraft not only move, but they also shoot back and no two air-to-air scenarios are alike.

The F/A-18 typically carries four air-to-air weapons; three missiles and the gun that is used in strafing can also be used to shoot down other aircraft. The name of the fighter game is to shoot the bad guy down well before the two aircraft ever see one another. This is usually accomplished with radar guided missiles, but as capable as modern day technology is, nothing is fail-safe. Since most missiles can't kill at close range which is approximately inside a mile, the gun is the last defense or offense in a close fight.

Most of the squadron's fighter training concentrates on strategies to achieve realistic kill solutions. While the actual mechanics of shooting down another aircraft are important, getting to a position where a missile or gun can be successfully fired is by far the most difficult. A pilot has to track the target on three computer displays, monitor aircraft systems, and achieve a firing solution. All this must be done while keeping an eye on possibly three other friendly aircraft—while moving through the sky at almost the speed of sound. When all the bells and whistles of the F/A-18's warning systems kick in, the pilot can easily become overwhelmed. The two weeks spent in Key West is every nugget's first opportunity to see just how difficult it is to be a real "TOPGUN."

To assist visiting squadrons in training, the Navy permanently based an adversary squadron in Key West. While I was with the adversary squadron in the Philippines, it was completely different. The adversary squadron in Key West, VF-45, was dedicated solely to air-to-air engagements, while the Philippine squadron only devoted a small amount of time to that mission. To help visiting squadrons make the most out of their training dollars, VF-45 provided both instructors and planes. The pilots of VF-45 were the best in the fleet, and all were TOPGUN graduates. (VF-45 has since been disestablished.)

Key West, Florida in May is hot and steamy which are generally not the best flying conditions. Aircraft engines perform much better in cooler temperatures and ocean environments are not conducive for corrosion control. Key West, however, was unique because planes operated in the plentiful local flying areas without disrupting commercial aircraft traffic flows. Air-to-air training also requires perfect weather, and cloudless skies are one of the benefits of Key West. Lastly, the aircrews of course love the party atmosphere always prevalent year-round in Key West. The Navy even maintains a hotel for military personnel only half a mile from the world famous Duval Street.

Key West is the home of one of popular music's most famous singers, Jimmy Buffet. His songs about life in the islands, drinking, and women are favorites of naval aviators, who can recite almost all the lyrics to his songs. Jimmy Buffet equally loves to hang around naval aviators because he also is a pilot. When he is in Key West, he has an open door policy for Navy pilots, who have spent many a night at his house.

During my detachment, while most of the guys, both students and instructors, spent all of their free time sampling the Key West lifestyle, I usually stayed behind in the hotel. My energy level plummeted with the heat and I found myself exhausted all the time. I knew something was seriously wrong when I would steal away to the ladies' room to take quick naps between flights. Despite sleeping eight or nine hours, I woke up still very tired and could not wait to go back to bed. I promised myself that after carrier qualifications in a month, I would see a doctor.

Naval aviators have their own doctors called flight surgeons. Flight surgeons are recent medical school graduates who have completed their internship but have not selected a specialty. They receive a six-month aviation physiology course as an introduction and their tours as flight surgeons are usually their first. Because flight surgeons have the power to keep a pilot from flying which is called grounding, aviators avoid them like the plague. Hours are spent sitting around the Ready Room telling flight surgeon horror stories. Even the most minor of colds will ground a jet pilot for days, and when aviators are diagnosed with serious diseases like diabetes, the results can sometimes be permanent grounding.

While I was in Key West, I knew I was sick from something, but I did not think it was serious. I thought maybe I contracted a mild case of mononucleosis or I was anemic. I only had one more month of training and I did not want to see a flight surgeon until I was finished. I knew grounding would likely result for at least a few days and I wanted to postpone that if possible. I also did not want to be viewed by my male counterparts as weak and not able to "hack" the program. In hindsight, my hesitancy to see the flight surgeons was not the smartest move I ever made.

Needing a lot of sleep was not the only reason that I didn't hang out with the other pilots in Key West. The similarities between the Philippines and Key West did not stop with the weather. It seemed that a little bit of the "Sex Disneyland" atmosphere was prevalent as well. At the end of a day of tough flying, the instructors told the students to meet them at the local strip bar for the day's debrief. The guys gathered in these "tittie" bars and actually discussed the recent training evolutions as if it was a business meeting. Of course, they took breaks to ogle the more well-endowed girls or those women that were particularly flexible or talented. I stayed in the hotel and slept instead of meeting the guys. Because of my experiences in the Philippines, I had absolutely no desire to take part in that behavior again. I wasn't passing judgment on the guys who liked to go; I just didn't feel like watching my peers drool.

The behavior that surprised me in Key West far more than the tittie bar debriefings were the abandoning of wedding rings. No stranger to Navy pilots cheating on their wives, I was shocked at how many of both the instructors and students left their rings behind in the hotel. These pilots played games just like those in the PI, and despite my worldliness, I was taken aback. While I knew it went on, I suppose I never thought it happened in the United States. I had not seen this side of the instructors and the students before, so I was shocked and surprised. I quickly learned that these men led a double life, and when they were out of the local Jacksonville area, they acted as if they were free agents.

The person that disgusted me the most was "Peeper." He got his callsign because he was caught trying to watch another female officer through her keyhole while on a bombing detachment. He was quite proud of his voyeuristic and illegal conduct and wore his callsign like a badge. Peeper's main argument for not allowing women on ships was his lack of ability to concentrate with women around. He enjoyed telling me that while starting up the plane, he found it hard to concentrate if a female plane captain assisted him. Peeper admitted that he found himself just staring at her breasts through her white T-shirt and fantasizing. He became visibly aroused just relaying the story, and I really wondered then if men and women would ever really be able to work closely together. I could not believe how sexually driven he was and how he let it affect him in his job.

In Key West, Peeper was the man to beat. He came into work night after night on the town and described his past evening's conquests. The fact that he was married with children didn't seem to faze him at all. He loved "doing fresh young meat" and the guys loved hearing about his sordid rendezvous. I was disgusted and found it impossible to respect these individuals. I tried to hide my disdain, but I have never been able to sport a believable poker face. I was mostly disappointed so much in individual behavior but more in the fact that I could never get away from the sleazy side of aviation. I thought I left all that immoral behavior behind in the Philippines; however, it was clear to me during those two weeks in Key West, that illicit sex and tittie bars were a permanent part of the fighter pilot business.

Another similarity to the Philippines was the drinking and flying. Many years ago, the Navy instituted a "twelve hour bottle to throttle" rule to provide guidance to those pilots who like to imbibe. The Navy determined that a pilot should be completely free from all effects of alcohol only twelve hours after the last drink. As anyone who has ever drunk to excess can validate, just because a person stops drinking does not ensure he will be completely sober in twelve hours. Because many aviators abused this system—some doing ten shots of Tequila in the last few minutes before the witching hour—the Navy decided to make the drinking policy even more strict. The Navy now has a "twelve hour bottle to brief" policy. This means that the pilot must be completely alcohol free by briefing time, which in reality only adds maybe two hours to the sobering process.

In the Philippines, I saw outright flagrant violations of this drinking policy by aircrews of all types of aircraft. The jet community certainly does not have the corner on the drinking market—all Navy aviators were encouraged to drink to extreme excess in the PI. I knew pilots who flew who probably exceeded the legal drinking and driving limits. I never respected those pilots who violated this rule, but because most of them were senior to me, there was little I could do. Just like the rampant prostitution, flying while still legally drunk did not seem to be a big deal.

Again I was gullible in thinking this behavior was just accepted over-seas. In Key West, the night before an exercise that involved all the pilots, the instructors wanted the students to join them for a "roll off" (a popular dice game for all types of officers in the Navy). The game involves rolling dice. A cup of five dice is passed around, and the person who rolls the highest number of similar dice gets to leave the group. The last person remaining has to buy everyone else drinks, so this is expensive for the unlucky final soul.

All the students and instructors were playing, so the loser would have to buy almost thirty drinks. As we started the roll off, I looked down at my watch and noticed that every single one of us would break the twelve-hour rule if we drank. I nervously watched the instructors as the roll off ended. The instructors gleefully ordered a round of drinks and started another roll off. When the waitress took my order, I simply said, "Diet Coke, please." Despite the fact that everyone else was flagrantly violating the drinking rules, I didn't feel comfortable doing it myself. When the word spread that I was not drinking, both students and instructors teased me about my straight-laced behavior. I just drank my coke and said nothing. After all was said and done, well over three rounds of drinks were ordered, and we were only ten hours from our brief time.

Struggling to fit in socially was actually the easiest part of Key West. My declining health was starting to significantly impact my perform-ance. I initially started my Key West training with two flights where I shot my own wingman down (all simulated). I was struggling with multi-plane engagements and using my radar. The F/A-18 radar, while impressive, is not fail-safe. I locked up an enemy fighter and took a sim-ulated missile shot. Unfortunately, the radar lock broke halfway through the missile's time of flight and switched to the best available target, which twice turned out to be my wingman.

The solution to preventing this is position. A pilot needs to fire when his wingman has cleared the area. Because planes are significantly far apart, typically around a mile, it can be difficult to see the wingman. When I fired, I could not see my wingman and thought he was clear, but he wasn't. I found out later that at this point, I was so ill that my vision was deteriorating.

I felt very bad about shooting down my wingman. I wasn't the only student who made that mistake, but I seemed to be catching on a little slower than everyone else. Because I received the proverbial "ass-chewing" after one of these flights, I was very hesitant to take shots on my next flight. My instructor for this flight, Hawk, made it clear early on that he didn't like me when he said, "I don't give a f—k what you think!" I was very intimidated by his open dislike and still literally gun-shy after my last event where I waxed my own wingman.

Hawk and I flew a similar flight to the last, in which we tried to maneuver to shoot down an enemy fighter. Procedurally, I flew the plan correctly, but because of my last flight, I refused to take a shot unless I was absolutely certain I targeted the right guy. Because I overcompensated, I shot no one on that flight. Hawk was furious and decided I needed my third SOD. Although I knew he hated me, I also realized I had not yet mastered the shooting doctrine and welcomed the extra training.

The instructor for my next flight was "Barney." A happy man with a Santa Claus belly, Barney was one of the best instructors, priding himself on his students' successes. Barney sat me down and methodically went through the scenario. He showed me exactly where I went wrong in my other flights and how to correct my mistakes. No other instructor ever took the time to tell me precisely what I needed to do to improve. Because Barney understood the thought processes of students so well, he recognized almost instantly that I was not paying attention to the right instrumentation. I listened very closely to Barney and because he was so friendly, I responded with amazing results. When Barney and I flew together, I always flew my best flights and this extra training flight was no different. I flew an almost perfect flight, always maneuvering for the correct shot and not exhibiting any of the mistakes of the past. When we landed, Barney told me he did not know what my problem was with Hawk, but as far as he was concerned, I aced the flight and needed no more extra training. I was overjoyed because the flight went so well and I finally felt as if I made a break through.

That week I flew some of the best flights of my short F/A-18 career. During the multi-plane exercises (four good guys versus four bad guys), I always seemed to shoot down the same enemy fighter who was a VF-45 instructor. Not only did I shoot him down, but I shot him down with the gun, which is the most difficult kill to make. I know he hated me because every time we landed, all the other guys would unrelentingly pick on him. They taunted him in a singsong voice with "you got gunned by a girl." I winced every time I heard this because I knew he hated the humiliation, which was made even worse by my gender.

Gunning a guy was not the only gender issue that came up while I was in Key West. One morning, the publication of an article in the newspaper, *USA Today,* would forever change my life. Linda Chavez, opposed to women in combat roles, wrote an article on the Kara Hultgren debacle. The article focused on another female F-14 pilot that trained with Kara. Chavez referred to this girl as "Pilot B" and alleged that she was not qualified to fly. With Elaine Donnelly's help, Chavez's article detailed Pilot B's training record, which showed she experienced some difficulties through training. Chavez alleged that a double standard for women existed and the Navy was allowing unqualified female pilots to fly.[10]

The article sparked a lively discussion in the Ready Room. I was the only woman and despite my presence in the room, several instructors jumped on the Chavez bandwagon. They made it quite clear they thought women didn't belong in fighters and when the conversation turned to me, I decided to leave. I did not care to hear my or any other woman's performance picked apart in a room of my peers. I acutely felt the pressure of the fishbowl environment and felt my departure was my only option. As I headed down the hallway, I saw the same article posted in the main entryway that led to VF-45.

I was very disappointed to see this article so prominently displayed. Next to the article was an even larger sign posted that said, "Read and Heed", with an arrow pointing to the article. Not only was it posted for all to see, the sections about women not qualified as fighter pilots were highlighted. Up to this point, I was really impressed with the professionalism of the VF-45 pilots. Compared to the adversary pilots I flew with in the Philippines, these pilots were gods. Now this same inflammatory article was posted for all to see by the VF-45 pilots. The message was clear. The VF-45 pilots also agreed with Linda Chavez and thought women should not be flying in combat.

Without thinking, I carefully removed the article and took it two doors down to a friend of mine who was a pilot in VF-45. Mark Dunleavy and I were friends since our days at the Naval Academy. After graduating in 1988, we went through primary flight training together. Mark went on to fly F/A-18s immediately after flight school and I went on to lesser jobs to wait my turn. Mark was a legacy and one of the Navy's golden children. His father, also a Naval Academy graduate, was Vice Admiral Dunleavy who at the pinnacle of his career headed all the air assets of the Navy, a very powerful position. Unfortunately, Admiral Dunleavy's career ended abruptly when he was forced to retire early because he was implicated in the Tailhook '91 scandal. Since female aviators were often seen as evil and militant feminists who were responsible for the Tailhook debacle, it is likely that both Mark and his father held no love for women in naval aviation. However, despite any ill will Mark might have harbored towards women pilots in general, he always seemed nice to me and I truly respected him. I never thought Mark would let his father's situation color his personal judgement, but I would again prove to be wrong.

I showed Mark the article and told him how disappointed I was that such a professional squadron would make such a statement. He danced around the issue, eventually telling me that the article was only posted because of general interest even though there were no other articles of any kind posted, but that he appreciated my input. He agreed that posting it, especially with the highlights, might convey the wrong message. After our brief discussion about the article, we chatted for another twenty or so minutes about mutual friends and the latest gossip. I left the article with him to do with as he pleased and went to the bathroom to take a quick nap.

The next day, the last big exercise for the Key West training detachment was scheduled. My class simulated an entire strike package, complete with fighter escorts. VF-45 pretended to be the bad guys and tried to prevent us from reaching our target. The flight was originally scheduled for early in the morning, but because of maintenance problems, we didn't take off until 5 PM. As all ten of our planes were headed out, I was unbelievably tired, my stomach was killing me, and I hoped the flight ended quickly. It was the last flight of the detachment and despite how sick I felt, I was going to complete.

Because our flight of four needed to have an instructor in one of the planes, an instructor was randomly assigned to my back seat. (Usually we flew alone.) I was leading a section of two planes and when we entered the training area, we needed to find the other two planes and join them. We successfully joined the four plane division and then held, waiting for the attack signal. As we were holding, we turned into the sun, which was low on the horizon. I lost sight of the two planes next to me and told my instructor. He didn't say anything and this made me even more nervous with my close proximity to other aircraft. Because I was blinded by the sun, I turned away trying to increase our separation. I over-controlled the turn that caused my wingman to turn away even harder. The flight of four was separated and the entire strike was delayed while we tried to regroup. When we did finally get back together, the strike went as planned with no more major incidents.

If I thought I felt ill when I took off, I felt ten times worse when I landed. I was humiliated because I delayed the entire strike. All my good flights were completely negated by this bad one. In the debrief I was thoroughly chastised by all the parties involved and the flight event was completed. My instructor knew why I made my mistake and did not think it was as grave as I thought it was. He told me "these things happen all the time" and he felt comfortable that I successfully completed not only the flight, but the entire two-week training exercise as well.

That night everyone headed out to celebrate. I did not feel up to it due both in part to my massive screw-up and the physical ailments that had been plaguing me for weeks. I stayed in that night and was in bed by 8 PM. The next day, we packed all our gear and flew back to Jacksonville. I was unhappy with the way the detachment ended, but I knew I learned a lot and was now focusing on carrier qualifications. When we returned to our base, I remained at the squadron several hours to complete a stack of paperwork and other administrative items. I headed home late in the afternoon. When I got home, a message was waiting for me on my answering machine. I was to come back to the squadron immediately to receive another SOD.

I turned right around and sped back to the squadron. I knew what was coming. Apparently the instructors had a group meeting and decided that I deserved a SOD for the previous day's flight. Just like the retroactive SOD from Fallon, it is very unusual for a SOD to be issued after a flight has been debriefed as satisfactory. This is in fact what happened again. My instructor completely reversed his previous decision and issued me a SOD for the flight. As he handed me the paperwork, he could not even look me in the eye. There was little discussion—he just asked me to sign the paperwork and then told me to see the Training Officer.

I knew I was in deep trouble. I just received my fourth SOD and because of all the previous discussions about "Pilot B" and unqualified women pilots, I knew the guys were closely watching me. The Training Officer asked me how I thought my training was going. I told him that

I was learning, but that I thought I needed any extra practice. I finally admitted that I was not feeling well and told him I probably needed to see the flight surgeon. He responded by trying to persuade me to voluntarily resign my position as an F/A-18 pilot. He told me he didn't think I belonged there and that I should look for other employment. I was speechless. I just poured out my heart to him, and he responded with veiled threats.

In the end, he told me that my next step was a Human Factors Board. (HFB) The purpose of this board is to determine if any external factors might be affecting a pilot's performance. Because the members of the board are supposed to look at medical and emotional issues, one of the four board members is a flight surgeon. I was not upset with my future HFB, I fully expected it and felt I deserved it. I figured I would be chastised for not bringing medical problems to the attention of the flight surgeon sooner, and then returned to flying in a probationary status once the medical issues were resolved.

I reported to the flight surgeon the next day. Dr. Kirk asked me how I was feeling and I told him everything. I told him how tired I was and how my stomach was aching. After listening to me, he decided to run some tests for ulcers. He then asked me how I thought I was holding up mentally. I told him about the article incident and the fact that at seemingly every turn, the guys enjoyed bashing Kara and other women pilots. Even though Kara and I were not in the same squadron and 3000 miles separated us, the ramifications of her crash were still impacting my instructors' perceptions. Dr. Kirk sympathized with me and said he knew it was hard to be one of the first women to go through this program. It was a positive meeting and I felt better when I left his office.

The next day I read the flight surgeon's report concerning our meeting. It was very supportive of me. Dr. Kirk thought I assumed complete responsibility for all my mistakes and stated I possessed a "strong positive attitude." He also stated that he thought I had no medical problems and that the tests would show nothing wrong with me. Dr. Kirk thought the HFB was warranted not because of any medical problems, but because of the stress in general.

Two days later the Human Factors Board was held. I was a little surprised with the quickness of the board. The ulcer test results were not yet back so there was no real answer about my medical status. However, I reported to the boardroom with a positive attitude and ready to move ahead. The board consisted of one senior pilot, two flight instructors, and Dr. Kirk. The head of the board was a Commander who was not an instructor and was not from VFA-106. He was a friend of the Commanding Officer's and was obviously repaying a favor.

When I walked into the room, I was surprised to see the Commander wearing a filthy uniform and sunglasses on his head with a bright pink croakie around the back. His military bearing was the most unprofessional I had ever seen in a senior officer and I was alarmed. He wore his sunglasses on his head throughout the entire board's proceedings, and I got the distinct impression he was not taking this very seriously.

The Surfer Commander started by asking me a few innocuous questions about my personal life. After a short discussion of my desires to remain in the F/A-18 community, the Commander launched into a thirty-minute lecture. The HFB was supposed to be a fact-finding body, but the Commander did most of the talking with little input from me. He began by telling me he did not think I belonged in F/A-18s because of the trouble I experienced in flight school. Even though I my grades were far above the average in flight school, the Commander seemed to think I never deserved my wings in the first place.

There was never any real discussion about any issues that could be affecting my flight performance. The other two instructors said very little and when Dr. Kirk was asked for his input, he said lab results were pending and nothing more. The only events the Commander really wanted to discuss were my confrontations with Lizard in Fallon and the Chavez article in Key West. He was outraged with my conduct in both and made sure I knew he did not support me at all. When he finished lecturing me, he told me that as far as he was concerned, there were no human factors issues and he did not think I should be flying. The next step he said would be a FNAEB.

FNAEB stands for Field Naval Aviator Evaluation Board. It is the one administrative procedure that all pilots fear. The recommendations of a FNAEB can not only end a military flying career, but a civilian one as well. FNAEBs are usually reserved for those pilots that exhibit heinous flying performance and carry a stigma that is far reaching in a pilot's career. I only knew a few people that ever experienced FNAEBs. Most were pilots that experienced serious difficulties landing on the boat or those that flagrantly violated rules and regulations. A pilot in my Philippine squadron who landed without extending his landing gear went through a FNAEB as did another pilot who was responsible for the near-death of a junior pilot.

Not all pilots who go to a FNAEB lose their wings. There are actually six possible outcomes of FNAEBs ranging from no punishment to the loss of all flight qualifications and the right to even wear the gold wings in the future. Some pilots are reassigned to other aircraft; this is what happened to my former roommate, Shannon. After her difficulties landing on the boat, she went through a FNAEB and was reassigned to a land-based aircraft. Some pilots are awarded extra training, especially if they have previously been outstanding pilots but need a little extra time.

I was very worried about the recommendation of my Human Factors Board to send me to a FNAEB. The fact that I was going was not my primary concern—I knew my flight performance deteriorated over the past few months and I personally felt like I needed extra training. I was not feeling well and I knew the three years I spent out of the cockpit while at graduate school left me behind my peers. What I was troubled about was the tone of the HFB. There seemed to be absolutely no real concern to address either my medical or flight related problems. The Commander of the HFB did not think I "deserved" to be flying F/A-18s and clearly wanted me out of the program. The review of my case was not objective and since the FNAEB board members would be drawn from the same pool, the future looked grim.

I went home after my HFB, stunned and very concerned. I called a former Marine F/A-18 pilot friend of mine for his opinion. After we discussed the recent events at length, he agreed that the HFB seemed rushed and not at all impartial. He told me to write a letter to the Commanding Officer who originally convened the board to voice my concerns. I wrote a two-page letter, summarizing my views of the board and the unmistakable biases, especially of the Commander. I concluded my letter to him, "My feeling after Key West and the Human Factors Board is that this community does not want me here and this review process (FNAEB) will be extremely difficult." I had no idea how prophetic this statement was.

I gave the Commanding Officer this letter the next day. Two days later, he handed me the official report of the Human Factors Board. I was not surprised to read the final recommendation for a FNAEB, but there were several statements that were very telling. The first was the statement concerning my medical condition, "LT Cummings does not appear to have any significant external circumstances that would affect her ability to perform…" The other comment that infuriated me was, "She has an overly familiar relationship with one if not more instructors whereby she calls them by their first name…. [the instructor/student] relationship has possibly degraded to an unprofessional state in a few circumstances."

One of the flight instructors (who was my same rank) and I were in the same company during our time at the Naval Academy. After calling someone for many years by his real name, it is sometimes very hard to call this same person "boner." He also equally sometime slipped and called me Missy instead of Shrew. Up to this time, I did not know that this was such a heinous crime. My flying career and health were on the line and the HFB decided my most egregious mistake was my calling an instructor by his first name?

The innuendo that an improper relationship existed between me and one or more instructors really angered me. I may not have been the best pilot, but I prided myself in behaving like an officer. I deeply resented the accusations of "sleeping my way to the top" and knew that if I were a man, this would never have been an issue.

I again consulted with my male F/A-18 pilot friend. After reviewing the HFB's report, he told me I should again write the Commanding Officer. I was clearly being held to a different set of standards and he also predicted the upcoming FNAEB would be very tenuous at best. He told me I needed to publicly document these problems, because the outcome of the FNAEB might not go my way.

I heeded his advice and for the second time in less than a week, I wrote my Commanding Officer another letter. I addressed all the conflicting statements and veiled accusations, clearly stating that I thought the board was prejudiced and negligent. It appeared to me that the HFB completely lost sight of its original charter to determine if any external factors could be affecting my flying. Instead, the board focused on trivial matters hardly indicative of my flight performance. In my last paragraph, I asked that he remove the HFB report from my record. I was not asking him to overturn their decision (which he could have). I was confident that a more objective FNAEB panel would return me to probationary flight status. I felt the HFB was nothing more than a character assassination and certainly unprofessional. It therefore should not be part of my official record.

When I presented the Commanding Officer with my second letter, he concurred. He agreed that the Human Factors Board was less than professional and said it would not be a part of the record. He then told me he received a phone call from the flight surgeon. The lab results finally came in and they showed that I was losing a significant amount of blood somewhere in my gastrointestinal track. The doctor's guess was that I had ulcers.

I was disappointed yet relieved in the same moment. The potential diagnosis seemed serious but finally there was an explanation as to why I was feeling so ill. I then asked the Commanding Officer, "Well then it's true that I have a medical condition that probably affected my flight performance, so the Human Factors Board was wrong. Does this mean I will still go to a FNAEB?"

Most certainly I would still go, the Commanding Officer assured me. Despite the fact the HFB did not wait for the lab results, and in spite of the fact the board was obviously biased, he felt I still "deserved" a FNAEB. I asked if the FNAEB could be delayed long enough for me to seek medical attention. He refused this request, telling me the FNAEB would begin in a few days and I could address the medical issues afterwards. Unlike the Human Factors Board, the FNAEB would take three to five days. I was assured it would be a very thorough yet objective review of my flight performance.

Again I was amazed at the callousness and apparent rush to push me to the next step of dismissal. Just as in the HFB, why was I not allowed to get medical care for obviously critical problems before a flight performance evaluation? Why did just a few days matter so much to these individuals? Lab tests confirmed a relatively serious condition that no doubt affected my flying performance. It was clear to me the medical problems were going to be ignored, at least by my squadron. So my next step was a visit to the flight surgeon.

I tracked him down in his office and confronted him with the news. I thought it odd he did not tell me and instead, broadcasted the news without my permission. If he did not think my condition was important enough to discuss in the HFB, then why did he think it was important enough to tell my Commanding Officer? When I started asking him these questions, he stammered and did not look me in the eye. He knew his misdiagnosis might potentially cost me my career. To make matters worse, I was not allowed to see any specialists about my medical problems. He eventually agreed to my requests to see an internal medicine doctor and scheduled an appointment, which would take place in the middle of the FNAEB board.

I drove home that day dazed and confused. Not only was I going to a FNAEB board, but what was worse is that my serious medical problems were essentially ignored. If the HFB was any indication of the tone of the FNAEB, I was in big trouble. For the first time in a very long time, I went home and cried. All my dreams of deploying on aircraft carriers and eventually finding my way to the space program were quickly disintegrating.

The next Sunday, I went to the church I attended for some time. I went with a group of friends I knew from Monterey. They knew what was happening and provided me with an incredible amount of support and understanding. As we were leaving the church, I could not believe my eyes. The Surfer Commander from my HFB was standing on the steps waiting for me. He also was a member of the church and saw me during the service. He reached out to hug me and wished me good luck in the upcoming FNAEB. I recoiled at his fake attempts at Christian love. I was still very angry that he ignored my serious medical conditions, and since I just read his scathing attacks on my integrity and piloting skills, he was not my favorite person. My friends, both male and female, were also shocked at the pseudo-display of affection by this senior officer and all were speechless. Why would this man who held such obvious contempt for me try to hug me in church? The group consensus was that he felt guilty about his role in the HFB and that was his lame attempt for forgiveness. It would be many years before I forgave him or anyone else involved in this sordid affair.

Chapter Twelve

Reality Check

There is no question that prior to my FNAEB, my performance was inconsistent and lacking in some areas. I knew it and wanted nothing more than to correct my deficiencies. But how were the other pilots measuring up? Was I the only person making mistakes? What was happening with some of the guys? The reality was that other students and many instructors were committing much more serious flying mistakes. These airborne blunders cost the taxpayers millions of dollars but were basically ignored by the senior officials involved.

During the same time frame as my FNAEB, another pilot who went through flight school with me also was transitioning from a different aircraft. Slime had almost 2000 hours in another tactical jet, so his transition should have been relatively smooth. One night he was taxiing to the runway and decided he did not need his taxi light. It was a squadron mandatory procedure to use the taxi light for safety reasons. For whatever reason, Slime decided the taxi light requirement did not apply to him, and subsequently ran off the taxiway. He damaged several taxiway lights and the landing gear of the plane, causing thousands of dollars worth of damage. Slime, definitely in the boys club, received a slap on the wrist and nothing else.

Another more senior aviator, Dawg, was also transitioning from an older attack aircraft. Like Slime, he had nearly 2000 hours in a tactical cockpit and well over 100 carrier landings. While I was suffering through Key West, Dawg made a routine landing, but thought something went wrong on the landing roll out. He inadvertently shut down one engine and blew both tires when he pulled the emergency brake and used too much brake pressure to stop. The blow out of the tires caused the plane to swerve sharply off the runway and into a field. Dawg was very lucky that day and walked away. The F/A-18 is known for flipping once it leaves a prepared surface, especially on blown tires.

Yet again, because Dawg had prior experience, his mistakes were overlooked. No SOD was issued, and in fact, his nearly fatal escapade was the big joke of the squadron. As the instructors did a skit about the accident in front of the entire squadron and hammed it up, I felt a little bitter that his mistakes were fun and games, but my lesser errors might cost me my career. About a year later, Dawg deployed on an aircraft carrier. One night, as he was making his final approach to the carrier, Dawg flew into the water, and the wreckage was never recovered. I can't help wondering that had the instructors paid closer attention to his mistakes and maybe sent him to a FNAEB, he would still be alive.

The younger guys were by far not making all the mistakes; the senior pilots had their fair share of screw-ups as well. The most talked about incident during my time in training was the Admiral Allen canopy incident. The head of all the Navy's air assets for the Atlantic region, Admiral Allen was a very powerful and influential flag officer. Despite the fact he was a navigator and not actually a pilot, therefore not qualified to pilot the F-18, he was allowed to fly any airplane he wanted because he owned them. Of course this is in direct violation of every safety rule the Navy has established over the past seventy-five years, but hey, he's the head honcho and Admiral Allen got whatever he wanted.

So Admiral Allen decided he wanted to fly one of my squadron's two-seater F/A-18s. Everyone kowtowed in response and sprang into action. In no time, he had a brief cockpit checkout in the simulator and then the admiral was in the front cockpit of a plane he had no idea how to fly. Because Admiral Allen was not a pilot, the squadron wisely decided to put an instructor in his back seat. As the Admiral and the young officer taxied out of the parking area, headed to the runway, the Admiral decided to put the canopy down. In a moment of sheer thoughtlessness, the Admiral grabbed the wrong handle and jettisoned the canopy. Good thing he didn't make that mistake in-flight! Cost to the taxpayers for an Admiral's joyride that never left the ground? Well over one hundred thousand dollars.

Also during this same period, one of the best "friendly fire" stories took place over Bosnia. Two F/A-18's wrapped up their patrol over Bosnia and headed back to the carrier. The pilot of the lead plane of the carrier was the Commanding Officer of the squadron and his wingman, "Spuds" McKenzie, was making his first cruise. The "Rules of Engagement" for that area dictated that all F/A-18s would always have their arming switch on in the case of emergencies. In the F/A-18, if the arming switch is on and the trigger is pulled, a missile will come off the rails. Like a wild dog in a meat market, the missile will try to kill the first plane it sees, no matter whose side it is on.

So as the planes went "feet wet" (transitioned from land to water), the CO told Spuds that since they had extra gas, they would engage in some training. They engaged in a 1-v-1 dogfight, and Spuds got the jump on the Commanding Officer. Spuds was a nugget so he was pumped that he was about to get a lock on the more experienced senior officer. Spuds out maneuvered the Commanding Officer, and "got the tone" which means he was within range for a kill. He immediately pulled the trigger, and much to his chagrin, a real missile came off the rails and headed for his Commanding Officer. Spuds forgot to dearm his missiles on the "feet wet" call and now he was about to kill the man who wrote his evaluations.

Whenever a real weapon is either shot or dropped from the F/A-18, a camera is automatically activated to record the event. Spuds watched breathlessly as the heat seeking missile tracked his CO. God was smiling on Spuds that day because the missile ran out of momentum just as it reached the CO's plane and fell just short of impact. The CO, completely unaware of his near demise, radioed Spuds to join back up and head home. Spuds, realizing someone would eventually notice a missing missile, told his CO in flight that a missile "fell off" his plane. His Commanding Officer, no dummy, asked if it fell off or did he shoot it off? Spuds meekly told him he shot it off.

When they landed on the carrier, the CO walked straight to Spuds' plane and confiscated the tape that recorded the entire event. He put it in a tape player and watched in horror as Spuds almost killed him. He was understandably angry at Spuds, but after he calmed down, he decided that "boys will be boys" and Spuds is still flying today.

Not all pilots in my squadron were so lucky with mishaps. The instructors in my squadron routinely found themselves in expensive and embarrassing accidents. Instructors of VFA-106 are supposedly chosen for their expertise and professionalism. In truth, assignment to various squadrons is very much "who you know" and is just as political as any corporate assignment. One day, two of these "golden hair children" found themselves in quite a predicament that was hard to explain.

Two instructors, Horse and Ozzy, took a two-seater F/A-18 to a small airfield in western Florida for the weekend. Because the runway was shorter than the regulations required, they requested and received a special waiver to land at this airport. After a fantastic weekend of fun in the sun, they met at the airfield to prepare for the quick flight home. The weather was clear in Jacksonville so landing at home wouldn't be a problem. However, the weather for takeoff was far less than desired.

Earlier that morning, thunderstorms swept through the area and dark, ominous clouds still filled the horizon. To make matters worse, the last shower dumped a vast amount of water on the airport in just a short time, leaving huge puddles of water scattered across the runway and taxiways. The pilots, eager to get home (what aviators call get-home-itis,) decided to press a borderline situation and take off anyway. The F/A-18 is incredibly capable with two powerful engines and a superb radar. What could go wrong?

They lined up on the runway and jammed the throttles into after-burner. The plane accelerated quickly and all seemed normal. In just a few seconds, the plane was ready to lift off. At 147 knots (166 mph), the plane drove through a large rain puddle in the middle of the runway. The pilot was trying to lift off but nothing happened. The puddle they went through was so big, it actually drowned out both engines. Horse and Ozzy found themselves in one of the worst predicaments a pilot can face. They were still moving down a runway at 120 mph, but since the engines flamed out, they couldn't take off. On most normal Navy runways, the plane can still stop because the runway is long enough. Unfortunately, this runway that required a waiver was almost half as short and there was no way they could stop in time. They departed the runway around 100 mph. They should have ejected because of the F/A-18's tendency to flip on unprepared terrain, but they elected to ride it out.

What they didn't know was that at the end of the runway, the terrain dropped off sharply, into a fifty-foot cement reservoir. God smiled again on these two who were now four-wheeling in a thirty-five million-dollar fighter jet. They eventually came to stop, right side up, unscathed. The plane however, was not so fortunate. After several million dollars worth of repairs, it was back flying. Always supportive of his instructors, the Commanding Officer was not happy with the accident, but allowed both pilots to continue to fly and instruct fledging fighter pilots.

The best example, however, of the double standard in naval aviation, is the story of the revered MIG-killer, Cowboy. In 1991, during Desert

Storm, Cowboy was one of the few lucky pilots who actually had the opportunity to shoot down an enemy aircraft. While the Iraqi's were no real threat in the air, any confrontation with an enemy aircraft armed with missiles is dangerous. Cowboy was a nugget pilot when he shot the MIG down and was immediately catapulted into hero status. Air-to-air engagements are extremely rare, and except for the brief Libya encounter in 1989, no military pilot had seen real "combat" since Vietnam.

From that moment, Cowboy could do no wrong. He received the choice jobs and was earmarked early on for greater things. After his Gulf War triumph, Cowboy rotated to VF-45 as an adversary pilot in Key West. On a sunny day with not a cloud in the sky, Cowboy took off on a solo mission. After receiving clearance for takeoff, Cowboy raced down the runway with his engines in afterburner. Just after rotation, Cowboy felt something odd. He didn't have any engine warning lights and no audio alarms went off—he just felt the aircraft settle towards the ground. Concerned that he might be experiencing some kind of catastrophic failure, Cowboy elected to eject. He pulled the ejection seat handle between his legs and with the force of 220 G's, he was rocketed clear of the plane.

The seat and parachute worked as advertised. As Cowboy floated to the ground, he expected to see a fireball that was once his F/A-18. Instead, he watched his plane, which is usually smarter than the pilot, execute the takeoff flawlessly and climb to a safe altitude. The plane continued to fly itself out to sea. It eventually ran out of gas and plunged harmlessly into the ocean.

The accident was clearly pilot error and the Navy determined this in an official investigation. Because the plane continued to operate on its own for quite sometime, it was obvious there was no catastrophic failure. Cowboy ejected out of a perfectly good airplane. Cost to taxpayers for a feeling? Thirty-five million dollars. What about the future of Cowboy? Because of his hero status, not one person blinked an eye. Cowboy's reputation, a little tarnished, held strong and he continued to not only fly, but also instruct students. Cowboy will no doubt command a squadron of F/A-18s one day, if not an entire air wing.

The Navy would like the public to believe that these "accidental" losses and mishaps like the LCDR Stacy Bates crash in Nashville that killed four innocent people, are one-time anomalies. The truth is, LCDR Bates is only one of many pilots who are allowed second and third chances, at the expense of millions of dollars and civilian lives. The problem lies within the bravado that must accompany individuals who risk their lives every day, and the culture of the excessively macho fighter pilot environment. Military aviation unwittingly breeds reckless behavior and a devil-may-care approach to life. For example, senior pilots often berate less experienced pilots for not having any "balls" and occasionally goad these nugget pilots into "flathatting." During my flying career, this type of flathatting was encouraged and expected. Senior pilots turned a blind eye to this behavior, again with the excuse "boys will be boys."

The Gondola incident in Italy is a perfect example of this phenomenon. On 3 February 1998, a US Marine EA-6B was flying in a mountainous region in Italy. It was flying well below the authorized altitude and much faster than the approved maximum speed. The pilot and navigator elected to deviate from their course and fly through a valley which unbeknownst to them, was home to one of Italy's most popular ski resorts. Dropping well below the authorized altitude, the pilot flew through the resort valley and in doing so, sliced a gondola cable with the tail of the aircraft—sending twenty innocent civilians to their deaths who were in a cable car suspended three hundred feet above the valley floor.

I laughed several weeks later when a general in the Marine Corps said in all his thirty years of flying, he never knew of any pilot going below an authorized altitude. It always amazes me when senior officers can lie so effortlessly to the press. During my time in both A-4's and F/A-18's, we were routinely encouraged by senior pilots to turn our "squawk off."

On every aircraft, there is a transmitter that tells the local controlling authorities what the plane's altitude is. This transmission is called a squawk, and when this piece of equipment is turned off, controllers have no idea what a plane's altitude is.

Not only was this procedure to turn the squawk off encouraged by senior and instructor pilots, many of these flights were videotaped for posterity. Most squadrons have a video compilation of these "illegal" flights, which are set to music. They are very cool and highly motivating. The maneuvers include incredibly low flying, acrobatic stunts, and other such showman type flying. Most pilots keep an individual copy as a remembrance of "the good old days." The crew of the EA-6B was no different, and the video camera found in the cockpit after the accident would be their death knell. Interestingly though, by the time the accident investigators got the tape, it was mysteriously erased. For this, the pilot and navigator were essentially convicted of a felony—obstruction of justice. While found innocent of the twenty manslaughter charges, the pilot was sentenced to six months in prison for his role in the destruction of the tape. What about his superiors who knew and encouraged such flying? They just watched from the sidelines, thanking God it wasn't them.

So as I was preparing for my FNAEB, I thought of these recent squadron mishaps and felt somewhat comforted in the "misery loves company" theory. I didn't rejoice in the others' misfortune, but it was somewhat consoling to know that my mistakes were not nearly as serious and very salvageable. I knew I was behind but I still had no idea how serious my medical problems were or their impact on my flying. I figured I just needed extra training because of my three years out of the cockpit. If it took a FNAEB to get extra training, then that was just fine with me.

I was nervous going into the FNAEB, especially after my first meeting with the senior member of the board, CDR Ackerman. We met a day before the official starting date to go over the preliminaries. When he "read me my rights," alarm bells went off in my head. I was not allowed a military lawyer; however, I could have an "advisor" present. This advisor would not be allowed to address the board and could not speak to anyone else but me. I knew a FNAEB was a serious matter, but I did not realize the word lawyer would ever enter the picture. I never considered it prior to the preliminaries. I thought my FNAEB was to concentrate on the problems I was experiencing and how to correct them. I knew after the preliminaries that I was on a mine infested playing field.

I asked my former Marine F/A-18 pilot friend to accompany me. He was savvy, experienced, and knew the game. I knew he would be the calm in the storm. Unfortunately he traveled with work and could not juggle his schedule to make it work. However, he was engaged to a close friend of mine from the Naval Academy, Michelle. She was a navigator with an S-3 squadron also based at the same airfield with the F/A-18s. Originally the board was scheduled for three days and I was grateful she took the time to observe the FNAEB in place of her fiancée. Because of the Human Factors Board and the reading of my rights, I was very nervous about the tone of the FNAEB.

The Commanding Officer, Captain Moffit, made it very clear he did not think I should be flying. Since the CO is the person who orders the board and chooses the board members, he can certainly stack the board in his favor. When the CO sets the tone prior to a FNAEB that he doesn't want a pilot, that pilot is history. I knew this going into my board, but always the optimist, I felt the truth would come out and I would soon be flying again.

The Field Naval Aviation Board consists of four members. The senior member is usually a Commander (O-5). My senior member, CDR Ackerman, was another F/A-18 pilot who was on the Airwing staff. The other two pilots on the board were instructors from VFA-106. One instructor was a guy I knew from the Naval Academy, Nose, and the other was a pilot I flew with while stationed in Japan. His callsign was Zoomie because he flew for the Air Force before switching over to the

Navy. I did not know either very well and thought nothing of their presence on the board. The final member of the board is a flight surgeon. He is assigned to the board as a medical consultant, especially if medical issues are a factor. I vaguely knew the flight surgeon, who was not the same flight surgeon who sat on my Human Factors Board. I had not really interacted with any of the FNAEB members so I had no real opinion of them.

During the preliminaries for the FNAEB, CDR Ackerman told me I was allowed to ask instructors to testify on my behalf. When I asked him how many instructors I needed to testify, he told me three was the usual number. I found three instructors whom I flew repeatedly with and asked them is they would support me at the FNAEB. All three were very supportive and agreed to speak on my behalf. So on the first day of the FNAEB, I was told my three choices would be the first people to testify. Not sure of the usual format of a FNAEB, I readily agreed. CDR Ackerman also told me the proceedings would be tape recorded by not one but two recorders.

The first instructor to testify was Luke, the same instructor who earlier said that I was a dog. We flew together often and the flights were always outstanding. Luke was a superb instructor who knew how to reach out and make students understand some of the more ambiguous problems. He was a senior officer who was highly respected in the squadron. He held all the qualifications a pilot could hold and was essentially an instructor's instructor. I felt that Luke's speaking on my behalf would carry a lot of weight with the other instructors.

In his statement to the board, Luke stated, "I have observed many NATOPS check rides, and I was duly impressed with her systems knowledge during the brief. Airborne, I was again impressed with her emergency procedures and decision making in an extremis situation. I considered the evolution significantly above average..."

He was asked to address my ability to socially interact with the other pilots. I thought this was an odd turn in the line of questioning, but I was pleased with Luke's response, "Shrew is quite capable of accepting a good natured ribbing, as well as administering one…LT Cummings' gender was never an issue, and I am confident it will not arise unless another officer were to make unprofessional intimations." He went on to say he would be glad to serve with me in the fleet.

I felt better after Luke's testimony. Since he was such a senior pilot and so highly regarded, I felt his words would have a lasting impact. The next instructor to testify was Barney. He was the same instructor who explained to me just what I was doing wrong in the air-to-air phase, which led to some superb flights. He was another senior instructor who was qualified in all phases of instruction and looked at as the wise man on the mountain. Barney was a squadron favorite both professionally and socially so I felt good that he was on my team.

Barney was complimentary of my flight performance overall, but again, instead of concentrating on flight related issues, he was asked about my socialization skills. Both Michelle and I started to see a clear pattern. The FNAEB members did not want to look too hard at the flying issues, they wanted the "dirt." Barney responded to these questions by stating, "It is my opinion that LT Cummings is carrying too much baggage by appearing to bear the weight of the whole female community on her shoulders…"

Barney knew how much the pressure on me was increased by the death of Kara Hultgren, and he too saw the change in the way I was treated by the guys. He always told me to just shake it off and ignore the guys. I tried my best but it is very hard when the instructors who vehemently oppose women in combat aircraft are the same instructors who are supposed to assign objective grades.

The last of the "good guys" was Rooster. He was a Marine instructor pilot who witnessed the entire Fallon incident with the Commander. Despite his close evaluation of my flying performance during several events, he was not asked to comment at all on my flight performance. The only questions the board asked him were related to the confrontation that occurred between Lizard and me. Rooster said, "LT Cummings formally apologized to [Lizard]...everyone left that meeting pleased that all the issues relating to the verbal assault charge had been resolved...I recall speaking to LT Cummings on numerous occasions following this incident when she expressed to me her regret concerning this issue and the publicity it had attained."

He went on to agree with Barney that I was putting too much pressure on myself, especially after the JAG investigation over the Fallon incident. In his written statement, he said, "I believe she takes her training too seriously and is in need of lightening up a little." He said he thought I needed to take a swig of Jack Daniel's before a flight to relax a little bit. I couldn't have agreed more. During my flights I was very tense, especially after all the trouble started. Because Rooster cared about his students, he recognized this trait of mine. Because of his unassuming nature, when I flew with Rooster, I flew very well.

After the three good guys spoke, the board took a break. Michelle and I thought it was going well, despite the board's unusual interest into my social interactions. We both agreed that it was odd that so much time was spent on my personal dealings with others instead of the obvious more important flight related issues. During the next segment of questioning, instructors that were chosen by the board would testify. I was not allowed to know ahead of time who would be testifying "against me," so the rest of the proceedings were a mystery to me.

After the break, it was Elvis's turn to testify. Behind Elvis's back, the students called him Iago after the annoying parrot in the recently released Disney movie, Aladdin. Elvis took great pride in giving the students a hard time about everything, but because his voice was so irritating, no one paid much attention to his rantings. As soon as Elvis began his rehearsed testimony, I knew I was in serious trouble.

Elvis's testimony began with a fairly accurate portrayal of my flight performance. Despite having only flown three flights with me, he said I was inconsistent. One day I would fly extremely well, but the next day

I would make uncharacteristic mistakes. Despite his hearsay based opinion, I agreed with him. Those days I felt well, I flew well. Those days that I tried to steal naps in the ladies' room were not the best flying days for me.

After a brief discussion of my flying abilities, the discussion turned again to my social skills. Elvis was outraged that I used someone's first name instead of his callsign. He felt that I constantly violated "Ready Room Etiquette" by sometimes forgetting to use a callsign instead of a first name. I found this particularly hypocritical on his part because he often referred to other pilots by their first names. He also stated that he "heard" I was confrontational with other instructors although his personal experiences instructing me were positive.

The callsign versus first name business in the Human Factors Board report confused me, but at least now I knew where it was coming from. I was shocked and concerned that such a trivial issue was turning into a central focus point for my FNAEB. I was struggling in some training areas and I desperately wanted to do better. Why were we wasting so much time on such inane topics? Elvis was only the beginning of a long train of personal attacks.

The group of witnesses the next day that testified were a complete surprise to me. The board chose to interview other students and instructors that never flew with me. I was completely dumbfounded. Why would other students be allowed to testify about my flight performance? Even more disturbing were the instructors that testified who never flew with me.

Peeper, the student who loved to watch women through keyholes, was the first student to testify. He readily stated, "I did not have the opportunity to fly with her so [I cannot] comment on her overall performance." He was however, asked to comment on the instructors' treatment of me. I though this was a very strange occurrence. Peeper was still a student going through training. What was he going to say? He certainly was not about to say anything negative about the instructors since they were the ones questioning him. His comment was that the instructors' professionalism was "impeccable."

The other student who was asked to testify was Lizard. Again, he knew nothing of my flying performance. His testimony, which appeared very rehearsed, centered on our social interactions in Fallon. He submitted a three page written statement, of which one entire page was devoted to the length of my hair. He also addressed the "verbal assault" incident, again denying any wrongdoing. He summarized his written statement by saying he would not want to serve with me in the future because of my "questionable allegations" towards him. Interesting enough, after I queried him, he reluctantly admitted that he knew I begged the Commanding Officer not to hold the JAG investigation. He said, "[she stated] she did not wish to jeopardize my career in any way."

The last person to testify before the board concluded for the day was an instructor who never flew with me, Rat. His testimony contained some very enlightening information. For the first time in the FNAEB proceedings, my master's degree from the Naval Postgraduate School was mentioned. Rat was irritated that I wanted to be an astronaut one day. I knew right away where this was coming from. The only person I ever discussed my NASA desires with was Road, a fellow student who also aspired to be an astronaut. I only knew Rat in passing so it was obvious Road told him about my astronaut dreams. Clearly he and a number of others were very resentful of my NASA goals, which is very ironic because a large number of astronauts come from the Navy's tactical aviator ranks. Apparently it was acceptable for the male pilots to aspire to the rank of astronaut—but it was a sin of unspeakable magnitude for me to consider it.

Rat, who admitted hearing all these statements third hand, went on to complain about my hair and said I was resentful of criticism. He openly acknowledged he never really talked to me and had never flown with me. Despite his lack of interaction with me, he went on to say he would not want to serve with me in the future.

Rat's entire testimony was ludicrous. It was incredulous that someone who readily admitted he had absolutely no interaction with me in the squadron was testifying against me. There was no doubt at this point in the proceedings what was happening. The instructors did not "like" me. Very little time was actually spent discussing my flight performance, which should have been the primary focus. Instead, the majority of questions dealt with my social interactions, conversations, and life goals. One instructor even said he wouldn't want to serve with me not because of my flying skills, but because "she's no fun to hang around."

As mad as I was that these instructors were focusing on trivial matters, I didn't really have much time to dwell on the injustices. The FNAEB was temporarily suspended because an internal medicine doctor reviewed my medical record and was very alarmed. Several weeks after lab tests indicated something was wrong with me, I was finally allowed to seek medical treatment for what the doctor thought might be an ulcer. I was amazed at my bad timing and luck. Not only was I now facing an antagonistic and fated FNAEB, but I was also simultaneously struggling with very serious health problems. I never understood adversity better than I did at that extremely low point in my life.

While the FNAEB members were deliberating over the mountain of evidence they accumulated and what their next move would be, I was in the hospital so the doctors could have a look in my stomach. When I went in for the Endoscope, I was nervous. I don't like sedation and I was to be knocked out for the procedure. After a long day in the hospital, the doctor briefed me on his findings. My stomach was grossly normal, meaning it looked fine with no ulcers. I looked at him quizzically. What did this mean? If I was losing that much blood, where was it coming from? He told me, "the other end." I was still a little groggy and didn't quite catch on. He told me he wanted me to come in the next day for a lower GI series. It wasn't until later when I came to my senses that I fully realized what was involved.

I showed up the next day really dreading the morning. There is nothing more humiliating than a lower GI series, otherwise known as a barium enema. During the course of the test, I heard the doctor say, "What's that? Hmmm, I am going to have to get someone else take a look at this." I knew I was in trouble when a team of radiologists came in. They were very focused, not on my gastrointestinal track, but on a huge mass that appeared on the X-rays.

After some low whispers and much discussion, the doctors told me what they thought. It appeared that a tumor was growing on my right ovary. They weren't sure exactly what it was but it wasn't supposed to be there. They concluded the barium enema and rushed me to the ultrasound room. Because Navy medicine is socialized health care, whenever a patient is rushed, it means something is seriously wrong.

While the doctor was performing the ultrasound, he began to assuage my fears. I immediately thought of cancer and he told me, "Well, we can't be sure right now, but I don't think it's malignant. Usually tumors this large on the ovary are benign. They are what we call teratomas. However, you are definitely going to need to see a surgeon about this." My surgery was scheduled for three weeks later and the FNAEB would reconvene immediately.

I was very nervous about the upcoming surgery. After I left the hospital, I went to the clinic to find Gonzo, the flight surgeon from my FNAEB. I was concerned how this might affect my flight status and I hoped he could provide me a better explanation. The doctor at the hospital told me I was likely to lose my right ovary and I was unsure how serious that might be.

When I told Gonzo what the doctors said, he said nothing. He asked me to leave the room while he made some phone calls. He brought me back in to tell me my medical problems would have no impact on my FNAEB. He said my condition was not serious and would not answer any more of my questions. I was summarily dismissed, now concerned not just about the FNAEB, but also with the potential outcome of my pending surgery.

As I was leaving the clinic, I ran into Kevin. The last time I saw him was in Fallon when we curled up on my bed and he told me he was "f—king lethal." He was waiting on his wife who was getting her annual physical. He asked me how everything was going. I told Kevin that not only was I in the middle of a FNAEB, but I was facing, at the minimum, the loss of an ovary and potentially something more serious. What I said to him did-n't even register because he cut me off, saying, "I am sure you'll be fine. Let me tell you my great news."

Kevin was clearly very excited and I figured something really big was on the horizon. I asked, "Is your wife pregnant?" He wrinkled his face in obvious distaste and said, "No, nothing like that. I got TOPHOOK of the quarter!!!!!!!" Kevin looked at me, waiting for the joyful accolades he thought should follow. The TOPHOOK award goes to the person who has the best landing grades for a given period. TOPHOOK of the quar-ter is nothing to sneeze at but the awards that really carry a lot of weight are the TOPHOOK of a cruise or of the year awards.

I looked at Kevin in disbelief. I just told him my wings were on the line and I was having serious surgery to remove a tumor and the best he could say was, "I got TOPHOOK of the quarter?" This was his fantastic news? I knew right at that moment the person I used to think was my soulmate no longer existed. The caring and compassionate Kevin died and was now replaced with a shallow, self-centered Stepford pilot. He didn't care about anyone else but himself and had really lost touch with reality. I cried as I drove home that night, mostly because of the stress of the FNAEB and pending surgery, but Kevin's complete conversion to the "dark side" really got to me as well.

When I got home, I did some research and found out that ter-atomas are also called dermoid cysts. These typically large tumors originate from epithelium cells that are responsible for the growth of hair and teeth. I was comforted to read that my condition was not life threatening. The general surgeon later told me he would make a small bikini line incision and remove the tumor. They would send it to the lab to be checked for malignancy right away. I would be out of commission for about a month, but my recovery should be complete. The only drawback would be the loss of the ovary. I wasn't eager to have any children so I wasn't too concerned.

After I calmed myself reading about my condition, I refocused on the FNAEB. I did not know how many more instructors would testify and was still unsure where the whole process was headed. Because we had not really discussed any flight-related issues, I felt that I was being punished for my heinous callsign sins and the Fallon incident. I still felt sure the board would recommend probation, especially in light of the unfolding medical conditions. I was obviously a sick person who probably shouldn't have been flying these past few months. I looked forward to bringing the FNAEB to an end, having the surgery, and getting my life back on track. How naive I was!

The next day of the FNAEB consisted of more testimony from instructors who did not support me. I was infuriated that the deck was so clearly stacked. The board members encouraged every person that testified to relay all rumors they heard, even if they were unsubstantiated. I was also quite cognizant of the fact the senior member of the board told me to find three witnesses to speak on my behalf, yet they found ten people to testify against me. Several of these instructors testified that, in their opinion, I was a below average pilot. I found it interesting that these were the same instructors who graded me well above average on the flights they personally flew with me.

What I found most disturbing were the phrases repeated by almost of all the pilots who testified against me. It was clear to my advisor, Michelle, and me that someone was telling them what to say prior to their official testimony. Many of their repeated phrases sounded mantra-like; "She's aggressive," "She's confrontational," and "She doesn't fit in." Many of the testimonies were very similar, especially those of instructors who couldn't offer specific instances of any poor performance on my part, only that they "heard" I was difficult.

The absolute most ludicrous testimony came from Comet, the same instructor who was responsible for blowing the "verbal assault" issue out of proportion. He was also the same instructor who originally passed me on my NATOPS checkride and then rescinded the passing grade three days later. During his FNAEB testimony, Comet did not really address the actual checkride. The primary gist of his allegations centered on what happened when I confronted him about changing the grade.

Comet, a man who stands 6'4" and weighs approximately 240 pounds, testified that I stormed in the Ready Room and dragged him to the navigation room. He then said I backed him up against a wall, stuck my finger in his chest, and had a "one-way conversation" with him. As Comet was relaying this story, it was difficult to suppress my laughter at his ridiculous allegations. I could not believe Comet was lying so blatantly. What originated as a professional discussion now had become a scene from the movie *Fatal Attraction*.

I also found it very funny that a fighter pilot who outweighs me by a 100 pounds and is a foot taller was telling everyone that I threatened him. Michelle also found his testimony comical but we were even more shocked when one of the board members interrupted, "So what you are saying Comet is that LT Cummings bullied and intimidated you?" He replied in a meek, browbeaten manner, "Yesssss, she did."

During the next break Michelle and I shared a good laugh over his comments. A seasoned fighter pilot and a supposed killing machine just testified that a short, blond girl practically raped him. It was so outlandish that I never even suspected anyone would take him seriously. I knew Comet was going through a very rough divorce and chalked his behavior up as hatred towards all women. Little did I know that his testimony would be the backbone of the board's case.

Comet then went on to testify that I was the worst pilot he ever flew with, despite the fact that he personally graded me well above average on all our flights together. He also suggested to the board that I was sleeping with a senior officer in another squadron. I had no idea who he was talking about but it was clear he believed I was sleeping my way through the program. This comment really angered me because I had not dated anyone in almost a year and wondered how these guys dreamed up these ridiculous scenarios.

Comet finished his testimony by telling the board I was keeping a journal in which I recorded everything that occurred in the Ready Room. At first, I did not know what he was talking about, but as he continued I remembered the event. One Saturday afternoon, I was the duty officer. This required me to be in the squadron all day, with absolutely no one else around and nothing to do. I took my laptop with me and spent part of the dead time catching up in my journal, a hobby I have had since I was six.

Comet stopped in the squadron to check his mail and stopped to talk with me. I let him read part of my journal in which I was writing about a friend's divorce. He went on to tell me all about his divorce, including such specifics as child support payments, lawyer's fees and other sordid details about his break up. One of the reasons I confided to Comet about the Lizard affair was because he spilled his guts to me that day and I thought we were friends. Clearly that was not the case because he went on to say in the FNAEB that I was "immoral" for keeping a journal and I was only doing it to later file sexual harassment charges.

Comet's farcical testimony wrapped up the instructors' part in the FNAEB. All that remained was my testimony before the board, which would be held the next day. Typically, this final portion of the FNAEB takes about an hour and is used to clarify any outstanding questions the board members might have. For my FNAEB, which was already setting never before seen precedents, I testified for five hours, fielding questions that ranged from my private life to my career goals. Yet again, very little time was spent actually discussing flying issues. It seemed that the board was far more interested in my life outside the squadron.

Several members of the board spent a lot of time questioning me about my time in the Philippines and also in Monterey, California. They were particularly interested in how I got my callsign, "Shrew." Both Michelle and I thought it odd that the board seemed preoccupied with events that occurred five years prior. However, not ever having experienced a FNAEB before, I did not know what was SOP (Standard Operating Procedure).

As far as my time in VFA-106, the two events that received the most attention during my testimony to the FNAEB had nothing to do with flying. The first concerned the supposed "verbal assault" charges against Lizard. Despite the fact that I reiterated I wished it never occurred, each of the board members chastised me further for almost ruining the career of a senior officer. The senior member of the board offered the most enlightening but chilling parallel. He wanted to know what I would do in the future if I had a poor landing on the carrier and the Commanding Officer threw me up against a wall in his frustrations with my performance.

I was speechless with this hypothetical situation. It never occurred to me that physical violence was something I would encounter as an officer. I stumbled my way through an answer, stating that I of course would just take it and say nothing. What else was I going to say in front of a group of men in complete control of my destiny?

The second focus point for the FNAEB was the article incident that occurred during the Key West detachment. Most instructors mentioned the incident in their testimonies and they were clearly outraged that I ever said anything about it. The board members also again expressed their displeasure with the way I handled the situation. They were angry that I removed the article from the very public board, despite the fact that I only removed it to show it to another male pilot and left it with him. I was truly bewildered with the animosity over this incident. I never said anything to anyone about the article except to my supposed friend and peer, Mark Dunleavy. During the FNAEB, the chain of events in Key West became clear. Mark apparently told not only his squadron mates about our discussion, he also told several instructor pilots in my squadron. Whether intentional or not, Mark sealed my fate because it seemed that this one incident was the final straw that led to my FNAEB. Maybe the Tailhook affair and his father's fallen angel status impacted Mark more than I thought.

One of the board members tried to explain everyone's anger with the following analogy. "Let's say you went to a barbecue at a friend's house. While you were in the kitchen, you saw an article on the refrigerator about abortion you did not agree with? Would you take it down? I knew I was in a lose-lose situation so I told the board I accepted their point and knew I was in the wrong. However, I was deeply disturbed with the underlying concepts. My seniors and peers saw nothing wrong with posting derogatory articles against women in very public government spaces. One instructor said it best when he said I violated the squadron's "sacred ground" by removing the article. That apparently was the feeling of even the most senior officers. I knew then that it would be a long time before women would ever be accepted into the fighter pilot ranks.

After the grueling five-hour inquisition, I was allowed to leave. Both Michelle and I thought my testimony went well, especially in light of the extreme statements of some of the instructors. We both took notes throughout the entire proceeding, but put them aside. Despite the negative slant of the board, we both thought it was just a tool to punish me for my transgressions. We agreed that I would probably be awarded probation status, especially in light of the unfolding medical problems.

The next day, I started to suspect that maybe this assumption was not correct. The senior member of the FNAEB briefed me that a member of the board was contacting other pilots from VC-5, my squadron in the Philippines, to testify. I later found out that one of my FNAEB members was a close friend of the same pilot in VC-5 whose job I was given because of his incompetence. It was not unheard of to ask a previous Commanding Officer to comment on a pilot's previous performance but contacting peers from several years earlier for statements was extremely rare.

The picture started to clear for me. The board was attempting to discredit me by any means possible. Because they did not really have enough flight related information to remove me from flight status, they were trying to annihilate my character and reputation. I expressed my concerns to the senior member, who was a man in his mid-forties. I will never forget how he looked me straight in the eye and said, " I know this board got out of hand. I am not sure about a lot of the testimony, but I know and respect Luke. If he says you're a good pilot, then I am inclined to believe him."

I felt a lot better after our talk and left his office again feeling positive about the outcome. The senior member was cognizant of the shenanigans of some of the guys and would rise above the fray to do the right thing. What I did not know was how malleable he was and how other people's opinions swayed him.

The next afternoon I was called in to report to the boardroom. The decision was in and it was formally read aloud. I was told to stand at attention in front of the board members while the following verdict was read:

1. The Board unanimously recommends that LT Cummings' flight status be terminated under category B. If allowed to continue service in naval aviation, she will sooner or later be the cause of the loss of aircraft, or loss of life, or both.

2. The Board further unanimously recommends that LT Cummings' flight status be terminated with prejudice under sub-category 2. Her pattern of making misleading and false official statements is dishonorable to naval aviation. To allow LT Cummings to retain the insignia of a Naval Aviator would be offensive and disrespectful to the tradition of honorable Naval aviators who have proudly worn the badge.

3. Based on an overwhelming preponderance of evidence against
LT Cummings' integrity, the Board unanimously recommends that
the Commanding Officer of Strike Fighter Squadron ONE ZERO
SIX consider further investigation.

As the verdict was read, I was in shock. After the Commander read
the results, I was dismissed. I about-faced and walked out of the room.
As I walked to my car, I began to understand the full ramifications of
the verdict. The board recommended that I not only lose my flight status, but also that my hard-earned wings of gold be stripped from me. In
addition, I had absolutely no idea what the board meant by false official
statements. Not once during any of the proceedings did anyone confront me with conflicting testimony. Finally, I realized that the board
meant for me to go to a court martial for "evidence against LT
Cummings' integrity." Through the course of the FNAEB, I witnessed
several instructors blatantly lie about their dealings with me, suffered
through some of the most humiliating moments of my life, and MY
integrity was called into question?

I did not shed one tear that night. I knew whatever they were accusing my of was untrue and I would be able to prove it. Always the fighter,
I vowed that I would battle this absurd FNAEB, all the way to the Chief
of Naval Operations if needed. Over the next few days as I struggled to
develop a plan of attack, my physical state deteriorated quickly, and my
surgery loomed on the horizon. Without a doubt, it was the lowest
point in my life.

The potential impact of the corrupt and malicious FNAEB on my
career sometimes overwhelmed me. My distress and fears were only
made worse by my realization that maybe my four years at the Naval
Academy were nothing but propaganda and brainwashing. All the
preaching and teaching about honor and integrity rang hollow in my
ears. There wasn't anything honorable about watching both my peers
and superiors lie so blatantly and try to burn me at the stake. This

FNAEB was heart wrenching not only because of the possible blow to my career, but it was the moment in my life that I realized what disillusionment, hypocrisy and mental indoctrination were really all about.

Chapter Thirteen

The Demoralizer

The recommendations of the FNAEB members are fortunately not final. Like every administrative procedure in the Navy, all senior officers in the chain of command must review the board's recommendations. The Chief of Naval Operations, the number one man in the Navy, is the only person authorized to remove a pilot's wings. This appeal process can take several weeks at a minimum and sometimes can drag on for a year or more.

My first step in the appeal process was to actually receive a copy of the FNAEB report. Once I received the report, I was given five days to respond. The senior officer review would take place once I rebutted the FNAEB. The week I was forced to wait for a copy of the report was the longest week of my life. I was left completely in the dark the entire week, and not one person from VFA-106 spoke to me about the board or anything else for that matter.

So I waited. Not one person from the squadron offered any words of encouragement, either for the FNAEB or my upcoming surgery. I slept and ate very little. I knew my flying career was over along with my future in the Navy. I was a Naval Academy graduate with a master's degree in Astronautical Engineering and hundreds of flight hours. It was a bitter pill for me to swallow that a few individuals could so easily destroy my career.

When I finally received a copy of the report, I sat down in a nearby office and quickly perused it. In less than ten minutes of scanning the report, I knew there was no way the recommendation would stand. The report was so poorly written and so clearly biased that I knew that no senior officer would attach his name to it. In just those ten minutes, my stomach knot went away, my appetite came back, and I knew I had better than a fighting chance. These guys were going down. I was a trained killer and I was going to show them what the word fighter really meant.

Before I started my rebuttal, I consulted with two very important people. The first was my friend, Andy, who was a former F/A-18 pilot. He was very astute about such dealings and provided me with some sage advice, "Don't bring up the sex issue. You are being harassed and discriminated against, but if you play the sex card, it will take away from your credibility. Just simply relay that what occurred is wrong and completely unprofessional and leave it at that. They will get the message."

The second person to give me wise advice was a Navy lawyer. Once I received the report, I took it to a Navy JAG that specialized in defense cases. When I showed the FNAEB report to him, he belly laughed. He said the Navy would be in big trouble if such a flagrant piece of discrimination were to hit the press. He told me I shouldn't worry too much because truly the FNAEB was ridiculous and someone in the chain of command would stop it. He also instructed me very carefully how to write my rebuttal. He told me to go line for line through the FNAEB and point out every error, inaccuracy, rumor, misleading statement, etc. He echoed the male pilot's sentiment about the sex card. He told me to rise above all the Neanderthal behavior and write the most professional, unemotional rebuttal possible.

I worked non-stop for the next five days formulating the rebuttal. I read the report very carefully and took copious notes. Navy reports are broken into three sections: findings of fact, opinions, and recommendations. This quasi-legal format is used for all types of reports ranging from personnel matters to accident investigations. As I combed through the FNAEB's Findings of Fact (FOF), it was clear that most of the statements were not factual; they instead were based on rumor and hearsay. The board members were clearly on their own agenda because many of the FOFs conflicted with witness statements included in the report.

The next section, the Opinions, is supposed to be taken from the FOFs, without any hint of emotion. The Opinions of my FNAEB were unbelievably prejudiced. Addressing my medical problems, the board ignored my upcoming major surgery and stated, "LT Cummings was not subject to excessive external life stresses that would adversely impact her flying performance..." Instead of addressing flight related issues, the FNAEB felt the need to revisit the Fallon confrontation. "In the Board's opinion, LT Cummings' conduct during the events which occurred at Fallon was unconscionable" and "LT Cummings has demonstrated an overly aggressive attitude toward senior Naval Officers..."

It was clear the board completely lost sight of its mission to examine flight related issues when it offered the following opinion, "LT Cummings' pattern of recurring confrontations coupled with her disregard for military and personal courtesies attests to poor development of interpersonal skills. This pattern is inconsistent with naval aviation, is disruptive to both unit cohesiveness and the establishment of a familiar working environment..."

Essentially my career was over because the warriors of VFA-106 did not like my lack of "personal courtesies." These were the same group of guys who like to burp and fart in front of each other and feed on poking fun at one another. I found the comment about "unit cohesiveness" very interesting. It reminded me of the remark the TOPGUN instructor (whom I was now flying with) made to the Presidential Commission on the Assignment of Women in the Armed Forces only two years prior. *"We don't believe that you can act as a unit unless you keep it the way it is, where it's the bonding—it's that intangible, the bonding, that makes a*

*squadron good, better, and we don't believe you can have that go on if we
have females in aviation.*" It seemed that this same group of people who
felt women prevented unit cohesion and bonding were now taking steps
to lessen the impact of their intrusion.

It was in the Opinions section that I finally found out what alleged
false official statements I made. There were conflicting testimonies
about flight qualifications I received while flying in the Philippines. I
thought the board was unusually interested about my tour in VC-5;
now I knew why. One of the FNAEB members, Zoomie, was a good
friend of one the whoremongering pilots in VC-5, Spider, who didn't
like me. Zoomie tracked Spider down in a dead end job in Texas and
asked him to testify that I was a poor pilot and liar. Since Spider was the
same person whose job I was awarded after he was fired, he was only
more than glad to help. Spider's life had not gone well after he left the
Philippines. The Navy was forcing Spider out, not for flying performance, but because he was such an incompetent officer.

I could not believe the FNAEB report based its accusations of false
official statements on the testimony of a disgruntled peer that dealt
with cloudy issues over three years ago. The board did not ask my former Commanding Officer from VC-5 or me to clarify any conflicting
issues, because they obviously just wanted to hang me. To prove my
innocence, I contacted my former CO and he supported my statements
concerning my qualifications. In his written statement, my former
Commanding Officer stated, "As her CO, I was very glad to have a junior officer of her caliber working for me; if I could have cloned her, I
would have."

Despite the flagrant and obvious flaws of the report, the board summarized their findings with the following statement, "It is the considered opinion of this Board that LT Cummings would present an
unacceptable airborne safety hazard and would destroy the good order
and morale of a fleet squadron. It is further opined that LT Cummings,

through her lack of integrity, is not suitable for service in any other naval aviation community."

I laughed when I read this statement. Yet again, this group of fighter pilots who supposedly constantly stared death in the face and emerged the victor was at my mercy. Apparently I single-handedly could do what Tokyo Rose could not, that is destroy military discipline and demoralize an entire branch of the Navy. I wish I knew prior to this time that I was so powerful.

After a good chuckle, I read the witness statements which made my blood boil. Each witness was presented with two options concerning his testimony; he could submit a written statement, or the board would summarize his oral statements from the tapes. Michelle and I took extensive notes throughout the proceedings so we knew who said exactly what. When I read several of the instructors' written statements, I was stunned. Many were dramatically different from their verbal testimony. The statements of the instructors who made positive remarks were completely changed. New topics that were never discussed in the board were introduced, and other witness statements were added from people who did not testify before the board.

I was furious that these bunglers accused me of lying while they were clearly tampering with witness testimonies. As mad as I was, when I realized this, I knew I would win the battle. Not one but two recorders taped the FNAEB. Anyone listening to the tapes and then comparing them to the written testimony would know that these hypocrites broke the law.

As I read through the individual witness statements, the last one that caught my eye was from a person who did not testify in front of the board. A person by the name of CDR Campbell submitted a written statement in lieu of personal testimony. I did not know anyone named CDR Campbell and had no idea how he related to me. When I started to read his statement, I was appalled. This Commander was the same person who accosted me outside the library at the Naval Postgraduate

School in Monterey, California to tell me he did not want my kind in his community. We were both in civilian clothes at the time so I did not know who or what rank he was.

Reading his letter was both enlightening and deeply disturbing. How did this person who never flew with me, who never worked with me professionally, and whom I didn't even know have the opportunity to testify whether or not I should be in the Navy, much less a pilot? Then I remembered. He threatened me that day by telling me he contacted the F/A-18 training squadron in California so they would be ready for me. I never gave his threats a second thought because I was headed to Florida. After I told him I was going to Jacksonville, he apparently contacted someone in the squadron to make sure they were also ready for me.

As I read his statement, so many cloudy issues became clear. CDR Campbell contacted another pilot in VFA-106, before I arrived for training, and set the stage. When the first hint of opportunity presented itself to send me to a FNAEB, the instructors jumped on it. One of the members of the FNAEB, a friend of CDR Campbell's, asked him to make a statement in an attempt to portray me as a troublemaker from years back. In Campbell's statement, he said, "[I] offered advice and information about the community. The conversation lasted no more than ten minutes with the following noted: All comments were taken defensively. My approach was resented. Her professionalism deteriorated. Nothing was accomplished. LT Cummings obviously needed to fall on her sword."

Reading his twisted account, I actually started to feel better. Now I knew where some of the hostility came from. True, I was set up before I even started training in the F/A-18, but at least now I knew just how far these guys would stoop to remove an outsider. CDR Campbell's statement alone told the story of collusion and machination in VFA-106. What I found most disconcerting was how proud the pilots were of their obvious biases and ruses. These were people who carried thousands of pounds of death and destruction at their fingertips. I found it amazing they resorted to such childish behavior against a fellow officer. Certainly the phrase "Officer and a Gentleman" was now a concept of the past.

After reading the report carefully, I started my rebuttal. The words flowed effortlessly and the actual writing was extremely cathartic. After I finished, I felt a heavy burden lifted from my shoulders. Though I was dealt a serious injustice, I could prove how malevolent and corrupt the board members were. I was a new person with hope that someone in the Navy would put a stop to this insanity.

I took the lawyer's advice and rebutted the entire report painstakingly line by line. I pointed out the majority of the seventy-eight Findings of Fact had nothing to do with my flight performance, which was supposed to be the reason for convening the FNAEB. I gave several examples of the board's preoccupation with my personal life and refuted all of the supposed false statements. I also highlighted the important medical issues that were completely ignored, and that several of the verbal testimonies were entirely opposite from the written ones.

Another very important point of my rebuttal was the actual appointing order from the Commanding Officer to the members of the FNAEB. Military law dictates that FNAEBs are administrative bodies only, stating, "The board is neither a judicial nor disciplinary body, and shall make no recommendations for disciplinary action as a result of its evaluation." Because my FNAEB recommended the Commanding Officer investigate my supposed crimes, they were stating that both judicial and disciplinary actions should be taken against me. The board member's failure to grasp the basics of their charter was clearly manifested in the totally lack of objectivity and professionalism in the report itself.

I summarized my rebuttal with the following,

> *"I greatly appreciate the opportunities given to me by the Navy and I have done my best over eleven years of service to be the finest*

*officer possible, upholding integrity, accountability and loyalty. I
feel my abilities and talents are neither appreciated nor desired in
this community. In fact, I feel this FNAEB process so far has been
an attempt to assassinate my character, destroy my credibility and
to end not only my flight career but also my naval career. I respectfully request you investigate these events and reconsider the board's
recommendations. I also respectfully request the tapes of the board
be forwarded and reviewed by an impartial third party and that I
be temporarily reassigned to another unit pending resolution of this
very complex matter."*

I asked both Andy and the lawyer to check over my response. Each
made a few comments but both thought it was very professional, factual, and unemotional—exactly opposite of the FNAEB report. My
friends, who heard about the FNAEB, rallied to my defense. Several senior officers wrote character witness letters, all expressing dismay over
the outcome of the FNAEB.

A Test Pilot School graduate and a lab partner at Postgraduate
School wrote the following, "LT Cummings is a dedicated, professional
naval officer. She is talented and assertive and the kind of aviator that
deserves the chance to fly a first rate fighter/attack aircraft...I find it
interesting that naval officers that have neither flown with LT
Cummings nor worked with her professionally have input to her
FNAEB board."

A former Commanding Officer wrote,

> *"If I could describe her in a few words, they would be; honest,
> intelligent, dedicated and professional...she is a total professional
> who will work as hard as she can to perfect her flying skills or
> become a better officer."*

Yet another Commander whom I worked for wrote, "LT Cummings
very favorably impressed me as an officer and leader whom I would be

pleased to have under my command." I appreciated the outpouring of support, especially from those senior officers with well over twenty years of experience. I hoped that the senior officers reviewing my package would appreciate the words of their peers and realize the FNAEB was completely and utterly flawed.

The last piece of documentation I submitted was a written statement from Michelle, my advisor who sat throughout the entire FNAEB. I was so grateful she was a witness to all that occurred and her testimony was invaluable in proving the overt biases of the FNAEB. Michelle addressed all the contradictory statements, discrepancies, and the focus on my personal life instead of flying. She pointed out that most of the negative testimony was based on rumor and hearsay and named those instructors who were the greatest offenders. She concluded her statements by also asserting,

> *"I am confident that once the audio tapes and the board's proceedings are reviewed, higher authority will choose to disregard the recommendation of this board and return LT Cummings to flight status."*

I then submitted my package to Captain Moffit, the Commanding Officer of my squadron who was the next person in the chain of command. My package would go to him, then the Wing Commander, and then to the Admiral who was in charge of all naval air forces on the Atlantic Coast (called AIRLANT) who was Admiral Allen. If the Admiral did not overturn the FNAEB, then it would go straight to the Chief of Naval Operations for final disposition.

Because removing a Navy pilot's wings is such serious business, I was allowed the option of discussing my FNAEB with each senior officer in the chain of command. I elected to exercise this right because I wanted both Captains and the Admiral to look me in the eye and tell me the FNAEB was fair and impartial. Because I was one of the first women fighter pilots, I knew this case was an attention-getter and I was not going to back down.

Several days later, Captain Moffit called me in to discuss his recommendation. Because he appointed the board, he enjoyed the latitude to ignore the FNAEB's report, reconvene another board, or change the recommendation. I personally felt he should reconvene a more objective board but the word in the squadron was that Captain Moffit didn't like women and wanted to see me gone. Because of his suspected attitude, I was nervous about our meeting. I was even more concerned when Captain Moffit asked me to meet with him in a completely separate building from the squadron.

When we sat down, he looked at me with a biting stare and said, "You should have been a lawyer." I actually took that as a compliment because it meant he reconsidered the board's recommendations. He then handed me his written endorsement that said,

> "LT Cummings has proven she can safely operate Naval Aircraft in certain environments. I therefore disagree with the Field Board's recommendation of Type "B" classification. The Field Board's recommendation of termination of flight status "with prejudice under sub-category 2" is not justified nor warranted. LT Cummings has done nothing in her career which would bring discredit upon naval aviation or the US Navy."

He went on to recommend that I be assigned to another aircraft. He did not specify what type, just some other aircraft other than an F/A-18. I was of course immensely relieved but I knew right away what his angle was. My former flight school roommate, Shannon, was recently kicked out of a tactical aircraft and reassigned to a more benign transport platform. It seemed the fighter community broke the code for getting rid of women; FNAEB them so they would be sent to a support flying community.

I then asked Captain Moffit why he didn't reconvene a board if he disagreed so completely with the recommendations. He told me that despite the board's "problems," he felt they got to the root of the matter. In a very condescending tone, he told me I would do much better in another community and it was a mistake that I was ever sent to F/A-18s in the first place. He then told me because the recommendation no longer involved stripping me of my wings, Admiral Allen had the final say, and so it would not go to the Chief of Naval Operations.

Before Admiral Allen reviewed my case, I was required to see the Wing Commander, Captain Fleming. Another week later, Captain Fleming called me in to discuss my case. Unlike Captain Moffit, he had not written an endorsement. He wanted to speak with me first before he made a decision. Captain Fleming wanted to know if I was still studying and practicing in the simulator. I laughed bitterly. I told him that my time was monopolized with fighting the FNAEB and seeing doctors. I reminded him what apparently everyone else either forgot or ignored; I was scheduled for major surgery in less than a week.

As his line of questioning continued, it was clear he was considering a further change to the recommendation. He wanted to send me back to flying F/A-18's in the same squadron. I think he truly felt I was dealt an unfair blow, but I told him I did not at all feel comfortable with going back to VFA-106. The instructors showed what they were capable of and I did not think I would be treated fairly or professionally if I returned. Because of my request for reassignment, Captain Fleming assigned me to his staff. Although a less formidable environment, I still felt like I was sleeping with the enemy.

Captain Fleming then dismissed me and told me to come back the next day. When I returned, he told me he changed his mind and was going to concur with the recommendation from my squadron commander. He felt both the Navy and I would be better served if I switched to another aircraft. I was not surprised and almost relieved. The

thought of being thrown back into the fire was not something I wanted
to consider.

I kept my father, who recently retired after thirty years in the Navy,
abreast of all the daily happenings. He was infuriated with the turn of
events. He could not rest until he did something to help me so he
decided to write a letter to Vice Admiral Allen, AIRLANT. The following is an excerpt,

> "To say I am concerned would be a gross understatement. I am
> outraged by the statements, by the charges, and the several contra-
> dictions by the witnesses. I requested a personal friend (a retired
> Commander and a Naval Aviator), who is familiar with these pro-
> ceedings, to review the documents. His reply, "They are on a witch
> hunt." From the tone and the areas examined by the Human
> Factors Board and the FNAEB this was not about aviation skills by
> any definition. This was about a personal vendetta, personal
> grudges, and bubbling cauldrons. The results of the Human factors
> Board were not allowed; a good indication the entire evolution was
> headed in the wrong direction from the start. It's interesting that a
> young officer who graduated from the Naval Academy, completed
> flight training, completed a tour in the A-4 Skyhawk, graduated
> from the Naval Postgraduate School and is a pack plus officer, has
> in six short months turned into Axis Annie who is threatening to
> inflict strike damage on the entire F/A-18 community.
>
> I find that the manner in which the board was conducted and the
> position taken by the members to be morally and professionally
> untenable. This has not been about holding a Human Factors Board
> and a FNAEB to determine the best for the Navy or an officer. This
> board was held with the overtones of a court-martial and conducted
> with extreme prejudice which, in my opinion, was the same way the
> training was conducted. I believe this to be part of a systematic effort
> to degrade, demoralize, and destroy another officer.

Twelve years ago LT Cummings had a choice of the Air Force Academy or the Naval Academy. Twelve years ago I recommended the Air Force because I feared this day would come. I did not think the Navy was prepared to offer a bright young girl a meaningful career. For some time I thought I was wrong, but apparently not."

After I read my dad's letter, pride and love welled up in me. The old adage, "The apple doesn't fall too far from the tree" held true here. His sense of outrage and injustice so closely mirrored my own that I was amazed at how linked we were in sprit. I always thought of my dad as "old school" and not too thrilled with the influx of women into the military. Now he was leaping to my defense, to protect his child who had been so clearly wronged by the organization to which my dad devoted thirty years.

After Captain Fleming attached his endorsement to my FNAEB package, he sent it to Admiral Allen for the final disposition. In the lull between reviews, I was to undergo surgery. Because of the seriousness of abdominal operation, I was to receive a month of convalescent leave. The continuation of the FNAEB review was put on hold while I recovered.

I was very nervous about the upcoming operation to remove the unusually large tumor on my ovary. Because my mother could not leave her job for an extended period of time without losing pay, my sponsor from the Naval Academy decided to help me through it. Sponsor families are assigned to each midshipman at USNA to provide a home away from home. I was still very close to my sponsor family and considered them surrogate parents. When Trish arrived the day before my surgery, I nearly sobbed as she hugged me. The past few weeks of the FNAEB inquisition and the medical problems took their toll on me and I was a wreck. I was very happy to see a friendly familiar face.

The squadron, including the flight surgeons, showed not even the most remote hint of compassion concerning the upcoming surgery. After assigning me to his staff, Captain Fleming told me to stay home until he contacted me with the Admiral's decision. The message was clear; the squadron wrote me off and wanted nothing more to do with me. Because of the squadron's cruel attitude, I was very surprised when Gunny visited me in the pre-op room. Gunny, short for Gunnery Sergeant, was a senior enlisted Marine who ran the flight equipment shop. Not only did Gunny and I work together, we had a little cooking competition going. He boasted that he was a far better cook than any woman. Not one to let a challenge pass, I bet him that I could surpass his culinary skills. I was a true Southern woman who made homemade biscuits, so no man, especially a Marine, would top me.

This rivalry led to the popular Officer vs. Enlisted Cookie Bake Off. We both made dozens of cookies and then asked the flight equipment junior enlisted personnel to decide. No doubt they loved the free and plentiful food, but these young sailors were no dummies. They worked for both of us so they cleverly decided to say our cookies were equally delicious. However, whenever Gunny wasn't around, they told me mine were the best! (They probably did the same for him!)

After my FNAEB, I turned in my flight gear and told Gunny about the board and pending surgery. Because no one else seemed to care, I thought he would fall in line as well. When he poked his head in my room, I was genuinely taken aback. He told me he heard all the rumors and knew better. Gunny said he was pulled aside by one of the senior officers in the squadron and was specifically told to no longer speak to me or associate with me in any fashion. Gunny, in the military for almost twenty years, recognized right away something was amiss. Despite the order of a senior officer not to speak to me, he decided to stop by the hospital and let me know not everyone hated me. He told me he had never seen the squadron go after someone so ruthlessly and really felt sorry for me. I appreciated his comments and gesture. I was glad to know someone was thinking sanely and knew I was not the Jane Fonda of the 1990's.

Despite the positive vein of the Gunny's visit, I was disturbed by the order not to speak to me. If a Commander would seek out an enlisted man to tell him to avoid me, then what were the other instructors and students told? Gunny and I talked a little more about the squadron's perceptions of me, and then it was time for me to go to surgery. As I was hooked up to the IV's and prepared for the anesthesia, I was grateful I would be unconscious for a while. Since the FNAEB, my brain was in constant motion and I needed a break.

After what seemed like seconds, I woke up in the recovery room, feeling like a freight train just ran over me. I knew that abdominal surgery involved a fairly large section of the body, but I didn't think I would be in such pain. When the doctor came in to check on me, he told me why I was in so much discomfort. While he suspected the tumor was large, he was startled with the actual size. He originally made a small incision, thinking the tumor was about the size of a golf ball. It turned out the tumor was as big as a grapefruit and weighed three pounds. Because it was so large, he essentially performed a C-section to remove it. Instead of the expected small incision, I now sported a four-inch laceration across my belly that was held together with metal staples.

I was moved to a regular room later that night and Trish was at my bedside to comfort me. The next day, I managed to get up with some help and move around. When I proved to the doctors I was stable enough to go home, they let me go. As I was waiting for my discharge papers, the doctor wrote out my convalescent leave papers. Despite the fact he previously told me I needed a month to recover, he instead only gave me a week. I was surprised as was his resident doctor accompanying him on rounds. When queried he replied, "Your command asked me to return you to work as soon as possible. Apparently they need you for some reason."

I was infuriated. I could not believe the squadron now mandated my recovery period. I wondered what was in store for me if I was only allowed a week to recover? When I called Captain Fleming, I found out. Admiral

Allen, stationed in Norfolk, Virginia, wanted to see me as soon as possible. I hoped to be back to normal soon, but I knew a week was not enough time to recover. Later that night, a friend of mine who is an OB/GYN doctor called to check in on me. When Steve heard what happened, he was outraged. He told me that the standard of care recommended four to six weeks recovery period for this type of surgery, especially for such an unusual case. I decided not to say anything and go along with the Navy's plan. I wanted nothing more than to put the FNAEB behind me and I would be able to travel regardless.

My week of recovery was slow. Trish and I rented movies and walked a little bit. The best part of the week was letting Trish drive me around in my Jeep Wrangler. Trish, a woman accustomed to driving Mercedes, rose to the occasion and after a week was ready for a Jeep Jamboree. I tried not to think too much about the FNAEB because when I did, I felt worse. After a week passed, I was able to get around on my own and I sent Trish home. I was to leave in just a few days for Virginia so there was no reason for her to stay.

The night I dropped Trish at the airport, I felt very ill. I chalked up my sick feelings to the increased activity and decided to go to bed early. Sometime in the middle of the night, I woke up and my head was pounding. When I couldn't get back to sleep, I decided to go to the bathroom.

That was the last thing I remembered when I woke up on the bathroom floor. I was dazed and confused. Why was I on the bathroom floor and why was my head pounding? Light filled the room so dawn came and went. When I was able to focus, I sat up and looked around. Blood was everywhere—I immediately thought of my incision. When I looked at my belly, the staples looked fine and there was no blood. Still disconcerted, I reached up to rub my head that still was pounding. As I ran my hand through my wet and sticky hair, I figured out where the blood was coming from. When I passed out, I hit my head on the way down. I now sported a gash across the back of my head that was still bleeding.

I called a neighbor who rushed me to the hospital. After stopping the bleeding and taking X-rays, the doctors determined I suffered a concussion. They decided my loss of consciousness was due to my recovery from surgery. The X-rays didn't show anything alarming so they agreed to let me go home. Now I really felt ill. I was still moving slowly from the surgery and my head permanently ached. When I crawled back into bed that night, I curled up in the fetal position, wondering what I did to deserve such punishment. Unfortunately my trials were far from over.

Three days later I was packing for my trip to Virginia. I was forced to buy a new suitcase on rollers because I could not lift anything and wondered how I would get around once in Norfolk. As I was doing laundry, I felt a searing pain in my abdomen. I immediately sat down and looked at my incision. The staples came out just a few days prior and now half the incision burst open and pink fluid was gushing out of the exposed wound. For the second time in three days, I was rushed back to the emergency room.

After the doctors drained the wound, taped it back together, and put me on antibiotics, they let me go. The surgeon later told me I was lucky I was getting all this free health care. I certainly didn't feel lucky. I had a four-inch open abdominal wound, not to mention the massive lump on the back of my head. To make matters worse, all my hair around the cut fell out. I was supposed to be getting better, not worse. Obviously a week of recovery was not enough.

Despite all my surgical complications, in just two days I was on a plane headed to Norfolk, Virginia. My mother was finally able to take some time off and she drove from Memphis and picked me up at the airport. I was in no condition to drive myself. Because of the head injury and the wound opening, I was on Percocet, a narcotic. I was so thankful she would go through this with me. I never thought I would be so happy to have her near.

When I reported to the Admiral's office, I was legally intoxicated, hardly able to walk up a flight of stairs, with an abdominal wound that was still weeping fluid—quite a sight. When I checked in, I was told I would not see the Admiral for a few days. First, I was to go through another review board. I thought I was going to pass out when I heard this. I couldn't take another FNAEB, especially with all my medical problems. The staff officer saw my discomfort and offered assurances that this board was not going to be like the FNAEB. This board consisted of all senior officers who wanted to clear up a few issues.

I was given a day to prepare for this new board. Instead of preparing yet another defense, I decided I would offer my resignation in place of any arguments. I was exhausted both mentally and physically. The thought of a replay of the first FNAEB board made me nauseous. I discussed my resignation with my mother, who wholeheartedly supported me. She never objected to my fast life in the Navy but the years of uncertainty and worry took their toll on her as well. She supported whatever made me happy, but she wanted me out of the Navy that was causing so much pain and anxiety.

When I was taken into the boardroom the next day, I was calm and composed. The Percocet kicked in which probably made me seem completely detached. The board consisted of various Commanders (O-5's) and Captains (O-6's). Some of the members were fighter pilots and some were pilots from the support communities. Two doctors sat on the board as well as a lawyer. I was a little intimidated to be sitting at a table full of senior officers but I made my decision and was resolute.

The senior member of the board, a Captain, began the proceedings by asking me what did I think the Admiral's decision should be? I looked him straight in the eye and said, "I am not sure what the Admiral should decide in lieu of the FNAEB report. I think the FNAEB was completely bogus, but I am only a Lieutenant, so my opinion doesn't count for much. But whatever he decides, I don't really care. I would like to offer up my resignation instead of continuing these proceedings. I am tired and I don't feel well. I think it would be in both mine and the Navy's best interests if I were to just leave."

The members of the board nervously looked at one another. It was clear they did not anticipate the white flag. Another Captain jumped in and said, "So what would you do when you left? Fly for the airlines?" He was clearly insinuating I was merely trying to jump ship for the more lucrative commercial airline industry. I replied, "No, although that would be an option. I think I would like to go back to school and finish out my Ph.D. I am not in this game for the money, I enjoy learning and it appears that's my best area."

The board again appeared confused. I am sure they were accustomed to people begging and pleading to be allowed to return to flying in the Navy. This same group of people just kicked Shannon off the USS Eisenhower and sent her to transport aircraft. Shannon, always gracious, didn't fight it or raise a fuss.

Slowly the questioning turned to my flight performance. The new board never really discussed the old board except for the audiotapes. They told me they transcribed the tapes and then showed me the enormous stack. They agreed there seemed to be some "discrepancies" and that perhaps the board was not completely objective. After only about and hour and a half, they let me go. I was pleasantly surprised. I thought this board would drag on for another day or two. I figured my game plan worked. They would concur with my squadron Commanding Officer and the Wing Commander that I should switch aircraft. It didn't matter to me really because I was already scanning the Washington Post for a job.

The Admiral would see me in three days to give me his final decision. In the meantime, two other Captains on the Admiral's staff interviewed me individually. The first was the Admiral's Chief of Staff, Captain Lolli. He was a very empathetic person and tried to make me feel at ease as soon as I entered his office. It had been so long since a Navy senior officer treated me with respect and dignity that it actually caught me off guard. He started by profusely apologizing for the FNAEB and the behavior of the board members. His exact words were, "This is an embarrassment for the Navy."

Captain Lolli told me the transition for women had not gone as smoothly as he would have liked and he knew there were problems. Captain Lolli then addressed the resignation issue. He pleaded with me not to resign. He told me the Navy would be losing a fine officer and pilot if I left. We chatted for over an hour and the discussion ended on a very positive note. I was appreciative Captain Lolli seemed so concerned and so…. sane. I was beginning to think maybe all this was in my head.

The last senior officer I spoke with before seeing the Admiral was the Training Officer, another Captain. He was a jovial person, always quick with a joke and a smile. He sat me down and, even more than Captain Lolli, just talked to me like real person. He told me some stories about ridiculous FNAEBs of the past to give me perspective as well as to relieve my fears. He wanted to know more about the squadron atmosphere. I told him about the Hooter's incident and the definite change in the squadron atmosphere after Kara's crash. I told him it was hard to feel like a part of the team when the guys say things like, "I'd like to bend her over" in regard to a female enlisted sailor. My personal favorite phrase was when a guy was asked how his flight went. If it went well, he said, "Titties man!" The Captain agreed that might be a tough working environment.

He then addressed a topic I hadn't even considered. He asked, "What will you do if the Admiral sends you back to VFA-106 to finish training?" I had no response. I couldn't even think of such an outcome. After a seemingly long uncomfortable silence, I said, "If Admiral Allen makes that decision, I think the wise thing to do would be to send me to California to finish. I think it's fairly obvious VFA-106 hates me and I don't think I would be given a fair shake."

The Captain looked at me and knowingly said, "If he sends you back to the F/A-18, he's going to send you back to VFA-106. He will want to teach all those instructors a lesson about attitude and professionalism." I did not even want to consider what he was suggesting. I dismissed his implications because I was certain I would not be sent back to Hornets. I also felt no one in his right mind would send me back to the unit that produced my FNAEB that dripped with malice, venom, and intense dislike.

Two days later, I was standing tall in front of Admiral Allen, head of all naval air forces of the Atlantic. A very busy man, Admiral Allen only could spare a few minutes to deal with this truly trifling problem. He had many more real problems to deal with; the deployment of airwings to the always dangerous Middle East, budget cuts—all in a downsizing Navy. He asked me to sit and told me he thoroughly read the FNAEB, my statement, the endorsements, and my father's letter. He paused for effect and said, "I find this FNAEB completely preposterous. I disagree with the findings of fact, the opinions, and most of all, the recommendations." He went on to address some of the specific problems, more towards his Chief of Staff instead of me. I felt like a child in a room full of adults that were talking about me, but allowed to say nothing. With a dramatic flair, Admiral Allen read through all the possible outcomes of a FNAEB and then said, "So, the way I see it, I am left with no other choice but to completely overturn this FNAEB. I award you the A-1 status and will pretend this FNAEB never happened."

I could have been pushed over with a feather. I never ever once considered the possibility Admiral Allen would totally reverse the FNAEB. The Chief of Staff signaled me it was time to exit so I thanked the Admiral for his understanding and left. In the hallway, one of Admiral Allen's staff officers briefed me on the full meaning of his decision. The FNAEB in effect would be erased from my record as if it never happened. I would report back to VFA-106 and begin training again once I was medically fit. I just nodded, still in shock from the outcome. All thoughts of resignation were behind me. If Admiral Allen felt strongly enough about me to completely wipe the slate clean, then I owed it to him and everyone else who believed in me to try again.

I was very leery of going back into VFA-106, but I felt I had no choice. I would not bite the hand that fed me. I was given an opportunity to prove myself and get my career back on track. I decided to bury my doubts about the hostile atmosphere in VFA-106 and give it the old college try. I was a fighter pilot, not a quitter and I would persevere.

Chapter Fourteen

The Professional Patient

I headed back to Jacksonville, elated with my victory but very apprehensive of going back into the fire. Before I could resume flying though, I was required to get my "up-chit" which I knew would be no easy task. The "up-chit" is the official Navy medical clearance that allows a pilot to fly. I was still very tired and sore from the surgery and blow to the head. The surgical incision was very slow to heal and my headaches were getting worse. I chalked all these maladies up to my problematic recovery, never suspecting that much bigger medical problems were on the horizon.

My welcome back in VFA-106 was anything but receptive. The instructors were clearly angry that I was allowed to return. It was very obvious what everyone thought, "The only reason she was allowed to return was because she was a woman." I knew the road before me would be a long, hard one, but I truly felt that if I kept my nose to the grindstone, I would prevail.

One day while studying in the squadron, Elvis, one of the instructors that blatantly lied during the FNAEB proceedings, approached me. As the training officer, he was ordered to design a refresher syllabus to renew my skills. Elvis made it clear he hated me and was only doing what he was told to do. After he spit out his instructions through clenched teeth, he turned to leave. I heard that Elvis's wife recently gave birth to his first child, so before he left, I said, "Congratulations on your new baby. Is it a boy or a girl?" He glared at me and said "Girl." Not one to let a perfect opportunity slide by, I said, "Ohhhhh, a little fighter pilot! You must be so proud." He snorted and walked away. I have always thought it perfect justice that fighter pilots often only have girl babies. It is suspected that pulling a lot of G's in high performance aircraft significantly weakens the Y chromosome; hence the high number of daughters for jet pilots. Sometimes life's little ironies are too good to be true!

Finally my incision healed and I was ready for my medical examination that would return me to flight status. Three months passed since I flew in Key West and I was anxious to complete my training. I was still tired and experiencing headaches, so I was a little unsure if I was really ready to start flying again. I told the flight surgeons of my concerns and they too thought maybe I had not completely recovered. They decided that perhaps my blow to the head was the problem and scheduled a MRI. It would be the first MRI of countless others.

As I lay in the cramped cylinder with magnets spinning around, not able to move in the slightest, I knew something else was wrong. Even though the ulcer tests came back negative, the doctors prescribed large doses of Tagamet, an ulcer drug. My stomach still hurt and the headaches were a permanent part of my life. Usually very healthy and energetic, I now slept for sometimes sixteen hours in a row. In my heart, I knew I was not yet out of the woods, but on the surface, I completely denied it. In my mind, I could beat whatever was wrong with me and I was determined to return to flying in just a few weeks.

I asked the MRI technicians if they saw anything unusual. I learned later that although not doctors, these technicians know when something is amiss. They just smiled at me in a very empathetic fashion and said my doctor would call me. A week later, I was sitting in a neurologist's office. Dr. Hopkins asked me to perform a myriad of tests designed to highlight any neurologic dysfunction. I passed all the tests that examined the senses, but the one area I had difficulty with was my balance. When asked to close my eyes and march in place for a minute, I slowly spun around, completely unaware I was moving. It was also difficult for me to keep my balance on one leg. The doctors just quietly noted all these seemingly insignificant quirks.

After they put their heads together for a conference, Dr. Hopkins called me into his office and showed me my MRI films plastered around his office. Always the optimist, he told me he thought everything was fine but…It seemed my pituitary gland at the base of my brain was enlarged. When he showed me mine compared to someone else's, the difference was shocking. He mentioned the word tumor and for the first time, I was truly alarmed. Dr. Hopkins then told me the definitive answer would be in blood tests. He wanted to draw some blood and test it for all the hormones controlled by the pituitary. In a week, we would know for sure if I had a more serious problem.

One agonizing week later, I received the news. I needed to be on the next plane to Washington DC to be seen at Bethesda Naval Hospital. The blood tests were astonishing and alarming. Dr. Hopkins had never seen such perplexing levels of pituitary gland hormones. There was now even stronger evidence that I possibly had a pituitary tumor. In addition, my TSH hormones were so high, the lab could not measure them. TSH stands for thyroid stimulating hormone and they are the hormones the pituitary gland produces to control the thyroid gland,

My first thought was "What's a thyroid gland?" I knew the thyroid controlled energy levels but beyond that, I did not have the faintest clue. Bethesda is the Navy's premier hospital, Dr. Hopkins assured me. The specialists would be able to get to the bottom of my problems and answer all my questions. The swiftness of my departure scared me more than the actual news. I knew that in the military's highly socialized medical program, only people who are very ill are flown to Bethesda to be seen immediately.

I went to the squadron to pick up my airline tickets and tell the senior officers what transpired. It was clear I would not resume flying anytime soon, if ever. As I left, I was reminded of the cold shoulder I received after my ovarian tumor surgery. Not one person expressed any sympathy or any words of encouragement. The instructors were no doubt delighted and were probably high-fiving each other as soon as I left. Fate accomplished what they could not, stopping me from flying the F/A-18.

As I hurriedly packed, trying not to think about all the frightening unknowns, I heard an unexpected knock on my door. I was very surprised to find Barney, one of the VFA-106 instructors, at my door. In the frame of my doorway with a sheepish look on his face, Barney didn't look anything like the impressive fighter pilot I knew from the squadron.

Barney told me he heard about my quick departure to Bethesda and wanted to see me before I left. He wanted to apologize for all the shenanigans of the other instructors and also wanted me to know that not everyone hated me. We sat at my kitchen table and talked for a long time. We talked about the FNAEB, my trip to see Admiral Allen, and the alarming medical problems. I was grateful for his candor and obvious need to tell me the truth. His knowledge of the behind-the-scenes dealings was extremely enlightening.

Barney told me I was set up from the start. He believed that Captain Moffit, the Commanding Officer, engineered the entire FNAEB as an attempt to further his career. He told me the members of the FNAEB board were instructed by the CO to "go for the juggler." He encouraged them to dig into my past and reveal as much negative information about me as possible. In fact, Barney said Captain Moffit actually gave the FNAEB members information about my past that they were not supposed to have. Captain Moffit wanted me gone and those were the instructions he gave to the FNAEB members.

Barney believed Captain Moffit set the board up to look sexist so that when it was his turn to endorse the recommendations, he could reverse them. In doing so, he would look like the big hero by senior officials, the man trying to put a stop to sexual harassment and gender discrimination in the fighter community. Barney said the FNAEB members were very angry with Captain Moffit and felt they were sacrificed for his political career. Since Captain Moffit was in line to be selected as an admiral, Barney thought he was doing everything he possible to make it happen. In the Navy, promotion to the Admiral ranks is the ultimate boys' club and is quite political.

As I listened to Barney, I didn't know what to think. Why would Captain Moffit engineer such a fiasco and could this possibly have been all just an attempt for him to become an Admiral? Was my entire career so meaningless to Captain Moffit? While I didn't believe everything Barney told me, I could not deny some of his allegations. Why had Captain Moffit held the investigation about the ridiculous events in Fallon? Why had he rushed my case through normal channels, ignoring serious medical conditions, in an attempt to send me to a FNAEB? At the very least, I agreed Captain Moffit had some hidden agenda in his handling of my case.

As I flew to Washington DC, all my thoughts of squadron politics quickly dissipated. I was so consumed with the medical "what ifs" that I really didn't have much time to agonize over the ridiculous FNAEB and its implications for my future. There was something seriously wrong with me and I knew I might not be able to continue in the military, much less ever fly again. To combat some of the anxiety, I bought several medical books that described hormone diseases, the pituitary and thyroid glands, and the importance of the endocrine system.

Prior to my very focused reading, I never heard the word endocrine and had no idea an entire branch of medicine was dedicated to the diseases of the hormone system. Very much the typical engineer, I completely ignored the most complex design of all—the human body. I believed everything any medical person told me and didn't want to be bothered with the details. Just like a woman who takes her car to the shop because she doesn't want to deal with her automotive problems, if I felt ill, I just wanted the problem fixed with minimal fuss, as quickly as possible. It was this cavalier attitude that got me into trouble in the first place. I knew my hair had been falling out for some time but I thought if I ignored it, the problem would just go away. I find it amusing that even the smartest of people can be so very stupid about the basics in life.

I was a complete sponge as I read. Because I was so lacking in knowledge about the human body, my learning curve was very sharp. As I read, I was amazed to find out that the endocrine system is necessary for basic survival. Never having been affected by PMS or mood swings, I previously dismissed discussions about hormones and their effects as excuses or crutches to explain away behavioral problems. I learned over the next several years just how critical the endocrine system is and how its diseases can not only devastate a life but end it as well.

I primarily focused on the issue of a pituitary gland tumor, which was the tentative diagnosis of the doctors in Florida. As I read about the problems associated with pituitary problems, I started to really feel ill. Manifestations of pituitary diseases include loss of peripheral vision, adrenal gland problems, but the worst is the change in the bone structure of the skeleton, primarily in the skull region where the face literally expands.[11]

As I delved further into my research, I prayed to God that I would not be cursed with any pituitary affliction. Even if I did have a benign tumor in the pituitary gland, the solution would require surgery. The removal of a pituitary tumor is considered neurosurgery because the gland sits at the base of the brain. To remove the tumor, a neurosurgeon has to drill a small hole through the nasal passages and insert a tiny scope. Using microcameras, the doctors locate the tumor, cut it out, and pull it out the same hole. The surgery is very delicate and even the slightest waiver can cause permanent brain damage. If I did indeed have a pituitary tumor, my flying career would most certainly be over.

A little knowledge is a dangerous weapon because after my two-hour flight to DC, I managed to scare myself half to death thinking about the possible outcomes.

I was both relieved and scared when I finally met with the doctor at Bethesda Naval Hospital. As I sat in the waiting room, it was painfully obvious to me that I was the only person in the waiting room under fifty years of age. Not only were the women old, their faces were lifeless and pasty, and they moved slowly. Most looked as if just merely living seemed to drain them. Watching them, I wondered what was in store for me.

The doctors first decided to run a myriad of tests to determine just what was wrong. During the long days hooked up to IVs, I realized the scope of my ignorance concerning medical issues was profound. To me, the worst part of coping with serious illness was not the illness itself; it was the unknown. I decided the only way to deal with the overwhelming medical issues was to learn about them. I started asking the doctors and nurses to explain everything to me. Because I was subjected to so many grueling tests, I learned a lot not just from asking but intently observing as well. The doctors knew I was scared and they recognized that my way of coping with the stress was education. I was so intent on learning about the various aspects of the endocrine system; my doctors dubbed me as their "professional patient."

After meeting with the endocrinologists, I was sent to the neuro-surgeon about the possibility of a pituitary gland tumor. I was more than a little nervous while waiting to see the doctor. I knew there was some concern about my pituitary gland, but I thought surgery was a big jump for a condition that was only a possibility. The neurosurgeon was very excited to see me, a little too anxious for my comfort level. I was reminded yet again that since Navy doctors see a relatively healthy population, they get very excited when something rare and challenging pops up. I was just such a patient for my neurosurgeon. He briefed me on the complete operative procedure for removing a pituitary gland tumor. The topic was fascinating but I was very nervous while I was listening.

While we were discussing the intricacies of the operation, the neurosurgeon mentioned that two of his colleagues in the department were former F-14 Tomcat pilots. Trying to lighten up the very serious environment, I told him that if I needed the operation, I didn't want the former F-14 pilots assisting. All I thought of was the movie *TOP-GUN* and the scene where the F-14 aviators high five each other and say, "I feel the need for speed!" The doctor just looked at me as if I had lost my mind, and I then had to explain the joke (which is humiliating in and of itself). After my painstaking explanation, the surgeon gave me a half-hearted laugh and then pressed on with his discussion.

Eventually I managed to break in and ask if he really thought I had a tumor. He pulled out my brain MRI and hemmed and hawed over it. He finally said the film was inconclusive and since my thyroid had failed so completely, the blood tests would not truly be accurate for several months. I then fell into the wait and see category. After six months on the thyroid medication, I would be reevaluated and if the pituitary gland shrank and the blood tests stabilized, I would be out of the woods. The neurosurgeon seemed disappointed that my case was not cut and dried, but I was more than happy to let him perform brain surgery on someone else.

Finally after several exhausting days, all the initial tests were complete. The doctors said I was such an interesting case because my problems covered so many specialties. They decided to use my case to teach fledgling doctors on some of the more enigmatic aspects of medicine. Despite all the professional expertise in my corner, there was still a lot of head scratching. The blood tests indicated that without a doubt I was hypothyroid. The opposite of hyperthyroid, when a person is hypothyroid, the thyroid gland cannot keep up with the demands of the body.

The thyroid gland controls many metabolic functions in the body, which means it controls the rate at which several organs and systems operate. Thyroid hormones are critical for smooth operation of the brain, the heart, the digestive system, and many more. People who experience this disease are most likely extremely fatigued and lethargic; some gain weight, and in many cases are extremely sensitive to cold temperatures. The failure of the thyroid can range from slight to severe but in my case, my thyroid completely failed. I have what is termed as Hashimoto's Thyroiditis.

Hashimoto's Thyroiditis is an autoimmune disease, a phrase I became intimately familiar with over the next few years. Autoimmune illnesses, still a mystery to modern medicine, manifest themselves in many systems of the body. The one common thread between them is that the body turns on itself and kills important organs and tissues in the body. In Hashimoto's Thyroiditis, the body's immune system goes haywire and thinks the thyroid is a foreign invader. It produces antibodies to kill the thyroid, just like it would produce antibodies to kill invading germs. The death of the thyroid is usually not a sudden event. It typically takes years for the entire thyroid to die and in some cases, the loss is only partial.

What made my case so unusual was the extreme level of failure. The pituitary gland controls the thyroid gland, like the mainframe computer. When the pituitary gland senses the thyroid operating below normal, it sends the Thyroid Stimulating Hormone (TSH) to the thyroid as a signal for it to increase its output. The TSH level is in fact how doctors determine the level of thyroid failure. Most patients find their way into the doctor's office when their TSH levels double or triple. By that time, most people exhibit enough symptoms to make diagnosis fairly straightforward.

In my particular case, the doctors were astounded when they reviewed my lab results. My TSH levels were ONE HUNDRED TIMES the normal levels. The doctors were completely mystified why I was not in a coma. People with my TSH level many times fall into a myxedema coma, which can be fatal. What was even more astounding to them was the fact that I had been flying high performance aircraft. I was told that day that I was not well enough to even drive a car, much less a fighter jet. They were not surprised that I experienced trouble in the plane remembering clearances and keeping track of other aircraft. One of the first basic functions to be affected in hypothyroidism is cognitive function and in my extreme state, they were amazed I could put together coherent statements. They considered me one of their "Ripley's Believe It Or Not" patients for managing to live a fairly normal life despite the seriousness of my condition.

As the doctors covered all this with me, so many questions about the past few months were answered. My failed thyroid was responsible for the loss of my hair, my deteriorating vision, failing memory, and extreme fatigue. I was lucky to be still walking and considering how sick I really was, I was even more thankful that I never made any fatal errors in the cockpit that might have cost my life, or worse, someone else's.

Now that I possessed answers, I wanted to know what the solution was. The doctors were still worried about a few issues. They did not understand how someone so young could experience such a catastrophic thyroid failure, and the enlarged pituitary gland was still a point of contention. The endocrinologists speculated that my pituitary gland swelled in response to the incredible amount of TSH it was producing. The pituitary gland also controls the ovaries so the rapid growth of the ovarian tumor all started to make sense.

I also wanted to know what my thyroid problems meant for my flying career. The flight surgeons decided that if I did well on the thyroid replacement hormone and my pituitary gland shrank, I could start thinking about flying in six months. I was actually overjoyed with the news. Just two weeks prior I thought I might be having brain surgery and now if all went well, I would be back in the cockpit in no time.

One of the doctors treating me, John, was the husband of a friend of mine from the Naval Academy. After the diagnosis, I was immediately started on levothyroxine, which is a synthetic thyroid replacement drug. John wrote my initial prescription but his decision for the dosage was overridden. One of the more senior doctors decided to start me on the maximum dose instead of a much smaller dosage John recommended. Because John was not the senior doctor, he changed the dosage but it was clear he was not happy about it. Not realizing something was amiss I ignored the discussion. I was anxious to start my recuperation so as far as I was concerned, the more the better.

After the first day of taking the incredibly small, innocuous looking pills, I knew the road to recovery was going to be a long, arduous one. When I woke up the day after I started the medication, I experienced the first migraine headache of my life. Not ever having experienced such concentrated pain, I was unprepared for the severity and intensity of a migraine headache. I ended up back at the hospital, not able to open my eyes and overcome with nausea. Despite the clear and obvious link to the medication, the doctor who prescribed such a large dosage insisted that my headache was a result of some other ailment like the flu. He kept the medication at the maximum level and I was sent home with the proverbial pat on the head, "You'll be all right little girl. Just leave your health to us" was the insinuation. Confused and feeling worse than when I arrived, I headed back to Jacksonville. I thought all my health problems would soon be behind me, but in reality, I would face many more serious medical problems that would be the proverbial albatross around my neck.

I did not know what my status would be once I returned to the squadron. The doctors were clear, I would not be allowed to fly for six months. At the end of that observation period, if all my physical ailments were under control, I might be allowed to fly again. What would I do in the squadron for six months if not allowed to fly? The instructors made it quite obvious when I left that they hoped I never returned. I was truly out of the frying pan and back into the fire.

My reception upon my return to VFA-106 was expectedly icy and disapproving. Very few people, both instructors and students, spoke to me. I was blatantly ignored and treated as if I did not exist. The Executive Officer brought me in soon after my return to tell me his opinion of the events of the past few months. He told me that he talked at length with the squadron flight surgeon, the same one that submitted two very different statements to the FNAEB. The flight surgeon told him that my insolent and aggressive behavior was all attributed to my hormone problems. The message was clear; they were going to blame all my "social" problems on my hormone imbalance, a more politically correct version of blaming them on "that time of the month."

I was disgusted. After several weeks of intensive medical care, I was still struggling through my recovery. I was lucky to be alive and relatively in one piece, and now my command thought all my problems could be boiled down to simple female problems. I found it amazing the male pilots were always attempting to find an explanation to my "aggressive and confrontational" personality. Never once did it strike anyone that I was just like them and these characteristics, which were so objectionable in women, were in fact the same traits that they bred in one another.

As dismayed as I was with my Executive Officer's comments, I was equally in awe of what my new Commanding Officer said. While I was away, VFA-106 underwent a "change of command." The old CO, who was very much against my presence in the squadron, reached the end of his tenure and was replaced with a new senior officer, CAPT Rico Mayer. I was very leery of him, as my previous experience with an F/A-18 CO eventually landed me in front of a corrupt and shameless FNAEB.

CAPT Mayer made it quite clear when I walked into his office that he was not like CAPT Moffit, or anyone else in the squadron for that matter. He immediately put me at ease by telling me he thought the FNAEB was bogus and he would do everything in his power to put me back into the cockpit. CAPT Mayer completely understood my problems; his wife recently suffered through a similar thyroid experience and he saw first hand what devastation accompanied such an insidious disease.

I was totally overwhelmed by CAPT Mayer's compassion and sincerity. I entered his office expecting more of the same cavalier attitude that the XO displayed. Instead, I was absolutely caught off guard by CAPT Mayer's wisdom, understanding, and sense of fairness. When I walked out of his office, I found new hope that I would be able to regain my health and get back into the cockpit of the F/A-18 with at least a very small minority of support.

CAPT Mayer assigned me to the Administrative Department. He knew I had prior experience in this field but he also knew very few of the instructors ever ventured into the administrative offices. For the most part, I was sheltered from the hatred and derision of those individuals who loathed my sheer presence. Despite my scarce presence around the Ready Room and other flying activities, the instructors and many students made their feelings known. If I participated in some command project, very few people spoke to me and they made it clear I was not welcome at social functions. I responded by keeping to myself and working on the information systems security project that CAPT Mayer assigned me. While work was a lonely existence, I was battling many other very important issues. Instead of getting better, my medical problems were becoming significantly worse.

Just a few short weeks after my return from Bethesda Naval Hospital, bizarre maladies began cropping up during a time when I was supposed to show the greatest improvement. One night as I was sleeping, I awoke to a searing pain in my left shoulder that coursed like fire down my left arm. The pain was so intense; it brought tears to my eyes. I leaped out of bed and paced the floor, swinging my arm around and trying to massage the muscles. Nothing seemed to help, so I eventually resorted to taking some Tylenol with Codeine that remained after my ovary surgery. After a few hours, the pain subsided. I talked to the flight surgeon the next day who told me I just suffered from a spurious muscle cramp. He gave me some Motrin and off I went.

Every night that week, I was again awakened with the same unbelievable burning sensation. It eventually became so painful that I could not sleep at all. The Tylenol with Codeine was having little effect, and the Motrin was worthless. In addition, I developed a strange pain in my right leg. Occasionally when I was walking up or down a flight of stairs, a pain shot through my right leg so debilitating, I collapsed. After resting for a few minutes, the pain completely subsided and I walked again as if nothing happened. I finally convinced the flight surgeon that something more than muscle cramps was the problem and he agreed. After shooting my shoulder full of lidocaine, a numbing anesthetic drug, he then prescribed Elavil, an anti-depressant. He diagnosed me with a condition known as fibromyalgia, which affects primarily women. Fibromyalgia is a mysterious syndrome in which its victims experience pain in at least eleven of eighteen specific tender points throughout the body. The cause of fibromyalgia is unknown and antidepressants are often used because they minimize pain perception in the brain.[12]

I told the flight surgeon I did not think I had fibromyalgia. None of my pains were symmetric and they didn't feel muscular to me. I was sure the new onsets of pains, plus the intense migraines that had not abated, were somehow related to my thyroid condition and/or the medication. The flight surgeon scoffed at my layman's idea and insisted I try the anti-depressant. He also suggested that I might need to see a psychiatrist, hinting that I was not handling the turn of events very well.

I gave him the benefit of the doubt and tried the medication. The Elavil made me nauseous and knocked me out for fourteen or more hours. While the mysterious pains in my right leg and left shoulder substantially subsided, new ailments took their place. One evening after chopping vegetables for dinner, I tried to put the knife on the counter.

I was very surprised and alarmed when I could not let go of the knife. The fourth and fifth digits of my right hand froze into the curled position around the knife. They didn't hurt but I could not straighten them or move them in any way. The doctors just scratched their heads in amazement and after a few days, I slowly regained full use of my right hand again.

While the temporary paralysis of my right hand was a medical red flag, something even more alarming was taking place in my wracked body. With the mild but cooler temperatures of winter in Jacksonville, Florida, I was experiencing almost complete blood loss in both my hands and feet whenever I went outdoors. This painful condition, called Raynaud's Phenomenon, is a complete mystery to doctors. For some reason, when the body senses a drop in temperature, even a sometimes mild one, the blood vessels constrict and the hands and/or feet will turn white with the loss of blood. Eventually the blood will rush back to the extremities causing a bluish or bright red color, and the reintroduction of blood is very painful.

Some people with no underlying illness experience Raynaud's Phenomenon, but in many cases, it is a signal that something is seriously wrong with a person's autoimmune system. Because of my history, the flight surgeons finally admitted my increasingly alarming problems were out of their scope of knowledge and I was finally referred to several specialists.

The first action the specialists took was to review my medical record. They were shocked and appalled at what they found. They told me that I was given a "potentially lethal overdose" of the thyroid medication at Bethesda Naval Hospital. They were quite adamant that someone who was so severely hypothyroid should only have been introduced to the thyroid replacement hormone at very small dosages over a long period of time. The internal medicine doctor made the following comparison, "It is like taking an old VW bug and dropping a Ferrari engine into it. You are lucky you did not have a massive heart attack. This dosage level would have killed a woman who was not in good shape." Not surprisingly, later echocardiograms and EKGs of my heart showed a heart murmur where none before existed.

The doctors immediately took me off the antidepressant Elavil, telling me many women experienced the same reaction from doctors who were not familiar with endocrine or rheumatic diseases. Most women afflicted with these types of illnesses often hear "it's all in your head" and spend years bouncing from doctor to doctor before one realizes the true nature of the illness. I was lucky the problem was solved in just a few months.

After the doctors figured out my endocrine problems, they refocused on the rheumatic issues. Rheumatologists are internal medicine doctors who specialize in the diseases of the joints and muscles, which include autoimmune illnesses. Despite the discovery that my thyroid medication dosage was too high, I was still not out of the woods. Several blood tests came back with alarming results. In particular, my ANA test came back not just positive, but in a range that signified serious rheumatic illness.

ANA stands for antinuclear antibody. These antibodies are produced at the cell level to kill off the body's own defenses and tissues.[13] While the ANA test is an important test, it alone does not provide a diagnosis for any particular disease. It only means there is autoimmune activity present, which could lead to several debilitating illnesses like lupus, scleroderma, rheumatoid arthritis, and many other connective tissue diseases that are sometimes combinations. These rheumatic diseases affect primarily women, especially between the ages of 20–40 and range in severity to mild to fatal. Perhaps the worst aspect of these diseases is the unknown. Doctors do not know what causes them and have trouble predicting the progression of the diseases once identified.

One of the more difficult aspects of these rheumatic diseases for their victims is the actual treatment. Corticosteroid drugs are currently the most widely used medication used to treat a whole host of autoimmune diseases. These drugs take over the function of a person's immune system, in effect suppressing the body's out of control immune response. The problem with these drugs is what it does to the physical appearance of the patient. People who take large doses of corticosteroids for extended periods of time develop the "moon face." For most patients, their faces as well as their bodies, swell as a reaction and many experience dramatic mood swings, which are only exacerbated by the change in their physical appearance. For many, the treatment is as damaging as the disease itself. For severe connective tissue diseases that require high doses of corticosteroids, the drugs can actually lead to an early death. Sadly, in those extreme cases, if the disease doesn't finish off the unlucky soul, in the end, the treatment will.

After much debate, the doctors decided I needed to remain in an observation status for a few more months to see if I developed a more pronounced illness. The rheumatologists were mystified. Some of their patients with far less provocative test results were far sicker than I appeared to be. Despite my blood work, an occasional odd rash, and the Raynaud's Phenomenon, there was no obvious indication of a specific disease. It was clear something was happening to my immune system, but no one knew what it was or how severe it might be. The rheumatologists told me that I probably had a disease called mixed connective tissue disease. People with this disease usually show a mixture of confusing symptoms that at older ages, usually developed into lupus or scleroderma.

Lupus is a particularly frightening disease because it can be fatal. In lupus, a person's immune system will kill off its own tissues and organs including the heart, kidneys and brain tissue. Scleroderma, a related debilitating disease, causes tissues and organs to literally petrify from scarring, rendering them useless. The onset of Scleroderma is typically a painful, slow process that also causes skin, especially on the face, to tighten, almost like wax sculpture.

I was just as confused about my medical condition as the doctors. Just what were they telling me? Did I have one of these horrific and incapacitating diseases for which the treatment is almost as bad as the illness itself? I knew the loss of blood in my hands and feet was painful and I still felt exhausted all the time, but I didn't feel like I was on my deathbed. I refused to believe I had either of these diseases. I knew something was wrong with me but I had complete faith that I could beat whatever it was.

The told me not to worry—yet. While I was experiencing some kind of autoimmune attack, it was not serious enough to cause any permanent damage. They were concerned though because I was a time bomb waiting to explode. The future was uncertain; my body gave many indications that it could eventually develop a serious autoimmune illness like lupus or scleroderma, but for now, I was in no immediate danger. There was no way of knowing if or when any more life threatening manifestations would surface. However, the doctors were certain about one thing, women who did develop these illnesses usually experienced some episode of intense physical or mental stress that activated the disease. In fact, almost all autoimmune processes can be triggered and aggravated by stress.

I looked at them in amazement. All I needed to do to prevent a major debilitating illness was to lead a stress free life, in the Navy? Were they crazy? Even if I wasn't in the Navy, I was a type A+ personality so stress was a permanent part of my life. How was I supposed to fly fighters in a stress free environment? The doctors explained the importance of a proper diet, sleep, and staying out of the sun. An OB/GYN doctor also told me that I needed to put the ideas of motherhood away, at least for a while. Childbirth is one of the most stressful events a woman's body can endure and with all my autoimmune problems, now was not the time. Maybe in a few years when my immune system was healthier, but for now, kids were not a smart idea.

The news about my childbearing inadequacies didn't even faze me. I had not dated anyone in over a year and a relationship culminating with children seemed an incredibly remote possibility. As far as I was concerned, this news would be a great way to relieve my mother's angst over the fact that I was not married and she didn't have any grandchildren.

During my medically down time, I reconsidered what the doctors said about stress and its potential impact on my health and on my career. I knew the most prudent course of action would be to find a more stress free life. I considered my options. There was a distinct possibility I would not be able to fly carrier-based aircraft again. I could ask to fly a less demanding aircraft, I could change careers in the Navy and become an engineer, or I could get out of the Navy altogether.

Working in VFA-106 during my medically down status was not doing anything to alleviate my stress. I was amazed at the childishness that was rampant in the squadron. The FNAEB was almost six months old, and after major surgery, I was still struggling with very serious medical problems. Except for CAPT Mayer, there was little compassion or even common decency from the instructors and students. I thought time would help people forget, but instead, the hatred seemed to build. I finally decided to take matters into my own hands. It was clear there would be no mercy, no camaraderie, or at the very least, a professional working environment in the squadron. I still faced at least six more months of recovery and life in VFA-106 was a living hell.

I started examining my options. If I found another unit that needed me, I could transfer on a temporary basis. Because of my engineering background, I looked for a Navy command in the local area that needed someone with my background. A Captain in Washington DC who was sympathetic to my plight put me in touch with the Commanding Officer of the Naval Aviation Depot (NADEP) in Jacksonville, CAPT Don Rice.

The Navy currently has three NADEPs located across the country. They are the Navy's versions of civilian aircraft rework and maintenance industrial complexes like Boeing or Northrop Grumman. Primarily civilians run them with a skeleton crew of military personnel to oversee the operations. NADEP Jacksonville recently expanded to more than twice its original size so it was in dire need of officers who could handle the immense increase in workload.

I was nervous when I went to speak with CAPT Rice, because I knew how reputations precede people in the Navy. My experience was anything but pleasant at VFA-106 and I was afraid of what might follow me to NADEP. In the end, all my concerns and worries were for nothing. CAPT Rice and the entire officer compliment of NADEP enthusiastically welcomed me with open arms. They were so desperate for help that they didn't care about my background. I would immediately begin working with the legal office investigating waste, fraud and abuse complaints and union disputes. There was much work to be done and I was both glad and relieved that I was needed so desperately.

I was very impressed and completely overwhelmed by the NADEP reception; it was almost like night and day compared to VFA-106. The other pilots and officers treated me like one of the guys and the civilians bent over backwards to make me feel like I was part of the team. It was not lost on me that while no one spoke to me at VFA-106 social functions, the NADEP officers actively sought me out not only for organized functions, but informal dinners and outings as well.

I look back on my time at NADEP with nothing but fond memories. I was a cherished and valuable member of a team and after my time at VFA-106, I recognized how important it is to feel wanted. My enjoyment with my work and my peers at NADEP tremendously impacted my health. The doctors were right; many of my problems were exacerbated by stress because in just a few weeks at NADEP, many of my mysterious maladies disappeared. My hair grew in over the bald spots and thickened, the strange rashes I developed vanished, and I started exercising again and gaining energy.

In the ensuing months of my recovery, I had to clear one more medical hurdle before I could be considered fit to fly. The doctors were happy with my seemingly miraculous improvements but they decided to do a bone scan to find out if any of the autoimmune activity affected my joints. If my bone scan came up clean and my overall health continued to improve, I would be back in the cockpit.

The bone scan is a nuclear medical procedure. I was injected with a radioactive compound, which was then absorbed by my skeleton. I was now the X-ray machine, radiating to a film. I knew something was wrong only a few minutes into the test when the technicians called in a doctor immediately. I saw this before with the ovarian tumor and my brain MRI. If doctors call one another with, "Hey Bill, you need to come take a look at this!" and consult in low tones, the patient has every right to be worried.

Lying on the table, unable to move due to the ongoing scanning procedure, I could not imagine what was so urgent. I feared they must have seen something pretty serious to act so quickly. Finally someone asked me, "Does your left shoulder and right knee hurt you?"

I was completely caught off guard with this question. Just a few months prior, both those areas gave me nothing but excruciating pain. I always thought the problem was muscular and since then began seeing a massage therapist and chiropractor. The pain had almost subsided and only made itself known occasionally. My shoulder had been throbbing recently, but I thought I was just getting old.

When I was allowed off the table, I finally got to see what all the fuss was about. A normal bone scan will show the skeleton in light gray shades. Problem areas will be highlighted in deeper shades of gray depending on the level of abnormal activity. My bone scan was fortunately completely normal in my joints but two very black spots appeared just above my right knee and in the upper part of my arm.

Even though I was a layman, it was quite clear something was wrong. I still did not grasp the meaning but feared the worst when I was in a CAT scan machine that very afternoon. I was reminded that Navy medicine only acts that quickly when the doctors fear the worst. As I lay in the tube with the machine humming and spinning around me, I reflected on the possible outcomes. I heard the doctors talking sarcoma, which is their fancy and detached way of saying cancer.

Cancer? Surely they were joking. I was young—maybe not as healthy as I used to be but certainly not ready for chemotherapy, balding, and maybe even death. It all seemed very surreal and I felt totally detached from my body—like I was looking at the situation from a God's eye view. I knew that a person with bone cancer was in serious trouble, especially if it spread. It seemed as if I could not break free from these doctors and their diagnoses were becoming progressively more serious. Brain tumor, possibly lupus, and now bone cancer. It was more than I could bear. I was totally paralyzed with disbelief that something so life threatening could actually be happening to me.

The CAT scan did not alleviate anyone's fears; in fact, the local ortho-pedic doctors were more convinced than ever that I was facing cancer. There was discussion of possible radiation and chemotherapy, very scary words that I refused to take seriously. I don't think I am a vain per-son but as any woman would, when I heard the word chemotherapy, I first thought of my hair. Trying to cope with my worst fears, I told the doctors I always wanted to know what I would look like as a red head.

The Jacksonville orthopedic doctors decided my case was too complex for them. I would be sent to San Diego to see the Navy's expert on bone cancer and most likely face immediate surgery. If any malignancy existed in that arm, I would lose the entire bone. That night as I lay in bed, unable to sleep, I began a transformation. I promised God that if I made it through this next medical hurdle, I would change. Someone later referred to me as a "foxhole Christian" which is partially true. Sadly for many peo-ple, it takes a traumatic experience to instill a true desire to change. I think many people who are faced with their own mortality reflect on their lives and make the leap into greater depths of spirituality.

I promised God I would spend more time with my friends and fam-ily. I would try to right all the wrongs of the past and I would make a conscious effort to be a better, more giving person. I was reminded and ashamed of the hurts I caused other people due to my own selfishness and I wanted to make amends. In the days that followed, I called many people I hadn't spoken to in years to try to heal some old wounds. I was ashamed that at 29 years of age, I spent my entire life focused purely on myself and my future achievements. Somewhere I missed the big picture of what life was all about. All my adult life I focused on flying and furthering my career in the Navy. What if I had bone cancer that spread? I would have probably less than a year to live and when I died, could I say I left the world a better place?

The "Missy Cummings Reformation" which began in Monterey, CA had now come full circle. Since my time in Monterey, occasionally a stray thought nagged me that maybe I was leading a purely selfish life and maybe the life of a swaggering, brassy fighter pilot was not what God intended. The competitor and perfectionist in me always rejected these thoughts with the rationale that I was "serving my country." Now after years of denial, I was forced to take stock of my life. I often thought my continuing medical problems, especially since they were getting more serious, was an attempt by God to get my attention. Because of my stubbornness, I now faced one of the most lethal forms of cancer. If God wanted my attention, He had it now.

In the days that followed, a calm actually came over me and instead of obsessively worrying and fretting over what could be, I acknowledged the possibilities with optimism. I finally accepted that I needed to change and if I did indeed have cancer, then I would fight it one day at a time. In my heart I knew it was not my time to go. While my faith in God wavered through the years, it was strong now. The next few months might not be easy, but I had fought too many battles to lose now. The FNAEB truly tested my faith and in some respects, paved the way for me to cope with this far more serious dilemma.

When I reported to the Navy's premier hospital in San Diego, this faith was tested almost immediately. The plain X-rays clearly showed something amiss, which was not a good sign. The next test the doctors wanted to perform was a MRI. While the CAT scan showed deformities in the bone, the MRI showed more soft tissue abnormalities. The doctors were specifically interested in the bone marrow. Cancer in the bone marrow would essentially be a death knell.

By now I was the proverbial old hat in the MRI. I knew by now that if the MRI ran longer than expected, the technician was attempting to obtain more scans of the problem area. This MRI lasted over an hour, so I knew they were concerned. As soon as they finished, I walked over to the computer screen where several scans were displayed while they were printing. Again, I was no doctor but it didn't take a brain surgeon to see the scans were not normal. The most inexperienced eye could see that a lesion was growing from the very top of my humerus down the bone towards my elbow.

One of my very close friends from the Philippines who was a pediatrician at the hospital met me to take a look. Her first comment was "wow" and then there was silence. We just looked at the MRI and then at each other. What was there to say? She told me that if the absolute worst happened, I could live with her through treatment and she would be there for me. I appreciated her concern and charity but it all seemed so surreal. How could this have happened? I was once a healthy naval officer, jet pilot, and athlete. Now I was facing the loss of major bone, possible radiation and chemo.

For the first time since all the medical horrors began, I went home that night and cried. What had I done in my life to deserve this? Was it the less-than-chaste and liberal life I led in the Philippines? Was this the payback for life in the fast lane? Despite my sometimes lapse in judgment, I always tried to be a good person. Hadn't I paid my dues with the appalling FNAEB and assassination of my reputation? Like so many other people facing dreadful diseases, all I could do was wonder why this was happening to me.

It took a few days for the doctors to huddle around the MRI and finally come to a consensus. With my newfound attitude, instead of dwelling on the terrible possibilities, I went hiking. The San Diego area is an amazing recreation region, providing countless changes of scenery, and new sights and smells. I spent many hours hiking along the beach, through fields, up mountains, in some kind of trance trying to make sense of my life and my place in the world. I found my wanderings very inspiring and spiritual.

Standing on a mountain top with the wind whipping around me, looking out over the sparkling Pacific Ocean, I felt peace and serenity. Despite all my trials and tribulations, I still was blessed. I lived a life and accomplished tasks most people only dreamed of and people who cared about me and would do anything for me surrounded me. Even if I only had a year left to live, it had been a fast, furious, and incredibly exciting life. My only regret was that I never really gave back and that I, for the most part, was a taker, not a giver. True, I was serving my country, but ending my career in a hospital bed was not what I envisioned.

Finally after my quasi forty days in the desert, the doctors called me in for their opinion. They apologized for the delay but they decided to consult with civilian specialists in the San Diego area. My MRI and X-rays provided an interesting and enlightening forum for discussion and training. The doctors concurred that the lesion was indeed a tumor, but all indications were that it was benign, something called an enchondroma. It was unusually large but they were almost certain it was not malignant.

Despite the occasional throbbing, the tumor had not caused any significant pain since I started my thyroid medication. In fact, there was some discussion concerning the link between the two. The doctors speculated that the tumor had probably been there for some time, but the sudden introduction of a metabolic drug into my severely hypothyroid state caused rapid growth of the tumor, which accounted for the intense pain I originally experienced. They considered performing a biopsy but decided against it. If they took a section of the tumor, my arm would be significantly weakened and they weren't sure what type of tissue would fill in the hole. They decided to leave well enough alone.

Not only was I not facing surgery, but also the doctors saw no reason why I shouldn't start flying again. There was a chance I could break my arm if I ever ejected, but many aviators break some part of their bodies on ejection. The doctors were much more concerned about my lifestyle of skiing and mountain biking. The risk was significantly higher of me injuring myself off duty than on.

Before they let me leave, the orthopedic doctors were very clear about one more aspect of my tumor. If my arm ever started to hurt again for long periods of time, especially if it woke me up at night, I was to see a doctor right away. While the tumor looked benign now, these types of tumors had about a 5% chance of turning malignant. With that warning, I left, almost in shock. I prepared myself for the worst, and now I was given a fairly clean bill of health. Not only did I not have cancer, but also there was a chance I could fly again. I was filled with so many emotions at one time; it was very difficult to sort through them. I had been on such an emotional roller coaster for so many months; my head was literally spinning. Just two weeks prior I was considering wigs for chemotherapy and now I had the opportunity to fly again. I hardly knew how to respond to the events of the past few weeks.

After celebrating the unbelievable news with my friends, I flew back to Jacksonville to meet with the flight surgeons. I had now been in a medically down status for over a year and was desperate to get my career on track. The flight surgeons told me I faced an extensive medical review board to regain my flight status. From this review board, one of four outcomes would result. I could regain normal flight status, I might be restricted to land based aircraft, I could be limited to only multi-crew aircraft and lastly, I might not ever be allowed to fly again.

I was still so grateful I did not have cancer, I was just glad that I was given the chance to fly again in any capacity. I wanted very much to return to fighters but more than anything, I just wanted to fly again. I would gladly fly any aircraft but despite all the nastiness that occurred in VFA-106, I wanted desperately to return to the life of a fighter pilot.

I loved flying the F/A-18, pulling a lot of G's, dropping bombs and most of all, landing aboard the carrier. In my renewed excitement for flying, I quickly forgot the doctors' warnings that my body was a potential time bomb and my promises to live a more charitable life.

I was on an emotional high and in my sheer joy just to be alive and well, I thought if I was allowed to return to F/A-18s, all the instructors would understand the impact of my medical conditions. In essence, I thought they would forgive and forget and maybe actually feel a little empathy for me. Despite all the hard lessons I'd recently learned, I was still very naive about the cruelty and hatred that permeated VFA-106.

Preparation for my medical review was a quick reminder of how much the squadron did want me back. Unfortunately, medical review boards are not based purely on medical issues. Like most boards in the Navy, the medical review board also has political undertones. For example, one male pilot with adult onset of diabetes was allowed to return to flight status despite the doctors' recommendations. Usually diabetes is absolutely disqualifying for flight status but because of his connections, he was allowed to fly a single seat aircraft despite the seriousness of his condition.

Captain Mayer, the Commanding Officer who supported me had been replaced with a new CO, CDR Gortney. Since we had never met, I was shocked when I found out the new CO was actively attempting to intervene and block my return to F/A-18s. He did everything possible to tarnish my reputation and bias the board of doctors against me. The FNAEB, which was now a year old, was again a central focus point.

I accidentally found out about Gortney's attempts to undermine my return to flight status from one of the doctors on the review board. The doctor told me it was very unusual for a Commanding Officer to fight to keep someone out of the cockpit; usually it was exactly opposite. Most CO's will go to the extreme to help their pilots at a medical review board. I was the first pilot to come before the review board in some time without the support of my CO and it was troublesome to the board.

To counter the attempts of the VFA-106 CO to stop my return to flight status, I asked the Commanding Officer of NADEP to write a letter on my behalf. Captain Rice was highly respected, and he wrote a glowing endorsement that sang my praises both as a person and a naval officer. I also appealed to the medical board to make their decision based on the medical facts alone and to ignore the clearly biased FNAEB.

In the end, I could not have asked for a more fair medical board. After days of testing and deliberation, I was awarded full normal flight status. One doctor told me after all my medical procedures and briefings, I should consider medical school after I finished flying. They were most impressed with my mental stamina to hang in the game for such a long period of time while facing such life threatening conditions. I was equally impressed with the board's sense of fairness and ability to see past all the venom of VFA-106. I heard nothing but horror stories about these medical review boards and expected a fight. Instead, for the first time in a long time, I was judged fairly and without prejudice. It was a good feeling.

I was now on my way back to the cockpit. Because I won full flight status, I elected to resume training in the F/A-18. I wanted nothing more than to fly fighters, make cruises on aircraft carriers, and really serve my country. I had a few reservations, especially after the CO fought so hard to keep me out but I decided to put my fears aside and jump back into the fire. I was still on Cloud Nine after the cancer scare and regaining my medical flight status. So many people fought to give me a second chance and I wouldn't disappoint them.

Chapter Fifteen

Never Say Never

As soon as I received word that I was medically cleared to fly again, I immediately went back to VFA-106 to find out when I would start flying. There was a great deal of confusion when I returned, and it was clear no one ever expected to see me again. I was told to just "hang loose" while the command formulated a plan for me. I knew something strange was afoot because there should have been no need for a special plan. Despite my up-chit, the command was stalling for some reason.

Finally I received word about my fate. While I was medically cleared to fly again, the Commanding Officer of VFA-106 felt uncomfortable letting me back into the cockpit of the F/A-18. Instead of resuming training in the F/A-18, I would be sent to Meridian, Mississippi for "refresher training" in the A-4. I thought this was a very odd turn of events. I logged over 500 hours of flight time in the A-4 and certainly had no problems flying that plane. Unfortunately, A-4's have no radar or no advanced weapon systems, so they would be almost useless in training me to fly fighters. While any type of flying has advantages, returning to the A-4 was not going to help me to master the F/A-18.

When I expressed my doubts, I found out the real hidden agenda. VFA-106 was not just sending me for a few refresher "back in the saddle" flight hours, I was to return to the aircraft carrier in the A-4 and prove myself with just three weeks of refresher training. I was a little stunned at first. The last time I landed on a carrier was seven years prior and I trained for months previous to that attempt. I had not flown an aircraft in almost a year and a half and with minimal training, I was going back to the aircraft carrier.

I was intimidated at first, which is the exact effect I am sure the F/A-18 commanders wanted. It was obvious I would be required to pass this impromptu and unprecedented test before allowed back in the cockpit of an F/A-18. I feel quite certain that none of the senior leadership that dreamed up this little "trial by fire" ever expected me to pass. They felt confident that I would fail at the carrier and they would then be justified in refusing to allow me back into the F/A-18.

I on the other hand, decided once and for all to show them what I was made of. Not only was I feeling physically much better but mentally, I was even stronger than before. These men did know the meaning of "trial by fire." I endured an unscrupulous FNAEB that not only tried to remove my wings, but end my naval career as well. I withstood two operations, countless medical procedures, and the threat of cancer. There was nothing they could throw at me now that would ever be worse than what I already suffered. As far as I was concerned, from that point on in my life, everything was gravy.

So I sucked up my suspicions and fears, and jumped in my Jeep for the long drive to Mississippi. As I drove, I felt my stomach tightening with the memories of my last time in Meridian during flight school. Several years had passed and I knew none of the same instructors would be there, but I could not shake the fear and trepidation that I felt as a naive and gullible student seven years earlier. When I was winged in the summer of 1990, I vowed never to return to Meridian. Now here I was, going back in pseudo student status almost a decade later. I was reminded of the old adage, "Never say never!"

When I arrived, imagine my surprise to find that some of the old instructors were actually still there. My stomach dropped when I was greeted in the Ready Room by one of my former instructors who was the bane of my existence. "How could this be?" I thought. The Navy rotates its pilots every three years. Why are these people still here? I later found out that some instructor pilots asked to return to Meridian in order to finish their careers, and some were reservists on their two week or weekend training sessions.

The fight-or-flight response in me took over and I took great pains to avoid these individuals who at one time represented the devil to me. To me, time stood still and I was back in the squadron seven years ago. What I didn't see right away was how time changed these instructors. They were now married with children, and had mellowed over the years. They were not the same hot heads I once knew.

One of the instructors who tortured me as a young student actually pulled me into his office one day for a talk. He profusely apologized for his behavior as my instructor years ago and told me that in his younger days, he was "full of piss and vinegar." I was greatly surprised but he genuinely seemed like a changed man. He also recently underwent serious medical problems and as a result, refocused his priorities. As we sat in his office and laughed over the events of seven years ago, the forgiveness and relief that swept through me was a comfort. I hated Meridian and dreaded this return, but in that hour of confession and soul searching, I knew that one moment made my return worthwhile.

Upon my arrival, it was painfully obvious to me that my reputation from VFA-106 preceded me. Ironically, those instructors from my time in flight school were actually the ones in my corner. The new instructors were now the ones that hated me and my overall reception at first was very hostile. The first words to me from the operations officer, the individual responsible for overseeing my training, were, "You must really have friends in high places to allow you this type of training." I was completely taken aback. I did not want to return to Meridian and certainly this was no "good deal" for me.

I asked the operations officer what he meant and he told me that VFA-106 called ahead of my arrival to make sure the flight school instructors "knew what they were up against." He knew all about the FNAEB and what a troublemaker I was. My stomach immediately felt like a knot again. I knew the VFA-106 senior officers did not like me but it was clear all was fair in love and war. They attempted to stack the deck against me before my arrival with well-placed phone calls. They told the Meridian instructors that I was only allowed to return because I was a woman. There was no mention of all my medical problems and the Meridian staff did not know I had been out of the cockpit for a year and a half.

I was very angry at first because I walked into a very difficult situation with little preparation. It never occurred to me that VFA-106 would go to such extremes to make my training so difficult. I was also very concerned because assuming I passed this test, what would my life be like once I returned to VFA-106? If they were willing to sabotage this phase of training, what would the next be like? For the first time, I thought my return to the fighter community was not such a clever idea after all.

What VFA-106 didn't count on was the number of instructor pilots who were friends of mine from previous duty stations. I knew many of the instructors when they were students with me in flight school and I flew with several in the Philippines. My friends and the old instructors were very sympathetic to my plight. One told me that he heard all about me prior to my arrival and just disregarded all the brouhaha as typical gossip. He did tell me that initially no one in Meridian wanted me there but once they found out about the medical aspects, most were understanding and ready to start flying with me.

After just a week or so of a very chilly reception, the instructors visibly warmed up to me. Many knew that I had more hours in the A-4 than they did and were very happy to fly with me. In fact, after I proved that I could fly the A-4 and was extremely capable, several instructors quibbled over who would fly with me. They appreciated flying with someone who knew what they were doing instead of a new student who was liable to scare them half to death.

My two weeks of warm up flying can be described as nothing but pure fun. I knew the A-4 and its quirks so well; it was like riding a bike. The simulator instructors were all the same and they were very complementary of my improvements in both rudimentary flying skills and mental judgments. It was a pleasure to show them that all their effort seven years ago actually came to fruition. I was amazed I had so much fun in an environment that seemed like hell to me seven years before. After a day of flying, I dined with my friends that I hadn't seen in a long time to catch up on all the gossip. What began as a potentially torturous situation turned into a very rewarding experience.

The only truly negative aspect to my return to Meridian was news we received one day while flying. One of my former instructors who returned occasionally for his reserve duty shot himself in the head the night before. I was shocked. I knew that suicide among naval aviators was not unheard of but this was the first time it ever happened to someone I had known. He was also someone I flew with and immensely respected. The greatest tragedy was the wife and two children he left behind.

I found it sad that I was back in the same chapel on base paying my respects to another fallen comrade. Almost to the day, eight years prior I stood in the same chapel grieving over the loss of my friend Steve who flipped his plane at the carrier during training. It was more painful though to sit through a ceremony for a pilot who has taken his own life than one who has crashed. Most pilots understand and accept the risks of flying, but most of us have a hard time understanding someone who ends his own life.

My heart went out to his wife and children and I was more deeply affected by the ceremony than I ever thought possible. The old instructors were not the only ones who changed; I also now was a more feeling and appreciative person. After the ceremony was over, the entire congregation moved to the steps of the chapel to wait for the "Missing Man" ceremony.

In naval aviation, especially in the jet communities, when a pilot dies, his squadron comrades put on the "Missing Man" fly-over after the chapel services. Four planes will fly low over the base and just as the planes reach the church, one plane will abruptly leave the formation, almost vertical as in an ascent to heaven. The other three jets continue to fly, but leave a spot for the missing man. To me, the ceremony is just as moving as hearing Taps played on a bugle. As I stood on those same steps and watched the Missing Man formation fly over again, I was reminded of how precious life really is.

I had to shake off the grief just as quickly as when I was a student because now I was about to start training for the carrier. There was only a short period of time to prepare for the last big hurdle in my quest to return to F/A-18s. The carrier training was just as intense as when I was in the squadron seven years ago. In no time, we completed our carrier qualification training and headed to Jacksonville, Florida where we met up with the carrier, the USS John F. Kennedy.

Due to budget cutbacks and age of the ship, the USS Lexington was no longer in service. Now students landed on whatever carrier was available, and for my class, the only choice was the USS John F. Kennedy, based near Jacksonville Florida. It was definitely bittersweet for me to be back at the same airfield with the F/A-18 squadrons. Despite my trepidation, I reminded myself that I was very familiar with the airfield and local course rules, so the return was actually to my advantage. The weather was hot but clear and all indications were that my first time at the carrier in seven years would go well. My practice sessions were strong and I felt very confident that I was ready.

As my flight of four headed out to the operating area in the Atlantic, just off the coast of Jacksonville, I was nervous but I did not have the same butterflies that I did so many years ago. Because I was very familiar with the operating area and the local controllers, I was amazed at how much more on the ball I was compared to my two carrier attempts as a student. No longer was I surprised when I saw the carrier for the first time and when we received our signal to "Charlie" (to proceed and land), I was ready and locked on.

We flew by the tower and I did my break maneuver, crisp and level. I set myself in position; I was number three to land. As the ship reported its course and speed periodically, I even managed to figure out the ship was in a turn. While the turn was ever so slight, I knew that if I didn't immediately correct for the ship's turn, I would overshoot the carrier when I tried to land. I knew that probably the new students would not figure it out, it was just too much information for someone seeing the carrier for the first time.

Sure enough, as my group rounded the corner, everyone but me overshot and had to wave off. I was the only person to successfully trap aboard the first time. As I slammed into the wires for the first time in seven years, my adrenaline surged and I felt wonderful. It wasn't a picture perfect pass but it was good. I actually knew what was going on, and I was so happy to be back on the carrier. I eagerly taxied over to the catapult (Cat), anxious to feel that 0 to 180-mph jump-start that was the best ride on the planet.

I was not disappointed, although the Cat shot was not as violent as I remembered from the USS Lexington. When I was a student, the USS Lexington boasted the shortest landing and takeoff area; hence the Cat shots were more powerful. The USS John F. Kennedy was a much bigger carrier with a longer deck. The tradeoff for a shorter and less exciting Cat stroke was the longer landing distance. Since a larger landing area makes the pilot workload easier, I was just as happy landing on the Kennedy. In no time at all, I banged out all my traps and Cat shots and headed back to the beach.

The word exhilaration can not even come close to the way I felt. I did it. Unlike the last time I flew an A-4 to the carrier, I knew I did well and knew I was a qual. My grades were much higher than when I was a student and my boarding rate was 100%. I passed my test with flying colors but more importantly, I knew I would be back in the F/A-18. I was set up for failure and responded with a resounding success.

As I shook the hands of the instructors from Meridian, I was reminded of how life often comes full circle. I dreaded my return to Meridian and was sure it would be a distasteful experience at best. I could not have been more wrong. Not only was it very positive, but it also allowed me to bring closure with my horrible memories from flight school.

My reward for good behavior and good flying was returning to the F/A-18. However, after all the shenanigans and interfering that went on prior to my arrival in Meridian, I was more than a little concerned about my reception in VFA-106. I shook off my worries with the "take it one day at a time" mantra. It worked for me so far, and I jumped through every hoop put in front of me. I knew my return to VFA-106 would not be a walk in the park but at least I knew I was capable of meeting the demands of flying. I would step up to the plate again and give it my best shot.

I vowed to return to VFA-106 a smarter, more outwardly humble pilot. I would try to be as invisible as possible and would only speak when spoken to. I would swallow my pride and turn myself into the quiet, demure church mouse they wanted to see. I not only wanted to survive in the F/A-18 world, but I also wanted to excel and I would do whatever it took to make that happen.

Chapter Sixteen

Back into the Hornet's Nest

When I returned to the squadron in the summer of 1996, I was greeted with cold stares and tight-lipped responses. Despite my outstanding performance in the A-4, it was clear I would not be welcomed in VFA-106 for quite some time, if ever. I expected a less than friendly welcome but I was unprepared for the open hostility. More than a year had passed since the FNAEB and many of the old instructors were gone. However, many of the core players who hated me were still around. I knew the waters were poisoned but I had no clue how deep and pervasive the squadron's animosity of me really ran.

A couple of my male friends who were pilots in other squadrons on the base pulled me aside to give me a few words of wisdom. They asked me if it was at all possible to switch to the West Coast. Both said they did not think I would get a fair shake in VFA-106 because the stories about me took on a life of their own. I told them I thought that the time I was away would have calmed the waters and make people forget the FNAEB from over a year ago. They shook their heads no.

Apparently, the passing of time had not healed the old wounds, it instead caused what I term as the "Babe, The Blue Ox" tall-tale phenomenon. Instead of dying away, the stories about me grew to fantastic proportions. My friends relayed to me stories about how I threatened to ruin careers of senior officials if I was not returned to flight status. They said the word on the street was that Congressman Patricia Schroeder, a well known women's rights advocate, was my champion and forced the Navy to bend to her will. No one knew about my medical problems or the corrupt FNAEB board, or if they did, they completely discounted the real facts in favor of the more juicy material.

Now I knew why my reception was much worse than I ever antici-pated. While I was away fighting for my life, the rumor mill turned me into the Jane Fonda of the 1990's. I was now an alleged , which is the anti-Christ of naval aviation. As I heard my friends tell these stories, I was aghast. No stranger to naval aviation and the fighter community, I knew what a death knell the label of a feminist would be. Completely untrue, I had no idea where the stories of my supposed political femi-nist connection came from. My guess is that the instructors wanted desperately to believe my return was not due to their own collusion and dishonesty in the FNAEB, but because I was a woman and pulled strings at the highest of levels.

I felt physically ill after my encounter with my friends. I was used to overcoming challenges but my reputation was a monster with a life of its own. No one knew the truth and worse yet, they didn't want to know. The male pilots' prejudices against women pilots that surfaced with the death of Kara Hultgren were now completely manifested and entrenched in the East Coast squadrons. Through my bogus FNAEB, their hatred of me was merely an outlet for their frustrations and anger against women pilots.

Despite my hostile reception, I did have one friend in the squadron, Vivian. She was not a pilot but was the new replacement administration officer and took many of my duties when I left for NADEP. She was sympathetic to my plight because she experienced the disparity in treatment every day in VFA-106. I told her what I heard and my fears about my upcoming training. I asked her about the new Commanding Officer, would he be fair? I was suspicious after his attempt to block my medical up-chit, but maybe I overre-acted. I wanted to know her thoughts.

Vivian just shook her head and told me she wasn't too sure about the new CO. She told me that in a moment of frustration, he said to her, "Vivian, don't take this the wrong way and I don't include you in this, but I really hate having women in this squadron." She also relayed to me a story about the CO's feelings on sexual harassment.

Other pilots noticed that one of the instructors, Slick, was paying more than just a little attention to one of the junior enlisted women, who clearly did not desire his advances. Apparently it was so obvious and disruptive, the other pilots turned him in to the CO. An investigation was held, and the results were appalling. Slick constantly hit on his young subordinate, despite both his position of seniority and married status. The squadron was in such an uproar over the matter, the CO decided to address everyone publicly. He told the officers and the enlisted, a group of over 600, that he would not allow this type of behavior and he would actively enforce the Navy's policy of zero tolerance for sexual harassment. He said Slick's career was over, end of story.

The Commanding Officer's actions would betray his words and during the ensuing legal proceedings, the CO not only dismissed any legal charges or proceedings against Slick, but he was in fact rewarded with an above average performance evaluation. Not only did Slick go unpunished, but also the CO made sure he would be promoted. The most detestable aspect of Slick's evaluation was the fact that the CO gave him an above average rating for the "Equal Opportunity" category—the one category in which Slick was an abysmal failure.

Vivian and I both knew what we were up against—a good ole boy CO who absolutely did not think women belonged anywhere but in the kitchen, barefoot, and pregnant. Just a few days later during an all-pilot meeting, the CO told us once our meeting was over, we would adjourn to the club so we could hit on the other pilots' wives. I just shook my head and wondered what was going through his mind. During one of these club outings, Slick pinned the wife of another pilot up against a wall and said, "I want to f—k your brains out." Of course the husband of the shocked wife tried to throttle Slick, but they were pulled apart and since Slick was one of the CO's fair haired children, nothing happened. So much for the "Officer and a Gentleman" requirement.

Armed with more knowledge than I ever cared to have, I began my training. It was as difficult as I thought it would be and sometimes more so. When I walked down the hallway, no one greeted me, despite my sugary sweet attempts. Worse still, was the blatant immaturity that seemed to overcome my fellow students and instructors when I entered a room. When I walked into the Ready Room, a hush fell over the dozen or more people already in it. There was a lot of blatant whispering behind my back and at first I thought it was kind of comical. Sometimes I actually went into the Ready Room to see how fast I could quiet it down or outright clear it. I was amazed at my newfound power.

After a few weeks of this infantile behavior, the humor wore off and it really started to affect me because it was actually impacting the quality of my training. If I sat down at a desk in the study room, whomever I sat next to made a big production of getting up and moving farther away. In group meetings, every seat around me remained empty. The novelty of having such an effect on people quickly wore off and I became more and more frustrated.

Finally after weeks of the cold shoulder treatment, the least likely candidate broke the silence. One day as I was walking into the squadron, I came face to face with one of the members of the FNAEB, Nose. I greeted him, just like I greeted everyone, expecting the usual dead stare or a turn away. Instead, much to my surprise, Nose grabbed my arm and said, "Missy, I am so very sorry for what happened. I can't apologize enough and if I thought no one was looking, I'd give you the biggest hug right now."

For the second time in as many months, someone I considered the archenemy was profusely apologizing for his behavior towards me. I was flabbergasted not only because I never expected to hear this apology, but also because Nose was so earnest in his apology. I actually felt tears welling up as I struggled to make sense of both the hatred I felt for him and the forgiveness that he so desperately wanted. We stood there for quite a while as we discussed the events from a year ago.

Nose told me that indeed the FNAEB had been directed from above, especially the part about pulling my wings. He told me that CAPT Moffit, the old CO, told them to "get me" by whatever means available, and remove me from flight status. Nose then told me something that made me feel nauseous. He said there was another person overseeing the board that I was not aware of, a representative from Admiral Allen's staff.

I couldn't make any sense of what he was telling me. Why would Admiral Allen, the same person who overturned the FNAEB, send a representative to monitor my FNAEB? Not only was that unheard of, it was blatant conspiracy. In addition, why would this representative encourage the board to lie and at best, misrepresent my situation? Nose shook his head in confusion as well and said we were all pawns. When I asked him why he went along with such nonsense, he said, "Well, it seemed like the right thing to do at the time. When Captains and above are telling you how to proceed, you do it." Nose said it made him nauseous to sign my FNAEB, knowing full well that he and several other instructors committed perjury in the process.

I knew Nose felt responsible for the outcome and his admissions of guilt were very therapeutic for me. After that day, I knew I at least one person in the squadron was my ally, at least for a little while. Nose decided to resign and was leaving the Navy, in part because of what he witnessed through my FNAEB. I was sad he was leaving because I would lose one of the only friendly faces in the squadron and someone who could give me a reality check.

Just a few days later, I was scheduled for my first simulator and the instructor was Nose. I was delighted because I wanted to show him what a solid pilot I was and prove my worthiness. As we sat in his office, talking about the simulator flight, he told me that several people came to him prior to the flight and said, "Did you see who you were flying with?" and "I feel so sorry for you."

While he relayed these stories to me, coincidentally, the phone rang. I was sitting right next to him so I heard both sides of the conversation. The person on the other line was another instructor who was responsible for scheduling. He profusely apologized to Nose for scheduling him with me, telling Nose, "I had to do it to somebody man, I am sorry it had to be you."

In a deja vu instance, I felt like I was in grade school and no one wanted me on his basketball team. These guys looked at flying with me as a fate worse than death and they were perpetuating the tall tales at every turn. Fortunately Nose was the consummate professional and didn't let the call faze him, but the significance of that call was not lost on me. I was not wanted and I would never be accepted, no matter what I did.

Shortly thereafter, all the officers were given a survey that evaluated the acceptance of women in the command. I filled it out truthfully, pointing to all these recent episodes as examples of harassing and demeaning behavior. When asked if I would leave the Navy because of the way I was treated, I answered yes. I knew my career was over, and my new plan was to finish my obligation and then leave. The events of the past few weeks proved to me that in such a tightly knit community, my future seemed very bleak.

Each survey was read by the Commanding Officer. When he got to mine, he called Vivian into his office. His response to my survey was, "I wish she would just resign then and quit wasting everyone's time." When Vivian told me this, for the first time since my FNAEB, I thought maybe my immediate resignation would be the best course of action. The CO clearly was not going to take any action to alleviate the situation and provide me with quality training.

I constantly reminded myself that the reason I decided to come back was my love of flying. Whenever I would get down, I forced myself to relive my moments at the carrier just weeks before. Just thinking about flying around the carrier made my heart race and temporarily refocused my attention away from my miserable work environment. My first flight in the plane was my initial indication that maybe my feeble attempts at self-brainwashing were not going to be enough.

I was happy to climb into the plane and I really looked forward to the excitement of an afterburner takeoff. I remembered how jazzed I was two years prior and looked forward to that heady feeling again. My instructor was relatively new so my hopes were high that he would be receptive to me. His reputation was one of joviality and easy going fun. Unfortunately, it was a side of him I never saw. He sat in the back seat and never said a word. I flew the flight almost as if I were alone and at some points I actually forgot someone was in the back seat.

While it wouldn't seem so bad for the instructor to remain quiet, it was very unnerving. It was uncomfortable flying with someone in my back seat who remained mute the entire time and only answered with monosyllabic responses when asked a question. When I landed and taxied back to the hangar, I was overcome with a feeling of sadness. It wasn't fun anymore, it was pure work. The lack of interaction drained me and it just wasn't the same no matter how much I pretended.

It was very difficult to gauge how well I was doing in my training. I knew that compared to my first time in VFA-106, I was doing much better and felt much more at ease in the aircraft. The silent treatment from the instructors remained the norm and it bothered me that in multi-plane pre-flight briefings, I was essentially ignored. It was clear I was on my own and that very little teaching would actually take place. Instead of looking forward to my flights, I dreaded the silence and ostracism.

In response to my hostile environment, I took solace in studying harder. I spent hours poring over the weapons and tactics manuals, thinking that if at least I was knowledgeable about the systems of the

F/A-18, I would gain the slightest modicum of respect. I continued greeting people in the hallway even though most were still ignoring me, pathetically overjoyed when someone said hello in return.

Instead of getting better over time, the level of abuse actually worsened. Despite my senior status, I was repeatedly assigned the most menial watch duties and always over a holiday. It was so blatant that even a few of my peers took notice. When the Christmas leave period was assigned, I requested the holidays off to join my family in Lake Tahoe. My request was approved in writing by all the departments involved with watch assignments, meaning I would not be required to stand any duty over the Christmas holidays.

I was quite surprised when I saw the December watch bill and saw my name on it Christmas Eve. I went to great lengths to have my leave approved and despite the approval in writing, I was still assigned a holiday duty. When I asked the watch officer who was responsible for scheduling, about his decision, he brusquely pushed past me and barked, "You figure it out!"

I regained my balance in the middle of the hallway with my leave request that he approved just dangling in my hand. It was degrading and incredibly frustrating. Even if I followed all the rules and played their games, I still suffered in the end. I spent thousands of dollars on plane tickets and lodging for my family trip, and there was nothing I could do about the duty assignment.

My only option was to find a replacement, someone who would be willing to sacrifice his Christmas Eve. After much begging and pleading, I found another student willing to take my place—for a price. Quite the aspiring extortionist, another student recognized my dire situation and offered to help out, for money of course, and I willingly paid him. I felt the whole affair was cheap and sleazy but quite symbolic of my time in the squadron.

Despite the hell I lived in, I still hoped that someone would recognize my flying skills improved immensely, and just maybe the instructors and other students would warm to me. Four months passed since my return and I desperately needed even the slightest hope that the situation would improve. Change was right around the corner, but it wasn't for the better.

One evening after I finished studying, I checked the next day's schedule to see if I was listed for a flight or simulator. The simulator schedule was published and I was not on it. It was not unusual not to be scheduled so I thought nothing of it. I called my class leader later in the evening for him to reconfirm that I was scheduled for nothing. He also told me I had nothing the next day.

At 0715 the next morning, my phone rang. It was the squadron and they wanted to know where I was. I missed a scheduled simulator and was in big trouble. I was to get my butt into see the Training Department Head immediately. I jumped into my Jeep and sped to work. What did I miss? I saw the schedule and did not see my name, and my class leader, a Lieutenant Commander, did not see my name either. What possibly went wrong?

When I walked into the operations office, I asked the scheduling officer what happened. One of the more junior officers looked around and then pulled me into a side office. He told me that the schedule changed late the previous evening and I never saw the later copy. He apologized to me and said that he never meant for me to miss anything. Just before I left, the scheduling officer said, "I don't know what you did but the instructors really hate you. They are gunning for you so watch out."

So there it was—a staff officer now vocalized what I always suspected. I tried to shake it off as I walked to the Training Department Head's office. He was a senior officer in the squadron who was very powerful and his callsign was Shaft. He was the same pilot diagnosed with diabetes so I thought maybe he would be more understanding. I was totally unprepared for his attack when I walked into his office. Shaft handed me a pink sheet. They were going to issue me a SOD (signal of difficulty) for missing the simulator. He said, "I don't care what your story is and don't even try to tell me, I don't want to hear it. You missed an event, you get a SOD, PERIOD."

I just looked at him in shock with my mouth wide open. A SOD was a very serious punishment; it is what eventually leads to another FNAEB. They are usually reserved for flight and safety related offenses. In addition, I knew for a fact that guys missed scheduled simulators all the time for various reasons and not once did they ever receive a SOD. When I looked at the paper, I knew an appeal was impossible. The Commanding Officer already signed it. My fate was signed, sealed, and delivered and no one ever heard my side of the story.

I was very upset that evening and cried over the phone to a friend. I didn't know what upset me worse, the SOD or the fact that someone close to the instructors actually verbalized their hatred for me. What Hell had I created for myself? I tried so hard to fit in since my return. I laid low, never complained, stood my duties, and suffered through countless episodes of humiliation. It was not lost on me that I volunteered to come back, because I thought it was what I wanted. I started to reconsider my earlier thoughts of resignation.

Was this what I wanted, REALLY? At some time in the past, I truly enjoyed flying but as of late, I started to dread anything that dealt with VFA-106. I reminded myself that I still really enjoyed working at NADEP even though I wasn't flying. The happiest times in my life were when I worked with people who wanted me on their team. When I was in the Philippines, the only time I was happy was when I was either flying or with my friends, not socializing with my fellow pilots. Had I missed the boat? Should I have swallowed my pride and never insisted on flying F/A-18s again? I agonized over my choices and the what-ifs.

Just a few days later, something happened that made my muddled view of the squadron only become more painfully clear. One day, as I was in the squadron preparing for a flight, I heard a big ruckus in the hallway. All the students and instructors were hustling out to the flight line. I asked someone what was going on. A mid-air collision I was told, two of our F/A-18s collided while mock dogfighting. Miraculously, no one was hurt and both planes were able to limp home and land.

The tow trucks brought the planes into the hangar and everyone wanted to take a look. I joined the mad rush, just as curious as everyone else. It was rare for two planes to collide and both return. Usually someone is forced to eject or even killed, and at least one plane crashes. Now we would have the opportunity to see the collision damage of both planes. Everyone stood around and armchair quarterbacked the probable events. As I looked at the aircraft, it was clear that the pilots of both planes were extremely fortunate. It didn't take a rocket scientist to figure out what apparently happened. Instructors who were honing their skills to fight against the students flew the two planes. The planes were dogfighting and one outmaneuvered the other. The aircraft in the rear was chasing the other plane, attempting to get a gun solution. A precarious position to be in, the plane closing for the kill has only a small window of time to fire. Once the safety bubble of 500 feet around the target has been penetrated, the attacking aircraft is supposed to terminate the engagement.

For whatever reason, the pilot attacking did not recognize his high rate of closure until it was too late. At the last second, he tried to pull away, but almost like hitting a car from behind, the offensive plane rammed the lead plane. In another aircraft that wasn't fly-by-wire, the results would most likely have been far worse. Because the F/A-18 flight control computer is so superior, it was able to correct for the damage on both aircraft, allowing the pilots and planes to return home safely.

Whenever an accident occurs in naval aviation, an investigation is immediately launched. In most military aircraft accidents, pilot error is to blame and it was clear from the damage that this was true yet again. The culpable pilot usually faces some type of disciplinary hearing, which is typically a FNAEB. Depending on the circumstances, the pilot is either returned to flying after some retraining, or he loses his flight status altogether. No one knew what would happen to the pilot who rear-ended the other jet but such a blatant error did not bode well for his future.

I found out the accident pilot's fate from a very unlikely source, Rick, the squadron flight surgeon. During a routine paperwork visit, Rick remarked that the accident pilot owed me a debt of gratitude. I couldn't possibly imagine what he meant. Rick then told me that he was responsible for examining the pilot immediately after the accident. The accident pilot complained of many of the same symptoms that I exhibited just prior to my FNAEB. Because of everything that happened to me, Rick was able to immediately recognize indications of thyroid trouble. He ran the blood tests, which came back with the instructor pilot's thyroid levels ten percent above normal.

At first I felt partially comforted that at least someone benefited from the months of my medical misery. Prior to my case, endocrine diseases received little if any attention in the almost all male world of tactical aviation. In fact, my flight surgeon went on to tell me that due to my predicaments, they were also able to recognize a case of lupus in another male pilot. My heart went out to these pilots because I knew what they were struggling with and the uncertainty they felt for the future.

As the events unfolded however, I was rankled with the squadron's response to the accident. When the Commanding Officer was informed of the medical problem, he decided that the accident pilot should not be blamed for what was clearly a medical issue. There would be no FNAEB and no black mark on the pilot's record. In fact, he was treated like a hero who survived a near death experience. The other pilots went out of their way to make the accident pilot feel like part of the team and as if the accident was no big deal. As soon as the doctors gave him the thumbs up, the pilot resumed flying.

The irony of the situation gnawed at me. This pilot collided with another plane, causing hundreds of thousands of dollars worth of damage. Because of the grace of God, he was still alive. No doubt his medical problems were a factor but his thyroid gland was only out of limits by 10%. My thyroid levels were one hundred times the normal and I truly had faced life threatening medical problems. Despite the fact that I never caused an accident and should have been in a coma, I was forced to endure an incredibly humiliating and corrupt FNAEB. I didn't wish ill on the accident pilot. I was glad that he was able to get back in the cockpit in just a few weeks. It was a hard to pill to swallow though as I watched the instructors show him so much compassion, while they displayed nothing but malice and animosity for me.

One evening after a long day of flying, I checked the schedule. Flight training follows the building block process of learning and every flight has a prerequisite flight that must be completed. When I saw the schedule, I immediately noticed an error. I was scheduled to fly a flight for which I did not have the prerequisites. I didn't think it was a big deal, I would just tell the duty officer which was the standard procedure.

When I approached the duty desk in the Ready Room, I noticed the duty officer, an instructor pilot, was engaged in idle chitchat with a buddy of his. I politely waited on the periphery for him to finish and when he did, I made an effort to explain the situation. He abruptly cut me off and literally started screaming at me. He yelled and cursed at me for my supposed lack of preparedness and berated me for my lack of professionalism. He made no sense and sounded like a raving lunatic. However, the Ready Room was full of instructors, egging him on and very much approving of his dealings with me. It was obvious to me the duty officer was peacocking for the other pilots who no doubt felt I deserved treatment much worse than a little yelling. The whole scene was very surreal and a little scary to me. I stood mute, shocked as I watched the Dr. Jeckyll/Mr. Hyde transformation.

When the phone rang, diverting his attention elsewhere, I turned on my heel and walked away, fuming and humiliated. The situation was so antagonistic in the squadron that I could not even do my job without blatant verbal abuse. I could handle the ostracism both in the cockpit and in the wardroom. However, with the unfair duty assignments, the bogus SOD, and now the verbal lashing in the Ready Room, it was clear the situation wasn't getting better, it was getting exponentially worse. The hatred the guys felt for me was no longer manifesting itself in passive aggressive actions, now they wore their derision for me like a badge of honor.

That evening, I went home and wrote my letter of resignation. I just couldn't take it anymore. All I thought about was that if I stayed, I faced three more years of service with these same hateful individuals. Who was I fooling? I would never have any kind of meaningful career in the fighter community. It was hard enough for a woman in such a macho environment, much less a woman who was rumored to be incompetent and considered the anti-Christ. I always thought performance is what counted, and as soon as everyone saw that I was flying well, they would back off. It never materialized. Despite all my accomplishment and improvements, I was the squadron leper and anyone caught befriending me would suffer the same fate. Despite my love of flying and desire to be on the tip of the spear, I could not go on in VFA-106. After all my medical trials, I learned that life was too important and too short to waste it on individuals who are petty and self-serving. I needed to leave the Navy and move on with my life or I would go crazy.

The following is an excerpt from my letter of resignation:

> *My ludicrous and slanderous FNAEB held in June of 1995 has continued to have a severe negative impact on my reputation and career which, at this point, are both unsalvageable…After spending five months in the squadron since my return, very little has changed in a positive vein. I would describe my current environment as hostile with prevailing animosity. The command and the community absolutely do not support me, and minimal toleration seems to be the agenda. Several "fleet pilots" have told me that it would be in my best interest to request a coast change, while others in VFA-106 have cautioned me about certain instructors' opinions. In fact one person*

felt the need to warn me, "The instructors are gunning for you." The general consensus is that the only reason I was allowed to return to training was because I was a woman, not due to any merit.

My father is a former marine and sailor, dedicating thirty years of his life to the Navy. I am a Naval Academy and Naval Postgraduate School graduate and have been a top notch performer throughout my entire career. The Navy has been the only life I have ever known, and I intended to dedicate thirty years just as my father did. I will always be very grateful to the Navy for allowing me to reach my full potential and providing me with opportunities I never dreamed possible. However, the events of the past two years have destroyed my faith and trust in my peers and senior leadership, and I have lost complete confidence in the system. The bottom line is that even flying one of the world's greatest fighters is not worth the daily humiliation, abuse and ostracism. I want to end this chapter of my life and move on to a more positive, receptive and rewarding career.

I did not hand in my letter the next day. After sleeping off my emotional temper-tantrum, I decided that I should think long and hard about such a final decision. I was a Naval Academy graduate who always intended to make the Navy a career. I had now served a total of thirteen years—four at Annapolis and nine as a commissioned officer. I was a top ranked performer and despite all my trials and tribulations, I persevered. I worked so hard to regain my seat in the F/A-18, was I really ready to give it up? Should I raise the white flag or was this just some type of childish response on my part? I decided to talk to a couple of my friends who also flew F/A-18s for their opinions.

After I showed them my resignation letter, they both agreed that it was probably the best thing to do. I was a little shocked. I somewhat hoped that they would rally to my side and try to motivate me to stay. Instead, they told me what they saw from the male perspective. They both said that when I was not around, the guys loved to talk about how much they hated me, in fact it was somewhat of a little game they played. The instructors were in fact gunning for me they said, and vowed to make my life miserable. I never had a fighting chance and they were personally dismayed with the intense hatred and contempt their peers exhibited towards me.

After my talk, I felt even more defeated and sure resignation was my only choice. I thought about transitioning to another job in the Navy but I was too senior for the jobs I wanted. At that point, I been a naval officer for almost nine years and was a Naval Academy graduate. Since I was seventeen, I planned to make the Navy a career. It was a hard pill for me to swallow that I failed at something. Up to that point, I succeeded at everything I attempted, but now I was forced to make a choice. I could continue flying fighters, have no life, and be hated by my peers. In contrast, I could leave, which would mean no longer flying the aircraft I loved, but it would mean I might find some happiness.

There was yet another aspect of my life that I had been ignoring. The strain of the intense training and the stress of the hostile environment started to physically show. The old feelings of exhaustion began to creep back into my days. Anyone with some type of autoimmune disease will attest to the fact that exhaustion associated with these diseases is unlike any other. Not just a sense of tiredness, these feelings are deep inside the muscles and bones. For me, nausea almost always accompanied the overwhelming fatigue. When these periods occurred, I felt like I must lie down or I would collapse.

I chalked the exhaustion up to stress and consciously made an effort to get more sleep and eat better. When the mysterious rashes began to crop up again along with the loss of blood in my hands and feet, I knew I made the wrong decision to return to fighters. The doctors warned me that my lifestyle would control the onset of a connective tissue disease and it looked as if they were right. When I worked in a positive, cheerful environment, my health flourished. Now that I was back in the

Hornet's nest, my body could not keep up with venom that inundated me at every turn.

The old feelings of exhaustion were not the only old malady to return. The deep ache in my arm returned with a vengeance. In the previous months since my return to VFA-106, I occasionally experienced a dull pain that ran the length of my left arm but I wasn't too concerned. The doctors told me the large tumor in my arm would probably cause an occasional ache. They told me the only time I should be concerned was if the pain repeatedly woke me up at night.

The first night I woke with the pain coursing down my arm didn't alarm me. "Just one of those things" I told myself. One time is no big deal. As it occurred more and more frequently, I started to worry. With the return of so many old symptoms, I convinced myself it was all stress related. Once I left VFA-106, life would be better and all these problems would just go away. I knew that night pain was a sign that a tumor could be cancerous, but I refused to believe after all I had been through, I would now develop cancer.

As I was struggling with this internal debate, my mother called to tell me my grandfather, Pappy, was dying. The family was mustering at his bedside in Pensacola, Florida to say good-bye. I immediately took emergency leave from the squadron and raced to Pensacola. The situation with my grandfather had been tenuous for some time, and not just physically. Unfortunately my step-grandmother did not approve of my grandfather's side of the family and we were estranged for many years. Now after years of squabbling, both sides of the family tried to make amends over the deathbed of my grandfather. It was sad and pathetic and it only added to my grief over my career.

When I walked into Pappy's house, which I had not seen, I was overcome with sorrow. Why was life like this? Why did we spend so much time building walls, digging trenches, and hurting one another over such incredibly trivial matters? I walked to Pappy's bed, which was a hospital bed and saw him for the first time in many years. Despite the weight he'd lost, he looked remarkably young. At 80 years of age, Pappy sported a full head of hair, which was still mostly brown. The biggest change was the oxygen machine assisting him in breathing.

Like so many people of his generation, Pappy smoked his entire life. He quit in his 60's when so much medical evidence for lung cancer gained media interest, but the damage was already done. He did not have lung cancer, but the forty years of smoking took their toll. Now his lungs were paper thin, as delicate as a spider's web. They could no longer provide Pappy with enough oxygen to breathe. The supplemental oxygen kept him alive but the doctors did not think his heart could handle the strain for much longer.

I sat next to Pappy and held his hand. He was very glad to see me and we just held hands, while I tried to carry on a one way conversation. For Pappy, speaking took too much effort, so I filled in for both sides. It was very difficult for me watching my grandfather die. I rarely stopped chastising myself for not making amends sooner. Had I learned anything from all my surgeries and medical problems? I made all these hollow promises to God that not only would I make my life better, but other people's as well and what came of these promises? I wasted years in this Hatfield/McCoy battle and now I was watching my grandfather die.

The next day, Pappy was feeling better and he wanted to speak with me. He started telling my brother and me stories about his past. An officer in the Navy, Pappy was Admiral Nimitz's meteorologist during the World War II Pacific campaigns. When we were younger, he never really spoke of his time in the war and we didn't know enough to ask. The families became estranged during my time at the Naval Academy and I never had the chance to ask him about his experiences once I was in the Navy. Now, on his deathbed, he seemed to need to talk about it and relished the fact that I was another naval officer. I was fascinated with his stories and descriptions of people and events that I only read about in history books. The more he talked, the sadder I felt for all the lost years. It broke my heart to watch him struggle and gasp for breath as he talked. We never tried to stop him though, we all knew he wanted to share his thoughts before he died.

While I was there, I told my family I was thinking about resigning from the Navy. Military service in my family was a tradition and I did not want to disappoint my family or have them think of me as a quitter. I wanted to follow in both my grandfather and father's footsteps and serve my country. I wanted to be like them, but most of all, I wanted them to be proud.

My mother was the first person to weigh in on the decision. She wanted me to leave. She knew the toll that the Navy had taken on me, both mentally and physically. I was her only daughter and she agonized over my crazy life and seemingly endless predicaments. She wanted me to come home for at least a little while and wanted to see me for the holidays again.

My uncle, a former Air Force B-52 pilot, was also at the bedside of his father. He was now a vice president for a major airline and a general in the National Guard. He asked me about the squadron life, and I told him how miserable I was and my doubts about my future. Without blinking an eye, he told me to leave it all behind and fly in the civilian world. He told me it wasn't worth all the misery and he would see to it that I had a job if I wanted it.

I was very grateful, not for the job offer, but for his matter-of-fact attitude about leaving the service. In fact, I was a little taken aback by my family's overwhelming response to leave. I had no idea my distress was so evident to everyone else. My mother, also a victim of an autoimmune disease, reiterated the doctors' earlier concerns. How far was I going to push a potentially bad situation? What was I trying to prove? As far as my family was concerned, I already proved myself. I had been a pilot now eight years, earned a master's degree in Astronautical Engineering, and was a fighter pilot, even if it was only for a short time.

I dreaded telling my family that I was thinking of leaving so I very much appreciated all their words of encouragement and their rallying behind me. I stayed in Pensacola for another day and then returned to Jacksonville. As I left, I kissed my grandfather on the forehead and told him I loved him. He squeezed my hand and told me he loved me too. It was the last time I ever saw him alive.

On the long drive home, I churned through all the events of the past few weeks. I was miserable in the squadron, and many nights I lay in bed wishing I died in one of my previous surgeries. Despite my love for flying, I dreaded interacting with all those individuals who clearly hated my mere presence and were in control of my future. My mysterious medical maladies were back, and I was quite certain the stress of my situation was a major contributor. The pain in my arm was worsening, and I was certain it was psychosomatic. In addition, my grandfather was dying and I never really got to know him because of my dedication to my career and my fierce pride. I had very little to show for my life except for my personal accomplishments and a series of failed relationships. In a moment of rare clarity driving down I-10, I was deeply ashamed of my selfishness and superficialities.

As I drove, I thought of two of my favorite passages. The first was a quote from Van Wyck Brooks, *"How delightful is the company of generous people, who overlook trifles and keep their minds instinctively fixed on whatever is good and positive in the world about them. People of small caliber are always carping. They are bent on showing their own superiority, their knowledge or prowess or good breeding. But magnanimous people have no vanity, they have no jealousy, and they feed on the true, and the solid wherever they find it. And, what is more, they find it everywhere."*

Somewhere along the path of my life, I lost my way. I was not the magnanimous person who loved life; I was now a bitter, angry person who hated waking up in the morning. I was then reminded of my second favorite quote, written by Richard Bach, *"We generate our own environment. We get exactly what we deserve. How can we resent the life we've created for ourselves? Who's to blame, who's to credit, but us? Who can change it, anytime we wish, but us?"*

The only person who could change my miserable situation was me. Despite the wrongs heaped upon me, I was still in control of my life. I loved flying, especially the F/A-18, but I could not stand the ostracism and abuse surrounding me. I was amazed at how quickly I forgot all the recent lessons God taught me about humility, the sanctity of life, and His grace in my quest to prove I was just as good or better than the next fighter pilot. Now, I was in pain both physically and mentally and I could only blame myself for continuing to submit myself to such torment.

So I did the hardest thing I have ever done in my life. I looked deep inside myself, swallowed my pride, and turned in my letter of resignation the next day. Despite the stern tone of my letter, I was not overly angry or bitter. I accepted the hand that life dealt me and decided the best course of action was to start over. I did not want my career to end in tumultuous accusations, I just wanted to leave and begin a new life in more promising surroundings.

Chapter Seventeen

Needs of the Navy

Despite the agony I went through prior to submitting my letter of resignation, I was relatively at peace with myself once I gave it to the Commanding Officer. Because the squadron fought so hard to kick me out before, I thought the senior leadership would rejoice in their victory and help me pack my bags. The climate of the Navy was one of downsizing in the post-Cold War era, and officers were leaving left and right. I was sure my departure would be quick and painless, with little fanfare. I was so certain in fact, that I started interviewing for civilian jobs and making plans to move away. I was completely unprepared for the fight to come.

As expected, I was ordered to report to the Commanding Officer, CDR Gortney. My letter was strong and pointed an accusing finger at my chain of command. I knew he would be unhappy with the tone but would no doubt celebrate my imminent departure. When I sat down in his office, he told me I never gave him the opportunity to fix the squadron and the problems I mentioned in my letter of resignation. I told him I didn't blame him or even the current batch of instructors. The previous Commanding Officer sealed my fate by ordering the corrupt FNAEB and ensuring the insane rumor mill about me was only perpetuated. I told him he inherited an unfortunate situation and instead of fighting it, I was ready to resign.

CDR Gortney then went on the offensive. He told me that because of my remaining one-year commitment, I had a choice. I could stay in the squadron or I would face a desk job as a pseudo-secretary on a carrier out to sea. This particular job is one most feared by aviators and is considered modern day torture. The unlucky recipient does nothing for the six-month cruise but menial paperwork while watching the other pilots fly. It is the ultimate form of punishment for fighter pilots and is the definition of hell.

I was completely blind-sided and totally shocked. I knew for a fact that the Navy was releasing officers early all across the nation due to the drawdown, and never once did I think my relatively tiny commitment would be an issue. I was even more angered by his response because I also knew CDR Gortney recommended early releases for several other officers. In fact, one fellow Lieutenant owed two years but was allowed to leave the Navy for a lucrative airline job. I also knew another male pilot in the airwing that was released early even though he took the bonus, which obligated him for four more years.

The bonus is a large sum of money the Navy pays to its pilots who are contemplating leaving. Taking the almost $100,000 bonus obligates the pilot for another six years and this pilot was allowed to leave in the middle of his commitment, owing thousands of dollars and years in commitment. The reason he was allowed to go? He attended TAIL-HOOK and his promotion was delayed as a result. No charges were ever brought against him, but because of the delay, the senior pilots felt sorry for him. They decided to let him go without any payback of time or money because of his career was ruined!

All these thoughts flew through my mind as I considered my Commanding Officer's words which were essentially a threat. CDR Gortney was upset that if senior officials saw my letter of resignation, his career would be in trouble. He made it quite clear that if I proceeded with my letter, I would be getting coffee for senior officers on a carrier. I was offering to leave with little hassle and now, my Commanding Officer was going to fight me to save his reputation.

The CO then told me to report back the next day and he would brief me on his final decisions. I gladly left, confused with the turn of events and wondering if he really possessed the power to back up his threats. All I wanted to do was raise the white flag and instead of accepting my defeat, my squadron was going to rub salt in the wound.

The next day, I returned at the appointed time and was met by the CO and Shaft, the Training Department Head who hated me. Despite the early release of other male pilots, CDR Gortney told me he decided to recommend me for immediate sea-going service. In addition, he presented me with two papers to sign. One suggested I would not file sexual harassment charges against the Navy and the other was a document that maintained I was turning in my coveted wings of gold, in effect never allowing me to fly again in the Navy or the civilian world.

I looked at them in disbelief. Did my blond hair make me seem like a complete idiot? They must have thought I was pretty stupid to even offer up these ridiculous documents. There was no way I would ever sign away my rights to be a pilot. I earned my wings with more blood, sweat, and tears than most pilots ever suspected existed. I did nothing wrong to merit the stripping of my wings, I was just merely trying to resign. The other male pilots in the squadron released early were never asked to "turn in their wings." Something was amiss and I was not happy with the turn of events.

I of course refused to sign the form giving up my wings. I did however sign the form suggesting I would not file sexual harassment charges. It was not my intent to spark a big brouhaha; I just wanted to leave. If I filed charges, a long legal process would only impede my departure and I just wanted out as quickly as possible. While I thought I would have an indisputable legal case, I wanted nothing of it. I did not want to instigate a messy sexual harassment suit and I didn't want to be a part of all that ugliness.

As upset as I was, I kept my composure. The CO was not the final approving authority for sea duty. My case would be ultimately decided in Washington DC and I felt certain any sane person looking at my case would recommend my immediate departure. It would not benefit anyone to have a long drawn out legal battle that would again embarrass the Navy. I was sure the senior officers would understand the gravity of the discrimination in the squadron and my charges, and allow me to leave.

After I submitted my letter of resignation, there was a stir in the instructor ranks. Word spread quickly that I resigned and I am sure there was much rejoicing. CDR Gortney, no doubt happy but also angry at my attempt to resign, ordered me out of the squadron immediately. I happily found work at my old command, NADEP, and picked up where I left off only six months prior. Everyone was happy to have me back and I was again amazed at the difference in the two environments. Interestingly though, just two days later, I received a phone call that was very enlightening.

Out of the blue, one of the instructors called me. I was very surprised, especially because it was Bull, the same instructor who testified at my FNAEB that I was no fun to hang around. He was also one of the instructors who made a big point of ignoring me and pretending I didn't exist. I didn't even know what to say beyond hello and it was pretty clear to me he had been drinking. In my experience, people are painfully honest when they have been drinking. Bull was no different and was a man who needed to relieve his guilt.

Without my prodding, he started profusely apologizing for his behavior towards me, both past and present. He heard that I was resigning and felt partially responsible. He never meant for things to go as far as they did and he wanted to let me know how sorry he was. I asked him why he changed his witness statement at my FNAEB. Bull told me that the FNAEB members approached him before and after the board to let him know of their "plan." Even before my FNAEB, the board members formulated a plan to vote for my removal and followed through to the very end. Bull told me he and several others were presented with bogus statements to sign and they went along because they didn't want to go against the clear direction from the board members.

I could not believe the confession I was hearing. I always suspected the conspiracy at my FNAEB but I never thought I would hear someone acknowledge it. I was greatly relieved to hear Bull's admissions, especially when he told me I never had a chance upon my return. He also thought the FNAEB and the continuous rumors damaged my reputation beyond repair. He confirmed that the instructors were gunning for me and it was extremely unlikely I would ever have a fair shake in the fighter community. He complimented me on my tenacity though and told me I had more "balls" than any of the pilots he knew.

Instead of becoming angry as I heard more and more of the details, I started to feel very sad. I realized I wasted precious time and energy in a situation that was doomed from the beginning. The level of corruption during my FNAEB and following events was frightening and I was only more convinced that my immediate departure was the best course of action. My worst suspicions were now confirmed. A few individuals who were only trying to support their own political agenda against women in combat destroyed my career. In the process, I suffered unparalleled humiliation, struggled with very serious medical problems that were initially ignored, and eventually lost my career.

The unfairness of the past two years weighed heavily on my heart and I questioned God again, "What had I done to deserve all this?" It was not lost on me that medically, I was still not out of the woods yet. Just before I submitted my letter of resignation, I saw the flight surgeon and told him about the recurring night pain in my arm. He was concerned but not overly alarmed. He wanted me to have another bone scan which would show any changes in my arm. I did not say anything about the medical problems either in my letter of resignation or to the

Commanding Officer. I did not want to cloud the issue or lessen the impact of my letter.

The flight surgeon needed my medical record to make some annotations but the records department initially couldn't find it. After searching high and low, they finally found it stuffed in the bottom of a filing cabinet. When they opened it, there was a note inside it to have me recalled immediately. Three months prior, some of my routine blood work came back with alarming results. My white blood count plummeted to an all time low and several other parameters were grossly out of limits. Another doctor flagged it for follow up, but somehow my record was misplaced. For the second time in my career, serious medical problems were overlooked, whether intentional or not.

I was an old pro for my second bone scan. After lying perfectly still for almost an hour while I radiated to a film, I saw the results. The tumor in my leg was now cold, meaning it barely showed any activity at all. Unfortunately, the tumor in my arm was as black at night and looked like it centralized over one point, possibly in the bone marrow.

The scan, coupled with repeat blood work that showed an alarmingly low white blood count, worried the doctors. They immediately sent me for a CAT scan and a MRI. The CAT scan, which shows bone abnormalities better than MRI's, did not show any conclusive changes. However, the MRI was quite worrisome. I was used to the football huddle by now, but when I read the report, I knew I was in trouble. The report stated, "Abnormal bone marrow signal in the proximal left humerus. The possibility of a malignant lesion would be a consideration. Biopsy is recommended."

So there it was. Cancer was now a real possibility. My orthopedic doctor was worried but he did tried to assuage my fears. His primary concern was Hodgkin's Disease, which is a cancer of the lymphatic system that can sometimes be manifested in the bone marrow. In addition to my night pains, my severely depressed white blood count was a symptom that could spell trouble. If I did have cancer, he told me, the tumor and the surrounding bone would be completely removed. A steel rod would then be implanted in my arm and I would follow up with some chemo and radiation.

My doctor in Jacksonville was a distinguished surgeon, but he did not specialize in bone cancers. I would be sent to Washington DC to see the only military orthopedic oncologist on the East Coast who was an Army doctor. I was in shock with the news. Because of the onset of pain, I knew something was wrong but the sudden seriousness of my situation was overwhelming. I quickly forgot about my problems with the squadron and attempts to resign. Medically, I would not be allowed to leave the service until this matter was resolved, and it would be several months before that would happen.

Unbeknownst to me, the Navy never intended to let me go regardless of my medical problems. Just one day after finding out my tumor was very possibly malignant, I received a call from my detailer in Washington DC. The detailer is the person in the Navy who assigns every officer his next duty station. He is a mid-grade officer and is really just a messenger. More senior officers above him actually control the billets and the detailer is just a pawn.

My detailer told me I had eighteen days to pack my bags, move across the country to Washington State, and report aboard the USS Nimitz for immediate deployment. I was more than a little shocked—I was completely dumbfounded. He went on to explain my letter of resignation was rushed through all the bureaucracy of DC and was subsequently denied, no questions asked. Furthermore, the Commanding Officer of my F/A-18 squadron wanted me out of Jacksonville immediately.

I still could not make sense of what he was saying or formulate any real thoughts or questions. I slowly told him I didn't think I was eligible for sea duty because of pending medical problems. He was a little terse with me and pressed me for the reason why. I then told him the doctors thought I might have Hodgkin's disease and at the very least, I faced an operation to perform a biopsy. The biopsy was scheduled in three weeks so I thought I would not be able to execute any orders.

When he heard the word cancer, my detailer immediately changed his demeanor. He was apologetic and told me he would discuss my case with his superiors. Nothing was set in stone yet, and he would call me the next day. I went home a dazed and confused individual. Why was my letter of resignation denied? Other Lieutenants in my squadron were allowed to resign owing much more time than I did. Why would the Navy deny my resignation and then try to send me to sea immediately, knowing full well I was scheduled for surgery? I could not possible be that valuable. Was this some kind of sick act of revenge and who was driving it?

I anxiously awaited my detailer's phone call the next day. I really didn't think the personnel people would follow through with their ridiculous plan. My Commanding Officer was seemingly following up with his promise of immediate sea duty orders. I also could not believe the Navy would act so rashly with such an accusing letter of resignation floating around. If I accused them of discrimination before, they were certainly making that allegation true now, especially in light of the medical problems. To my knowledge, five male pilots were released from obligations early to pursue careers in the civilian sector. I should have been no different.

When the detailer called, I knew I was in trouble because he first apologized. He told me that his superiors were going to send me sea immediately. They would consider my medical problems only if they received word via official Navy medical channels which takes a month or more. I told him my orthopedic doctor would call him but he said that was not acceptable. Only the archaic snail mail system would be permissible. So I was to move coast to coast right away, despite the scheduled surgery. When the official medical messages were received in about six to eight weeks, the Navy would reconsider my case.

I was furious at their obvious little game and their blatant waste, fraud, and abuse. I wondered if part of the original plan of my Commanding Officer and the senior officers in DC was to send me to sea as soon as possible to keep me quiet. It would be very difficult for me to make my case against the squadron if I was in the middle of the Pacific Ocean with very limited communications. In addition, the Navy would spend thousands of dollars moving me 3000 miles when they knew full well I was facing surgery in Washington DC. When I expressed my frustration and concerns to my detailer, he gave the Navy's standard brainwashed excuse, "I am sorry Missy, but that's needs of the Navy."

His last comment really made me flip my lid. The Navy was so desperate for paper shufflers at sea that they "needed" to send a person underway who faced cancer and surgery immediately, with no input from the doctors? This whole situation now crossed the line into the absurd. The situation in my squadron was a textbook case of harassment, discrimination, and abuse. I volunteered to resign because of the incredibly hostile environment created in part by a conspiratorial FNAEB, which was now confirmed. My male counterparts were released early, and despite my serious medical issues, I was not allowed to resign. Instead I was the most "needed" person in the Navy.

As I hung up the phone, a thought came to me. In the past, I was unjustly accused of calling the Navy's 800 number for reporting harassment and discrimination. Maybe now was the time to make that accusation true. All I wanted was to be left alone to obtain proper medical treatment. After the biopsy was over, maybe we could discuss possible options but right now, I needed to stop the Navy from sending me out to sea.

I explained my situation to the Commander who answered the Hotline complaints, but he didn't seem sympathetic. In fact, after only a brief recounting of my situation, he said that as far as he was concerned, I did not have a valid complaint. I responded, "You don't think being sent to sea with such short notice when I am scheduled for surgery is unusual or deserves any attention?" He replied no and I wondered what episode of *The Twilight Zone* I was in.

I found it incredulous that the Commander was not going to take any information from me or look into my situation in the least. He was a senior officer for the Navy's Inspector General's office, the branch of the Navy that is responsible for investigating itself. If they were not going to at least hear me out, what options did I have?

Well, I had one more option, but I really did not want to use it. I knew I could call my congressman. That drastic move is not well received in the military because it means a congressional inquiry. This was my silver bullet and would commit me down a very serious path. I did not want to do it, but if the Navy forced my hand and did not let me finish my medical treatment, I would make that call. I told the Commander exactly that and I was very shocked when he replied, "Calling your congressman is your right and if you feel the need, then just go ahead. You will not be satisfied with the results if this office investigates."

I felt like I was slapped in the face and triple dog dared. I thought the Navy was a little smarter about potential media bombshells like my case. Instead of handling my complaints delicately, the Commander was basically calling my bluff. Now I understood how the TAILHOOK investigation totally spun out of control. I was incredibly frustrated not just with the brush off by the Inspector General, but also because I was trying to use my chain of command to solve this problem. I did everything by the book, with disastrous results. That sentiment also seemed to describe my entire career in the Navy. So with great resignation, I picked up the phone and called my congressman.

My congressman from Tennessee was receptive and said he would initiate an inquiry. The political officials to really come through for me however, were my dad and Congressman Asa Hutchinson, a republican from Arkansas. My father, a retired naval officer, was a county judge in Arkansas. Because of his close working relationship with Congressman

Hutchinson, my dad gave him a call when I told him about the imminent set of orders to sea.

My dad was only too willing to help me. A 30-year veteran, he also
could not believe the outrageous turn of events and the chutzpah of my
Commanding Officer and the personnel officers in DC. Congressman
Hutchinson, the modern-day knight in shining armor, didn't just start
an official inquiry, he started a fire. He held various meetings with
Admirals and Undersecretaries of the Navy who were more than a little
uncomfortable answering to a member of Congress. Congressman
Hutchinson accomplished what I could not—to make the Navy take
notice of this absurd situation and hold them accountable.

Because of the congressional interest, my immediate orders to sea
were held in abeyance and the Navy Inspector General (IG) was ordered
to begin an investigation. I was very leery of the objectivity of the Navy
IG; they made it clear in my earlier phone call they did not think my situation merited an investigation. I have also never seen an investigation
of this type ever leave the complainant with an intact reputation or
career. The Navy IG serves to protect the Navy's interests, not those of
the little people who dare step out of line.

I breathed much easier after my temporary stay of execution. I could
now concentrate on the tumor in my arm and quit worrying about
moving across the country. Just days after the congressional inquiry
began, I reported to Walter Reed Army Hospital in Washington DC. I
was very nervous when I met the orthopedic oncologist, Dr. Peters. I
expected him to be an older doctor with gray hair but imagine my surprise when I found out he was even better looking than George
Clooney, made famous in the TV series ER. If my tumor was cancerous,
at least the doctor treating me was gorgeous!

Dr. Peters was concerned about the tumor. The MRI's clearly showed
change in the bone marrow and my blood work was very unusual. He
wanted to do the biopsy immediately. The worst I faced was a malignant
tumor. He repeated the earlier doctor's explanation of the process of a

total malignant tumor resection, which would be followed by chemo and radiation. Dr. Peters did not mean to alarm me, but the MRI films did not look promising.

On the operating table for the third time in two years, I prayed to God for good results. I wondered if maybe I pushed my limits too far this time. I couldn't help feeling that if I had not returned to the fighter community, my health would not have degenerated. Maybe this was yet another reminder that I made a poor choice and it was time to grow up.

A few hours later, I woke, fighting the nausea and mind numbing effects of anesthesia. Despite my old pro status, I never grew accustomed to the uncomfortable feeling of coming out of the drug-induced sleep. I fought hard though, because I wanted to desperately leave the hospital. I was alone and had to prove I was fairly functional before I could leave.

Dr. Peters came in as soon as I was fully conscious to tell me the results. The initial biopsy indicated the tumor was benign, but the more definitive lab results would say for sure. I breathed a sigh of relief until he said "but…" Even if the lab results came back benign, I was going to have to endure another operation. He did not feel comfortable leaving the tumor in my arm, even if the lab results showed it to be benign.

The four-inch long tumor had penetrated more than half way through my humerus, well into the bone marrow. The doctor had never seen such an aggressive non-cancerous tumor. While probably still benign, it was behaving like a malignant tumor and it needed to come out. Once the more conclusive lab results came back, a decision would be made on how to proceed, but until then, I needed to rest and prepare for major reconstructive surgery.

I left the hospital feeling somewhat relieved but still apprehensive. Major reconstructive surgery? That didn't sound appealing but given my other option of malignancy, I should consider myself lucky if that was the worst that happened. That night, I stayed with my former roommates from Monterey who now lived in DC. My old boyfriend

Scott, from Monterey was also passing through town that night, so all three of them plus their two dogs climbed in my bed to console me. I was in a fair amount of pain both mentally and physically and they wanted to comfort me. As the six of us lay in the bed, reliving old memories, I felt at peace with so many caring people around me. All would be well and I would come through this, scarred and wounded maybe, but I would be just fine in the end.

Soon after my return to Jacksonville, the lab results came back. The tumor was benign, but I would be going back in just a few weeks to have the tumor completely removed. I felt as if a huge weight was lifted from my shoulders. Despite the looming surgery, I was grateful once again for my near miss with disaster. I vowed to recommit myself to my year old promises to live a more productive life. However, to do that, I just needed to leave the Navy, but it was proving to be a major hurdle.

A preliminary inquiry was held in my squadron over my letter of resignation. In an unbelievable and amateurish approach, questionnaires were disseminated to the pilots and support officers. It reminded me a lot of the notes we passed in grade school: Do you like me? Check Yes or No. Some of the laughable questions included: "Would you want LT Cummings in your squadron?" and "Do you feel LT Cummings is too outspoken? A troublemaker?" So much for trying to find the facts and maintaining an objective approach. Many people confessed that the only information they could provide was based on hearsay and one person interviewed actually stated, "I'm answering questions that are influenced more by rumor than fact given my experience."

My favorite question and the one that actually demonstrated the true feeling in the squadron was, "Do you agree that women should be flying the F/A-18 Hornet? Please explain." Many of the responses were either "no comment" or statements such as "It's not my job to determine policy (i.e. NO)." However, I was quite surprised that many pilots actually spoke their mind and here are a few of the more choice responses:

"Yes,…not necessarily off aircraft carriers. The issue is combat, I wouldn't want my daughter in combat. It's not a question of ability, it's about my preferences."

"Not in combat."

"For the USMC, my answer would be no. They are not fully qualified."

"Yes, but not in combat."

"Personally, I believe women have no place in combat."

"There is no gain to our fighting force by adding a very small number of females to the cockpits. However, it has and will continue to be a significant operational and financial burden to implement females."

"No, I personally believe that females in a fighter squadron can only be a disruption."

"Sure, but not on a carrier or in combat."

"Women should not fly in combat."

"We've been told they can, so they will"

"No, the most important part of our job is espirit de corps/wardroom chemistry and a woman by human nature, will irrevocably alter that."

"The logistical, social, and integration NIGHTMARE outweighs any overall benefit that women provide."

"Yes, but I don't believe women should be in combat."

"Personally, I don't agree with that. I have a problem with sending women to combat."

"If it were totally up to me, I would say no. I think that they would have somewhat of a disrupting affect on an all male squadron."

It is crucial to remember that these individuals were instructors, the same people who were supposed to be objectively grading the performance of students, both male and female. While they would probably say they could separate their personal beliefs from their professional actions, subconsciously, is that really possible?

Once the preliminary inquiry was completed, the Navy IG started its primary investigation soon after my return from the hospital. I flew to

Norfolk, Virginia where I was literally put on the witness stand to testify just like in a trial. I thought about taking a lawyer with me but decided against it. Instead, I asked another male aviator to accompany me as a witness, Jim, a Lieutenant Commander. From my FNAEB experience, I knew how important a witness was and this time I wanted a man by my side. I did not want my case to boil down to gender, even though much of what happened to me was gender based. Crimes were committed and I wanted those people responsible held accountable and gender issues would only cloud the matter.

I was grateful for Jim's presence because he gave me a reality check. As I told my side of the story, Jim was appalled at the chain of events. He took copious notes through the proceedings, concentrating on the questions asked and the demeanor of the investigators. Halfway through the interrogation, it became clear that the investigators were not looking for truthful answers or facts. In the typical IG fashion, the victim is made into the culprit. I was blamed for the atmosphere in VFA-106 and it was my fault that ostracism existed. Just like the FNAEB, my "abrasive" personality was faulted for all the problems that I clearly created. I was also reproached for not bringing my problems to the attention of the Commanding Officer sooner and not giving anyone the opportunity to fix the problems. I was chastised for contacting my congressmen and not responding to the "needs of the Navy."

After a day and a half of the IG's condescending reprimands, I was allowed to leave. As I left, both Jim and I agreed the results would point to me as the perpetrator and there would be no justice. Jim felt that the board's purpose was to prosecute me, not gather any facts. Despite the unmistakable wrongs and the criminal activity of personnel in VFA-106, the Navy IG would protect the institution of the Navy and hang me out to dry. I didn't lose a lot of sleep over the biased investigation though; my career was over and was long over before the IG stepped into the ring. It just depressed me that the concept of accountability in the Navy was just a sham and I sacrificed my career for pathetic, indifferent yes-men who lacked moral fortitude.

The investigation actually took over a year to complete. The investigators spent hundreds of man-hours and tens of thousands of dollars to amass a document that refuted everything I said. Instead of attempting to address the facts of the investigation, the main focus was to portray me as the derelict and singularly responsible for everything that happened, just as Jim and I suspected.

With the conclusion of the investigation, the Inspector General sent me a letter, explaining the findings. Vice Admiral Gunn, the head of the Inspector General's office, was very biting and condescending in his remarks. He said all of my allegations were unsubstantiated and was quite clear he felt the blame was squarely on my shoulders for any inappropriate conduct. I was accused of "insulating" myself from my fellow pilots, and intimidating the instructors. He basically told me I got what I deserved for not "interacting positively in the group" and that my difficulties were a direct result of my "self-fulfilling prophecy" that I would not be welcome.

I was expectedly furious with the results. Just as during my FNAEB, the critical and factual issues were ignored to concentrate on the more nebulous issues of my personality and social interactions. I decided to request the supporting documents under the Freedom of Information Act to find out just how the investigators and Admiral Gunn came to their biased and ridiculous assertions.

After I received the over 1000 pages of the investigation, I read through the witness statements, which were quite enlightening. I found it interesting that many pilots and instructors that never met me were interviewed for their opinions. The investigators profusely apologized to every person they interviewed and the basic gist was, "Sorry we had to bring you in for something so distasteful, but we are only doing our job." They made it clear from the very beginning they thought I was just a histrionic female and there was no real basis to my complaints.

As I read through the report and the supporting documents, I was very interested to read many of the findings. Bull, the instructor who called me to confess the conspiracy of the FNAEB, actually admitted the same information in a sworn statement to the investigators. He told them the names of the instructors involved and the circumstances surrounding the false witness statements. This was significant because it is a felony in the military to sign a false, official statement against another officer. Despite the admission of a crime, the Navy IG investigators just bypassed this information as unimportant. The Navy Inspector General is supposed to be an internal checks and balances. Despite the proof of criminal conduct by a naval officer, they chose to do nothing. This was my first indication when reading the report that justice was not the intention of the Navy IG.

In response to my allegation that I received a SOD (signal of difficulty) for missing a simulator that no one else received, the investigators did determine that six years elapsed since anyone was issued a SOD for missed events. They noted many people missed simulators during the previous six years, but no one was ever punished for this infraction. I may have received unfair treatment, they acknowledged, but I was not discriminated against. Their stretch to find the squadron innocent was unbelievable and I wasn't really sure what definition of discrimination they were using.

In response to my statements that I was ostracized, the Navy IG said those charges were unsubstantiated as well. Apparently through the course of their interviews, they did find a pervasive attitude that the only reason I was allowed to return after the FNAEB was because I was a woman. Both my peers and the instructors admitted they ignored me as much as possible and several agreed that I was ostracized. The Navy IG was required to explain this situation, but if they said I was ostracized, they would be substantiating one of my charges. Since their charter was to refute all of my charges, they needed to find a different, more bland explanation. Instead of ostracism they said, I was merely "professionally distanced."

As I read, I laughed out loud over this one. I think someone must have earned a medal for coining the ludicrous phrase of "professional distancing." The Navy's investigators were so desperate to prove me wrong, that in the face of clear evidence, they chose to use a Clintonish twist of words to minimize an adverse situation. Every time I read the phrase, "professionally distanced", I remembered the TOPGUN testimony to Congress that bonding is considered essential to performance in fighters.

After brushing my claims aside, the Navy released the following statement, "*This case highlights the very difficult leadership challenge of professional distancing between individuals who work together...In [Cummings's] case, hundreds of hours were expended investigating the repercussions created by professional distancing. Although not criminal behavior, it negatively affected the people involved, the command, and ultimately, the Navy...It is recommended that the Navy Leadership Continuum address the issue of professional distancing both by commands and individuals. Areas for examination and discussion include how to prevent it; how to stop it, once started; and the detrimental effects associated with it. Professional distancing must clearly be identified as contrary to our core values of honor, courage, and commitment.*"

The irony and double talk of the situation disgusted me. The Navy refused to admit any guilt in my case but they wanted to address the issue of "professionally distancing" throughout the Navy because it violated the core values of honor, courage, and commitment? I knew better. The Navy was again just giving lip service to its core values and never intended to truly address the issue of ostracism, or in its words, "professional distancing."

The most interesting aspect of the Navy IG's report was actually what it did not say. The crux of my case was the debate over my letter of resignation. I felt my resignation was unjustly denied, and I was immediately ordered to sea despite the early release of five other male pilots from my airwing. I suspected the entire affair was retaliatory for my accusing and damning letter of resignation. Since so many of my male peers were released early, I felt this was a clear case of discrimination.

The Washington Times printed a series of articles about the early release of a male pilot from my airwing despite the fact he owed the Navy two years and several thousand dollars. Even in light of this public disclosure of the pilot's release, the Admiral in charge of naval personnel told my congressmen that absolutely no officer had ever been released early under his tenure. I could not believe the Admiral lied so blatantly, especially when the proof was in the Washington Times.

This was a fairly easy case for the Navy to investigate. I gave them names of officers released early and the newspaper articles from the Washington Times. All the investigators needed to do was check with the separations branch of the Navy to find out the exact details. Surprisingly, this was never done and in fact, there was never any investigation concerning my allegations of resignation discrimination. Since my claims were neither refuted nor supported, I can only surmise that either the investigators unintentionally neglected this critical point in their investigation or purposefully left it out. Whatever their motive, the main purpose of the congressional inquiry was never investigated.

The Navy's answer to the congressional inquiries was actually very amusing and illuminating. While the IG's letter to me was condescending and accusing, the Admirals were smart enough not to take that approach with congressmen. Instead the Navy told them, "The investigation did not substantiate LT Cummings' allegations...[however] we are particularly sensitive to complaints from a young Naval officer such as LT Cummings, who demonstrated at the Naval Academy, the Naval Postgraduate School, and in her subsequent duty assignments, that she is a very talented, committed, and intellectually gifted young woman."

In true political doublespeak, they complimented me while simultaneously saying I was out to lunch. I wondered if they ever truly understood the irony of having an outstanding officer resign under such circumstances. Did senior naval officials really expect everyone to believe the Navy was completely blameless, especially when the officer in question possessed such a credible record?

I wish my saga in the Navy ended with the release of the Navy IG's results, but alas, the Navy was not quite through humiliating and punishing me for daring to step out of line. Just a month after the conclusion of the Navy IG interviews, I was back in Washington DC, preparing for the reconstructive surgery for my arm. While the Navy was formulating their "professional distancing" argument, I was facing real and sobering decisions.

During the preparatory procedures for the resection of the tumor, Dr. Peters told me I needed to make a very important decision. The tumor in my arm was so large, that when they removed it, my humerus would not be able to support the weight of my arm without some assistance. I was given three choices: a bone graft from my right hip, a steel plate, or a cadaver transplant.

Let's see—bad, worse, and even worse still. When presented with such a lovely array of choices, I can't even verbalize what I was feeling. I definitely did not want a steel plate in my body. I knew it would have to be replaced periodically and frankly, I never wanted to see another operating room again as long as I lived. I also didn't want to become a card-carrying member of the Airport X-ray Machine Alarm Club. The thought of having part of a cadaver in me thoroughly grossed me out and I didn't even consider it at first. I didn't want the bone graft both because that would mean two operations instead of one and I would not be able to walk for a few days. None of the choices really appealed to me, so I asked the Dr. Peters what he thought was best. He agreed the bone graft from my hip was not the best choice. He preferred steel plates but he thought I should give the cadaver transplant more consideration. Eventually the foreign bone would be replaced by my own and if all went well, I would never have to have another operation.

After a lot of consideration, I agreed to have the cadaver transplant, but only if they made me better, stronger, faster…(a quote from the Six

Million Dollar Man TV show). My doctor looked at me as if I had lost my mind and I again had to explain the joke and tell him I was just kidding. Boy, was it tough to joke with these doctors.

Two nights before my surgery, I decided to call my answering machine in Jacksonville to check my messages. I was very surprised to hear Bull's voice. Again it sounded like he was drinking, and he was rambling off some sort of apology about a book. He told me he never said the things the author attributed to him and he was very sorry for everything that happened. He never meant for everything to get so out of control and was sorry I was the one that would suffer. He ended his message by telling me the name of the book, *Bogeys and Bandits*, by Robert Gandt.

At first, I had no idea what Bull was talking about and thought maybe he was really losing his mind in a drunken stupor. Then I slowly started to remember. During my initial training in VFA-106, a civilian author was permitted to hang around the squadron for months. My Commanding Officer actually instructed us to cooperate fully with Gandt and treat him as if he were one of the class members. I vaguely remembered speaking to him a couple of times about trivial topics such as previous duty stations and hobbies, but I never really even knew what his proposed book was about.

I raced to the local Barnes and Nobles to find the book and see why Bull felt so guilty. I found the book and started to read. As I read, I was horrified. I was not just mentioned, I was a main character and the only bad guy of the book. Gandt detailed my FNAEB, several of my flights, and alleged interactions with various individuals in the squadron. Gandt painted me as an incompetent and socially inept. I wasn't just the sole antagonist; I was the ultra-feminist who was only allowed to fly the F/A-18 because I was a woman.

If Gandt had attributed these hateful qualities to just any girl flying Hornets, I would not have been so upset. However, he took great pains to make sure everyone who read the book knew who I was. He

described me personally to such detail; he even listed my undergraduate degree in math and my master's degree in Astronautical
Engineering. He described my appearance, the car I drove, and my
supposed thoughts about life as a female fighter pilot. He changed my
name to avoid a lawsuit—instead of using my real callsign Shrew, he
named me Shrike. Gandt wanted to make quite sure that anyone reading this book could easily find out my identity.

Since I spoke to him only a handful of occasions, I was shocked at the
level of detail. His stories about me were outrageous and misleading.
Gandt either twisted the truth until it was no longer recognizable, or
when he needed a little more conflict between his characters, he just
completely made up a story about me verbally castrating a male. In his
depiction of me, when I wasn't trying to push the feminist agenda, I
somehow did the Dr. Jeckyll/Mr. Hyde and Gandt portrayed me as a
svelte, sexual creature dancing my way through life. The split personality he gave me was ludicrous and the message was clear: Women do not
belong in the cockpits of fighters; they are merely sexual creatures just
looking for love in all the wrong places. Some of his passages about me
were absolutely laughable and if I hadn't been so mortified, reading his
pseudo-tabloid story might have been amusing.

*"Sometimes she thought it would be so nice just to be…a girl. That was
all. Just be a girl and wear pretty clothes and go dancing and have men
open doors for her. She would take long bubble baths and have her hair
permed and go to the theater. She would meet men who did not feel threatened by her and who respected her for what she was. She might even find
the right one, and if she did, she might even consider starting a family."*[14]

I really chuckled over this passage, realizing what a ridiculous and
sexist depiction this was of me. Gandt, just like so many other manly
men, could not grasp the fact that women who fly fighters do it not
because they are trying to prove something. They do it for the same reasons men do; because they love flying and love serving their country.

The publication of this book was my ultimate nightmare. Even though I was no longer in my squadron, my reputation throughout the Navy would be destroyed. Once I was finally allowed to resign, I planned on flying with the reserves, which was filled with many of the same pilots listed in the book. Because naval aviation is such a small community, this book and its insults would forever hound me. With this book, I would never be welcomed into any community in the Naval Reserves and I would be the laughingstock among any group of pilots.

I was equally upset over what this book would do to my chances of flying for the commercial airlines. Gandt was a Delta pilot and several of the people who helped him write the book were also commercial pilots. Most commercial pilots are former military pilots and once the word was out that I was the Jane Fonda of aviation, I would be blackballed from the world of commercial aviation as well.

As angry as I was over the potential harm this book could do to my future, I was even more infuriated with the Navy's role in the publication of the book. In his acknowledgments, Gandt thanked my entire chain of command, which included of course my Commanding Officer, the Wing Commander, and last but not least, Admiral Allen who turned out to be an old friend of Gandt's. He also thanked two instructor pilots from my squadron for helping him write the book. One of these pilots was one who made my life hell in the squadron and lo and behold, the other was a member of my FNAEB.

It was obvious from reading the book that Gandt possessed copies of my training records, the FNAEB, and several other official documents about me. It didn't take a rocket scientist to figure out many, if not all of the people Gandt thanked, gave him my records and personal information so he could write a very damaging account about me. These documents that were given to Gandt are protected under the Privacy Act and it is a federal crime to release these records without authorization.

The more I thought about the book and the people involved, the clearer the events of the past two years became. I was always amazed at the level of animosity that greeted me upon my return to the squadron and I never understood how time made life worse instead of better. Now I knew. After I left for my intense medical treatment, Gandt stayed with the squadron another six months. The two instructors who helped write the book were still around when I returned. No doubt they were the source of the continued bitterness and wild stories that I was only allowed to return after Pat Schroeder forced the Navy to bend to her feminist agenda.

What was even more disturbing to me was the possibility that Gandt significantly influenced not only my training syllabus but also the FNAEB itself. At worst, Gandt could have been coaching his two co-writers, one of whom was a voting member of my FNAEB, to bring out all the personality issues, including the fact that I was an intimidating demoralizer. At best, the FNAEB members knew an author was watching over their every move. Still angry about the Hultgren crash and women in fighters in general, in a show of vindication, the squadron made a huge spectacle of my case to prove to each other and the author that they would not tolerate a woman in their midst.

My worst fears were confirmed when I later found out Gandt was actually an active participant in my FNAEB. While the FNAEB was in progress, Gandt communicated with not only one of the FNAEB members who was helping him with the book, but he also discussed my case with both the Commanding Officer and the senior member of the FNAEB. It was not only unethical to discuss an on-going review board with a member of the media, it was also downright criminal. No wonder the FNAEB was so tainted and corrupt—the motivation, direction, and leadership from the very beginning was biased, malicious, and nefarious.

While I feel the author is very much responsible for his lack of journalistic ethics and attempts to dramatize his story just to make a buck, I feel the Navy is the biggest culprit in all of this. Taxpayer dollars funded Gandt's research, including a ride in a F/A-18, a trip to an aircraft carrier, all his medical and physiological support, and hundreds of man-hours for interviews. The Navy encouraged this author to shadow me, allowed him complete and free access to the squadron, and even gave him my personal records protected under federal law after allowing him to participate in my FNAEB.

The most disgusting aspect of the Navy's involvement was that I was forced to return to the same squadron. The Navy individuals involved knew full well that my environment would be extremely hostile, and much worse once the book was released. I find it unconscionable the Navy intentionally destroyed my career, committing several crimes in the process, and then denied my resignation while letting others go. In light of the book, I was even more astonished with the Navy IG's findings that while I was treated unfairly, I was not discriminated against, and that I was not ostracized, I was merely professionally distanced, which was primarily my fault anyway.

I contacted the Navy IG immediately after reading the book, so they could incorporate this very critical aspect into my case, which I feel proved true everything I alleged. Their response? The investigators denied any person in the Navy violated the Privacy Act and in their typical fashion, blamed me for the information that appeared in the book. They again intimated that I deserved all the hateful press in the book for my "many complaints." In an incredibly unethical gesture, during the active phase of the investigation, one of these supposed objective Navy investigators actually published an online review of the book. The review just wasn't encouraging, it was absolutely gushing. I knew then that I never had a chance for a fair and impartial investigation.

What about the still pending orders to the secretarial job at sea? After congressional intervention and the furor I raised over the book, the Navy decided that maybe I wasn't a seaworthy sailor after all. The orders were permanently cancelled and I was allowed to seek medical care without further intervention.

My spirits going into the surgery were just about as low as a plane just about to hit the back of a carrier. As I laid on the gurney in the pre-operative holding area, I prayed to God to take me during the surgery. I saw no more reason to live. I spent my entire life trying to serve my country to the best of my ability and in turn, I was rewarded with betrayal and public humiliation. My entire life was a sham and I had nothing to show for it.

I was so severely depressed that not surprisingly, my recovery from the operation was slow. Coming out of anesthesia was difficult, and the pain in my arm was incredibly intense. The removal of four inches of bone with a cadaver pack is no easy task. During my recovery, I cried and cried, not just because of the pain, but also because of the book and the realization that the Navy I tried to dedicate my life to, sold me out—lock, stock, and barrel. My mom held me, bathed me, and dressed me through the difficult weeks of recovery, crying almost as much as I did. It broke her heart to see her only daughter who at one time wanted nothing more than to be an admiral, suffer from so much mental and physical anguish.

Slowly but surely, through the weeks of recovery and physical therapy, I started to regain the fighter spirit that propelled me throughout an amazing career. Instead of wallowing in self-pity, I vowed to fight the recent injustices and to do that, I would have to first be physically strong. So despite the physical and emotional difficulties, I made a solid and speedy recovery.

Just a month after the operation, I received a very strange phone call from my detailer. He wanted to tell me the orders to the carrier were officially canceled and the Navy wanted to offer me a new set of orders. Would I take a prime set of orders as an NROTC instructor at Penn State? They desperately needed a female aviator with a master's degree to fill a billet and this would allow me to serve out my time. I found the change in the demeanor of the personnel office humorous. Just two short months prior, the seventh fleet could not sail without me and now, a NROTC unit would wither away if I didn't go.

Really all I wanted was to leave the Navy. I felt I had endured enough, but because I still faced many follow up appointments in the hospital, I decided to take the orders and not push the resignation issue anymore. I would not be employable to the civilian sector for some time, so the year or so at Penn State would allow me to heal and start seriously job hunting.

As I drove to Pennsylvania from Florida, I stopped in Washington DC to check in with the doctors and attend a retirement ceremony. Captain Rosemary Mariner, the second most senior woman aviator was retiring. While we never served together, every female aviator knew about Rosemary. She was outspoken and I am sure that just like me, her peers called her aggressive and abrasive. Regardless of the perception of her personality, she was a pioneer and helped pave the way for hundreds of aviatrixes behind her. I wanted to attend her retirement ceremony out of respect and as a form of therapy to help bring closure to my own career.

The ceremony was touching and I felt fortunate to watch a chapter of history close. After Rosemary was "piped ashore" which is the Navy tradition of sounding a whistle as a senior officer departs a ship or retires, the entire gathering moved to the reception. I was thrilled to see so many of the other "female fighter firsts" in naval aviation. I did not expect them to be there since most were stationed on the West Coast.

These were the same women with fresh, young, and hopeful faces just a few years before. It was such a bittersweet reunion and all of us looked as if we had been through hell and back. Now we were all tired, cynical, and still trying to figure out what just happened in our lives. We shared stories, caught up with the latest happenings, and consoled each other. The West Coast women told stories similar to mine and it actually made me feel better to know I was not the only one.

As we discussed the events that occurred since the repeal of the combat of the exclusion law, one aspect became very clear. As a whole, the first group of women in fighters had not fared very well. There were initially eight of us; two F-14 Tomcat pilots and six F/A-18 drivers. Kara was dead, the other F-14 female pilot had been grounded for two years and was still fighting her FNAEB. Four of the remaining seven hired lawyers to protect themselves, and two F/A-18 women requested transfers out of their squadrons as soon as possible.

As the reception concluded, we said our good-byes and wished each other well. After a pause in the pleasantries, one of the F/A-18 women left us with a comment that rang so true, it was painful to consider. She said, "You know, we may have won the first battles, but they are winning the war."

Of the original group, only three decided to make the Navy a career, and of those, only one intended to remain in the fighter community. 88% of the first group of women fighter pilots, hand chosen by the Navy for their superior skills and proven outstanding records—the best of the best women—would leave the fighter community. Perhaps the Navy should have taken a harder look at their self-termed phenomenon of "professional distancing"—it seems I wasn't the only victim after all. The Navy's first wave of women in fighters suffered the same fate that many military historians know so well—the first wave in an invasion always gets massacred.

Chapter Eighteen

The Other Split Tails

Conspicuously absent from my story of flying fighters is interaction with other women pilots. Unfortunately, I was the only woman in my squadron during my time in Jacksonville. It was difficult as the only fish in the bowl and I was certainly the lightening rod for any spurious anger against women in combat roles. When the original eight women were selected to fly fighters, the plan was to distribute them evenly in the East and West Coast squadrons. The intent of the Navy detailers was to pair women together or at least station them in the same airwing. They flew either F-14 Tomcats or F/A-18 Hornets and deployed on two carriers. The East Coast women were on the USS Eisenhower, formerly nick-named the Ike, but when women were stationed on the ship, it became known as the "Dyke." The carrier for the West Coast women was the USS Abraham Lincoln. The guys couldn't come up with some negative spin and finally settled with the "Babraham" or "Babe" Lincoln.

While my squadron troubles seemed never-ending, the other women were having just as many problems. All of us struggled at one point and it was never easy, especially after Kara crashed her F-14 trying to land aboard the Lincoln. All of us felt the derision and raw hatred that was very much directed towards all female aviators after the crash, but no one more so than Carey Lohrenz. She was the remaining female F-14 pilot after Kara died.

The F-14 is not an easy plane to fly and it does not have all the fancy bells and whistles of the F/A-18. It is a plane that requires constant attention and is not user-friendly. Its notorious record of flight control and engine problems did not rest well with the aircrew. For the most experienced pilots, the F-14 is challenging and Carey was just a "nugget"—a new pilot.

Despite her outstanding performance in flight school during which she received several awards, Carey struggled through various aspects of her Tomcat training. Carey was accelerated through the program, which did not help her, but contrary to popular belief, she was not rushed through training merely because she was a woman. Many other men were accelerated through the pipeline during the same time. Often when pilots are in training, the Navy will identify certain individuals who will be making immediate cruises—these pilots are known as "must-pumps." Carey fell into this category because she was assigned to the USS Abraham Lincoln, which was slated for the next deployment to the Gulf. Since this was the only West Coast carrier with women aboard, there was no other assignment choice for her.

Just like Kara Hultgren and almost half of the male pilots, Carey disqualified in her first attempt at the carrier. She rallied on her second try and improved immensely. Qualified, she was ready to set sail for her first deployment to the Persian Gulf. Carey was not Chuck Yeager and she never professed to be. She was a nugget pilot with a lot to learn but she was qualified.

While Carey was deployed on the Babe (USS Abraham Lincoln), the same articles about Kara's flying qualifications that plagued me in Key West were distributed throughout the carrier at lightening speed. These articles not only claimed Kara was unqualified, they alleged that Carey had no business not only flying on a carrier, but in any aircraft whatsoever. Carey was thinly disguised as "Pilot B" in the article, but her identity was painfully obvious to the most casual observer since she was the only remaining female F-14 pilot.

It was clear from the article that parts of Carey's F-14 training jacket were leaked to Elaine Donnelly, the sole member of the Center for Military Readiness. The Privacy Act protected these records, just like my flight records, and whoever leaked them committed a federal offense. Since officers in her training squadron were the only personnel with access to the records, it was obvious one or more played a role in this crime. What was so damaging about this and subsequent articles was that the clearly biased and subjective portrayal of Carey painted her as an incompetent, and only allowed to fly because she was a woman. The articles ignored Carey's successes and improvements and were her death knell when passed around the carrier.

Up to the illegal release of her records and the subsequent publication of the defamatory articles, Carey was improving in her carrier landing skills. When she was handed copies of these articles circulating among her peers, she was absolutely mortified, just like I was when I read the book. For Carey though, the timing could not have been worse. She, like every other pilot, was under intense pressure to perform well. Now Carey was forced to deal with the added pressure of these deriding and accusatory articles influencing everyone around her. The articles were the number one topic of discussion in the airwing and male pilots let it be known that she was an outcast in their midst. Some even openly taunted her with her now well-known public persona as "Pilot B."

Carey's performance subsequently declined over the next month. The ostracism worsened and she lost a significant amount of weight. Instead of providing her the least amount of support, her senior leadership did nothing to stop the vicious rumor mill about the articles. No one was under more pressure than Carey, and instead of rallying to help one of their pilots who was clearly wronged, the Navy just left her to flail on her own. Instead of trying to implement some damage control over the defaming and extremely damaging articles about Carey, the

Airwing Commander held mandatory pregnancy testing and told the women he did not support sending them into combat.

After a month of trying to overcome the damage done by Elaine Donnelly's assertions, Carey was sent to a FNAEB. The articles clearly impacted the board members who voted to remove Carey from carrier flight status. Carey was not the least proficient pilot in the airwing; there were five others whose landing grades were worse, but she was the first pilot in the airwing kicked off the ship. In fact, two male pilots with similar poor landing grades were sent to a more benign Human Factors Board instead of the career-ending FNAEB. The senior aviation admiral in Carey's chain of command upheld her FNAEB, and instead of allowing her to fly another aircraft, the Admiral decided to permanently ground her.

I am sure Carey was overwhelmed with the sequence of events. A Navy officer illegally released her records for publication, which unquestionably impacted both her performance and the perception of her skills. The humiliation and badgering she suffered from the prejudiced release of her records eventually led to her permanent removal from flight status. Instead of defending Carey to the press or attempting to punish the officer(s) responsible, the Navy remained mute, no doubt hoping all the controversy would just go away. Just like I was, Carey was left to fend for herself after the Navy betrayed her, and in the end, she also lost her career.

Like the fighter pilot she was, Carey was not about to accept the hand she was dealt and she decided to fight the Navy in a court of law. When Carey lodged her complaint that she was treated unfairly, the Navy first responded with an Inspector General (IG) investigation. The first investigation was so unprofessional and shoddy that the IG was forced to reconvene another one. After almost two years, the report was released.

Just like I did, Carey alleged that she was subjected to an intensely hostile work environment and she was a victim of discrimination. Just like in my case, the Navy IG completely and utterly denied any wrongdoing on anyone's part in the Navy. They unsubstantiated her claims of hostile work environment because the Navy's official definition of hostile work environment was lewd jokes, sexually disparaging remarks, display of sexually explicit material, and requests for sex. In the Navy's view, because none of those events occurred, neither Carey nor I experienced a hostile working environment.

Webster's dictionary defines hostile as unfriendly, not hospitable, antagonistic (actively expressed opposition). Apparently having our personal records illegally released to members of the media in order to publicly humiliate Carey and me and destroy our naval careers does not meet the Navy's definition of hostile environment. At least in my case, the Navy admitted I was "professionally distanced"; Carey did not even get that much of an admission of guilt.

Just as in my investigation, the Navy IG did admit some policies were applied unequally against the women pilots in the airwing and there were instances where the women received harsher treatment compared to the men. However, just as in my investigation, the Navy IG maintained the unequal policies and treatment were not gender biased or even discriminatory. The similarities between the two investigations were both depressing and disturbing.

During the course of the inquiry, the investigators determined the identity of the officer who released her records. LT Pat Burns was a flight instructor with an axe to grind and took it upon himself to have Carey removed from flight status by whatever means possible. He justified his cowardly actions stating that he tried to use the Navy chain of command, to no avail. LT Burns maintained that only after attempting to bring his opinions to the attention of his commanding officer, did he seek out Elaine Donnelly to try his case in the press.

There exists no official or unofficial record that LT Burns ever attempted to contact any senior officers before giving Carey's records to Ms. Donnelly. LT Burns' Commanding Officer categorically denied ever discussing this case with LT Burns. Additionally, all other flight instructors in the squadron also denied that LT Burns ever brought up his concerns to them. In fact, the instructors interviewed testified no direction or pressure was ever put on them to pass the women. Despite the clear and admitted crime of LT Burns, he was not punished for his behaviors by anyone in the Navy.

Because of this inaction, Carey also alleged that the Navy did nothing to punish the individual(s) for releasing her documents to Elaine Donnelly and committing a federal crime. In response, the Navy IG made the following statement, "The allegation that the Navy improperly did not investigate the disclosure of LT Lohrenz's training records or attempt to correct the public record in UNSUBSTANTIATED."

In the Navy IG's report, the senior officials responsible for overseeing the investigation decided not to either further examine LT Burns' crime or punish him in any way. They excused their apathy by stating any further inquiry would "cause more institutional harm than good." After reading that statement, I wondered why the military even had a judicial system since we apparently excused away blatant crimes if they were just a little too messy and might give the Navy a black eye.

Eventually, a year later when Carey filed civil charges against the Navy for violating the federal Privacy Act law, the Navy was forced to take action against Burns. Despite his criminal background, he was recommended for promotion to a Lieutenant Commander. His promotion was finally blocked, not by any naval officer, but by the Honorable John Dalton, the Secretary of the Navy. Dalton, a civilian who is the President's naval advisor, is responsible for overseeing both Navy operations and policy.

I would like to believe that Mr. Dalton was really moved to refuse Burns' promotion because of his criminal behavior. However, I can't help but suspect Dalton did it only because a nasty court case hung over his head. In Dalton's statement to Burns, he said, "*I find that you intentionally violated the Privacy Act by releasing the personal training records of a fellow officer to an individual outside the federal government who lacked authority to receive such records…I expect all our officers in the Navy to exhibit our core values of honor, courage, commitment…. Your actions were not honorable, in that you violated federal law by releasing records of a shipmate knowing that such information would be used to humiliate the officer involved."*[15]

I found Dalton's mantra of the Navy's core values of "honor, courage, and commitment" extremely hollow and hypocritical. I was glad that some punishment was meted out for Carey's sake, but when I thought of my own situation, I was disgusted. My entire chain of command helped an author write not just a transient article, but also a nationally published book humiliating me. I was not a marginal pilot, but one that by the Navy's own account, was above average. Not one person involved in my case was punished and the Navy categorically denied both any wrongdoing or that I suffered any harm other than "professional distancing."

As a result of both Carey's lawsuit and intense media scrutiny, she was eventually allowed to return to flying. She was restricted from flying carrier-based aircraft and was forced to settle for a twin engine propeller plane that transports the Navy's VIPs. Once a fighter pilot, Carey was relegated to flying around those admirals who originally showed her no mercy.

On the warpath, Carey prevailed in her court battle over the Navy's violation of the federal Privacy Act of 1974. The Navy, not wishing for another media circus over a fallen female aviator, settled out of court. In an ironic twist, Carey was forced to resign from the Navy as part of the settlement. Her struggle to resume flying for the Navy to which she also dedicated her life was essentially for naught. She, like me, was forced to leave the Navy for no other reason than infringing on hallowed ground.

In addition to her lawsuit against the Navy, Carey also sued Elaine Donnelly, the one woman right wing conservative think tank called the Center for Military Readiness (CMR) An interesting fact that came out of the legal proceedings was the origin of much of Donnelly's funding.

Apparently, the Association of the United States Army, which boasts a membership of 75,000 officers, gave her more than $25,000 over a six-year period. Many retired Admirals and Generals, including two former Marine Corps Commandants support her.[16] Clearly many military officers in influential positions are not yet ready to accept women in combat roles.

While Carey and I suffered through the most public and overt career assassinations, the other women fighter pilots were struggling in their own battles. Not long after Carey was sent home, another fighter female was sent to a FNAEB. She managed to maintain her flight status but she was eventually passed over for promotion. It seemed as if the men who hated the women's presence figured out a new way to force them out. If they couldn't find something wrong with the women's flight perform-ance, they would get their pound of flesh professionally or personally.

Every year, a formal ball is held on each coast to honor all the F/A-18 Hornet pilots and participation is mandatory. Not only are all the pilots in attendance, but the supporting officers and all significant others are present as well. It is the largest social event in the fighter community and is generally a wild and crazy event. Drinking is paramount and everyone gets pretty rowdy. During this ball, junior officers traditionally perform skits to poke fun at senior officers and other pilots who make silly mistakes. Usually the jests are made in pure fun and everyone has a good time. However, this ball that included the female pilots was dif-ferent. During one skit, some of the pilots performed a skit about the personal appearance of one of the women pilots. It was so vicious and so humiliating, her squadron Commanding Officer and the Wing Commander were both forced to issue her a formal apology.

In another instance, one of the female fighter pilots, Jane, was selected as a TOPGUN alternate. It is quite an honor to be selected to attend TOPGUN and competition for the billets is very fierce. A woman has never attended the prestigious school so Jane would possibly be the first. Each squadron is allotted a periodic quota and pilots within an individual squadron compete for the slots. Jane was very pleased to earn the alternate slot because that meant her chances for future selection would be much better.

Jane was even more excited when she found out the primary candidate was not able to attend, so the TOPGUN slot was hers—or so she thought. While she was preparing to attend the school, the first woman to do so, the squadron quickly and covertly convened another selection board and nominated another male pilot instead of Jane. The rumor was that the guys didn't want the coveted warrior billet to be "wasted" on a woman, so they sent a male pilot in her place. The squadron Commanding Officer could have intervened and allowed Jane to exercise her right to go, but he didn't. In fact he was the final approving authority on the decision so he absolutely knew what happened. The boys' club was firmly entrenched at the highest levels and the "No girls allowed" sign hung where everyone could see it. Jane eventually resigned her commission in part because of this incredibly unethical and blatant discrimination. Despite the Navy's very public stance that women have been successfully integrated in aviation, to date, not one woman has still been allowed to attend the flying portion of TOPGUN.

Another one of the women, touted as the only chick that could really fly the Hornet, experienced problems of her own. A true Chuck Yeager in every sense, Tammy was a naturally gifted pilot who was clearly heads and shoulders above the other women—and the men. Unfortunately, during one port call, Tammy was rumored to have slept with another F-14 pilot in her airwing. Regardless of the truth, the rumor swept through the ship like wildfire, and the supposed Don Juan was inundated with snide remarks. In addition, a group of male pilots designed a T-shirt to commemorate the event, and distributed it to dozens of aviators in the airwing.

The T-shirt depicted a macho F-14 plane with bulging muscles mounting from behind, a feminine F/A-18 with long eyelashes. Emblazoned across the front was the caption, "Go Airwing Early!", a

takeoff on the male pilots' favorite saying of "Go Ugly Early." The inti-
mation was clear—the airwing women were ugly and repulsive, and
should be used and quickly discarded for nothing but sexual pleasure.
Tammy, as gifted as she was, did not escape the humiliation that was so
familiar to the rest of us.

The female fighter pilots were not the only group of women aboard
the carriers who suffered. As mentioned previously, Shannon, an EA-6B
pilot was summarily removed from the carrier for poor landings while
another male with similar grades was given a second chance. Another
female EA-6B pilot turned in her wings after a particularly vicious
FNAEB, which was followed by the ever-familiar ostracism and overtly
hostile environment. For those few women pilots who were married,
within a couple of years, most were divorced.

The Navy wasn't the only military branch integrating women into
combat roles during this time period. Both the Army and Air Force
assigned women to combat air units, but seemingly, they did not have
the same difficulties the Navy did. Well after Kara's death, an Air Force
female A-10 pilot crashed and was killed during training. Unlike Kara's
crash, there was no public outcry that she was unqualified and no one
in the Air Force felt it his personal mission to discredit both the fallen
aviatrix and all other women pilots as well. There was however, one
highly publicized problem in the Air National Guard.

Major Jackie Parker, a former Air Force test pilot, was the first female to
fly the F-16, the Air Force and Air National Guard's premier fighter. When
she unexpectedly resigned from her National Guard unit, an investigation
was held. Unlike the Navy's unwillingness to admit any wrongdoing, the
National Guard investigators openly acknowledged finding an incredibly
hostile environment, which coincidentally began with Kara Hultgren's
crash at the carrier. They even detailed an in-flight conversation between
two male pilots where one pilot said he would like to see Major Parker,
"shot…in the stomach, so she would die a slow death."[17]

As a result of the National Guard investigation, Major Parker's Wing Commander was fired and another senior officer was demoted. Apparently the National Guard investigators did not hide behind some ambiguous, narrow definition of "hostile environment" and recognized Major Parker's situation for what it was. For all the lip service the Navy gives to the concept of accountability, it seems that the National Guard was the one military branch actually practicing it.

In the aftermath of Kara's death and the subsequent problems the Navy experienced integrating women into combat aircraft, there was one small glimmer of hope for acceptance and appreciation. No doubt seeking closure to an incredibly painful loss, Kara's mother, Sally Spears, decided to write a book about Kara titled, *"Callsign Revlon."* Sally wrote the book from not only her perspective as a mother, but she also used Kara's detailed journals and interviewed Kara's close friends to portray the real Kara, which was acutely overlooked in the wake of her death.

Kara's vivaciousness, zest for life, and even her flaws came to life in the book, and the book was a fitting tribute to the first woman combat pilot to die. The book received glowing reviews and was actually quite successful in the commercial market, appealing to a wide and diverse audience, not just the "good ole boys club." I think the success of Sally's book proves the American public prefers a real story of disappointment and triumph to a contrived depiction of a castrating feminist's attempts to demoralize the Navy's fighter community.

Chapter Nineteen

Making Sense of It All

When I first arrived in State College, Pennsylvania after my surgery, I was very unhappy. The Navy not only destroyed my career but also helped publish a book that maligned and humiliated me. Instead of letting me resign under the cloud of humiliation they created, I was required to serve out my remaining commitment as a Naval ROTC instructor who was responsible for molding the Navy's future officers. It was incredibly ironic that after all that happened, I was now supposed to promote the same organization that I despised.

It was very difficult at first to separate my professional and personal feelings. All I wanted to do was leave the Navy and instead, I was preparing the Navy's future officers. To effectively do my job, I would have to bite my tongue and put on a happy, pro-Navy face. Fortunately the other NROTC staff members were absolutely wonderful so the transition was not as difficult as I thought it might be. This was the first time I worked with officers from the surface and submarine branches of the Navy and I was pleasantly surprised. I soon realized that my bitterness towards the entire Navy was unfair. Despite my miserable experiences in aviation, there were still many good officers in the Navy who were professionals, and couldn't care less whether I was a man or woman.

Since I missed the total college experience while at the Naval Academy, it was exciting and rejuvenating to be a part of one of the largest universities in the nation. In an amazingly short period of time, I started to climb out of my depression and look forward to the future. Every college campus is overflowing with life and energy, and Penn State was all that and so much more. I don't think I could have made the smooth transition into the civilian world however, had it not been for a psychology class I took at Penn State.

When I reported to Penn State, I learned I would be teaching the Navy Ethics and Leadership class in the spring semester. Again the irony was not lost on me but instead of dwelling on the negatives, I decided to take a graduate level course titled Psychology of Leadership in preparation. What started as an attempt to better educate myself on the theories of leadership turned into transforming therapy that truly helped me bridge the gap between bitterness and understanding. The psychology class helped turn my anger into quiet resignation and made the agonizing loss of my career a little easier to bear. I was then able to finally start the forgiveness process that was necessary for moving forward with a happier and healthier life.

The purpose of the class was to examine the current models and theories of leadership from a psychological perspective. After thirteen years in the Navy in various leadership roles, I was fascinated to learn the theoretical aspects, especially in light of all I recently experienced. I was particularly riveted by two extremely interesting psychological phenomena that directly impacted my life of flying fighters; groupthink and gender prototypes.

Frederick Nietzsche once said "madness is the exception in individuals, but the rule in groups."[18] History proves that the herd mentality or "groupthink" is a powerful force that is not easily overcome. From the Holocaust to the Civil Rights efforts to the most recent Hale-Bopp comet suicides, groupthink has appalled and shocked outsiders who inevitably ask, "how could this happen?" Although my situation was not nearly as drastic, I found myself asking the same questions.

As I studied the groupthink phenomenon, I was overwhelmed with its applicability to many important junctures in my naval career. The male midshipmen openly mooing and oinking at the female midshipmen, the overwhelming participation in prostitution in the Philippines, and my FNAEB—all were examples of groupthink. This phenomenon was not just a factor, in many cases it was the driving force. The common thread between all these experiences was not necessarily that the participants were men; the link was the composition of the group, which was that of military personnel.

The military, especially officers, is one of the most homogenous groups of our society. Uniformity and conformity are by nature, two of the most defining characteristics of the military. These are not harmful qualities; they are absolutely essential for the discipline and motivation required to send young men and women into combat. The military could not survive without them, but just like almost every absolute in life, uniformity and conformity are also double-edged swords.

Groupthink, firmly entrenched in military decisions, is almost a necessity in the fighter community where uniformity and conformity are paramount. Groupthink is part of the fighter pilot culture and to some extent, is needed to maintain the rigid military structure. The intangible bond that is created in groupthink is the same bond that propels these warriors into battle, makes them risk their lives for one another, and die for their country. To an extent, the blind commitment to the unit is absolutely critical for the success of dangerous and life-threatening military operations.

History has repeatedly illustrated that the tight-knit nature of military communities is an inherent hotbed for groupthink. In recent news, Tailhook is perhaps the most notorious example. Dozens of women were assaulted by naval aviators who quickly closed ranks when accused of criminal behavior. These men, who individually were law-abiding

citizens and defenders of our nation, somehow lost their separate iden-
tities and reverted to their most base, animal instincts when in a group
of their peers. This did not happen because they were members of the
military, it happened because they were members of a very cohesive and
uniform group.

My FNAEB was almost a textbook example of the groupthink phenomenon. For true groupthink to occur, a group of individuals must be
faced with a decision, and my FNAEB was a breeding ground for groupthink. By the Navy's own admission, my FNAEB was "fatally flawed."
Designed to review the flight performance of aviators, my FNAEB
somehow became an attack on my personality rather than an objective
performance review. Witnesses were introduced who never flew with
me and oral testimony was altered when transcribed. Most alarming,
the board members coerced witnesses to sign false statements about me
and were in contact with a member of the media for his input. How
could these officers, who swore to uphold and defend the constitution,
commit such crimes?

The elements of groupthink were quite obvious in my FNAEB. When
I spoke with a board member, Nose, more than a year after the fact, he
was extremely apologetic about his role. When I asked him why he went
along with such a malicious and deceitful attack against me, he replied
that senior officers basically forced him to lie. Nose told me once he
showed signs of dissenting, he was removed from any more decision-
making processes in the FNAEB. Nose admitted he rationalized his and
the others' actions by telling himself that the senior officers knew best—
that's why they were in charge. The instructor who admitted to both the
Navy Inspector General and me that he signed a false witness statement
echoed these same thoughts. Both men did not want to appear to be
anything but team players, despite the fact that they committed crimes
in doing so.

As these facts unfolded, I grew very angry and bitter because to me,
my FNAEB was clearly a conspiracy. I was incensed with the Navy for

letting the board spin out of control, and also for not punishing the officers who committed the crimes. My FNAEB was the crucial event that touched off the derision, hatred, and ostracism that doomed my remaining time flying fighters. I originally felt my career was essentially derailed by a group of criminals who were rewarded by the Navy for their conspiratorial efforts. It wasn't until I took the Psychology of Leadership class at Penn State, that I realized I was wrong. The FNAEB was not a conscious conspiracy; it was groupthink run amok.

Groupthink was not the only psychological phenomenon that helped shape the tragedy that devastated my career. Even more pervasive and insidious were the concepts of prototyping and gender stereotyping. A prototype is a model or a construct that an individual forms to classify and categorize a newly received piece of information. Prototypes can change over time and experience, but they always remain the basic building blocks of sense making. A prototype can be as fundamental as a young woman holding a baby, and assuming she is the mother. They can also evolve into more complex models such as seeing a young black man with a bandana on his head and assuming he is a member of a gang. Prototypes are the basis for stereotypes, but are not necessarily negative actions.

As technology and the world around us grow more complex, prototyping allows humans to process a great deal of information very quickly. Categorizing behaviors, appearances, and situations is the human attempt to classify the world in which we live—a way to control an otherwise chaotic life. In the military setting, as well as in any organization, categorizing helps all levels of personnel comprehend their often complicated and dangerous environment, thus reducing the fear and anxiety of the unknown. This is especially true of fighter pilots who face overwhelming tasks and perilous, life-threatening situations.

Unfortunately, the categorization processes of prototyping can many times become skewed and develop into biased, very subjective stereotypes. Stereotyping is not a conscious decision to discriminate; it is the

fatalistic and inevitable aspect of prototyping. One of the most prominent examples of stereotyping in our culture is that of gender stereotyping. The military by no means has the corner on gender
stereotyping. It exists in almost all facets of our culture—the business
world, medicine, academia, law enforcement, etc. While I knew this, it
wasn't until I took the class on the Psychology of Leadership did I learn
how truly pervasive gender stereotyping was.

In a recent Fortune 1000 survey, polls revealed female executives
believed that the bias of gender stereotypes is the primary factor preventing them from advancing to corporate leadership.[19] I was surprised to find that there actually existed a plethora of both qualitative
and quantitative studies that supported these women's beliefs.[20] Even
more interesting, especially in light of my attempts to fit in with the
fighter pilot community, I learned that women are negatively perceived
when they exhibit masculine traits.[21] Thus the fated life of a female
fighter pilot—to do her job, she must act like a man but be rejected
because of her those same qualities she must have to survive.

This very interesting psychological finding directly related to my flying experiences. During my FNAEB, I was shocked at how much of the
testimony revolved around my personal interactions and my supposed
abrasiveness and aggressiveness. When one of the instructors stated I
bullied and intimidated him, I knew the situation had crossed over into
the absurd. As a fighter pilot, wasn't that what I was supposed to be? At
times, I was severely lectured for not "getting my fangs out" and taking
charge of a situation. Then, when I did, I became an aggressive bitch
who intimidated and bullied the men around me. I was in between the
proverbial rock and a hard place.

During the psychology class, I learned of a critical gender
stereotyping case that not only sounded eerily familiar but one that also
eventually found its way to the Supreme Court. In 1982, Ann B. Hopkins
was a candidate for partnership with one of the big-eight national
accounting firms, Price Waterhouse. With more billable hours than any

of the other 88 candidates eligible for partner, she was personally responsible for bringing in accounts worth more than 25 million.[22] Despite her outstanding performance, she was denied partnership, which was granted to over half the male candidates.

A year later, Hopkins was still not promoted. Her evaluators said she was "macho" and needed a "course at charm school." She was counseled to "walk more femininely, talk more femininely, dress more femininely, wear make-up, have her hair styled, and wear jewelry."[23] She was further described as aggressive, abrasive, and difficult. As I read the summary of the Hopkins case, I felt as if I was reading my FNAEB report and the book, *Bogeys and Bandits* again.

The phrases "LT Cummings has demonstrated an overly aggressive attitude," and "LT Cummings has a reputation for abrasiveness" were repeated almost like mantras. In my FNAEB, I even had the distinction of single handedly "demoralizing" the entire warrior culture of military fighter pilots. In the book, I was plain-faced, confrontational, and a "one woman blitzkrieg." I was amazed that the descriptive phrases of Ann Hopkins were almost identical to those used to depict me. Two women, in two very different fields, were both accused of exhibiting those qualities that were deemed critical for the success of males, yet were unacceptable in women. The similarities were both comforting and frightening.

As a result of the denial for partnership, Hopkins eventually sued Price Waterhouse (PW) for violation of Title VII of the 1964 Civil Rights Act, which is the federal law that prohibits discrimination in the workplace based on sex, race, religion, or national origin. She prevailed at both the federal district and appellate courts, and eventually the Supreme Court heard her case. Gender stereotyping became a central issue in this case and as a result, there was significant expert testimony from psychologists who specialize in this field.

Social psychologist Susan T. Fiske testified that "stereotyping is most likely to intrude when the target is an isolated, one-or few-of-a-kind individual in an otherwise homogeneous environment." She also stated

that stereotyping occurs when groundbreakers move into non-tradi-
tional groups, in part because the attributes of leaders (and fighter
pilots)—aggressive, competitive, driven, tough, and masterly—are not
typically expected of women and those who behave these ways are
often disliked[24].

All levels of the justice system, including the Supreme Court, recognized that Ann Hopkins' social skills, which were considered abrasive for
women but expected of the men, became the primary focus for her evaluations instead of her business-generating aptitudes. Additionally, during
the PW partner selection process, the courts recognized that "the opinions
of people with limited hearsay information were given equal weight with
the opinions of people who had more intensive contact."[25]

Again I was shocked to see the uncanny similarities between Ann
Hopkins' evaluation and my FNAEB. Hearsay, rumor, and gossip were
the basis of my FNAEB; well over half the official "findings of fact" had
no factual basis whatsoever. In addition, instructors, students, and officers who never worked with me testified to both my aggressive and
abrasive personality and my supposed inability to fly. It was amazing to
me that Ann Hopkins' case was so similar to mine despite the vast difference in our chosen career fields. The one common denominator was
clear though; we were both women in an extremely male dominated
group who did not want us to be like them.

The federal district court ruled, "The firm of PW refused to make
Ann Hopkins a partner. Gender-based stereotyping played a role in
this decision."[26] The appellate court upheld the district court's ruling,
but PW appealed to the Supreme Court. Ann Hopkins prevailed again
and in her defense the Supreme Court stated, "In the specific context
of sex stereotyping, an employer who acts on the basis of a belief that
a woman cannot be aggressive, or that she must not be, has acted on
the basis of gender...An employer who objects to aggressiveness in
women but whose positions require this trait places a woman in an

intolerable Catch 22: out of a job if they behave aggressively and out of a job if they don't."[27]

I wondered if this dichotomy ever occurred to those pilots and senior officers in the fighter communities. When a woman acted like them, she was an aggressive bitch, yet many women were marked below average on their evaluations because they failed to "get their fangs out." After my return to the squadron, I was pulled aside one day by a senior officer and told to drop my "Shrew" callsign. He told me it was too harsh. I later laughed at my impossible situation. The guys I flew with had callsigns like "Bull" and "Thrasher" but my callsign of Shrew was a little too harsh for their sensitive palates?

A civilian English professor at the Naval Academy made an astute observation concerning this inherent double standard when he said, "the *structure* in which all contacts take place is deeply male—and thus, hardly by chance, both deeply misogynistic and deeply homophobic. In blunt terms (how self-evident this appeared a generation ago, and how inflammatory today!), the military is an organization set up, not coincidentally, by men, for men....Perhaps worst of all, pretending that the military is truly integrated punishes the women who are victims of such willful head-in-the-sandism: They are invited in on the surface, but kept out by the understructure, where real change must occur."[28] Because of the superficial acceptance of women fighter pilots which is really just mandatory tolerance, it will be a long time before a woman will ever be able to successfully command a squadron of fighter pilots.

The psychology of female and male pilots has been a hot topic since the repeal of the combat exclusion law. In 1996, the Air Force sponsored a study which stated in the final report, "we expected to find significant male/female differences with our cognitive tests, but we didn't...Men are generally thought to have stronger mechanical skills, while women are thought to possess stronger verbal skills, but we didn't find any evidence of that among Air Force pilots."[29] In addition, they discovered that the IQ's of the men and women were essentially identical. Despite

the recent debate over the abilities of women to fly, the report concluded "The bottom line is, a pilot's a pilot."

Despite the quantitative and objective scientific evidence that
women are just as capable as men in combat aviation, and the proven
successes of the women pilots in all branches of the military, many still
refuse to believe women belong in the cockpit. One of the most vocal
opponents of women in combat is James Webb, a former Naval
Academy graduate. A Vietnam War hero and popular author of military
fiction, Webb has not made the transition for women pilots any easier.

My first exposure to James Webb was during my time as a midshipman. In 1987 when I was at the Naval Academy, Webb was sworn in as
the Secretary of the Navy (SECNAV) on the Academy grounds. Several
companies of midshipmen were stationed in a semi-circle backdrop in
honor of the incoming SECNAV. After the companies were formed,
Navy and Marine Corps officers swept through the ranks, pulling out
every woman who might be seen by Webb from the podium and dismissed them from the ceremony. Webb has long been an opponent of
not only women at the Naval Academy, but also women in the military
and especially those in combat platforms. The senior officers at the
Academy apparently agreed with him and went to great lengths to
ensure Webb would not have to set eyes on a female in uniform. Both
Webb's disapproval of women in combat and the Academy's willingness
to support him were omens of what would transpire once the combat
exclusion law was repealed.

In a recent interview with PBS, James Webb offered an unconvincing
reason for his opposition to women on combat ships. In response to the
question, "Have they [the Navy] been bringing women too quickly into
the military?" Webb replied, "I spent the night on a helicopter ship. And
my bodyguard got up at 2:30 in the morning to walk along the corridors
and just sort of make his mid-morning patrol, whatever. He walked by
several toilet facilities, and he reported to me the next morning. He said,
"I've never seen anything like this in my life. At 2:30 in the morning,

every single head (bathroom) was backed up with 20 guys, with a copy of Playboy magazine, waiting for their five minutes of privacy." Now, you inject a 10 percent female crew into that environment, and you've got some really volatile leadership challenges."[30]

Even someone as intelligent and well spoken as James Webb is not immune to stereotypes and shortsighted conclusions. To assert that women do not belong on ships because they would somehow interfere with the male need to masturbate or the inability of Navy men to control their sexual urges is an insult to both men and women. Men may have more urgent sexual needs than women but "cruise socks" will always be around, regardless of the presence of women. (Cruise socks are special socks that men pack in their seabags. They use them for masturbation in their racks (beds) while at sea to minimize the mess).

Recently the American Spectator, a self-proclaimed "national anti-radical" conservative magazine, published a series of articles vehemently opposing women in combat. In response to the furor over whether or not Kara Hultgren was qualified to fly the F-14 Tomcat, the ultra-conservative online magazine stated, "Hundreds of thousands of dollars have been wasted, six people are dead, and at least one career has been destroyed—all to produce two female combat pilots…"[31]

Somehow in a twisted misogynist perspective, the author decided that the insertion of women into combat aviation was somehow directly responsible for the mistakes of LCDR Stacy Bates. He was the F-14 pilot who attempted to show off in Nashville and lost control of his plane, crashing into a neighborhood, killing five people. I found it amazing that the author made connection, in effect absolving LCDR Bates of his deadly errors and pinning the blame instead on the women pilots. Somehow the less-than-objective author forgot to mention that LCDR Bates previously crashed another F-14, well before women were ever injected into the equation.

The American Spectator comment about the destroyed career refers to LT Burns, the officer who committed a federal crime in giving LT

Carey Lohrenz's training records to the press. Apparently women pilots were again responsible for his illegal actions and therefore, LT Burns's promotion was unjustly withheld. I find it amusing that this author and those like him will be the first to invoke the victim syndrome when it fits their purposes. I am surprised that the female fighter pilot community has not been compared to Delilah, tricking men with their womanly wiles and robbing them of their strength!

Perhaps the most extreme and disturbing stereotypical view of women in combat recently came from a former naval aviator, Gerald Atkinson. He wrote a book titled, *"From Trust to Terror: Radical Feminism is Destroying the US Navy."* In his self-published book, he asserts that the feminist movement is assaulting naval aviation with threats, intimidation, and a "reign of terror." Atkinson further opines that "The feminization of the US military is occurring under a coordinated 'social engineering' agenda that would serve as a model for a New American Civilization—one that would destroy the traditional family, be hostile to traditional religion, and attempt to 'remake' human beings through the use of 'thought control'—right out of Stalin's Soviet Totalitarian handbook."[32]

Amazing. Somehow naval aviation and the entire US military is the epitome of Orwell's *1984*, all because women want to serve their country and fly airplanes. Just like I was termed a "demoralizer" in my squadron, Atkinson feels the presence of women in the hallowed ranks of aviation will not only destroy the military but also undermine the very foundation of democracy on which this country was built. To this end, he stated, "The US Navy is sinking under a radical feminist assault. What the Japanese could not accomplish at Pearl Harbor and what tyrannical forces of Soviet communism could not accomplish during the Cold War is being accomplished by America's radical feminists and their allies in the Executive Branch and in Congress with support from the nation's mass media. The US Navy is being torpedoed by the very government it serves. While the American people sleep!"[33]

The funny part about the brouhaha forged by Elaine Donnelly, James Webb, Gerald Atkinson and the remaining opponents of women combat pilots is that the joke is on them! For all the grandstanding and warnings from the ultra-conservative soapboxes about the frailty of women, their inability to assimilate in the all-male culture, and the encroachment on the hallowed concept of male bonding, women actually transitioned into combat planes despite all their misguided efforts.

As the rest of us debate the pros and cons of women in combat, women in the Navy are flying on and off aircraft carriers every day, carrying live missiles, and flying combat patrol missions over Bosnia and Iraq. While dissenters continue to dispute females as prisoners of war, both the Army and Air Force have women pilots stationed on the front lines, doing the exact same job as the male combat pilots. Not only are these women flying critical sorties, but without them, all three branches of the military could not meet their mission requirements.

In recent years with the booming US economy, the military has witnessed a severe and alarming decrease in both initial recruitment and retention of officers and enlisted. Both the Air Force and the Navy are experiencing extreme pilot shortages that have left both services critically undermanned and ill prepared for volatile and unpredictable world crises. Even if Congress passed a law right now ordering women out of combat roles, the Navy could not afford to let them go. Without the 51,000 officer and enlisted women who make up 13.5% of naval active duty forces, the Navy would come to a standstill. As a nation who is privileged to have an all-volunteer military, women have become an integral and vital resource that the Navy can ill-afford to lose. In addition, the Census Bureau predicts that after the year 2000, women will actually make up a majority of the country and are now a significant resource that can no longer be ignored or thought of as second rate.

In fact, several recent studies have shown that integrated units perform as well as all-male units. In the Navy, women are assigned to 68 combatant ships and 57 support ships.[34] Women fly every aircraft in the naval inventory, including all the fighter and attack planes. Several women in different aircraft have won the prestigious "TOPHOOK Award", the highly coveted distinction for the best landings on the carrier. Most importantly, in 1998 women combat pilots passed the first real test of fighting skills; they dropped bombs and flew combat missions over Iraq and Bosnia. Despite a rocky start, women made the transition into the warrior ranks and are now an integral part of our nation's war fighting machine. I may have been a casualty from the first wave, but at least I have the satisfaction of knowing I helped pave the way.

In 1996, the Navy commissioned a guided missile destroyer and named it the USS Hopper, the first time in modern naval history a warship was named after a woman. Rear Admiral Grace Hopper, a pioneer in computer technology, was responsible for bringing the Navy into the computer age. She was recalled out of retirement twice because her expertise was in such dire need. Unfortunately she died in 1992 and was never able to appreciate her legacy.

Despite the ugliness of my experiences in the Navy, when I reflect on the amazing successes of women since the repeal of the combat exclusion law, I am proud of both my contributions and the Navy in general. I know for a fact that as a result of my medical problems, flight surgeons are now trained to recognize endocrine and autoimmune diseases, which affect not only women, but men as well. I also know that without a doubt, the women behind me in the F/A-18 community had it much easier.

One day as I was between tests in the hospital, one of the women who started training in VFA-106 after I left, Laura, profusely thanked me for making it easier for her. Laura recently flew with one of the instructors who lied about me during the FNAEB. During one flight, upon her return to the airfield, she became disoriented and nearly caused a mid-air collision. She was certain she would be severely punished for her mistake, but she wasn't. Laura was not let off the hook because she was a woman; she was just treated like a normal student. The male pilots routinely were not tarred and feathered for an occasional blunder so finally some measure of equality was achieved.

I felt both happy and sad when Laura relayed this story to me. I was glad that maybe all my pain and suffering actually helped someone else but I was depressed that I was the sacrificial lamb. Sometime I think if it were possible, I would go back and do everything differently. Maybe instead of choosing jets in flight school, I should have selected helicopters. My girlfriends in the helicopter communities seem to be much happier and more accepted by their peers. I also sometimes wonder if I made a mistake in selecting F/A-18s after the repeal of the combat exclusion law. Maybe I should have selected a multi–crew aircraft, but my pride and ego got the better of me. Without a doubt though I know my biggest mistake was trying to act just like one of the guys when I flew fighters. Knowing what I know now, I should have been the quiet, demure little lamb the men wanted me to be.

I often reflect on the Machiavellian question, "Does the end justify the means?" and wish I truly understood it as a young, junior officer. If I had been smarter, I could have changed my persona while flying fighters long enough to eventually rise to the position where I could have made a difference. I should have kept my mouth shut, brought cookies in the morning, and laughed at the degrading jokes. I should have flirted more, never teased the men, and cheerfully accompanied them to the strip joints. In short, I should have been seen, but not heard.

It may sound absurd, but the women fighter pilots who were mousy and inconspicuous were the ones who were the most successful. My anecdotal experience only confirmed what psychologists and sociologists already knew; women who take on the masculine qualities of aggressiveness, competitiveness, and independence are shunned by those they are merely trying to emulate. Maybe I would have been selling out but if I had kowtowed, but I would be flying missions over

Bosnia today. Hindsight was not just 20/20, for me, it was like looking into the sun.

During the course of the Navy IG's investigation, one person said that my self-esteem was too high. It is actually amazing when I reflect on my past life as a fighter pilot that I have any sense of self-worth at all. I actually took that comment as a compliment and felt I achieved some measure of success. I can honestly say I reached my full potential in the Navy and feel that I learned some critical lessons about life that most people don't realize until it's too late, if ever. However, I can honestly say that I never again want to hear the phrases, "character building experience" or "what doesn't kill you, only makes you stronger."

Sometimes I think Kara was the lucky one. True she died in the prime of her life, but she died doing something she loved more than life itself. I often envy her for not living to see the aftermath, to see not only her peers ruthlessly turn on her but also watch the institution of the Navy to which she dedicated her life betray her as well. I often reflect on my oath of office to the Navy in which I swore to uphold and defend the constitution of the United States against all enemies both foreign and domestic. Little did I know that all my battles would be on the home front, against my own team for nothing more than just wanting to be one of them.

My good friends and supporters try to console me and congratulate me as a trailblazer, someone who really made a difference. That may be true and I don't feel like my life was wasted, but when I see a plane overhead or I see F/A-18s on CNN, I can't suppress those wistful, yearning feelings to still fly one of the world's greatest fighters.

As I separated from the Navy and left the Penn State NROTC unit, I was sad that my naval career came to such an unexpected and tragic ending. I had hoped to make the Navy a career just as my father did, and maybe someday reach the rank of admiral. Since my naval career was a ship dashed on the rocks, I worked hard at Penn State to make sure that I prepared the midshipmen for the rocky road ahead. I did the best I could to make sure they did not make the same mistakes and that the midshipmen, both male and female, would be the finest officers the Navy ever commissioned.

My proudest moments at Penn State came when I received my course critiques. Overall they were glowing and the mids seemed to understand that I was really trying to teach them more than just words from a book. My anger and bitterness against the Navy started to melt away when I read the following: "LT Cummings is one cool lady. She is definitely a model officer." and "LT Cummings is a wonderful teacher and I've learned more from her than any other professor at Penn State. I'd like to be an officer like her someday."

That's poetic justice. The woman who was once called the demoralizer left the Navy with a legacy of little Missy clones. Fortunately though, for those women behind me, the fat lady has left the stage and hell has a glacier climate. Women are now officially warriors and there is no turning back.

Epilogue

The Navy and I finally parted ways in early 1999, almost exactly two years from the time I submitted my original letter of resignation. Interestingly though just prior to my departure, the Navy awarded me with a prestigious Navy Commendation Medal for my outstanding teaching and advising efforts at Penn State. How ironic that I was the onetime demoralizer and bane of the Navy, and then was later honored for my efforts in molding the Navy's future officers.

After wandering the country for six months and much soul searching, I decided that I was best suited for academia where original thought and intellectual curiosity are encouraged instead of suppressed. I took a position as a professor in the nationally ranked College of Engineering in Virginia Tech, and now teach in the Engineering Fundamentals division. I hope to continue my teaching excellence and motivate both men and women to reach their full potential.

My last few years in the Navy left a deep scar that will no doubt color my views towards both the Navy and fighter pilots for many years to come. However, in an effort to turn my lemons into lemonade, I began speaking across the country to students, professional societies, and other interested groups about my experiences as one of the nation's first female fighter pilots, the impact of gender stereotyping, and the importance of mentoring. Hopefully through inspiring others, my sacrifices and struggles in the Navy will become meaningful and helpful to others, especially to those future trailblazers.

Glossary

ADMIN: administrative, usually refers to a department or division of personnel. Also means a room that a group of aviators rent for a party.

AFB: Air Force Base

AI: Aviation Indoctrination, a five-week introductory course prior to flight training.

AIRLANT: the Admiral in charge of the entire Navy's air assets for the Atlantic region.

ANA: Anti-nuclear antibodies that are produced at the cell level to kill off the body's own defenses and tissues.

Bar Fine: A prostitute or hooker.

BOQ: Bachelor Officer's Quarters. A dormitory for officers.

Cat: The catapult on an aircraft carrier that propels aircraft off the deck.

CMEO: Command Managed Equal Opportunity Officer

CMR: Center for Military Readiness, an extremely conservative think tank that opposes women in combat.

CO: Commanding Officer, the officer in charge of a Navy unit.

Det: A detachment, usually of aircraft or personnel that leaves the main unit for an off-site mission.

DOD: Department of Defense

DNA: Designated Naval Aviator, a pilot who has earned his wings.

EO: Equal Opportunity

FAA: Federal Aviation Administration

FAM: Familiarization, a stage or a flight that is designed to acquaint a pilot with the rudimentary aspects of a plane.

FCLP: Field Carrier Landing Practice

FOF: Findings of Fact

FNAEB: Field Naval Aviator Evaluation Board, which in theory is a peer evaluation of a pilot's performance.

FRS: Fleet Replacement Squadron, which is the intermediate step between flight school graduation and assignment to a fleet squadron.

Gouge: good deal or good information

G-suit: Pants that inflate to keep blood from pooling in pilot's legs.

Head: Navy slang for bathroom

HFB: Human Factors Board, an informal board that supposedly investigates medical or emotional problems could be affecting a pilot's performance.

HUD: Heads Up Display. A projection of critical flight information in the pilot's windscreen view.

IG: Inspector General, the branch if the Navy that is responsible for internal investigations.

JAG: Judge Advocate General. The term is used to describe both Navy lawyers and legal investigations.

LBFM: Little Brown F—king Machines, Philippine prostitutes.

LSO: Landing Signals Officer, the person on the ground that provides assistance to aircraft landing on a carrier.

MIG: A Russian fighter.

MIR: Mishap Investigation Report, a written, highly subjective assessment as to the cause of an accident.

NADEP: Naval Aviation Depot, an organization that is responsible for the major overhaul of naval aircraft.

NAM: Navy Achievement Medal

NAS: Naval Air Station

NATOPS: Naval Aviation Training & Operating Procedures Standardization

NATTC: Naval Air Technical Training Center

NFO: Naval Flight Officer, the person in the backseat of an aircraft who is a navigator/systems operator.

NPS: Naval Postgraduate School

NROTC: Naval Reserve Officers' Training Corps

Nugget: A young, inexperienced pilot

O Club: Officers' Club.

PI: Philippines

Qual: Qualified

Ready Room: The room in a squadron where pilot meetings and general socializing takes place.

Round-eye: A Caucasian woman

SDO: Squadron Duty Officer

SERE: Survival, Evasion, Resistance, and Escape. Refers to the school aviators attend to learn how to become prisoners of war.

SNA: Student Naval Aviator

SOD: Signal of Difficulty, a flag that documents difficulties a pilot is experiencing.

SOP: Standard Operating Procedure

TACFORM: Tactical formation, dynamic maneuvering of two or more aircraft in close proximity.

TOPHOOK: The pilot with the best landing grades aboard a carrier.

TSH: Thyroid Stimulating Hormone, the measure of how well a thyroid gland is working.

UCMJ: Uniform Code of Military Justice, the laws that govern military personnel.

USMC: United Stated Marine Corps

USNA: United States Naval Academy

WESTPAC: Western Pacific

XO: Executive Officer, the second in command of a Navy unit.

Notes

1 United States Navy: www.spear.navy.mil

2 www.philippine.org/prov01/bataan.htm

3 Dacanay, B. M. *Mt. Pinatubo: 500 Years After* (Quezon City, Philippines: Mass Media Publishing Corporation, 1991), p. 26.

4 *Ibid.* p. 20.

5 Zimmerman, J. *Tailspin* (New York: Doubleday, 1995), p. 142.

6 Vistica, G. L. *Fall From Glory: The Men Who Sank the U.S. Navy* (New York: Simon & Schuster, 1995), p. 209.

7 Chavez, Linda. "Did Navy policy cost pilot her life?" USA Today, 10 May, 1995, 13A.

8 Navy Safety Center

9 Chavez, Linda. "Did Navy policy cost pilot her life?" USA Today, 10 May, 1995, 13A.

10 *Ibid.*

11 Clayman, Charles B., M.D., Medical Editor. *The American Medical Association Encyclopedia of Medicine.* Random House, New York, p. 789.

12 Wallace, Daniel J., M.D. *The Lupus Book.* Oxford University Press, New York. 1995, p. 170.

13 Ibid., p. 25.

14 Gandt, Robert, *Bogeys and Bandits: The Making of a Fighter Pilot.* Penguin, New York. 1997, p. 164.

15 Scarborough, Rowan. "Navy Boss Censures Officers on Records." Washington Times, March 19, 1998, p. 10.

16 Freedburg, Sydney J. "Taking Aim at GI Jane." Government Executive Magazine. Daily Briefing, March 16, 1998.

17 McIntyre, Jamie. "The boys who didn't get it." CNN, October 21, 1995.

18 Nietzsche, Frederick. *Beyond Good and Evil.*

19 Catalyst. (1996). Women in corporate leadership: Progress and prospects. New York, NY.

20 Dubno, P. (1985). Attitudes toward women executives: A longitudinal approach. *Academy of Management Journal, 28,* p. 235-239.

     Eagly, A. H., Makhijani, M. G., & Klonsky, B. G. (1992). Gender and Evaluation of Leaders: A Meta-Analysis. *Psychological Bulletin, 111,* p. 3-22.

     Rosen, B., & Jerdee, T.H. (1974). Influence of sex-role stereotypes on personnel decisions. *Journal of Applied Psychology, 59,* p. 9-14.

21 Eagly, Makhijani, & Klonsky, p. 16.

22 Fiske, S.T., Bersoff, D.N., Borgida, E., Deaux, K., Heilman, M.E. (1991). Social Science Research on Trial: Use of sex stereotyping research in Price Waterhouse v. Hopkins. *American Psychologist 46:* 1050.

23 *Ibid.*

24 *Ibid.*

25 *Ibid,* p. 1051.

26 *Ibid,* p. 1049.

27 *Ibid,* p. 1055.

28 Fleming, Bruce. "Gay Poets, Women, and Other Threats to Group Loyalty at the Naval Academy." *The Chronicle of Higher Education,* January 30, 1998.

29 McGlohn, Suzanne, E. & King, Raymond, E. "Assessment of Psychological Factors in Aviation." Human Systems Center Public Affairs release.

30 PBS Frontline documentary, "The Navy Blues," original airdate, October 15, 1996.

31 The American Spectator Online Update, March 11-17, 1997. http://www.amspec.org

32 Atkinson, Gerald. *From Trust to Terror: Radical Feminism is Destroying the US Navy*. Atkinson Associates Press, 1997, Camp Springs, MD, p. 98.
33 *Ibid*, p. 99.
34 United States Navy—Women in the Navy web site, *http://www.chinfo.navy.mil*

About the Author

Missy Cummings, a 1988 graduate of the U.S. Naval Academy, received her Master's degree in Astronautical Engineering in 1994. A naval officer for ten years, she was one of the Navy's first female fighter pilots. She is now a professor in the Virginia Tech College of Engineering, Engineering Fundamentals division.